2016

D1035879

THE
HEART
OF HELL

THE
HEART
OF HELL

The Untold Story of
Courage and Sacrifice in the
Shadow of Iwo Jima

MITCH WEISS

BERKLEY CALIBER, NEW YORK

BERKLEY
CALIBER

An imprint of Penguin Random House LLC
375 Hudson Street, New York, New York 10014

This book is an original publication of Penguin Random House LLC.

Library of Congress Cataloging-in-Publication Data
Names: Weiss, Mitch.
Title: The heart of hell : the untold story of courage and sacrifice in the
shadow of Iwo Jima / Mitch Weiss.
Description: First edition. | New York : Berkley Caliber, 2016.
Identifiers: LCCN 2015036457 | ISBN 9780425279175 (hardback)
Subjects: LCSH: Iwo Jima, Battle of, Japan, 1945. | Iwo Jima (Volcano
Islands, Japan)—History, Naval—20th century. | United States.
Navy—History—World War, 1939–1945. | World War, 1939–1945—Regimental
histories—United States. | LCI (G) 449 (Ship)—History. | Landing craft—Japan—Iwo
Jima (Volcano Islands)—History—20th century. | Gunboats—Japan—Iwo Jima
(Volcano Islands)—History—20th century. | Sailors—United States—Biography. | World War,
1939–1945—Naval operations, American. | World War, 1939–1945—Amphibious operations. |
BISAC: HISTORY / Military / World War II. | BIOGRAPHY &
AUTOBIOGRAPHY / Military. | HISTORY / Military / Veterans.
Classification: LCC D767.99.I9 W438 2016 | DDC 940.54/2528—dc23
LC record available at http://lccn.loc.gov/2015036457

First edition: March 2016

PRINTED IN THE UNITED STATES OF AMERICA

10   9   8   7   6   5   4   3   2   1

Jacket design by Richard Hasselberger.
Jacket photo by Navsource Photo Archives.
Book design by Tiffany Estreicher.

Penguin
Random
House

To my father, Morris Weiss,
a member of the "Greatest Generation"

Courage is not the absence of fear,
but rather the assessment that something
is more important than fear.

—FRANKLIN DELANO ROOSEVELT

CAST OF CHARACTERS

LANDING CRAFT INFANTRY (G) 449

OFFICERS:

Lieutenant Willard Vincent Nash: The gunboat's first skipper, Nash was in his early thirties when he left his thriving legal practice in Saginaw, Michigan, to enlist in the navy.

Lieutenant Junior Grade Rufus Geddie Herring: The Roseboro, North Carolina, native joined the navy after graduating Davidson College. Beloved by his crew, he was only twenty-three when he replaced Nash as the gunboat's captain.

Lieutenant Junior Grade Byron Chew Yarbrough: A graduate of Auburn Polytechnic Institute (now Auburn University), Yarbrough was a well-respected leader who took part in some of the bloodiest campaigns of the War in the Pacific.

Lieutenant Junior Grade Robert Duvall: The ship's communications officer, the twenty-three-year-old Duvall was a newlywed who tried to write his wife every day.

Ensign Leo Bedell: The twenty-two-year-old Akron, Ohio, native was the youngest officer on the ship and a decisive leader.

Ensign William Corkins: The twenty-nine-year-old father of two enlisted in the navy because he didn't want to sit on the sidelines during the war.

Ensign Frederick Cooper: The son of a pastor, Cooper was a twenty-four-year-old high school teacher when he enlisted. He told his wife he couldn't stay home when so many of his students were being drafted.

Ensign Donald Cromer: After enlisting in the navy, he trained with Corkins and Cooper. The three officers joined the gunboat the same day in September 1944.

CREW:

Pharmacist's Mate First Class Henry Beuckman: The men called Beuckman Grandpa because he was the oldest man on the gunboat. But the thirty-seven-year-old from East Saint Louis, Illinois, had one of the most important jobs: He was the ship's only medic.

Steward's Mate Ralphal Johnson: The only African-American on the ship, his job was to serve white officers. But after discovering Johnson was a crack shot, the officers made him a gunner on the 20mm starboard gun.

Seaman First Class Junior Hollowell: A scrappy kid from rural Oklahoma, he enlisted when he turned eighteen. At the height of segregation, the white ammo loader became good friends with his African-American gunner from Decatur, Texas: Ralphal Johnson.

Seaman First Class Clifford Lemke: The teenager wanted to join the navy after the Japanese attacked Pearl Harbor, but his father refused to let him. A few months after his eighteenth birthday, Lemke enlisted, leaving behind his pregnant wife.

Seaman First Class John Overchuk: The Cleveland, Ohio, native joined the navy to make his father proud. He was outgoing and an excellent dancer, and the crew gravitated to Overchuk, who took the quiet Lemke under his wing.

Seaman First Class Lawrence Bozarth: A devout Christian, he asked to be an ammo loader to avoid firing weapons and killing enemy soldiers. The sailors would often seek out the eighteen-year-old Tulsa, Oklahoma, native to pray.

Boatswain's Mate Second Class Frank Robert Blow: A natural-born leader who everyone on the gunboat affectionately called "Joe Blow," the twenty-one-year-old impressed his shipmates by staying calm under fire.

Motor Machinist's Mate Third Class James Casaletto: A mechanic who could fix anything, he enlisted to escape a bad marriage.

Radioman Max Ball: A fisherman's son from Gloucester, Massachusetts, he was taking part in a U.S. Merchant Marine training program when the Japanese bombed Pearl Harbor.

Ship's Cook Second Class Clarence Kepner: One of the most respected men on the gunboat, he'd prepare special meals the night before combat.

Fireman First Class Norman Holgate: A shy eighteen-year-old, he enlisted to get away from his abusive father. At home, Holgate loved to tinker with cars and gadgets. On the 449, he worked in the engine room.

Seaman First Class Clarence Hoffman: A fun-loving street kid from Saint Louis, Missouri. When Hoffman tried to enlist early in the navy, he discovered a family secret that would haunt him.

Signalman Arthur Lewis: A twenty-year-old from Baltimore, Maryland, he was nicknamed "Horizontal Lewis" because he spent most of his off-hours sleeping.

Gunner's Mate Third Class Charles Banko: A gun crew captain, Banko was always getting in trouble. After being kicked off another gunboat, the eighteen-year-old from East Selah, Washington, grew a bushy red beard in defiance.

Seaman First Class Bruce Hallett: A gunner from Wenatchee, Washington, whose father refused to let him enlist before his eighteenth birthday, Hallett joined the gunboat the same day as his best friend: Banko.

Seaman First Class Charles Hightower: An ammo passer on the port side 40mm gun, the Russellville, Arkansas, native was cool under fire. His gun captain, Ralph Owens, became his best friend.

Gunner's Mate Third Class Ralph Owens: A gun captain, he always talked about his girlfriend Nina. His best friend was Hightower, and they'd often talk late into the night.

Seaman First Class Frederick Walton: A Southern California teenager, he was one of the youngest sailors on the gunboat. Even though his family tried to stop him, Walton enlisted after high school.

Seaman Second Class Robert Minnick: A high school baseball star in Akron, Ohio, he turned down a contract to play minor-league baseball for the Cleveland Indians to enlist in the navy. The eighteen-year-old joined the gunboat just weeks before Iwo Jima.

HOME FRONT:

Betty Jones: A twenty-four-year-old single woman from Cordele, Georgia, she became pen pals with one of the officers on the gunboat. She was a smart and prolific writer, who poured her heart into each letter. She worked in her father's pharmacy, but dreamed of becoming a nurse in Atlanta, Georgia.

Dorothy Wallace: A former press agent with CBS radio who worked at *Life* and other magazines, she went on a date with a girlfriend's brother, an officer preparing to join the 449. They stayed in touch during the war.

Mary Cooper: The twenty-two-year-old mother would listen to the radio every night in hopes of hearing good news about the war. Her husband, Ensign Frederick Cooper, was on the 449.

Elaine Butler: She was a teenager working in a San Diego, California, broom factory when a young sailor walked in the door. They spent nearly two weeks together in Southern California before he shipped out to Pearl Harbor.

GLOSSARY

TERMS FOR A SHIP

Port Side: Left-hand side of a vessel, facing forward

Starboard Side: Right-hand side of a vessel, facing forward

Bow: Front of a boat

Prow: Forward-most part of a ship's bow

Stern: Back or aft-most part of a vessel

Aft: At, near, or toward the stern

Deckhouse: A structure aft of the bow, used as a shelter. On the 449, the officers' quarters, galley, and mess deck were inside the steel building.

Fantail: Rear of a ship

Bridge: Outdoor platform from which the ship can be commanded

Pilothouse: Room with the ship's navigational equipment and steering controls

Mess Deck: Area where sailors socialize and eat

Galley: Kitchen aboard a vessel

Wardroom: Room where officers socialize and eat

LIFE IN THE NAVY

Crew's Head: Ship's restroom

Bulkhead: Walls of a ship

Gun Deck: A deck primarily used for the mounting of weaponry

Well Deck: Forward part of the ship between the deckhouse and the bow

Rack: Bunk, or bed, of a sailor

Liberty: A specific period of recreational time in which sailors would be allowed to leave the ship

Rating: A sailor's position. The equivalent for the army would be "rank."

Striker: A sailor seeking advancement to a specific rating, such as signalman or radioman. For example, a seaman first class would be striking for signalman.

TERMS FOR THE MEN

Skipper: Captain of the ship

Captain of the Ship: Regardless of rating, the commanding officer is always referred to as the "captain." He has total responsibility for the ship and authority over everyone on board.

Executive Officer: The second in command, he's the ship's administrator, responsible for all personnel on board.

Engineering Officer: Responsible for operation of the ship's engineering plant and electrical generation and distribution

Boatswain's Mate: Generally considered to be the senior enlisted rating in the navy and expected to be the most capable seaman on board

Seaman: Generally referred to as "non-rated" personnel, he could be assigned duties in any of the non-engineering divisions. Most seamen were assigned to the Deck Force, meaning they were at the beck and call of the boatswain's mates.

Machinist's Mate: Responsible for the operation and maintenance of all of the equipment in the engine room

Black Gang: Men who work in the engine room, typically motor machinist's mates and firemen

Electrician's Mate: Responsible for the ship's electrical and distribution systems, including power and lighting equipment

Quartermaster: Provides assistance to the navigator and maintains the deck log while the ship is under way. He often steers the ship.

Signalman: Responsible for visual communications between ships by flashing light, flag hoist, or semaphore

Radioman: Responsible for all electronic means of exterior communication. Available methods included voice radio, Teletype, and the old-fashioned Morse code key.

Pharmacist's Mate: Medical person aboard an LCI, equivalent to an army medic

INTRODUCTION

FEBRUARY 17, 1945

A CLEAR, BRIGHT morning. Rufus Geddie Herring, lieutenant junior grade, peered through binoculars at the tiny island in the distance.

Rocky coastline, deep gorges, high ridges. It bristled with Japanese machine guns, rockets, and thousands of soldiers, all of them well dug in. The Marines had their work cut out for them. So did his flotilla of little gunboats.

It wasn't the fortified coastline that worried Herring the most. It was what stood behind it. Mount Suribachi towered 550 feet into the sky, dark gray, all heavy artillery and menace.

It was a natural fortress, a long-dormant volcano on the southern tip of Iwo Jima. The sight was breathtaking, Herring thought, something from a Hiroshige woodblock print. And from the top of Suribachi, the Japanese had just as clear a view of him. Spread out in all directions behind Herring's gunboat was the American fleet, complete with battleships, destroyers, and cruisers.

Up close is what concerned Herring as he and the rest of Flotilla Three, Group Eight—twelve very visible gunboats—moved slowly in the very shadow of the mountain. If the Japanese opened fire, they all were in deep, deep shit.

But they were in too far now. This was a critical scouting mission. Recon, two days ahead of a massive amphibious assault the United States was sure would alter the course of the War in the Pacific. The flotilla of landing craft infantry gunboats had been ordered to move close to shore and provide cover for an elite navy commando team. The frogmen would swim underwater and disable mines, then scout beaches in the shadow of Suribachi to ensure the sandy, black volcanic cinders could support tanks and other heavy equipment.

So far, everything was going fine. Still, Herring and his crew were uneasy. The Japanese commanders on the island were probably focused on the fleet in the distance. Surely someone up there had spotted the gunboats. But the flotilla had received no fire. Nothing.

It's too quiet, Herring thought.

With the binoculars dangling from his neck strap, he turned to his second in command, Lieutenant Junior Grade Byron Chew Yarbrough.

"One more time," Herring said.

Yarbrough nodded. Grabbing the handset to the ship's communication system, he touched base with crew in key positions. Ensign Leo Bedell in the engine room, where it was difficult to hear over the din of the diesel engines. Everything was running smoothly. Quartermaster Second Class William Vollendorf in the pilothouse said the gunboat was steering as usual. Ensign William Corkins on the gun deck said all was well with the gun crews. Yarbrough hung up the handset and gave Herring the thumbs-up sign.

Herring sighed. He'd been in battle before—the brutal Marshall and Mariana Islands campaigns—but this was his first combat mission as captain. He had learned from the previous skipper to take nothing for granted. Under fire, everyone had to know exactly what was expected.

Herring's job was simple: Lead by example.

Stay calm, he told himself. The crew was at battle stations, huddled behind their guns, weapons protected by only a two-inch shield of plastic armor. They waited, eyes fixed on the mountain. Maybe everything would work out. They'd get in and get out of there without any shots being fired. Maybe they'd all survive.

Something shook underfoot. Something shivered. Metal moaned. Water suddenly sprayed Herring in the face, and fear came blasting out of nowhere.

Everything changed.

PART ONE

PRE-MISSION

1

HIS BIG SEABAG slung over his shoulder, Seaman First Class Clifford Lemke stepped off the transport and bounded toward a dry dock at the other end of Pearl Harbor. The legendary, infamous Pearl Harbor! Lemke stood up straight and focused on the street ahead. There was so much to see, right here and now.

Just an hour earlier, an officer on the USS *Leon* had told Lemke, "Pack your stuff." Transfer. Say goodbye. Another ship, another crew was waiting for him there at the sprawling naval base in exotic Hawaii.

Lemke was stunned. He'd been part of the maiden crew on the *Leon*. He'd stepped on board February 12, 1944, the very day the transport ship was commissioned at the Bethlehem Steel Company dock back in Brooklyn, New York. Lemke was nineteen years old, a quiet, skinny kid from Wisconsin. During the three-month, five-thousand-mile voyage from New York to Pearl Harbor, he stayed up late playing cards with his buddies, bullshitting about baseball, girls, any subject that popped into their heads. Lemke mostly listened, but by the time they docked in Pearl Harbor, he felt he belonged.

Now he'd have to start all over again.

He took an inventory as he walked, and fought back the knot in his stomach: T-shirts. Pants. Socks. The already-threadbare mattress secured inside its hammock. All rolled according to spec, all tucked neatly inside the bag on his back. No sentimental goodbyes. Everyone knew this day would come.

The war was moving west across the ocean. Progress was slow, island by tiny island, toward the Japanese mainland. He was moving with it, toward God-knows-what. The progress wasn't coming cheaply, either.

The Pearl Harbor naval hospital had eleven hundred beds full of the wounded sent in from the ships fighting across the Pacific. The navy needed to replace the injured and dead, and Lemke was just one of the thousands stepping up. The *Leon* wouldn't leave Pearl Harbor anytime soon, but other ships at the naval base were getting ready to join the fight. The recruits aboard were being plucked away, reassigned, moved along.

Civilian Navy Yard workers darted between the dry docks, piers, storehouses, and oil depots. Lemke crossed the streets carefully, dodging jeeps full of sailors, Marines, and soldiers. Mess halls, headquarters, offices, most of them newly built—the 22,000-acre naval base sprawled over the entire southern tip of Oahu. All along the waterfront, hundreds of vessels were being repaired in dry docks and restocked with supplies. The navy wasn't just recovering. It was gearing up. Lemke could feel the energy. You didn't need military intelligence to know that America was getting ready to launch another offensive.

Pearl Harbor was everything Lemke had imagined, right down to the palm trees. Two-and-a-half years had passed since he'd first heard of the place, since the newsreels of the Japanese military strike had riveted him to his seat at the Rex Theater back in Park Falls, Wisconsin.

Life before that was relatively simple. He worked most days alongside his father, learning to make furniture and cabinets. At night he walked downtown. If he had enough money, he'd catch a flick with his friends. He'd dreamed of saving enough to buy a used car, and maybe even leaving Park Falls when the time was right.

Until that horrible Sunday, Lemke hadn't paid much attention to the events leading up to war. He was a kid, a sixteen-year-old high-school dropout living in a tough town still recovering from the Great Depression. Few people took much notice of foreign affairs.

Except his dad. Fred Lemke, a stocky carpenter with a broad nose, thick wavy black hair, and calloused hands, took a lively interest in the news. He was the son of German immigrants, eking out a living in a Wisconsin town founded by German immigrants.

The old man crouched over the kitchen table every day with the *Park Falls Herald* spread open, eyes fixed on the latest accounts of Adolf Hitler and Nazi Germany's growing military aggression. Fred snapped through the pages and shook his head, muttering. In the evenings he sometimes explained what was happening, while the family pretended to listen: When Germany surrendered at the end of World War I, it was forced to sign the Treaty of Versailles, a document designed to humiliate. A new German government was formed, but by the end of the 1920s, the nation staggered under massive unemployment and inflation.

Into this chaos stepped Hitler, a World War I corporal who rose to power with a fiery brand of nationalism, promising to tear up the Versailles Treaty and restore Germany to its former glory. He waged a vicious campaign of propaganda and terror against his political foes, and reached the pinnacle of power on January 30, 1933, when he was named chancellor of Germany.

Hitler kept his promises. He put Germany's industrial base to work rebuilding its military, and then he mobilized it. While the world looked anxiously on, Germany annexed Austria and Czechoslovakia. On September 1, 1939, Germany invaded Poland, and Europe stepped off the sidelines. World War II erupted, but Germany already had massive momentum. By the summer of 1940, Germany's military, backed by factories rolling out Panzer tanks and Messerschmitt planes, had swept across Europe in a lightning war, conquering most of the continent. Only Great Britain remained.

Back at the Lemke house, Fred sat with an ear against the cathedral-shaped Crosley radio, listening to CBS radio correspondent Edward R. Murrow describe the terror in London as waves of German planes bombed the city. Buildings crumbled. Fires consumed whole neighborhoods. But somehow, Great Britain held on.

The United States by then had started providing much-needed weapons and supplies, but how long could the Brits continue to resist?

It wasn't only England. The following summer, Germany launched an offensive against the Soviet Union, their former ally. Nazi troops were suddenly on the outskirts of Moscow.

In the waning days of 1941, with London and Moscow on the brink, Fred Lemke and most everyone else gave little thought to the Far East. Anyone with a newspaper or radio knew that Germany posed the biggest threat to the free world.

But reality was different. Japanese aggression in East Asia had been just as ambitious as Germany's in Europe. A decade before Pearl Harbor, the Japanese invaded Manchuria, and followed with a brutal attack on China in 1937.

Seeking to curb Japanese aggression, the United States in 1940 imposed tough economic sanctions, embargoing scrap iron, steel, and gasoline. Two months later, Japan retaliated by signing the Tripartite Pact with Germany and Italy. Suddenly, the Nazis had allies on the other side of the globe.

Even with severe shortages of oil and other natural resources, Japan's leaders decided it was time to displace the United States as the dominant Pacific power. On Sunday, December 7, 1941, Japan attacked the United States.

Most of America learned of the strike when a news bulletin interrupted their Sunday afternoon radio programs: "The Japanese have attacked Pearl Harbor, Hawaii, by air," according to the breathless announcers.

"Japan?" People shook their heads in disbelief and adjusted their radios. Was it true? Could it be possible? Newspaper special editions confirmed everyone's worst fears. The nation was stunned, and waited for the president's reaction. President Franklin Delano Roosevelt, the man who had guided the nation through the darkest days of the Great Depression, was now called upon to lead the United States through another crisis.

The following day Roosevelt addressed a joint session of Congress and told the nation via radio that the Japanese attack was "unprovoked" and "dastardly." He called December 7, 1941, "a date that will live in infamy."

The president was blunt. The strike had damaged American naval and military forces severely, he said, and "very many American lives have been lost."

"There is no mincing the fact that our people, our territory, and our interests are in grave danger," he said, adding that Japanese forces had attacked other American targets in the Pacific, including Guam and the Philippine Islands.

"No matter how long it may take us to overcome this premeditated invasion, the American people in their righteous might will win through to absolute victory," he thundered.

Congress responded. Later that day, they declared war on Japan. Four days later, Germany declared war on the United States.

With his parents and sister huddled by the radio for days, young Lemke sat quietly as journalists relayed the latest horrors from the Pacific. More than 2,400 Americans were dead. Eight navy battleships were sunk or heavily damaged. Nearly 350 U.S. aircraft were destroyed or damaged.

A wave of patriotism swept the country. Overnight, folks who had urged America to stay neutral became binocular-toting volunteers, watching the nighttime skies for enemy planes. During the day, men, women, and children watched for "suspicious activity."

Teenagers like Lemke were expected to join up. If you were an able-bodied male, it was your "patriotic duty" to enlist.

With Germany on one side and the Japanese on the other, it didn't matter which branch of the military you joined. Recruiting stations everywhere were flooded with men of all ages looking to do their part.

Clifford Lemke felt the same way, but he was too young to enlist. You had to be eighteen years old to be inducted into the army, and seventeen to join the navy or the Marines, and only then if you had your parents' permission. And as much as Fred Lemke despised the Japanese and the Nazis, he wasn't going to sign those papers. Not yet.

Fred had seen this before. He knew all about war, and the unrelenting public pressure to enlist.

Nearly twenty-five years earlier, the young men of Park Falls had been urged to take up arms, to fight the German "Huns" who not only threatened Western Europe but the American way of life.

Back then, Fred Lemke and his brothers faced a dilemma: Park Falls and most of the towns in northern Wisconsin were predominantly German. Their grandparents and parents spoke German. Most people had cousins and grandparents in the Old Country. They ate German food and sang German songs on the holidays.

The Lemkes knew their family history: Great-grandfather Herman, with a few hundred dollars in his pocket, boarded a ship in Bremen in 1867 with his wife and five children. They settled a vast expanse of land in Clark County, Wisconsin, where the dense forests and long winters reminded them of home. His son August took over the farm when old Herman could no longer follow a plow. Fred was the fifth of August's seven surviving children.

But in 1917, despite their deep ties to the Old Country, all four of the Lemke boys enlisted in the U.S. military. Fred was deployed to France with the U.S. Army Ambulance Service. Every day he picked up and transported dozens of wounded men from the front lines to field hospitals: soldiers with arms or legs gone, bodies mangled, ripped apart by shrapnel and machine-gun fire, or found choking on toxic mustard gas in the rat-filled trenches. His small truck had hard rubber tires with no give. The wounded groaned and shrieked with every bump and rut in the road.

By November 1918, the war was over. Casualties were staggering: In just over eighteen months, 53,000 Americans died fighting, and 63,000 more died from disease and accidents. More than 200,000 were wounded.

Fred Lemke had seen enough war for his lifetime, and he wouldn't succumb again to flag-waving nonsense. He knew it was just a matter of time before his son would be old enough to enlist on his own. He hoped this war would be over by then. Maybe his boy wouldn't end up like those young men who haunted his nightmares, choking on their own blood, praying for death.

Clifford Lemke didn't like his father's thinking, but there was little he could do but wait. By early 1942, some of his cousins and friends were already in basic training. And everywhere the teenager went, the war was there: Posters touted war savings bonds from storefronts. The drugstore on Main Street sold yellow toy-filled candy boxes emblazoned with an anti-aircraft gun and the message: "Remember Pearl Harbor!" Radio stations played patriotic songs, urging Americans to "protect our shoreline to the door line."

Even at the Rex, where Lemke used to find solace in the back row watching westerns, he couldn't escape. Movies like *Wake Island* with Brian Donlevy and *Flying Tigers* with John Wayne trumpeted American "fighting men." Before the features, Lemke sat through shorts directed by Hollywood giants, Frank Capra and John Huston among others, who positioned the war as a battle between good and evil. The nation's freedom, the American way of life, was at stake. Even Bugs Bunny and Elmer Fudd were in uniform . . . How could Lemke not feel guilty about being left behind?

By late 1942, Lemke was still working with his father, picking up odd jobs in town, when he read an advertisement in the newspaper that perked him up a bit. There were openings at a new munitions plant in Baraboo, Wisconsin, a city 225 miles south of Park Falls. The ad said the "need was urgent" for workers. New weapons factories seemed to be cropping up overnight, and the plants desperately needed employees to fill the shifts—they were even hiring women to work on the factory floors. Lemke told his father he wanted to apply.

His father gave his blessing. If his son was hired, at least he'd feel like he was contributing to the war effort. Clifford didn't have to worry about an apartment either, as there was plenty of housing for the plant's eight thousand production workers.

On a bitterly cold November morning, young Lemke packed his few belongings in his mother's tattered suitcase. Then he put on his fleece-lined jacket and hugged his parents and sister goodbye before walking out the door. He trudged a few blocks through the snow to the bus station and waited.

Lemke was scared. He'd never been on his own. He was an introvert and didn't know if he'd make any friends. But he was going to push himself. He had learned that from his father. The old man had put up with a lot over the years, but he never gave up. Lemke wanted to make the old man proud.

A few hours later the bus rolled into Baraboo and the Badger Army Ammunition Plant. Lemke's eyes lit up. Badger wasn't just a plant—it was a city.

It was fourteen hundred buildings sprawled over seven thousand acres, factories that produced explosives and propellants—smokeless powder for hand grenades, M1 rifles, and rockets—along with housing for workers, a recreation center, child care facility, hospital, and cafeteria.

Near the front gate workers changed from their street clothes into coveralls and lab coats. Miles of railroad tracks threaded through the place, loading up freight trains with ammunition for military bases and ports all over the country.

In the months before Pearl Harbor, the U.S government had seen war on the horizon and started planning and building ammunition factories. The army hired defense contractor Hercules Powder Company to design and operate the Badger plant.

As Lemke's bus pulled into the station, he glimpsed the supportive signs in storefront windows and buildings, including one of a man and woman in coveralls glancing proudly at the words: "We make the best powder in the world. Keep 'em shooting."

The place was overwhelming at first, but Lemke soon found his rhythm. Through the day he drove truckloads of propellant chemicals from the factories to storage areas. At night he slept in his own little room in a big company-run dormitory. He took care of himself, showered and shaved and had his hair trimmed once a week. He was surrounded by thousands of people, but Lemke was lonely. He kept to himself, saved his money, and marked the time until February 5, 1943: his eighteenth birthday. The news from the front was getting a little better—U.S. troops were sweeping across North Africa and striking back in the Pacific. But there was no end in sight.

And one day in the cafeteria, a perky girl with long brown hair sat down beside him. It was no accident that seventeen-year-old Eleanor Lois Boyd had targeted Lemke's table. She'd been watching him for weeks, she said. He was one of the few boys her age in the plant. In a place full of roughnecks and rowdies, Clifford was neat, clean, and didn't feel the need to call attention to himself.

Lemke was shocked into silence, but the girl happily chatted away to him: She worked at Badger to stay busy while her boyfriend was fighting in the Pacific. There wasn't much to do in Baraboo, but she asked Lemke if he wanted to get together one night, maybe go to a movie. Lemke was tongue-tied. He'd never gone out with a girl, but he sheepishly nodded his head yes.

They went to movies, took long walks around the factory and Baraboo. Sometimes, they walked to Devil's Lake and sat by the water's edge holding hands. When the weather was nice, they packed a lunch and hiked along the winding trails to bluffs overlooking the park. Lemke didn't ask about Eleanor's boyfriend. His eighteenth birthday came and went, but he put off enlistment. He was falling in love.

In early May, their story took a new turn. Eleanor was pregnant. They both were eighteen, old enough. If Lemke enlisted in the navy, they could marry right away, and no one would count too closely the months before the baby came.

They said "I do" before a justice of the peace on May 30. On June 5, Lemke reported to the Great Lakes Naval Training Station in Chicago.

The next months passed by in a blur of training and orders: Chicago, Maine, and Newport, Rhode Island, where Lemke learned his wife had delivered a healthy baby girl, Mary Jane.

By February 1944, he was a seaman first class, an ammunition loader, assigned to the *Leon*. He traveled from Brooklyn, New York, stopping in Roanoke, Virginia, and then through the Panama Canal, on the way to Pearl Harbor.

The navy brought him face-to-face with his need for order and cleanliness. He'd never been on a ship before he joined. He had to learn to live in close quarters with men from all over the country, something that triggered his social anxiety. Lemke missed his wife and his family in Park Falls. He had been in such a hurry to leave, to jump into the fire . . .

And here he was, in Dry Dock 4, Pearl Harbor. He stood in the shadow of Landing Craft Infantry (G) 449, the ship that would be his new home. He stared at the gunboat, then he felt a tap on his shoulder. He turned around and saw a familiar face.

"They got you, too," chuckled Seaman First Class Charles Vogel.

Lemke smiled. They had been shipmates on the *Leon*. Lemke didn't know Vogel that well, but at least someone he knew would be on board the new ship.

"Let's get this over with," Vogel said.

Hoisting their seabags, they walked down a long flight of metal stairs leading to the bottom of the dry dock where the gunboat was being outfitted. They climbed up a ramp to the deck. They stopped for a moment to scan the ship. "It's small," Vogel said. "Probably a third of the size of the *Leon*. *Leon* was new. This thing looks like it's been around awhile."

"Our bunks are probably smaller, too," Lemke added. Christ, he thought, considering the living conditions on board. Would they have fresh water? What about the head?

He took a deep breath, then followed Vogel to what amounted to a steel building standing tall amidships. Inside the deckhouse they saluted Lieutenant Junior Grade Robert Duvall, the gunboat's communications officer. Lemke and Vogel stood at ease while Duvall checked their names against his roster. The men were among a dozen or so new sailors set to join the ship in the coming days.

Duvall gave them no time to settle in. With their bags still slung on their shoulders, he took them to meet the commanding officer: Lieutenant Willard Vincent Nash. They found the man in a crowded, cluttered cabin, his brow knitted over a thick book.

Duvall introduced Lemke and Vogel. Nash set aside his book and told them to grab two metal folding chairs and sit down. At thirty-four, Nash was older than most of the men on the ship. Tall, handsome, and a bit reserved, he looked a little like film star Fred MacMurray. Like the actor, Nash hailed from the Midwest; he was born and raised in Saginaw, Michigan.

Back home, Nash was an attorney, a partner in a successful law firm. He didn't have to serve; he could have stayed in Saginaw, but that was out of the question. In April 1942, Nash enlisted in the Naval Reserve as an officer. His parents were surprised, but he had no regrets. He couldn't stay in a county courthouse office while America was out making history.

A hands-on skipper, Nash made sure he knew the name of everyone on board. It was important that every crew member know his role on the gunboat and what was expected of him. That's why Nash talked personally to every sailor who joined the crew.

Nash asked Lemke and Vogel to talk a little bit about their backgrounds.

Lemke told him that he was from Wisconsin, had a wife and baby girl, and mentioned that his father was a World War I veteran. The eighteen-year-old Vogel said he was from Indianapolis, unmarried, and working in a grocery store when he decided to enlist.

It was Nash's turn. He told them the gunboat was undergoing repairs in advance of a new campaign. He didn't have details about the mission, but when he did, he would tell them. And when LCI-449 was ready, the crew would be involved in heavy training exercises. If they had any questions, they should go to one of the ship's officers. With that, Nash said they were free to go.

Lemke and Vogel were passed on to Boatswain's Mate Second Class Frank Blow, a fast-talking twenty-one-year-old from Southampton, Massachusetts.

Blow showed them over the gunboat, talking mostly about the crew, as they moved below. He was a muscular man, six-foot-three, and had to duck low through the hatchways. He'd joined the boat in August 1943, as part of the original crew. He said the group was small but tight-knit. Just about everyone got along. "If you got any problems, come to me. I'll take care of it," he said.

Lemke asked if they'd been in combat.

Blow stopped and leaned against the deck rail. He smiled as he recounted their last mission. They'd been to the Marshall Islands, he said, part of a group of twelve gunboats that moved along the shores of occupied islands to provide cover for landing Marines. The Kwajalein Atoll, he recounted, drawing out the strange syllables—that's where the Japanese fired rockets at them, from bunkers no one could see. The sound was deafening. It was terrifying, they were so vulnerable. And it went on for hours.

"They threw everything at us," Blow said.

Days later, when they had taken the island, he recalled the stench of dead bodies, rotting in the sun—the unforgettable "sulfur smell of death."

Lemke and Vogel didn't say a word. A moment passed.

"Any idea where we're headed next?" Lemke asked.

"Only scuttlebutt. Nothing for sure," Blow said, stepping down off the ship to show them the big guns up front. "We usually find out at the last minute. But just look around," he said, indicating the stacks of munitions going into the hold, the armor being screwed into place. "Don't worry, you won't be bored. Wherever we're going, there's going to be plenty of action. The closer we get to Japan, the worse it's going to get."

Lemke felt his stomach twist again.

2

NASH STARED DOWN at the map on his desk. "This," he said, jabbing his finger at a tiny dot, "is where we're headed." Mariana Islands. Another endless cluster of islands dotting the central Pacific.

They looked like nothing at all, but they meant everything, at least for the next few weeks. They were the next step in the U.S. military strategy developed in the wake of Pearl Harbor.

On the morning of December 7, 1941, the Japanese didn't just strike Hawaii; their planes bombed the Philippines, Wake Island, Guam, and other U.S. posts in the Pacific, as well as British positions in Southeast Asia. Within a month, the Japanese had taken most of the Philippines and seized Wake Island and Guam. By the end of February, President Roosevelt had ordered General Douglas MacArthur to withdraw from the Philippines.

The Japanese kept up the pressure. They invaded the Dutch East Indies, Dutch Borneo, and Singapore. Their planes bombed Darwin, Australia. A Japanese submarine even fired on an oil refinery near Santa Barbara, California. Americans panicked, realizing that Japan was capable of bringing the war to America's doorstep.

U.S. military brass, unused to retreating, scrambled to maintain their dignity as the wily, ruthless enemy cut a wide swath across the Pacific, crippling America's battleship fleet and snapping up a chain of islands across the region. If the Japanese managed to fortify those islands, they'd form an impenetrable barrier to the U.S. Navy.

By mid-1942, with victory in sight, Japanese fleet commander Isoroku Yamamoto decided to deal a crushing blow. Yamamoto would take Midway Island, at the end of the same island chain as Hawaii. When the Americans rallied their few remaining aircraft carriers, his fleet would be waiting.

But U.S. Navy code breakers figured out his secret, and Admiral Chester Nimitz, commander in chief of the Pacific Fleet, got the drop on Yamamoto. When the Japanese destroyers and carriers slipped within attack range of Midway Island, they were met with waves of American planes. Four Japanese carriers went down, and two destroyers were badly damaged. The crippled fleet withdrew, and the United States celebrated its first decisive victory in months.

After the Battle of Midway, Nimitz and MacArthur, the commander of the Allied forces in the Southwest Pacific, grabbed the initiative. They devised an "island hopping" strategy, capturing and fortifying key islands, one after another, until Japan itself came within range of American bombers. The Americans would bypass strongly held islands and strike at the enemy's weak points.

As MacArthur pushed along the New Guinea coast with Australian allies, toward the Philippines, Nimitz crossed the central Pacific by way of the Gilbert and Marshall Islands.

Now American forces were poised to attack the Marianas.

Herring knew Nash had been poring over the maps for days.

"What do you think?" Nash asked.

"It's not going to be easy," Herring said.

The officers sat down by the desk. The cabin was cramped, cluttered with reams of navy paperwork, piles of books, and stacks of maps and newspapers. The skipper pulled out a pack of Lucky Strikes and a Zippo, lit the end of a cigarette, and inhaled deeply.

Taking the Marianas—an arc-shaped archipelago including the islands of Guam, Saipan, and Tinian—would be a major blow to Japan, he said. If that happened, U.S. troops would be a mere thirteen hundred miles south of Tokyo.

But the Japanese were dug in already. They'd fight to the last man. And the Marianas terrain was a little different than the other islands they had encountered: There were mountainous jungles with deep caves, perfect hiding places. And unlike many of the other islands, people lived on the Marianas. There were civilians to consider, residents, especially on Saipan.

Herring leaned back in his chair. When Nash was on a roll, it was like an opening argument in a Saginaw courtroom. All you could do was listen.

"We have another problem, ourselves," he told Herring. "Personnel. Have you seen the boys coming aboard? Nearly half the crew is new. Most of them right off the farm."

It wasn't news to Herring. Men who'd been along since the beginning and through the Marshall Islands invasion were being transferred to bigger ships—destroyers, cruisers, battleships—because of their combat experience. Now Nash had to train new men for the upcoming mission. They seemed to be getting younger all the time.

But the new crew was just like the last ones, and just like the ones filling all the gunboats. They came from different states and classes and backgrounds, but were all young adults. They were children of the Depression, too tough to be called boys, but still too green to be men. Most were seventeen, eighteen, and nineteen years old. They hadn't waited for the draft. Almost all enlisted right after graduating, or they dropped out and got their parents to sign. When Pearl Harbor was bombed, these guys were kids. They had to wait their turn. And while they waited, they saw what happened at home when their brothers, fathers, and uncles were killed in action in Europe or in the Pacific. They still signed up. They still wanted a piece of Hitler, or Tojo.

This was their first deployment. They'd been trained, but they'd need to lean on veterans for guidance. And the 449 veterans weren't much older than the recruits. Just look at the officers: Herring was a month shy of twenty-three; Duvall and Lieutenant Byron Chew Yarbrough, the ship's executive officer, had both just turned twenty-four.

Nash was the grand old man at age thirty-four. The only person older was Pharmacist's Mate First Class Henry Beuckman. He was thirty-seven. Nash smoked. Herring sighed.

Nash was right. The crew was young, but they'd pick it all up quickly, Herring said. He reminded Nash what they'd gone through since they boarded the ship in 1943. They'd been in deadly firefights off godforsaken islands. Hell, their craft had even been totally redesigned, and their original mission changed, during what was supposed to be a routine layover in San Diego. The officers were experienced tap dancers, Herring said, and the seamen always stepped up to every change of tune, too. The new ones would do just as well, he predicted. Maybe even better.

Nash smiled. Herring's optimism was infectious, one of the reasons Nash liked being around him. During their time on the ship, they'd grown close. Even with an eleven-year age difference, and their north-south roots, Nash and Herring had much in common. They were solid middle-class, college-educated. Nash got his undergraduate and law degrees from the University of Michigan; Herring got an economics degree from Davidson College in North Carolina. They came from prominent families—Nash's father was an attorney who served one term in the Michigan state legislature and was a delegate to the Democratic National Convention that nominated Roosevelt in 1932. Herring's father owned three banks and a lumber mill in rural Roseboro, North Carolina. Both were bachelors.

But their strongest bond was their love of sailing. When time allowed, they chattered on for hours about boats, rigs, wind, and the adventures they'd had under sail.

Herring's experience was limited to summers at his parents' lakefront cottage on White Lake, North Carolina, where the family kept a twenty-foot sloop. Herring had spent countless hours gliding across the lake, passing other cottages, tacking and turning into the breeze, before heading back to shore. It was like the line in the poem "Sea Fever" by John Masefield: All Herring needed was a "tall ship and a star to steer her by" to feel complete.

Nash understood Herring's pining for "a windy day with the white clouds flying." Sailing was in his blood, too, and for three years when he was a teenager, Nash's summers had been spent working on a thirty-five-foot gaff-rigged sloop, making weekend cruises to points on Saginaw Bay and Lake Huron.

After graduating law school in 1935, Nash devoted a good part of his free time to sailing a forty-foot auxiliary schooner called the *Sea Horse* on Lake Huron and Lake Superior, including the North Channel and Georgian Bay. That's where he really learned how to pilot and plot courses—the challenges of Great Lakes navigation and sailing were fine preparation for a navy officer.

When the Marshall Islands campaign wound up and their orders arrived for Pearl Harbor, Nash and Herring almost bought a small outrigger sailboat together, a native craft a local man had for sale. They plotted how to stash it on the 449, and discussed where and when they might break it out on the ocean. But after examining the craft, Herring changed his mind. "The boat turned out to be in bad shape," Nash wrote his mother. "So we didn't find out how many cans of salmon and packages of cigarettes" the boat's owner "would have held out for."

But Nash and Herring made a pact: After the war, they'd sail together somewhere. It didn't matter if it was in Saginaw Bay or White Lake, they'd go for sure.

But with the way the war was going, they could be fighting in the Pacific for years, especially if they had to invade Japan.

Nash crushed the end of the cigarette in an ashtray and pulled a fresh one from the pack, letting it dangle from his mouth for a moment like Humphrey Bogart. Despite the challenges of being on the 449, and the dangers, Nash was thrilled to be its captain.

He had fought hard for an appointment to the U.S. Naval Reserve. Nash was thirty-two years old when he applied in 1942. At the time, they were looking for younger applicants. But Nash continued to push—he didn't want to stay home. This was his chance to do something good. He knew how to frame a good argument, how to put the right word into the right ear. And with his sailing experience, he knew he'd be an asset.

Nash was finally accepted. After several months of training, he was assigned to a landing craft infantry (large)—an amphibious assault ship—that was being commissioned at a New Jersey shipyard. He was set to be second in command, but the man chosen as skipper failed an eye test. Nash told his sister he was "drafted to replace him."

Nash boarded his ship for the first time on August 25, 1943, at the Barber Shipbuilding and Drydock Company in Perth Amboy, New Jersey. Now, after the overhaul, it was almost unrecognizable.

That summer of 1943 saw the navy in a chaotic rush to build the hundreds of landing craft infantry (L) boats needed to deliver troops directly onto beaches. The crafts were critical on the Pacific front, where they were the only way for American forces to land on remote islands.

The craft was a variation of the landing ship tank, a stroke of genius naval engineer John Niedermair had only designed a year previous, in 1942. They made the Pacific "island hop" possible as the battle campaign stretched over thousands of miles of ocean.

The design was revolutionary. Each narrow boat had a large ballast system that was filled for ocean passage, then pumped out in shallow water. The amphibious crafts ran counter to traditional navy rules. Generations of captains were warned never to "founder on rocks and shoals," and now they could aim their craft straight onto them.

The landing craft infantry (L) was far from impressive-looking. It looked like an armor-plated barge with a steel house stuck in the middle and a conning tower on top. The quarter-inch steel hull was only 158 feet long and 23 feet at its widest. Two hundred men could fit inside the ship, and once the craft planted its bow on the beach, a pair of steel ramps dropped and the men inside could exit.

Nash described it to his mother as a "passenger ship, soldiers being the passengers."

And like a barge, the landing craft infantry (L) was a flat-bottom boat. Instead of gliding over water, it rocked with every heavy wave. Men prone to seasickness spent half their time leaning over the deck, vomiting into the ocean.

As the American forces moved west across the water, the Japanese extended their supply lines eastward. They used convoys at first to carry men and supplies to the islands, but American planes and warships were making that dangerous. During the Battle of the Bismarck Sea in March 1943, a squadron of American and Australian aircraft attacked a Japanese resupply convoy headed to Lae, New Guinea. It was a disaster for Japan: Eight transport ships were sunk, as well as four of the eight destroyers accompanying the vessels. Three thousand Japanese soldiers were killed, and all the supplies were lost.

The Japanese began using barges more and more to transport supplies and men, especially between islands. The barges posed a problem for American forces. They could operate in relatively shallow water, hugging the coastline to avoid detection. The U.S. military had to develop a shoal-draft boat not only to hunt and destroy the barges, but to protect assault troops as they hit the shore, island after island.

Commanders were finding that their pre-invasion tactics—heavy bombing from planes and artillery barrages from big ships—weren't reducing the overwhelming number of American casualties. When artillery shells fell, the Japanese lay low in heavily fortified and camouflaged pillboxes, trenches, and bunkers. Unless the installations took a direct hit, the positions were hard to destroy. Soon as the American barrage died down and troops began landing on the beaches, the Japanese regrouped and opened fire. The navy needed gunboats that could move close to the shoreline to provide close-in fire support for troops as they made their landing.

The landing craft infantry (L) was perfect for the challenge; with a top speed of sixteen knots, it could operate in shallow water, turn on a dime, and maneuver in tight places. The only thing missing was firepower; it had only a pair of 20mm guns. So at the end of 1943, the navy began converting dozens of LCI (L)s into gunboats.

They welded on additional 20mm guns, and added in some 40mm guns, too. Some models, like the LCI (Mortar)—fired 4.2-inch mortar shells. Others, like the LCI (Rocket) could fire hundreds of 4.5-inch rockets, one after the other. Unknown to Nash and the other crew members in New Jersey, the navy had built a prototype LCI (Guns) in Pearl Harbor and, after successfully testing it, decided to go ahead and convert nearly a dozen more in Hawaii and San Diego.

Nash's ship left New Jersey in August 1943, a plain-Jane LCI (L), and sailed straight into the new technology. What was supposed to be a quick stop in San Diego, California, turned into a complete makeover at the U.S. Naval Repair Base.

Nash wasn't told much. The crew was sent ashore for R&R, and when the work was finished, their ship was one of five newly minted Landing

Craft Infantry (G) boats. The ship suddenly bristled with hardware: one 40mm gun on the bow and two on the gundeck, and ten rocket launchers that fired 4.5-inch shells.

With the new equipment came a new mission. Before they left for Pearl Harbor on January 6, 1944, new crew members came aboard, including gunners and ammo loaders. Two weeks later, they joined an additional eight refitted LCIs in Pearl Harbor, and Flotilla Three, Group Eight was formed. For the next few weeks, the gunboats trained hard to master firing the 20mm and 40mm guns in all kinds of conditions. Then they headed to the Marshall Islands, where the flotilla proved itself under intense enemy fire. They sometimes sailed so close to shore that the after-battle cleanup crew picked Japanese rounds off the deck.

Now here they were in Nash's room, wondering when it would all end, when they could go back to their loved ones and living a normal life. When could they go sailing? Nash had expressed the same thought in a letter to his mother:

> *Our executive officer was one of the many who predicted that Germany would be out of the war by Christmas. Possibly the end of the war is like the end of the Depression; it was just around the corner for a long time. Guess it doesn't matter how long it takes, we have no alternative but to win it.*

Nash took another deep drag. There was one more thing, he told Herring. During the next mission, they'd somehow be involved with a new navy unit, a team of swimmers that would disable underwater mines and sneak ashore in advance of the invasion to scout the best places to land troops and heavy equipment.

Herring was puzzled. Swimmers?

Nash nodded yes.

It may have sounded odd, but it made perfect sense to commanders. Even though invasions were planned down to the very last detail, amphibious warfare in the Pacific was as dangerous as hell. After an island was bombarded by battleships and aircraft carrier planes, waves of amphibious crafts—some transporting troops, others carrying equipment—would begin moving from the line of departure, usually a few thousand yards offshore, in carefully timed sequence to designated points on the beach.

But as they got closer, especially in the shallow water, the crafts not only had to pass through direct enemy fire, but they had to dodge a series of natural and man-made obstacles: reefs, barbed wire, concrete blocks.

In the early amphibious operations, there was no surefire way of detecting and destroying underwater obstructions close to the beach, or determining the depth of water. And that guesswork had resulted in heavy casualties for U.S. troops. Nowhere was that more apparent than during the invasion of Tarawa in November 1943.

Tarawa, an atoll in the Gilbert Islands, was strategically important, a gateway of the U.S. drive through the central Pacific toward the Philippines. Marines were supposed to easily seize the tiny but heavily fortified Japanese-held island of Betio in Tarawa.

But problems quickly arose for the fighting units. Lower-than-anticipated tides on the morning of the invasion prevented some U.S. landing crafts from clearing coral reefs that ringed the island. Marines were forced to abandon their landing crafts and waded to shore, hundreds of yards away, through chest-deep water amid heavy enemy fire.

Despite major resistance from the 4,500 Japanese troops, who fought to the death, the 18,000 Marines finally took the island after a bloody, seventy-six-hour battle in which both sides suffered heavy casualties. Three thousand Marines were killed or wounded. Of the Japanese defenders, only seventeen survived.

Word of the heavy casualties soon reached the U.S., and the public was stunned by the number of American lives lost in taking an island that was only two miles long and three-quarters of a mile wide at its broadest point.

In the aftermath, U.S. commanders learned an important lesson: They needed better pre-invasion reconnaissance—they had to plot the underwater terrain between the line of departure and the beach so obstacles could be blown up or avoided.

Admiral Richmond Turner, commander of the amphibious forces in the Pacific, turned to Draper Kauffman, a bomb expert who had been training demolition squads at Fort Pierce, Florida. In early 1944, Turner ordered Kauffman to expand the units and head to Hawaii. The admiral wanted him to train five full-blown units, called underwater demolition teams, for the Marianas mission.

Nash said he didn't know all the details, what they'd be doing with the teams, but he'd find out in a few days at a briefing. Until then, there was nothing they could really do. They couldn't train because the ship was in dry dock for at least another week. They were still waiting for a few more new crew members to report.

It would have been a perfect time for that outrigger, Nash said and smiled.

He extinguished the cigarette in the ashtray and leaned forward. He expected the crew to work hard, but he also wanted them to enjoy the rest of their time in Pearl Harbor. Once they headed to the Marianas, no one knew what would happen. He couldn't guarantee a thing.

3

RALPHAL JOHNSON BUTTONED his cuffs, ready for dinner in the officers' mess. Three more minutes, and he'd jump up from his shadowy berth in the bowels of the boat and put in another shift in the wardroom. Eight hours at their beck and call. Serve their dinners, wash their dishes, swab down the dining room for the next day. Stand by smiling, in case the lieutenants needed a shoeshine, laundry, snacks.

Three more minutes. He leaned back into the too-short mattress and rested deep.

Johnson was a steward's mate, the lowest rank on the ship, a position reserved for black men. It was May of 1944, but the U.S. military was as segregated as the Jim Crow South. Negroes held menial jobs in every branch of the armed services—the shittiest jobs, and the most miserable housing. On a cramped gunboat like the 449, that was an achievement.

Sleeping quarters, "berthing areas," were steel bunks, four high on each side of a narrow-aisle room, with the top bunk almost touching the ceiling. Each man had a locker twelve by eighteen inches deep and four feet high, with clothing rolled up tight to fit. Under the bottom bunk was a space a couple inches high where crewmen stored their shoes. Steel beams and pipes crisscrossed walls and ceilings. Men were constantly tripping over one another's stuff, swearing, stinking, snoring. The rooms were brutally hot. And Johnson's bunk was worst of all, tucked against the engine-room wall.

"We lived in such a confined area that it was like being in a butcher block in a meat market," recalled Seaman First Class John Overchuk, a gunner on the 449.

The bathroom was a hellhole. The men shared two showers, four washbasins, a urinal trough, and six toilets, nothing more than a slat of wood with holes. Seawater ran continually beneath and flushed the waste over the edge. The ship could distill three thousand gallons of freshwater each day, but it was strictly rationed, mostly for drinking and cooking, because the distilling equipment broke down often, and no one wanted to be stuck on the ocean without freshwater.

Conditions were harsh, and the men griped and complained to one another. Everyone but Johnson. There were sixty-five white seamen and officers, but Johnson was the only black sailor on board the 449.

The nineteen-year-old from Decatur, Texas, didn't feel sorry for himself. He knew he was just as capable as anyone aboard, and he'd already proved that. When Johnson wasn't serving the officers, he was standing behind a 20mm gun on the starboard side of the ship, firing at targets during practice, or hammering Japanese positions during combat. There were all-black units in the military—some on the front lines—but an African-American was almost never seen in such a critical position in an all-white unit.

Still, the officers couldn't ignore that Johnson, a five-foot-seven, muscular kid, was a crack shot.

The fact that Johnson had even made it this far was no mean feat.

He was the oldest of nine children. His parents had been just teenagers when they got married; Roosevelt Johnson was nineteen; Dora, seventeen. They met in Venus, Texas, and soon moved seventy-five miles north to Decatur, where land was cheaper. Roosevelt, the grandson of slaves, dreamed of owning his own farm.

His goal was to work hard, save money, and buy land. He didn't want to become a sharecropper. That was nothing more than a step above slavery, he liked to say. All your profits went to the white landowner, and there was never enough money left at the end of the season. You were always in debt.

Decatur was a thriving little railroad town surrounded by farmland.

Cotton had been a major crop for years, but by the time Roosevelt arrived in the mid-1920s, the soil had been depleted. Roosevelt found work picking cotton, sometimes traveling more than a hundred miles, following the harvest.

His family lived in a small house on the black side of segregated Decatur, a place where everyone knew their neighbors and looked out for one another, recalled his childhood friend, Janet Minor. The community banded together to build a one-room schoolhouse on North Newark Street, but the conditions were second-rate. The students used "outdated, hand-me-down-books" from the white schools, and often there weren't enough chairs or desks in the crowded classroom. The school only went up to the eighth grade. If they wanted to continue their education, black students had to find a way to the "Negro High" in Denton, about thirty-five miles away.

Ralphal Johnson was a good student, but as the Depression set in, his father often pulled his son out of class to help him pick cotton. The boy hated it—he liked class and loved playing baseball after school with his friends. He was getting pretty good at it, too. He could scoop up anything hit in front of him, and could hit the ball farther than anyone in the neighborhood. But all the kids knew better than to talk back to their father.

Roosevelt and Ralphal were often gone for days, driving a beat-up Ford from farm to farm, looking for work. When they found a job, Roosevelt would motion for his son to get out of the car. It was time to get busy. Picking cotton was backbreaking labor. With long sacks strapped over their shoulders, the men stooped to pluck the white blossoms from their bristly stalks, then tucked them into the bag. Fingers and wrists were covered in cuts and scrapes, but the ache in their stooped backs was worst of all. Ralphal watched his father moving expertly up and down the long rows in the hundred-degree heat. He only took short breaks. At night the pair took rifles out beyond the edges of town to shoot rabbits or quail for the dinner pot. Once in a while, they even bagged a deer.

Roosevelt gave up on his dream farm, but by 1936 he had saved enough for a down payment to buy a small patch of land in town, Lot 1, Block 6. It was the perfect spot for a growing family. Soon, the Johnsons' house on East Brown Street became the center of the neighborhood, filled with kids who played in the yard. Ralphal and his best friends Lloyd Francis and Carl Coleman played baseball, wrestled, and boxed one another in a rocky field near the house.

They stayed in their own neighborhood. Unless their mothers worked as housekeepers for a white family, Decatur's young black citizens stayed pretty much out of sight. When they did venture downtown or out of town, whites wouldn't hesitate to call Ralphal or his friends some racially charged epithet: nigger, coon, pickaninny.

Public places in Decatur and Wise County were clearly divided into black and white, from the bus stops to the movie theaters. At the Ritz Theater, black customers climbed a ladder to "the buzzards' nest," a separate balcony area well away from white customers. At the Majestic, "Negroes" were steered to a small roped-off seating section.

Just walking to the movies—or anyplace in Decatur—could spell trouble. If you looked the wrong way at a white boy or girl, if someone thought you were "sassy," or "uppity," a beating sometimes followed. And beatings had a way of turning into lynchings.

The Ku Klux Klan was active throughout Texas, especially in rural communities where a handful of Confederate soldiers were still alive. The police helped preserve the status quo; no one knew just who the Klan members were.

Newspapers routinely published stories that reinforced the racial divide. In 1901, when President Theodore Roosevelt invited black inventor Booker T. Washington to dine with him at the White House, the local paper ran a piece written by an outraged local "poet." (The 234-word poem "Elegy" used the word "nigger" twenty-three times.) In 1934, six African-Americans were fined for playing blackjack and poker, and the judge scolded them, saying: "Those games are the White Man's pastime, and you negroes have committed a grievous violation of society by usurping the rights of the white race." The reporter then added a comment from one of the suspects as they were leaving the court: "No mo'e black jack or white jack for us. That jedge knows us niggers."

Reporters even used racial slurs in routine entertainment stories. When band leader Cab Calloway performed in Fort Worth, Texas, in October 1934, the *Wise County Messenger* said his "hot orchestra and distinctive style of singing is indebted to Southern pickaninnies for his song trick which has made him famous. It is called scat singing . . . supplanting the lyrics of songs with meaningless 'hi-de-ho' and 'do-de-do' are the best examples. First to do it were the colored urchins entertaining travelers at way stations to Southern resorts."

All of it took a toll on young Ralphal, who once threatened to slug the next person who called him "nigger." His father said there were better ways to strike back: Work hard, be successful, "love the Lord thy God with all thy heart." Roosevelt Johnson didn't want his son hanging from a tree.

The young man took his passion to the baseball diamond. After finishing eighth grade, he landed a job at a farm supply store. He joined the Decatur Cats, an African-American baseball team that traveled around the region, playing teams out of Dallas and Fort Worth. A second baseman with power and range, Johnson hoped to eventually make it to the Negro Leagues. But plans changed after Pearl Harbor. North Texas might call him "boy," but Ralphal Johnson was an American man.

Just after his eighteenth birthday a letter arrived from the local draft board: He was going to be inducted into the armed services.

He knew he'd probably end up in the army. After years of kicking around in dusty fields, the last thing he wanted to do was live in a foxhole. So Johnson made up his mind: he'd enlist in the navy. He'd never seen the ocean, or been aboard a boat, but he was ready to go. His mother broke into tears. His father said he knew this day would come. The war was in full swing; the military was taking heavy casualties and needed replacements.

Johnson's name appeared in the newspaper, on a list of local men "reporting for duty." Right after the word "Navy" and just before his name there was a word tucked in the middle: "Colored."

Johnson discovered quickly that the segregation of civilian life spilled over into the military. When he arrived at the Great Lakes Naval Training Station in Chicago in June 1943, he was assigned to Camp Robert Smalls, which trained African-American seamen.

The men went through the same rigorous training as white seamen on the other side of the sprawling base. But there was a critical difference: When white sailors finished boot camp, they usually continued with advanced training. When the black men finished basic, they were more often than not sent to be servants.

Johnson wanted to be a gunner—he'd learned gunnery basics in class, and his old quail-shooting skills gave him an edge over all the other shooters at the range. But he wouldn't be shooting where he was going, the officers told him. Instead, they trained him to be a steward's mate. Johnson was beside himself—he didn't want to spend the war shining shoes. The navy's orientation manual spelled out all the details:

> Steward's mates are in charge of the wardroom, pantries, galley and officers' rooms. Most of them are Negroes . . . Since they are constantly in rather close contact with officers and have frequent occasion to be in the wardroom and in the officers' rooms, there is a tendency to become too familiar with them, or perhaps too brusque with them. The officer should always be tactful in his dealings with the Steward's Mate. They are readily amenable to discipline if properly handled.

The navy had even put together a promotional movie glorifying the role of steward's mates. It included stock pictures of black men who'd taken heroic action in the face of enemy fire. When the Japanese attacked Pearl Harbor, steward Doris "Dorie" Miller rushed to the deck of the USS *West Virginia* and fired round after round from a .50-caliber anti-aircraft machine gun at dive-bombing Japanese planes. After hearing about the exploits, a new steward turns to the film's narrator: "And I thought steward's mates were just waiters," he says in awe.

"Well . . . you might call them that, but they're fighting men, too," the narrator responds.

Johnson knew it was bullshit. Negroes weren't fighting men. The navy intentionally kept them out of combat. They could only be stewards or mess cooks. In the navy's eyes, they were inferior—and that infuriated Johnson.

When Johnson finished boot camp, he received his assignment: Report to a newly built landing craft infantry (L) being commissioned in a New Jersey shipyard. After arriving, he introduced himself to Nash, Herring, and the other officers.

For weeks, Johnson kept to himself as he learned the ship's routine.

He overcame seasickness on the maiden voyage down to Panama and on to San Diego. Maybe when they got to Hawaii there would be a baseball team, or maybe he could box, he told himself. Heavyweight champ Joe Louis was black, and the army allowed him to box. He had to find something to help him pass the time.

When the craft was changed to a gunboat in San Diego, Johnson's outlook changed, too. They had a long trip ahead of them to Pearl Harbor, with plenty of equipment training exercises on the way, including firing the new guns. This was Johnson's chance to impress the officers with his marksmanship.

The 20mm Oerlikon was one of the navy's most versatile and powerful automatic weapons. It could fire up to 450 rounds per minute, the ammunition supplied from a detachable magazine. The gun could shoot planes out of the sky, or pierce an enemy pillbox on the beach a few thousands yards away.

Four men were needed to effectively operate the 20mm. They included the loader, who was responsible for removing and replacing magazines; the column operator, who raised and lowered the gun to find the best position for the gunner; and the sight-setter, who manned the telephones and kept the range set according to officers' orders. But the gunner was the most important member of the team. Standing behind the 20mm, his job was to aim and fire the weapon. During a battle, it was the hot seat as dive-bombing planes did their best to take him out.

The gunboat convoy left San Diego, and training began the second day out. Crews on the destroyers alongside dropped empty boxes over the side, creating floating targets.

The gun crews who had joined the 449 in San Diego got the first crack at the boxes. After they were finished, some of the other crew volunteered to shoot, including Johnson. Herring didn't know what to make of Johnson's action. He could have stopped him—he could have told him to return below—but he didn't. If Johnson was qualified, they could use him. The color of his skin didn't matter.

When Johnson strapped on the harness that melded his body to the gun, some of the men grumbled. Johnson ignored them. He settled in behind the weapon. He leaned against the shoulder rest and peered through the sight. There were the targets, clear as day. Just like quail, he told himself. He wrapped his finger around the trigger, eyed the target down the barrel, and squeezed. Boom! When the smoke cleared, they could all see the results: direct hits. When the destroyers released balloons into the air, the outcome was the same: Johnson didn't miss.

They had gunnery practice three times in the next four days, and Johnson was right on the money every time. Herring was amazed. Johnson seemed to have a natural feel for the weapon.

Herring shared his thoughts with Nash. Without question, Johnson was one of the best shots on the gunboat. With more training, he could become top class.

Herring knew they were skating along the edge of regulations. Negroes weren't supposed to fire guns. But this guy was too good to stay hidden below.

Nash listened carefully. He'd learned to weigh all the evidence before making a decision. This was no different. Race had a way of bringing out the worst in people, and some of the seamen might grumble or even create trouble. But if Johnson was as good as advertised, he could prove useful in the face of enemy fire. Nash agreed: Johnson would become a triggerman. But on one condition: He'd still have to perform his duties as a steward. And if anyone complained, or made any negative racial comments, that man would be disciplined.

Johnson did not disappoint. He had proved his mettle many times since that day, cool under fire during the Marshall Islands campaign. Whenever the gunboat hugged the shore, he stood at his starboard station, firing round after round. Whatever misgivings the crew might have had about a black cabin steward firing a gun in combat were blown apart like pillboxes.

If the people at home could see him, they wouldn't believe it, he thought with a smile.

He was a Negro gunner some days, yes. But today, right now, he was a steward. At 16:00, Ralphal Johnson jumped up from his bunk. It was time to go to work.

4

FRANK BLOW LATHERED up his chin and cheeks before a mirror in the head, getting ready. The bath area was cramped as usual, and men were waiting to use the sink and showers. But Blow wasn't going to hurry. Not when he was shaving. He wanted to look good. He had liberty, and you never knew what could happen in Honolulu. There were girls out there. You gotta look your best.

His buddies kidded him. Respectable girls didn't hit the nightspots— their parents locked them up. Blow knew that was true, but he'd take his chances. He didn't want to end up with the guys on Hotel Street, the city's notorious red light district. The gregarious Blow would rather get drunk and stagger back to the 449 than end up in bed with a prostitute.

The sailors called him "Joe Blow," a sign he was a good guy. But as a boatswain, Blow was one of the leaders on the gunboat. He gave out the daily work assignments for the seamen and checked to make sure they were done correctly. Blow could be a hard-ass if he felt you were slacking off. He'd get in your face, spitting out cuss words like a machine gun. You wouldn't make the same mistake twice.

By now everyone knew this could be their last liberty for a while. In a few days, the gunboat would be moved from the dry dock to a staging area in the harbor. Blow grabbed a group of buddies as well as a few of the new guys, and told them they were heading out for a night of action.

But Seaman First Class Bruce Hallett and Gunner's Mate Third Class

Charles Banko didn't know what to make of Blow. The two friends had reported together a few days earlier. The nineteen-year-old Hallett grew up in Wenatchee, Washington, a city on the Columbia River—his father grew apples for a living. Like Lemke, Hallett's father refused to sign papers for his son to join the navy, so he had to wait another year. When his time came, he was a 40mm gunner on a gunboat that saw action in the Marshall Islands. The boats were popular targets, strafed by dive-bombing Japanese planes. The planes came so close that months later, Hallett could still see the pilots' faces in his sleep.

The nineteen-year-old Banko was more of a rebel. His parents ran a little gas station in East Selah, Washington, and after he graduated high school, Banko visited the navy recruiting station and took the aptitude test for Officer Candidate School. He wanted to be a fighter pilot. He passed, but was told he'd have to wait until he turned eighteen. The thought of sitting around for six months didn't appeal to him. Banko asked what would happen if he enlisted in the navy that day—could he start Officer Candidate School on his birthday? The recruiter said yes. But after the papers were signed and his birthday arrived, the navy said no. Banko was bitter.

He was assigned to LCI-455, but trouble followed. He fought with the boatswain. He was caught stealing food from the galley while he was on guard duty, and spent a few days in the brig. Banko stopped shaving, his beard a defiance. A couple of times he didn't make it back from liberty on time. Finally, the commanding officer had had enough. He shipped Banko off to the 449.

But since Banko's arrival, he'd been on his best behavior. That was because of Hallett, one of Banko's roommates on LCI-455. He kept reminding his buddy of the fresh start.

"You don't want to screw up again," he'd tell Banko.

"Yeah, right," he'd mumble.

To most people, they were as opposite as they were close: Hallett was tall, thin, and easygoing, with a wide smile, the type of guy who had no trouble making friends. Banko was short with a round face and a bushy red beard. He could be a smart-ass, especially when he was drinking. But for all their differences, they shared a few things in common. They both grew up in small towns in rural Washington. They came from close-knit families and couldn't wait to enlist.

They bonded on LCI-455, staying up late, talking about their love of hunting and fishing. Hallett would listen as Banko recounted stories of how he and his two brothers would spend endless summer days casting lines in the Yakima River, trying to catch whitefish. Hallett would follow, telling Banko how he and his three older brothers would hunt deer and fish in streams in the Wenatchee National Forest. They'd talk about how far they'd come. Just a year earlier, Hallett and Banko were fresh-faced teenagers, hanging out in soda shops, borrowing their parents' cars to go on dates. Now they were tough combat veterans, ready to take their place on another gun crew: this one on the bow of the 449.

Hallett turned to Banko. "What do you think?"

Banko shrugged. They didn't really know Blow or some of the other guys. But what the hell: "Let's have fun," he said.

As darkness set over Pearl Harbor, Blow, Banko, Hallett, Lemke, and some of the others stepped onto the deck in their navy-blue suits and white sailor hats. Blow spotted little Lawrence Bozarth near the deck-house.

"You wanna go out on the town?" he asked.

Bozarth smiled and politely declined. Blow knew he would, but had to ask. He really liked the kid.

Blow waved goodbye and the group followed him off the ship. Bozarth watched as they disappeared into the night, then he headed to his room. Finally, it would be quiet for a while.

When he reached his bunk, Bozarth pulled a pocket-sized prayer book from his pants pocket and sat down. The book had a calendar inside, and beside each date was a Bible verse. The day he left his Oklahoma home for boot camp in San Diego, California—September 17, 1943—he had read the passage from John 14:18: "I will not leave you comfortless: I will come to you." His first big battle in the Marshall Islands, the day's word was from Isaiah 41:10, "Fear thou not; for I am with thee: be not dismayed; for I am thy God: I will strengthen thee; yea . . . I will uphold thee with the right hand of my righteousness."

The Word was his strength, but Bozarth was homesick and lonely.

Sitting in his bunk alone, he let himself feel how he missed his family. When he was down, they were always there for him, offering prayers and words of encouragement. He needed them now.

Bozarth was eighteen years old, and at five-foot-seven, 115 pounds, he looked much younger. He was only seventeen when he enlisted. He'd convinced his dad to give him permission to join, even though the family was devoted to nonviolence.

"Lawrence was so afraid he was not going to be able to do his part for the war effort and begged Mom and Dad to sign his paper so he could join the service. Dad finally gave in, but he did not want to," recalled Mildred Cosper, one of his three sisters.

Bozarth was the second oldest of six siblings. Their big family lived in Tulsa, Oklahoma, among a swarm of aunts, uncles, and cousins who were always stopping by their home. His grandpa was a pastor, and his father, a devout Christian, was a broom-maker.

Broom-making was still a handcraft then. Bundles of broomcorn, a type of sorghum grass that grew exceptionally well in Oklahoma, arrived on the factory floor in 350-pound bales. Workers sorted the stalks by length and color, then sprayed them with water to make them pliable. They then were shaped, flattened, inserted inside broom-heads, and sewed in place. Young Bozarth had learned to make brooms himself over the years, from watching his father work. The family didn't have a lot of money, but Lawrence and Leona Bozarth taught their children to work hard.

Their eldest son set an example for his siblings. He was passionate about golf—he kept a scrapbook of golfers: Byron Nelson, Ben Hogan—and he took a job as a caddy at a country club a few miles from home. He walked to work until he made enough money to buy a bicycle, then he handed over much of his earnings to his parents. With time left over between work and school, young Lawrence played with his brothers and sisters in the backyard. He cut and trimmed fishing rods, and took the kids down to the spring-fed creek where they could sometimes catch their dinner.

"We would sit on a tree that had fallen across the creek and watch the fish take our bait," Cosper recalled.

In the spring, he planted a garden. "I remember Mother saying, 'Son, you had better come in here and rest.' Lawrence was always a giver or doer. He was never idle," his sister remembered.

Dinner was the most important time of the day, with their father saying grace over the meal. Everyone was expected to sit down at the table— no excuses. Afterward they gathered around the radio, or played gospel records on their old Victrola.

The Bible was at the center of the Bozarth household, and Lawrence Junior knew large passages of the book by heart. Pearl Harbor brought the teenager to a spiritual crisis. Like most of the young men around him, he felt the need to defend his country, but he was deeply troubled by the thought of killing another human being, even an enemy soldier. It ran counter to everything he had been raised to believe.

In Matthew 26:52, Jesus said: "Put up again thy sword into his place: for all they that take the sword will perish with the sword." In Luke 6:27, Jesus urged his followers to "Love your enemies, do good to them which hate you." But if the Japanese and Germans won the war, what would happen to his country? His family?

He discussed it with his father one evening, over the kitchen table. Ma saw that something important was happening, so she took the kids out onto the porch to visit with their cousins. Inside, the old man just listened while his boy unloaded his concerns. He took his son's hands, and both men bowed their heads in silent prayer. When they opened their eyes, the son told his father he'd made up his mind: He was going.

The morning Bozarth left for boot camp, the family got up early for a big breakfast of eggs, bacon, toast, and coffee. Usually the breakfast table was filled with chatter and laughter, but that morning they ate in silence. When it was time to leave, Bozarth grabbed his bag, hugged his siblings goodbye, then jumped into the backseat of his parents' car. His mother and father drove him to the station. As they pulled away from the house, Bozarth glimpsed his brothers and sisters standing along the porch rail, sobbing. To cheer them up, he pressed his face against the inside of the car window and made a funny face. No one seemed to notice. No one laughed. At the moment of goodbye young Lawrence kissed his mom and dad, and promised he wouldn't abandon his Christian principles, and that he would come home safe.

The long ride to San Diego gave him plenty of time to think. Maybe there was a position in the navy where he could be useful but wouldn't have to kill anyone. He'd learned in boot camp how to load and shoot rifles as well as 20mm and 40mm guns. If he had to be on the front lines, maybe he could load the ammunition rather than actually fire the gun. He ran the idea by his commanders. They saw his sincerity and went along with his request.

Once he was assigned to the 449, the crew immediately noticed his humble, self-contained manner. He was polite, didn't cuss, never raised his voice. He whispered a prayer over his chow. He was physically small, but strong in a way that commanded their respect. They felt protective of him, like they would a younger brother. And they noticed something else: He carried his pocket prayer book with him, and read from it every night, along with his Bible. Soon, members of the crew sought him out during their quiet moments. They asked him about God, about scripture. Sometimes they prayed together.

Maybe Bozarth knew something they didn't. Maybe he had a line of communication with God. Maybe prayer could add an extra layer of protection in combat. It certainly couldn't hurt anything.

As the days went on and more men opened their hearts to his quiet witness, Bozarth began wondering if the Lord might have led him here for a reason. Maybe there was a call on his life. He'd find out soon enough, though . . . because for now his primary job was loading ammo. As he'd been told over and over in his lifetime of Sunday school and Bible studies, you had to wait for God to reveal his plans.

NASH COULDN'T SLEEP. The air in his cabin was sticky. The humidity in the tropics was unbearable. The blades of the electric fan pushed the hot, stale air in his direction. There was no relief. He was dead tired, but he knew it would probably be another long night of tossing and turning.

He ambled to his desk, opened the drawer, and pulled out a pen and paper. It was almost Mother's Day and he wanted to make sure she knew he was thinking about her. But as he stared at the blank piece of paper, his mind drifted to his hometown and the cool summer nights in Saginaw. It could get hot during the summer. No question. But at night, a cool breeze from Saginaw Bay would blow across the city. And if it got too hot, he could always take his boat out on the water and sleep under the stars.

For Nash, there was no place like Saginaw. His family was well known in the industrial city of nearly 83,000 people about a hundred miles north of Detroit, Michigan. His parents encouraged Nash and his two brothers and sister to do well in school and to give back to the community, to their country. That was one of the reasons Nash enlisted.

Saginaw was a thriving factory town whose economy was tethered to Detroit's automotive industry. Even during the Great Depression, people could find work there if they looked hard enough. The city had a Chevrolet parts plants that built transmissions, gear housings, and power steering pumps.

And when the United States entered World War II, the city's industrial base changed direction, producing munitions, ordnance, and components for military vehicles. The city was also home to a factory that produced .30-caliber machine guns, armor-piercing shells, and M1 carbine rifles.

Nash knew he had to get started on the letter. After Herring left, he had written to his sister Jean, his rock, his confidante. He could tell her anything and the words just flowed. He knew he couldn't write too much in a letter because every piece of mail was censored. Yarbrough, the ship's executive officer, examined every one and redacted anything that could give away their positions. "Loose lips sink ships," Yarbrough liked to say, repeating the government's slogan to keep people from inadvertently disclosing useful information to the enemy.

But Nash didn't know why he was having trouble now. He lifted his pen and began writing.

"Mother's Day greetings. Not necessary to tell you that I'd like to be home for the occasion, that goes without saying," he wrote, adding that he was going to send her a telegram wishing her a happy Mother's Day, but he was afraid it "might cause you some anxiety before you had a chance to open the envelope and read it." (During the war, people lived in constant fear of receiving telegrams because they were the main way families were notified that a loved one had been killed in the war.)

He had some good news to share: He had just been promoted to a full lieutenant.

And he thanked her for sending copies of the *Saginaw News*. They were helping him "keep somewhat in touch with the old home town. That way I should be in a better position to start practicing law again in Saginaw after this global war is wound up." Then he offered words of encouragement. "Spring should be with you soon, bringing with it birds, green grass, flowers . . ."

He paused for a moment. Winters in Saginaw could be dreary, with the extreme cold, snow, and foundries belching gray and white smoke against the pale blue sky. But at the first sign of spring, there was a rebirth—people opened their windows, listened to the songbirds, and spruced up their homes in anticipation of warmer weather.

Spring was always Nash's favorite time of the year. He wondered if the tulips and daffodils had started blooming at his family's house. Even though he was in his thirties, he still lived at home. He explained that he was there to help take care of his parents, who, in their mid-sixties, were getting up in age.

But his friends and family kidded him about not having a place of his own, saying he should get married.

When Nash found out that his younger brother Richard had just gotten engaged, he was happy. "Guess I'll be the only bachelor left in the family," he wrote his mother. "Am certainly glad he decided to get married. Can't see any point in waiting once you've found the right girl."

Nash had always had girlfriends, but it never reached a point where he wanted to get married. But lately, he had been thinking a lot about one girl: Dorothy Wallace.

She was Jean's friend and working as a writer in New York. His sister had reminded her brother that if he ever made it to the city, he should call her. She just knew they'd hit it off.

So when Nash went to New York in August 1943 to join the ship, he decided to call. He picked up the telephone in his Manhattan hotel room and dialed her number. When the female voice on the other end answered, he introduced himself. He said he was Jean Nash's brother. He was in town for a while, waiting for "a ship to be commissioned," and would she like to have dinner with him the next evening?

She said yes, and they agreed to meet at six at the Astor Hotel.

"I was not excited about the date," she recalled. "In fact, I didn't care whether I was on time."

After work, she had drinks with two friends at a bar next to her office in Times Square. Then she walked a few blocks to the hotel. She was a couple of minutes late, but when she walked inside she glimpsed a tall, slim man dressed in "whites," his navy uniform.

She was surprised. Many of her friends tried to set her up on dates, but they always seemed to end badly. The guys were either boring or unattractive. Nash, though, was handsome. And as they drank daiquiris, she realized that he was articulate and funny. They had the same taste in books, movies, and entertainers. They stayed at the crowded bar for a while, then walked about seven blocks to the Glass Hat restaurant on 49th Street and Lexington Avenue. They ordered soup and steak, but they were too busy talking to eat.

Nash told her to call him Vinnie and filled her in on his life. He was an attorney, a graduate from the University of Michigan, but if he had his way, he'd spend the rest of his life on the water. Dorothy said she also was a Wolverine, graduating with an English degree. She later moved to New York with her family—they lived in an apartment in Forest Hills. She was a former press agent with CBS and had worked at *Life* magazine. Now she was the East Coast editor for a company that published several magazines, including *Movieland*.

Nash asked if she had met anyone famous. Dorothy laughed and began rattling off an impressive list of clients at CBS: Ronald Reagan, Betty Grable, Danny Kaye, Frank Sinatra—the list went on and on. She handled their publicity in New York, escorted them to their appearances on live radio shows, and went to cocktail parties where they'd spend all night drinking, and if there was a piano in the room, they'd start singing. It was like that with entertainers: They always felt the need to perform, especially when they were drunk, she said. With her new job, every time a movie star was in town promoting a new film, they'd stop up to her office, hoping she'd write a story.

Nash soaked it all in. Dorothy was smart and witty. She wasn't a knockout, but there was something very attractive about her. She wore a black dress that hugged her thin frame. Her brown hair was soft, short, and curled. Her makeup was perfect, from the black eyeliner to the red lipstick. She had a warm and friendly smile. And she was close to his age, just shy of her thirtieth birthday.

After dinner, they decided to walk a few blocks uptown to English singer and actress Gracie Fields's new nightclub. The streets were teeming with people rushing from one spot to another. Soldiers and sailors in uniform walked in groups, heading to hotels or clubs with big bands, or looking for women. Taxis honked to move pedestrians out of the way. Men hawked newspapers and magazines from newsstands, while cops patrolled the streets looking to keep law and order. For Nash, it all added to the ambiance.

When they got to the club, it was dead. So they headed to another: the Monkey Bar at the Hotel Elysée. But Dorothy had an ulterior motive: The more time they spent together that night, the more she was attracted to Nash. But she was going to test him, or "try Jean's brother out," she later recalled.

The bar was dim and dark and crowded, but they managed to grab chairs near a piano. Moments later, singer Bruce Raeburn sat down at the keyboard. He began singing a bouncy melody, but the lyrics of "Hilda Was a Darn Good Cook" were risqué, filled with double entendre about what Hilda liked to do in the bedroom. The crowd roared with laughter, and when Dorothy glanced at Nash, he was in stitches, too.

When they left, he hailed a taxi for her and asked if he could see her again. She said yes. Two days later, they met again, this time for lunch, and talked about books and writers. They even shared plots for movies—what they would write if they had a chance.

She stared at the clock on the wall. It was time to get back to work. As they were leaving, he told her he was shipping out, and didn't know when he'd be back. He asked if he could write her. She smiled. "Of course," she said. He walked her back to her office building. When they stopped in front, he turned and kissed her. It was a short kiss, but he felt the connection. He didn't want to leave. He stood there and watched as she disappeared into the building.

Nash was so excited that he fired off a letter that night to his sister about the dates.

He knew Jean loved to write, so he suggested a plot for a short story, one that he had bounced off Dorothy earlier in the day. He explained that at sea, a navy officer serves as a censor, reading letters to make sure no one reveals the ship's location, mission, or other vital information. The letters are posted in unsealed envelopes and then the "censor does his stuff."

"But what would happen if the censor switched envelopes for two letters by one of his 'wolves,' one letter having been directed to his wife and children, and the second being intended for a single woman who doesn't suspect the true state of affairs and has been falling for his line about marrying her after the war is over," he wrote.

He said he wouldn't disclose how he "happened to get the thought," but the idea "intrigued him."

Since he left New York, Nash had been writing Dorothy letters, telling her about life on the gunboat. She wrote him back, too, sharing her latest celebrity tales.

Nash tried to turn his attention back to the letter that he was writing to his mother, but Dorothy was still on his mind. He couldn't remember the last time he had felt this way about a woman. Finally, he just gave up. He opened his desk drawer and put away his paper and pen. He couldn't finish the letter. Not now. All he wanted to do was close his eyes, and maybe, if he was lucky, he'd be back in New York—at least for one night.

IN THE SLEEPING quarters below, Blow was wide awake. His buddy James Casaletto was snoring loudly, sprawled out on the bed above him. So was Max Ball, curled up in a bunk on the opposite side of the room.

But Blow wasn't up because of the noise. It was because of the list in his pocket.

For all of his bluster, Blow was one of the most respected men on the gunboat. The officers depended on him: They only had to ask him once and the job would get done.

"He loved to have fun, but he was responsible. He always took care of business," Ball recalled.

Earlier that night, Blow and the others had hit several Pearl Harbor bars. They listened to music on jukeboxes, chased shots of whiskey with glasses of beer, and swapped stories before stumbling back to the 449. No girls. Just lots of drinking and bullshitting. Casaletto poked fun at his family life, his five kids and his crazy wife. Ball was his usual rowdy self: "No one better look at me the wrong way," he warned. Not to be outdone, Banko bragged about his troubles on LCI-455.

"They knew not to screw with me," Banko said, loudly.

"That's why they got rid of your ass," Hallett joked.

They all laughed.

When they returned to the 449, Casaletto and Ball fell asleep as soon as their heads hit their pillows. Not Blow. Instead, he pulled out a piece pf paper and scribbled a list of things he planned to do to prepare the crew for the next operation. He had learned that from his father, a quiet but stern World War I veteran who found peace in the green, rolling hills of western Massachusetts.

Frank Blow Senior was a farmer—he raised a few cows and pigs, grew corn and beans and other vegetables. He'd write down what he needed to do on scraps of paper, anything handy—wrappers, receipts.

Blow knew his father's story: He grew up in a French-Canadian town, toiled as a farmhand, pitched hay, fed barn animals. As a teenager, he immigrated to the United States, hoping to save enough money to buy a farm. But Frank Blow Senior took a detour. Swept up by America's patriotic fervor, he enlisted in the U.S. Army in 1917. Assigned to the 305th Infantry Regiment, Company A, he fought in some of the bloodiest battles of the war. When it was over, he returned to Massachusetts, married his girlfriend, bought a patch of land, and started a family. He rarely talked about the military. If someone asked, he'd shrug: "We got hit. We hit 'em back." You move forward in life. That's what he taught his son, the middle of three children. He encouraged his boy to always do the right thing. Take care of your family, he liked to say. And that's what Blow did when tragedy struck.

Blow was just sixteen years old when his father died unexpectedly in 1939. His mother, Helena, didn't know how they'd make it. He told her not to worry. Blow dropped out of high school and picked up odd jobs.

After the Japanese attacked Pearl Harbor, Blow wanted to enlist right away. He had just turned eighteen, but his mother begged him to wait. He did, landing a job as a plumber's apprentice. But by early 1943, Blow couldn't wait any longer. He told his mother he was leaving and enlisted on April 7, 1943.

Blow soaked up all the training, and his natural leadership skills drew the attention of the officers. He quickly advanced from seaman first class to boatswain's mate first class. Officers suggested to Blow that he'd make a good one himself. But he said no. He was having too much fun as an enlisted man, just being "one of the guys."

When the crew went out, Blow acted like a ladies' man to impress his buddies. With his muscular arms, playful smile, and soft brown eyes, the girls swooned. But what Blow didn't tell his friends was that he had no intention of straying. He had a girl back home, Mary Hodges. He'd met her at a dance in New York City, shortly before the gunboat sailed for the Pacific. She followed the ship down the East Coast. At every port, she was there. Mary said she'd wait for Blow; he promised he'd call her after the war, and Blow never broke a promise.

So now, sitting in his bunk, at the break of dawn, Blow was finally getting sleepy. He pulled out the piece of paper from his pocket, scanned the list one more time, then tucked it away. He knew he had to report for first shift soon. No matter how tired he was, he'd be up on time and ready to go.

5

NASH WAS GETTING worried. His gunboat had been stuck in Dry Dock 4 for nearly three weeks. He knew the 449 needed some work, but he'd hoped it would wind up by the middle of May. The delay had pushed back their participation in training exercises in Maalaea Bay. Even though he didn't have an exact date, they were still scheduled to leave Pearl Harbor for the Marianas by the end of the month. That meant they'd have to cram in a lot of training into a short time. There was nothing he could do about it.

Dock 4 was the biggest dry dock in the entire navy yard—1,089 feet long, 147 feet wide, and 59 feet deep. It worked like a lock in a canal, but with a wood-pile foundation and reinforced concrete walls, it could handle an aircraft carrier. Underneath were massive pumping stations so the dock could be drained of water when a ship was in place, and the water could be pumped back in when work was finished. Dry docks were like big, outdoor service stations, with huge overhead cranes to move steel beams and iron plates. The dry docks swarmed with thousands of electricians, welders, and riveters who arrived at dawn and stayed into the night reinforcing welds, overhauling engines, and repairing rudders, propellers, and shafts.

The 449 looked like a toy down in that huge dock, but major work was needed, even after its San Diego overhaul. Here in Hawaii the final upgrades were added on and bolted down, as fast as possible, extras like a sprinkler system to flood the ammunition compartments if the ship was hit by enemy fire. New ammunition storage spaces were created in the bow and amidships, with a ventilation system to disperse explosive fumes the ammunition leaked over time.

Even the new weapons needed upgrades. Permanent foundations were installed for the 40mm and new 20mm guns, as well as the rocket launchers. Properly founded guns were more accurate, and their "kick" didn't tear up the deck of the gunboat so quickly.

Two sets of quad General Motors six-cylinder diesel engines were torn apart and overhauled (eight engines total), along with the shafts that operated the pitch screws and the engine exhaust pipes. The fire and bilge pumps were rebuilt, and at the end of it all, a large part of the ship was repainted.

While the 449 was stuck in dry dock, the men had been upgrading, too, attending special classes for firefighting as well as first aid and radio operations. Almost all had attended the refresher courses. The new arrivals would go next. But Nash was concerned. He knew too many of them were still learning their way around the ship and trying to familiarize themselves with shifts, routines, equipment . . .

The gunboat's three levels were connected by a series of stairs and ladders. The crew's quarters and the engine room were on the lower level, or first platform. Above the first platform was the main deck, with a deckhouse in the middle, and above that was the gun deck.

Like the lower level, the main deck was crowded and cluttered, crammed with equipment and ammunition. With so many men rushing back and forth, it resembled a busy city street on a hot summer day. On breaks, shirtless men with their faces turned to the sun would rest in a section between the deckhouse and the bow: the well deck. They'd also catch rays on the fantail, the space between the deckhouse and the rear.

The deckhouse itself bustled with activity. Inside were the officers' quarters and the wardroom, where Ralphal Johnson served the officers' meals on white china with a blue pattern around the edges. In the galley cooks whipped up breakfast, lunch, and dinner, then filled the seamen's metal trays with food as they walked in a line past their stations. The sailors would eat in the mess area before heading back to their shifts, or bunks. Most of the gunboat's communications equipment was stored in the radio shack, and Beuckman took care of the sick and injured seamen in the "messing and clipping" room.

On the gun deck, two 40mm guns were mounted in the forward section, while two 20mm guns were positioned in the aft. Thin plastic armor surrounded the guns for protection, making the weapons look like they were sitting in tubs. Rising from the gun deck was a ten-foot-high circular structure with six portholes: the conning tower. Inside was the pilothouse, a room carrying the ship's navigational equipment, including a Sperry gyrocompass, which used the earth's rotation instead of the magnetic north to find geographical directions. (They were much more reliable at sea than a magnetic compass because they were unaffected by ferromagnetic materials, such as the ship's hull, which could change the magnetic field. However, the pilothouse had a magnetic compass for backup.) In the cramped room were levers for the helmsman to steer the ship, as well as the engine order telegraph, a machine that allowed him to signal the engine room with his desired speed and direction. (The device was operated by another sailor wearing headphones so he could hear orders from the bridge regarding changes in course and speed.)

On top of the conning tower was the bridge, a circular deck protected by a five-foot-high metal wall. The officers stood there during battles, giving directions to the helmsman as the action unfolded. The bridge had communications equipment, too, including a sound-powered telephone that allowed officers to stay in touch with crew in all parts of the ship. (All you had to do was push a button on the handset to talk.) During combat, officers on every deck wore headsets with microphones to keep in contact with the bridge. A signal light was mounted on the edge of the bridge to communicate with other ships.

Towering over the gunboat was the mast. (It was welded to the gun deck and attached to the side of the conning tower.) Like a clothesline with laundry, the tall pole was crisscrossed by a series of lanyards to hold up flags of various sizes, shapes, and colors to send messages between ships. At the very top of the mast: the U.S. flag.

The new arrivals would have to learn everything very quickly. As usual, Nash turned to Herring: "Can you take care of it, Geddie?" The skipper already knew the answer.

When Herring walked into the wardroom the next day, he spotted Nash with Yarbrough and Duvall. He showed them the new schedule for the crew.

Every gunboat, like every ship in the navy, had a clear hierarchy. The captain was in charge. As second in command, the executive officer was responsible for navigation, censoring outgoing mail, and disciplining the men who ran into trouble. The engineering officer supervised the sailors who operated the engines, while the gunnery officer was in charge of the weapons and ammunition supply. The commissary officer handled supplies, and the communications officer kept in contact with other ships in the fleet, and supervised flag, signal light, and radio communication. (Since there were only four officers on the 449, Duvall was responsible for communications and supplies.)

All worked closely with the noncommissioned officers, like the boatswain. He handled the day-to-day supervision of the seamen, conducting drills and ensuring that everyone knew how to use the vital items like fire extinguishers, life rafts, and storage lockers.

Herring was the 449's engineering officer, but he had taken on more than the usual amount of leadership on the gunboat. He didn't have to be asked to do things—Herring came up with ideas on his own. He got jobs done quickly, without grandstanding. The other officers didn't mind that he sometimes encroached on their territory—everyone liked him. He had a gentleness and sincerity that made others want to be around him. A wiry officer with a boyish smile, Herring reminded some people of the actor Jimmy Stewart, right down to his "aw-shucks" persona. He worked as well with the men in the black gang—sailors stuck in the grimy, sweltering engine room—as he did with his commanders.

That's the way he was raised.

Herring learned at an early age to treat even the lowly with respect. He "came up" in Roseboro, a small North Carolina town in a sea of tobacco, corn, and beans.

His father, Troy, owned a lumber company, and made enough money to open a savings bank that grew from one branch to three. He never turned anyone away who needed help. Herring's mother, Susan, was unusually cultured. She'd graduated from the Women's College of Greensboro, North Carolina, with a music degree. They were pillars of the town, builders of the United Methodist Church, involved in all kinds of civic activity.

Their house was the biggest one in town, two stories and ten thousand square feet, with columns in the front and a wraparound veranda, all shaded by a big magnolia tree. In the summer the family moved to another five-bedroom house at nearby White Lake.

Big Jenny and her husband Claude lived in their own wings of the houses and took care of the Herring family's day-to-day needs. They were "Negro help," but they became part of the family.

Then tragedy struck the Herrings. When young Herring was twelve, his father died of a heart attack. From the outside, he looked healthy, but his family said Troy had worked himself to death. He left the family enough money so they didn't struggle financially, and friends and relatives rallied to support the widow and her boys. Young Herring strapped on a smile while he dealt with the loss. His older brother Marvin had just started at North Carolina State University, leaving the younger boy alone with their distraught mother. He tried to be an upbeat, smiling kid who was full of life, the one thing that made her happy.

"Everybody just loved him," recalled Cora Essey, a childhood friend. "He coped with it very well. He was a strong young man."

Even though he came from a privileged family, he worked at the general store after school.

When the time came, he went to Davidson College, about 180 miles west of Roseboro. He became a cheerleader, joined the Pi Kappa Phi fraternity, and had an all-around great time. During the week he dressed up in a shirt and tie for classes. He only went home once or twice a semester, and when he did, he put on his old dungarees and headed down to the lumber yard or out to the garage, anything to get his hands dirty. He didn't bathe for days.

After graduating Davidson with a degree in economics in the spring of 1942, he joined the Naval Reserve as an officer. Within a year, he was assigned to the same landing craft infantry (L) as Nash. And just like he did back in North Carolina, Herring got along with everyone, from the skipper right down to the deckhands.

A sailor brought word up to the wardroom: Their boat would be finished tomorrow.

The officers stopped what they were doing. They all knew what that meant: With the repairs completed, they didn't have much time left in Pearl Harbor.

6

ASIDE FROM THE *toilets, censoring mail is the worst part of this job*, Yarbrough thought to himself.

A mountain of mail seemed to loom over one end of his little desk. As executive officer, he was responsible for scouring the crew's letters home, to prevent anyone disclosing sensitive information to family and friends. Sixty-five people served on the 449, and every afternoon they left dozens of letters folded in unsealed envelopes in a box by his cabin. Inside his room, before he slept at night, he read them each line by line, trying to decide if there was anything that could be of value to the enemy—a location, descriptions of weapons or equipment, or where they might be next week. Using a wide-nib pen and black ink, he obliterated as little as he could get away with.

Reading all those pages made him feel lonely. It seemed everyone on the gunboat had a girlfriend or a wife, someone to long for, someone to miss him. Everyone but Yarbrough.

Not that he didn't try. He was twenty-four years old, but still awkward around women. He was in good shape physically: five-foot-eight, 160 pounds. His eyes were blue, but prominent. He had a thick neck, big ears, and a widow's peak. He was self-conscious about a scar in the middle of his forehead, courtesy of a childhood bout of chicken pox.

All of the sailors carried pictures of their girlfriends and wives in their wallets, or had them taped to the wall by their bunks. When they talked about girls, Yarbrough had little to add. He'd met a girl back in San Diego, when the gunboat stopped there on the way to Pearl Harbor. For a week he took Dotty everywhere, to dinners and the movies. They made out a few times on the beach. He even wrote his parents, saying he was falling for a nice girl. When Yarbrough shipped out, she promised to write. He penned a few letters, but she never answered. It was embarrassing when his father asked about her. He wrote back:

You spoke of Dotty, the girl that I met in San Diego. I have been expecting to hear from her, but so far I have not. I don't know whether she has written or not. The mail is so confused . . . Maybe I was wrong about her, who knows.

But Yarbrough knew what had happened: He'd gotten the brush-off.

Yarbrough sat up straight, opened the first envelope, unfolded the first sailor's letter. He knew everything about Casaletto's troubled life—his wife Winifred, his five kids, the little house near Boston where the brood lived with Winifred's mother. Yarbrough knew Casaletto's wife complained that he wasn't sending home enough money. It was ironic—he knew so much about these guys, but aside from Nash and Herring, Yarbrough himself was an enigma to the rest of the crew.

Back home in Alabama he was a different man. In Auburn, Yarbrough was surrounded by a network of family and close friends he'd known from the cradle right up through college.

Yarbrough came from a prominent family: His father, Cecil, was a physician and politician. He served several terms as mayor and a term as representative in Alabama's House of Representatives. After America's entry into World War I, he enlisted as a navy medical officer.

Yarbrough's mother, Bertha, was a housewife who had graduated from Alabama Polytechnic Institute after the school first admitted women in 1900. He had five siblings—four brothers and a sister. It was a close family.

Yarbrough admired his father—he was a fighter. When state lawmakers tried to move the university from Auburn to Montgomery, the state capital, in 1922, he led a coalition in a highly public campaign to derail the plan. He recruited alums in the battle, and they launched a coordinated attack on the lawmakers who supported the measure. Under increasing public pressure, the lawmakers backed off, and that victory raised Cecil's stature even more in Auburn.

Cecil was a disciplinarian. When his boy was ten years old, his father caught him sneaking a smoke. "My dad gave me a whipping at that time, and I didn't forget it until I was old enough to know better," Yarbrough wrote to a friend.

When he was seven, his mother died of pellagra. At the time, the cause of the crippling disease was a mystery. (Later, it was found to be linked to an overdependence on corn as a staple food. Nearly three million people between 1900 and 1940 contracted pellagra, mostly in the South, and more than one hundred thousand died from it.) Yarbrough's mother had all the terrible symptoms: disfiguring dermatitis, diarrhea, and, near the end, dementia. His father, a doctor, was helpless. For young Yarbrough, it was crushing. She had doted on him. After her death, he felt lost. It didn't help when his father remarried less than a year later.

After graduating from high school, he went to API and joined Phi Delta Theta as a freshman. But he left the rowdy fraternity after a year because they drank too much. He recalled how his father had urged him to stay away from alcohol.

Yarbrough found solace in swimming—he loved the water. When he could, he'd head to the Gulf Coast with his friends. While there were girls in his circle—and he dated some—he didn't go steady. He just never felt comfortable.

He had just graduated with an agricultural engineering degree when the Japanese attacked Pearl Harbor. Like so many Americans, he was stunned, then angry. Within days, he enlisted in the navy. His father praised him, and told how he'd jumped at the chance to serve in World War I. Now his son was doing the same.

Yarbrough joined the gunboat the same day as Nash and the other officers. He liked them, especially Herring. They had more in common than their age—they grew up in the rural South, came from affluent families, had each lost a parent and graduated from college. But where Herring always seemed to enjoy himself, Yarbrough was homesick. He missed his family. His missed college football season when the campus was awash with burnt orange and navy blue.

"I was so happy in Auburn, and I would like it to be the same when I return," he wrote a family friend.

It was during those times when Yarbrough turned to swimming. Sometimes he rounded up a bunch of guys and, with sailors on the deck watching for sharks, jumped into the ocean. They'd swim and laugh and, for a time, forget about the war. But afterward, he'd come back to reality.

"I am one who likes to swim very much and you would think I would be in heaven here," he wrote in a letter home. "But it is not so because the water is very salty and the wind blows incessantly making the water very choppy . . . However it is better than no swimming at all."

Maybe his time on the gunboat would be easier if he had a girlfriend. It was one thing getting letters from his family and friends—another if they were from a special girl. Maybe that would happen. But he doubted it would happen anytime soon. Not where he was headed.

7

NASH COULD FINALLY feel the sea rocking under the keel. He scanned the dry dock paperwork and smiled to himself at the clean bill of health. "All work completed" and "ready for sea," the papers said. But as the ship turned to starboard, heading out to join the rest of Flotilla Three, Group Eight, on maneuvers, a deep grinding sound shuddered its way up from the depths and movement slowed. "Jesus," he muttered. *What now?*

The engine room shouted up the bad news: The gearbox on the starboard quad engine was out. They were losing power.

The long-awaited training in Maalaea Bay was probably out of the question. Nash turned to Duvall, the communications officer, and told him to get a message to the dry dock.

Duvall sighed. He knew why Nash was upset—the skipper wanted to get back in action. Duvall wasn't in such a hurry. He was still thinking about the last campaign—exploding shells and mortars, bullets pinging off the hull. He wondered if the next mission would be more of the same.

Walking into the radio shack, Duvall asked radioman Max Ball to contact the dry dock.

"What should I tell them?" Ball asked.

"We're stuck," Duvall said drolly.

He wheeled around and bounded outside. He needed a smoke. Leaning against a railing, he pulled a pack of Lucky Strikes from his pants pocket, fished a cigarette from the box, then lit the end with his lighter. He inhaled deeply, holding the smoke in his lungs for a few seconds.

Relax, he told himself.

It wasn't getting any easier.

Duvall was a polite, soft-spoken Kentucky boy. With his athletic build and a strong, handsome face topped by perfectly trimmed wavy black hair, he resembled Olympic swimmer and "Tarzan" movie star Johnny Weissmuller. Of the gunboat's four officers, Duvall was the only one who was married. He wrote to his wife nearly every day, but the letters only reminded him of their distance from each other. They were newlyweds when he boarded the 449 in early November 1943. He hadn't held her in seven months and didn't know when he'd see her again.

Duvall took another drag, then tossed the cigarette in the water. He quickly lit another. He missed her so damn much, talked about her all the time. His face would light up when he recounted how they met during their freshman year at Eastern Kentucky University.

The officers had heard the story so many times they could recite the details by heart: Duvall was in a crowded school auditorium, squeezing down an aisle to find a seat before the start of a play, when his leg brushed against a splinter on the back of a wooden chair. His pants ripped, a girl giggled. It was Evelyn Preston, a pretty blonde. She patted the empty seat next to her; Duvall slipped into the chair. When the play was over, she promised to sew his pants. The following day, he took her up on her offer.

They became inseparable, taking long walks on campus and sharing details of their lives. Duvall grew up in Frankfort, where his father worked for the state. His mother was a housewife, but she'd often help out her parents at their downtown department store. As a kid, he'd run around the store with his older brother. Duvall planned to major in business and his good friends called him "Bob." Evelyn was from Louisa, Kentucky, a small town on the other side of the state. She was majoring in education and loved the outdoors. She said she wanted a house one day with a backyard so she could work in the garden.

Within a few months, they broached the subject of marriage, but decided to wait until they both finished school.

But then the war complicated their plans. When Duvall started college, the nation was at peace. As he was getting ready to graduate in the spring of 1943, the nation was at war. Duvall wanted to get married, start his career, and have a family. He stayed up at night, wrestling with the issue: Should he enlist? Wait to be drafted? So many of his friends were already fighting. Hell, his own brother was serving. How could he stay home?

Duvall enlisted in June 1943 and, after months of training, got his orders: He was headed to the Pacific. He married Evelyn on October 20, 1943. Two weeks later, he was at sea.

The next few months passed by quickly. Training. Marshall Islands. More training. When he wasn't in combat, part of Duvall's job was procuring supplies for the gunboat. Using skills he learned in his grandparents' store, he'd wheel and deal with other ships to land fruit, ice cream, beer. No matter what happened during the day, he'd make sure he ended it with a letter, letting Evelyn know how much he loved her. In one, he said the day they "stood before the chaplain and pledged our love to each other will always be the happiest day of my life."

"Honey you have given me so many wonderful memories," he wrote, but added: "There just isn't any genuine happiness as long as we are apart."

He stayed busy to forget the loneliness. Still, there were times Duvall couldn't escape the pain, especially late at night, when he'd stand on deck, staring at thousands of stars stretched across the dark sky. He'd begin wondering if Evelyn was gazing at the same constellations, where she was . . .

A tugboat toiled up to tow the gunboat to Pier Baker 10 in the East Loch section of Pearl Harbor. Duvall tossed his cigarette and walked inside the deckhouse to tell Nash.

When they arrived at the dry dock, Nash got the news: Additional repairs. Mechanics couldn't predict how long it would take.

Damn, he thought.

Nash knew how important the training was, and wondered if the snafu would delay their departure.

Invasions were complicated. They involved thousands of moving parts: sailing schedules, tactical formations, target lists. There had to be sufficient ships and supplies, "everything from beans to bullets to bandages," as the

Marines liked to say. Every move, from the pre-invasion bombardment to landing troops on the beaches had to be carefully planned and synchronized, right down to the minute.

The Marianas campaign was no different. For weeks, the navy had been conducting extensive training exercises in advance of the attack. They'd coordinated cruisers, destroyers, battleships, and other vessels taking part in the opening wave, as well as the little landing crafts that would carry American fighting units to the shore.

The gunboats in Flotilla Three, Group Eight, were scheduled for several days of training. Nash knew the gunboats had to know the precise positions to take during the invasion to avoid collisions. Every position was charted. They had to be at specific points at specific times. No mistakes.

Part of the training called for target practice with live fire. Nash had some new gunners and loaders, and he wanted to see how they performed under pressure. It was critical for them to work together. Just as with the 20mm, special teams were assigned to the 40mm guns. Seven men handled the 40mm, and each one had a specific task. There were seats on each side of the gun: One was for the trainer, who moved the weapon side to side. The other was for the pointer, who used a lever to move the gun up and down, before pressing a foot pedal to fire the weapon. The others helped reload, passing round after round from the ammunition lockers, while the gun captain directed the crew.

Now his gunboat was out of action. It could take days to repair the transmission. They'd miss the exercises. He bit his lip and hoped to God this damn gearbox wouldn't sideline his ship from the entire invasion.

8

WHISTLING A LINE from "A String of Pearls," Clarence Hoffman bounded into the room and dropped his seabag. Not bad, he said to himself. He scanned the quarters and was ready to claim a bed, when he glimpsed a pair of legs on the bottom bunk. Squatting down, Hoffman smiled at the sailor: "What's cooking?" he asked.

Norman Holgate stared at Hoffman, then sat up. "Is this your bunk?"

"Nope, just got in," Hoffman said, then reached out his right arm to shake the sailor's hand. "I'm Clarence, but my friends call me Junior."

Holgate shook Hoffman's hand and introduced himself. This was his first day, too, he said.

"Do you know if any of these bunks are taken?" Hoffman asked.

Holgate shook his head no. But he said he'd heard that a few more new guys were reporting for duty and they'd all end up in the same place.

"We got the pick of the litters," Hoffman laughed.

Hoffman kept gabbing as he unpacked his seabag. Holgate didn't mind. It was a welcome diversion. He knew the gunboat was heading out into combat, but he didn't want to think about it. Not yet.

Holgate was a shy eighteen-year-old. He had a baby face, with light brown wavy hair and sad brown eyes. At times he looked lost, almost scared, like he was trapped in a nightmare and looking for a way to wake up.

Only a few months earlier, Holgate had been wasting away in a little farm town called Terreboone, Oregon. He enlisted with his brother Walt to escape from their abusive father. At times he wondered if he'd made the right decision. The navy wasn't exactly an improvement. It didn't help that he was assigned to the engine room.

As a fireman first class, Holgate's job was maintaining the engines and ensuring their fuel supply. He liked working on machines; at home he loved to tinker with cars. But the engine room was in the bowels of the ship, in a cramped, closed compartment full of diesel fumes, heat, and racket. The men kept a cutting torch nearby in case the gunboat took a hit and they got trapped inside.

Hoffman, the latest arrival, wasn't sure what he'd be doing on the gunboat. As a seaman first class, he could be assigned to any job on the deck. He didn't have a specialty, but was told he'd probably end up as an ammo loader.

Hoffman was almost the same age as Holgate, but they came from different worlds. Hoffman was from the streets of Saint Louis, Missouri. He was a tough, fun-loving kid who loved the Saint Louis Cardinals baseball team and big bands—Harry James, Glenn Miller, and Tommy Dorsey.

No one could have predicted he'd turn out this way. His father, Clarence Bergmann, died before he was born in 1927. A year later, his mother met a widower, Charles Hoffman, a World War 1 veteran. When they married, Hoffman adopted Clarence, and his surname thereafter was Hoffman. They didn't tell the boy he was adopted. A few years later, the couple had a child and named him Charles.

They lived in a working class Irish neighborhood of redbrick row houses and wood-frame two-stories. It was a fine neighborhood, and all the families knew one another. The parents sat on the front steps afternoons and evenings, chatting while their children played baseball, football, and marbles on the sidewalks and in the streets. Junior's best friend was Ollie Berger. They spent hours in the alley between their homes, shooting their BB guns at the trees.

"We became dead shots. We would hit birds while they were flying," Berger recalled.

Hoffman became a great pool player, too. One of his friends had a pool table in his basement, and he practiced so hard that he began hustling all the teenagers in the neighborhood.

Everybody knew when Hoffman was nearby: He was always whistling.

"Clarence had a talent for whistling . . . Whenever he'd walk through our alley, my dad would say, 'There goes Clarence.' My dad was a professional trumpet player and he knew how good Clarence really was," Berger recalled.

The neighborhood girls were drawn to his wide smile and outgoing attitude. Berger's little sister Lucille gave him his first kiss, and his first wink, too. He never forgot that kiss. They never dated, but Clarence always carried a picture of her in his wallet—she was his "girl next door."

Hoffman played the accordion and performed duets with his brother on the piano. Berger joined them with his trumpet, and the band played at neighborhood festivals, but their musicianship was usually limited to the living room.

Their repertoire included old songs from the Great War, special requests of Mr. Hoffman. "My Buddy," a melancholy ballad of friendship and trench warfare, was a particular favorite. It took Mr. Hoffman back again to an artillery unit on the front lines—the brave boys who died, and the ones he hadn't seen since they marched home from France.

Most of the neighborhood went to Southside Catholic High School and hung out near the Michigan Theater, where they'd sneak in through a back door when they didn't have enough money for tickets. It was there in the theater where Hoffman first heard the words "Pearl Harbor."

The movie was well into the first reel when suddenly the screen went blank. A man on the stage shouted the news: "Pearl Harbor has been attacked. Everyone needs to go home immediately!" For a moment, everyone just sat there. Nobody had ever heard of Pearl Harbor.

"Who's Pearl?" a boy shouted back. "Who's attacked her? Why's it mean we have to go home?"

The lights came up, and the theater manager explained from onstage: The Japanese had attacked America's fleet at the Hawaiian naval base and destroyed most of the ships. Everyone was silent, and as Hoffman and his friends walked home, they found themselves scanning the sky for airplanes.

Hoffman was only fourteen years old, but he ached to join the fight. He followed war news closely in the *Post-Dispatch* and radio broadcasts. When he turned seventeen, he asked his parents again about enlisting, but they were reluctant. The recruiters required his birth certificate along with his parents' written permission—and his birth certificate showed his last name was Bergmann.

So the time came to tell the boy the truth. He was stunned. They had lied to him. His father was really his stepfather. His brother was really a half brother. For weeks, he was quiet.

"I know this really bothered and confused him," Berger recalled.

Hoffman didn't understand why they'd hidden the truth from him, but he didn't want to leave Saint Louis on a bad note. So the morning he left, he hugged his father and kissed his mother goodbye. He told them he wasn't mad anymore.

He lied, but in the end the truth and lies didn't matter much. His anger faded with time, and his new life of regimented training was a healthy change. He began whistling again, and looking for any information he could find about the Cardinals. When he boarded the 449, he felt a jolt like a shot of adrenaline. This was it. He was really here. Now all he had to do was find the right bunk and he'd feel right at home.

A FEW MINUTES after dinner, Casaletto bolted to the gun deck, brushing by Bozarth on the way. When he reached the conning tower, he pulled a cigarette from his shirt pocket and squatted as he stared at the ships in the harbor.

With his self-deprecating sense of humor, Casaletto was one of the most popular guys on the gunboat. He could talk nonstop about any subject: his beloved Red Sox, cars, deep-sea fishing—striped bass and bluefin tuna. "You shoulda seen what I caught. This big," he'd say, extending his arms as far as he could.

But lately, Casaletto had been moping. He hadn't seen his kids in nearly two years. Hell, he hadn't gotten a letter from them in months. As usual, his wife was busting his balls, complaining about every little thing and, of course, asking for more money. It was tough trying to deal with family crap when you were so far away. So he'd started sneaking off more and more by himself, chain-smoking Chesterfields, trying hard not to think about his problems at home. But the more he tried to forget, the more he thought about everything. It was driving him crazy.

"No use," he muttered.

He lit the cigarette, took a few deep drags. He was ready to head below, when he heard two men talking loudly as they climbed the ladder. It was Blow and Ball.

"I knew we'd find you up here," Blow said.

"Yeah, Bozarth says he saw ya."

Casaletto shrugged. "Yeah?"

They told him they had a surprise for him in their room. "Come on, you'll feel better," Blow said.

Casaletto moved to the edge of the gun deck and flicked his cigarette into the water. He followed them down the ladder to the well deck, then to stairs leading below. When they got to their room, Blow opened his locker and fished out a full bottle of Scotch hidden under his dirty clothes. He offered his buddy a drink.

"I was saving it for a special occasion," he said.

Casaletto grabbed the bottle, twisted off the cap. He took a quick swig and scrunched his face.

"Feel better?" Blow asked.

Casaletto nodded yes, before handing the bottle back to Blow. They passed it around a few times, before Blow stashed it back in his locker.

Blow and Ball knew Casaletto had been feeling down—more trouble with Winifred. What better elixir than Scotch?

Casaletto said thanks, but he didn't need to say a thing. They'd been lifting one another's spirits since joining the gunboat in August 1943. When Casaletto, Blow, and Ball boarded the 449, they were strangers. But in a matter of days, they had become friends. Why not? They were tough-talking, hard-drinking guys who grew up in small towns in Massachusetts.

"We were like brothers," Ball recalled.

The 449 was like any other place where people are suddenly thrust together: the military, college. Sailors began associating with guys who had the same interests. Howard Schoenleben, William Tominac, and Glenn Trotter called themselves the Chicago Three—although only two were actually from the Windy City. (Trotter's home was Sheffield, Illinois, a railroad town 130 miles west of Chicago.) They were pranksters, Chicago Cubs fans who loved to ride the Southern boys, calling them hillbillies. There was the black gang, the guys in the engine room: Robert Carrell, Meredith Luckner, Alfred Fox. They were muscular, quiet men who became friends toiling long hours in sweltering heat with ear-shattering noise.

But Casaletto, Blow, and Ball seemed to be the most social. They'd go room to room, recruiting groups of sailors for marathon card games, or trips ashore to hit bars. Blow was the youngest of the three, barely twenty-one, but he seemed like the oldest. He was always making sure things didn't spin out of control.

The twenty-two-year-old Ball was a fisherman's son from Gloucester, Massachusetts. He was born on the ocean and worked with his father in the summers. He didn't like the long hours, especially when most of his friends were hanging out in town, trying to pick up girls, but it was a good living.

In his senior year of high school, he took part in a training program run by the U.S. Merchant Marine. He figured he'd serve a few years, then start his own fishing company.

Pearl Harbor changed his plans. If he had to fight in the war, what better place than at sea? At least he knew what to expect in the navy.

He finished his Merchant Marine training on Hoffman Island, New York, then enlisted in the navy, where he became a radioman. Beyond patriotism, Ball loved the comradery on the ship. Like Blow, he enjoyed going out with the guys. He never started fights. But when they got into trouble, he was the first to jump in.

For Casaletto, the navy was an escape.

His parents were hardworking Italian immigrants who settled in a small town a few miles north of Boston. The second oldest of eleven children, he left home as a teenager to find work to help his family. His life moved fast: At twenty, he got married to a neighborhood girl, landed a good-paying job as a truck driver, and became a member of the Teamsters Union.

By 1940, he had five children, but his marriage was falling apart. He spent long hours on the road, and while he was away, his wife found another man. Winifred eventually moved to her mother's house. She took the kids along with someone else: her boyfriend. The children stayed upstairs with Grandma, while Winifred slept downstairs with her lover.

The stress finally got to Casaletto. He quit his job and enlisted in the navy on August 15, 1942. Over the years, he had learned how to fix cars—anything with an engine. When the navy saw his skills, he became a motor machinist's mate, and he was now a key member of the black gang. Whenever anything went wrong with the engines, they turned to Casaletto.

But Casaletto was more than a good mechanic. He was a larger than life figure. In his early thirties, Casaletto was older than most of the others, but even the young sailors enjoyed his company. He told everyone he joined the navy because he "had five kids back home and a wife." They didn't know if he was kidding.

But lately, Casaletto was worried. Winifred was demanding more money. He was already sending home most of his navy check. What the hell was going on?

His friends could sense trouble. So Blow had decided to break out the Scotch to cheer him up, just like he did in early December, when Casaletto received a horrible telegram from the Red Cross: "Brother Died Thirty November."

That's when Casaletto found out that his sixteen-year-old brother, Billy, had died after being injured in a neighborhood football game. Casaletto was distraught—he felt like screaming and crying at the same time. It wasn't fair, he thought. He was in harm's way and his kid brother was supposed to be safe at home. Casaletto wanted to punch the wall, but Blow and Ball stopped him. Instead, Blow passed around the bottle. They stayed up all night drinking, listening as Casaletto recounted stories about his kid brother and his big crazy Italian brood, the Sunday dinners, the Italian festivals . . .

By dawn, Casaletto had calmed down. He realized something else that night: Ten thousand miles from home, he had found a new family. They were there for him that night, they were here for him now.

Casaletto smiled and turned to his buddies: The night was young. He suggested they grab a few guys for a card game. That's just what Blow and Ball wanted to hear. On the way to the deckhouse, Casaletto turned to his friends: "You know Ted Williams was robbed, right? He shoulda won the MVP in '41, but that stinkin' DiMaggio . . ."

PHARMACIST'S MATE FIRST Class Henry Beuckman rearranged the cabinet full of bandages, syringes, scissors, tourniquets, and morphine. Beuckman was the only medic on the gunboat. When the worst happened, it was his responsibility to keep sailors alive until they could be transferred to a ship with doctors. It was a heavy load, and he wasn't confident he could handle it. He prayed he wouldn't have to use his supplies or his skills in a battle situation.

But meantime, all he had to do was to look after the general health of the crew: provide first aid for cuts and burns, diagnose colds and flu, dispense medicines, and occasionally inspect the galley and other sections of the ship for sanitation irregularities.

His tiny office was always busy. Sometimes, it was sailors faking an illness to get out of some shitty detail, or asking for aspirins to take the edge off a hangover. Most of the time, it was legitimate. A few days earlier, ship's cook Israel Rosenbloom had wobbled in, complaining of being tired and weak. His joints were aching. After a quick examination, Beuckman tagged Rosenbloom as having "acute catarrhal fever," a respiratory catchall that included everything from the common cold to lobar pneumonia.

Beuckman isolated Rosenbloom from the rest of the crew and ordered the gunboat's other cook, Clarence Kepner, to take over. He didn't want the disease to spread.

Beuckman was thirty-seven years old, the oldest man aboard. The men called him "Grandpa." Beuckman was tall and stout, with a rugged face and a bald head that made him look older than his years. He could be gruff at times, but he dispensed sage advice along with pills. He warned the sailors to stay away from alcohol, smoking, and brothels— he didn't want any of them taking home a venereal disease to their wives and girlfriends.

Beuckman felt protective of "his boys," as he liked to say.

He was the moral compass of the gunboat. Nash depended on him. The two talked often, and the skipper sounded him out and took his advice on many matters. He might have dropped out of the sixth grade, but he was as smart as anyone on the gunboat.

Beuckman was intelligent and calm under fire. He was a no-nonsense petty officer with a "let's get it done" attitude.

The medic came from East Saint Louis, Illinois, across the Mississippi River from Saint Louis, Missouri. His father was a clerk at a department store, and Henry was only nine when racial tensions flared in July 1917. Union leaders, fearing that blacks migrating from the South were taking their jobs, staged protests that erupted into riots. Whites fired on African-Americans, and they returned fire, killing a white police officer. When the riots ended, more than one hundred black residents had been killed and their businesses and homes burned. Beuckman recalled the sky alight with flames, and his father warning them to stay inside.

With the outbreak of World War I, his father signed up for the draft but, at age forty, didn't get called up, something he always regretted. A year later, Beuckman's mother died. For Beuckman, it was a terrible blow. He was only ten, but he promised he'd do everything to protect his three younger siblings.

Beuckman dropped out of school and took odd jobs with the railroad, selling newspapers—anything to make money. His escape was baseball. He played with the kids in his neighborhood, and dominated the diamond. In 1924 he caught the attention of the manager of the Wagner A. C. baseball club. They brought him on as their centerfielder, and in his first year the team went almost undefeated.

But Beuckman had to find full-time work. His father didn't make enough money to support the family. A railroad company hired him on as a clerk, so Beuckman gave up baseball. He met a nice girl: Loretta Jones. They married, and formed a big family with their younger sisters and brothers. As the years passed and the Depression set in, Henry became the rock. Whenever they needed anything—money, a place to live—he was there.

When Pearl Harbor happened, he decided to enlist.

"It was all about patriotism," recalled his stepdaughter Susan Anderson. "He was the kind of guy who didn't sit back. He took things on."

He knew he didn't have to go, but Beuckman recalled how his father regretted not serving in World War I. "If you ever get the chance, take it," he'd told young Beuckman.

So Beuckman signed on for the Naval Reserve on March 23, 1942. Inspired by the navy corpsmen motto "In the midst of death, they wage a war for life," he told the recruiter he wanted to become a pharmacist's mate.

That meant weeks of specialized training, in fields far from his previous experience. He learned about life-saving trauma care, how to save lives aboard a ship and in the field. He learned his way around anatomy, X-rays, clinical laboratory tests, pharmacology, contagious diseases, sanitation, and fever therapy. It wasn't easy, but Beuckman enjoyed the challenge.

He'd been lucky. They'd all been lucky the first time out. They'd come under heavy fire during the Marshall Islands campaign, but no one on his boat was killed or even wounded. Beuckman liked to tell Nash that you have to pray for the best and prepare for the worst. He didn't know how long their luck would last. All he could do for now was make sure his supply cabinet was full and his skills were sharp. Time and fate would determine the rest.

9

BETTY JONES WIPED down the long countertop by the cash register, swept the floors, and pushed the chairs back under the tables. She switched off the lights and stood in the dark while the radio finished the last notes of "Satin Doll." She turned off the radio, locked the door, and headed home.

She hadn't counted on spending so much time, and so many late nights, at Edd Jones Pharmacy. It was supposed to be temporary, just a few hours here and there to help her father catch up.

She would do anything to help him out, it was no great sacrifice. But the more time she spent in the pharmacy, the clearer it became: She was stuck in Cordele, Georgia—"the Watermelon Capital of the World."

Betty was twenty-four. Every day it seemed one of her old high school friends sent a wedding invitation, or dropped in to buy baby aspirin or cough syrup for her children.

Betty Jones was bright and attractive, a nice girl from a good family, but she was still single. Her prospects weren't good as long as she stayed in Cordele. There were only seven thousand people in town, and the only men left were under the age of eighteen or over forty. All the men worth looking at were in the military. If she was going to find a man, she had to go at least to Atlanta.

But her home was here, and her job. Her mother was here, too. And her mother wouldn't allow her to leave.

Betty strode down bright, busy Main Street. It was a cool summer night.

Teenagers gathered outside the movie theater and examined the dummies in the window display at the B. C. Moore department store. A couple of ragtag cars cruised up and down the street, with kids sticking their heads out the windows, calling out for friends. She turned a corner and passed the library, the post office, and the Cordelia Hotel, down the dark street to home.

She stood at the front gate, not ready to go inside. It was a lovely, comfortable home, but it wasn't easy living there. Her mother was never happy. Betty had graduated from a two-year women's college and wanted to go on to nursing school, but her mother put her foot down. "That's not for you," she told her.

"I felt so bad for her," recalled Nancy Jones, her sister-in-law. "Her mother felt being a nurse was beneath the family." And she was just as negative about her daughter's love life and other interests.

Betty was petite and brown-eyed, always well dressed in quality clothes from Rich's and Davison's and other high-end Atlanta department stores. Her family were successful farmers and merchants, close-knit and protective. She had boyfriends, but nothing serious. None of them could measure up to her mother's standards.

Even as she told Betty "you're not getting any younger," she criticized every boy who came to call.

Betty was the eldest of the children, the responsible one, expected to set an example for her younger brother and two sisters. On Sunday, their big extended family gathered after church for a big dinner.

Every dinner, every birthday, every wedding, Betty was right there with her mother and daddy, but it was getting old fast. Her brother, Russ, had just been drafted. Her two younger sisters were in school, living their own lives outside the house.

That left Betty to care for Mother, who seemed to enjoy having Betty there to drive her on shopping trips or to her bridge club. When the servants quit—which they did all the time—Betty would have to fill in for them, cooking, serving at the table, and washing dishes until they found new colored help.

She took more hours at the store just to have some time for herself. She went to the movies. It wasn't so bad . . .

Betty lifted up on the gate so it wouldn't squeak, moved quietly up the walk, and let herself in the side door. Her parents were in the sitting room, listening to someone making a speech on the radio. Betty tiptoed upstairs and into her room, closed the door, and turned on her little radio to the station that played the blues: "Saint Louis Blues," "Blues in the Night," lonesome whistles blowing . . . The music was soothing. There was another world out there. But for now, she was stuck in this one.

AFTER A MEETING with the flotilla commanders, Nash bounded back to the gunboat. Big news. He headed to the deckhouse and spotted Herring standing on the bridge. Get Yarbrough, Duvall, and Beuckman to his cabin, he said. It's important.

The officers squeezed into the little room. Nash wasted no time. The gearbox was fixed. They'd found no other problems. The 449 was being released from Pier Baker 10 and would join gunboats berthed in another part of the harbor. One more thing: They had orders. May 30, off to the Marianas. Saipan would be the first target. The invasion of the Japanese-held island would commence June 15.

More crew was coming aboard before they left Pearl Harbor. They still had a lot of work to do before they set off, but at least they were no longer in limbo.

The officers let out a deep breath. They knew not to share the information with the crew. Not yet.

Details of military campaigns were closely guarded, and trickled down from the top. Admirals and top officers planned the massive logistics and movements, and only shared invasion information with other officers at the right time, to better keep the secret. The sailors were always the last to know.

The men had turned to leave the cabin, when a great, deep boom rocked the gunboat around them. Another great explosion tore through the air, and another. The officers rushed to the deck. The sailors ran to their battle stations. Nash scanned the horizon with his binoculars and glimpsed a massive cloud of smoke billowing against the deep blue sky across the bay. More booms, shouts from the boats nearby . . . The crew looked up to see if there were Japanese planes. It sounded like they were under attack.

Then they heard a message crackle over the radio: There had been an accident in West Loch, another part of the vast navy yard, a peninsula that was a staging area for ships in preparation for Operation Forager. Medical help and fire crews were scrambled, sirens wailed.

Nearly six hundred ships and craft were required for the first act of the invasion—and landing ship, tanks (LSTs) were a critical part of that amphibious armada. The crafts were able to deliver tanks, vehicles, and supplies directly onto enemy beaches. In West Loch, more than two dozen LSTs had been tightly clustered with their hulls and decks filled with ammunition, supplies, and materiel. Ammunition was being loaded on the fantail of one of the LSTs when an explosion triggered a series of blasts, ripping open other ships as flames engulfed men and machinery.

Explosions, accidents . . . Casualties, Beuckman said to himself. They'd need all available medical personnel. While the crew of the 449 watched, Beuckman told Nash he was going. He didn't wait for his response. He bolted to the road and flagged down a jeep, shouting out he was a medic. He jumped in the back and held on tight as the driver sped along a twisting road, using the thick black smoke as a marker. West Loch was on the other side of the harbor and there was no direct route.

Bozarth offered a prayer on deck. Lemke and Holgate didn't say a word as they watched the orange flames flicker in the sky. Even wise-ass Blow had nothing to say.

Nothing could have prepared Beuckman for the horrific chaos on the other side of the bay. Dozens of stunned sailors wandered the docks, their uniforms burned away. Others were on the ground screaming for help, their cries almost drowned out by the rising crescendo of ambulance sirens and ships' horns. Even more were in the water, screaming as they tried to swim to shore. The force of the explosions had blown apart wooden buildings. Fire crews were trying to fight the flames, but the heat was so intense they couldn't get close enough to make a difference. Some LSTs managed to move out to safety, but others began to sink. The roaring flames and smoke, the running feet of rescuers and victims, the shouted orders and shrieking brakes, and more explosions that seemed to tear the ground from under his feet . . . Beuckman couldn't help but think this was December 7, 1941, all over again. Lightning does strike twice.

Beuckman waded in to help a nurse pulling a gasping man from the water. A sailor nearby shouted and swore, demanding they help his friend—the friend was burned black, curled into a fetal ball, his struggle finished. Doctors and nurses, chaplains and regular sailors settled into their work, and as firefighters shouted and metal twisted and screamed, the wounded found their way to Beuckman's strip of concrete. He bandaged horrible shrapnel wounds, carried men to the ambulances, held sailors' hands as they died. How many hours was he there? How many men did he treat? He could never remember, ever after. It was all a blur.

The fires burned for more than twenty-four hours. When the smoke died away, the cost of the catastrophe was counted. One hundred and sixty-three men lost their lives, with another four hundred injured, including several fighting the fires. Six LSTs were destroyed.

The navy put a lid on the explosion—there was to be no reporting of the disaster. The public didn't need to know about it—not yet. It would stay a secret.

But the explosion left an indelible mark on the crew of the 449.

They were all shaken by the blasts, the sound of the explosions—and stories of badly burned soldiers begging to die. They stood quiet the next day when a haggard Beuckman finally returned, his uniform torn and filthy, stained with blood and stinking of diesel fuel. The medic stopped only to report himself present and wash his face and hands. Then he fell into his bunk, exhausted.

It wasn't combat, but it was war. Bad shit could happen at any time.

PART TWO

OPERATION FORAGER

10

LEMKE LEANED OVER the rail and retched. His throat ached. There was nothing left in his stomach, but he was queasy anyway. He appreciated now how the USS *Leon* had glided over the water. This tub of a gunboat crashed through the waves like a fullback plowing headfirst into a wall of linemen. On windy days, and especially during storms, it rolled back and forth like a carnival ride at the county fair. It spun you round and round until you upchucked a week's worth of chow.

Lemke tried not to think of carnival rides, or food . . . He'd puked every one of the 3,700 miles between Pearl Harbor and Saipan. It was bad enough they were heading into combat, but if this kept up, he'd be a skeleton before the first shots were fired. He thought about asking Beuckman if he had anything for nausea, but his buddy John Overchuk told him to tough it out.

"Nothin' you can do but get used to it," he said.

Great, he thought. Get used to it. Adjust.

Lemke clutched the rail and contemplated the awfulness of his life. It was bad enough when they were docked in Pearl Harbor, but the high seas only made it worse. He couldn't write a letter to his wife, because the motion made the words shift around on the page, which made him dizzy. Every time he put down his pen, it rolled off the table.

At dinner, he had to act fast to keep his food tray from sliding away. Not that the chow was any good. The two cooks, Clarence Kepner and

Israel Rosenbloom, were nice guys. But the grub was always the same: ground beef. Meatballs, hamburgers, sloppy joes, or some variation thereof. And you had to eat in a rush. With just four tables, only thirty-odd men could sit in the mess deck at a time, so there was always somebody waiting to sit down.

It was like that in the head, too. They lined up to use the toilets. It was "sit, shit, and go," and no matter how many times Lemke washed his hands, he never felt clean. He hated salt water. Half the time, he was showering in it. He washed his clothes in salt water, too, and hung them outside on a rope to dry in the salty air. They came out stiff. They never smelled quite clean, no matter how much soap he used.

And then he read "Survival on Land and Sea," a Navy-issued booklet about how to stay alive if something bad happened. Every sailor was issued one. Most used the pages for toilet paper when supplies ran low, but Lemke read his, over and over: "Since this war began thousands of men whose ships have been sunk or whose planes have come down in uncivilized areas of the world have made their way back to friendly territory," the book said, adding that the text was written by men who had actually lived in jungles.

"Survival at sea depends on three things: Knowledge, equipment and drill. With luck you may get along without one or the other of these, but the going will be tougher and the chances of telling your grandchildren about it not so good," the pamphlet warned. The most important factor in survival at sea is being prepared when the order comes to abandon ship:

Always have a sheath knife on a lanyard in your belt, a police whistle around your neck and a light pair of leather gloves in your hip pocket. Second, have a small knapsack or kit bag, with shoulder straps prepared so that you can take it to your battle station. This should contain a filled canteen, a flashlight with a transparent rubber sheath tied over it, a blanket, sweater, shirt and socks and a first-aid packet.

Lemke's kit was packed and ready. He'd memorized the pictures of edible and poisonous plants, as well as the dangerous snakes and spiders he might encounter out there.

Overchuk shook his head when he saw Lemke scrutinizing the pamphlet yet again. "That book is doing nothing but keeping you up at night," he told his roommate. "Don't think about the hard parts. Think about a cold beer, and pretzels. Tell me what you're giving your little girl for Christmas, once you get home. What about birthdays? What do you give a baby girl? Tell me about driving a truck. You drove a truck at that gunpowder factory, right? You going to drive a truck for a living, once you get back home?"

And then he'd bullshit to Lemke, talk on and on about all kinds of stuff, especially at night in their bunks. He knew the man was naturally fussy, a worrier, suffering too much with things that meant nothing. He hoped some chatter might take his mind off his troubles.

Much like Blow, Overchuk had taken it upon himself to look out for the guys—they were the leaders on the 449. Both were gregarious, fun-loving, but serious when it came to keeping the gunboat afloat and everyone alive.

They agreed with Nash: You had to be prepared. You had to know how to handle the equipment inside and out so you wouldn't panic under fire. All the way to the Marianas, the gun crews unloaded and reloaded the 20mm and 40mm guns, until each action was second nature. The black gang watched the engines closely, conscious of every change in pitch. Blow and the damage control crew conducted fire drills. Every man aboard had to know how to extinguish fires quickly, or the heavily armed ship could blow sky-high in moments.

They conducted signal drills, just in case they ever got into trouble. Signalmen knew how to use blinking lights and flags to communicate with other ships during radio blackouts. They had one of the best in Signalman Arthur Lewis, a twenty-year-old from Baltimore. The crew watched him practice on the bridge, moving the flags up and down and sideways like a cheerleader at a football game. His upright choreography on the bridge contrasted with his laid-back off-duty demeanor—he spent most of his off-hours in his bunk with his eyes closed. The men nicknamed him "Horizontal Lewis."

Staying busy kept the crew sharp, and helped them forget all the petty shit that could potentially overwhelm them.

In the wardroom, the officers prepared, too. The logistical details, lists, and maps were in good order, navigational devices had been cali-brated, and strategies had been reviewed and discussed. They were one of hundreds of ships and landing craft involved in the invasion, so they had to know their role as well as their navigational positions. They mon-itored radio traffic between the ships, and made sure they never moved too close or too far from their fleet formation.

Nash kept the men on alert, on the lookout for "planes with a big red circle on the side." During the Marshall Islands campaign, dive-bombing Japanese planes had strafed the gunboats. So at night, the gun crews rotated shifts at their battle stations.

Overchuk exuded confidence, but the nearer they came to Saipan, the more nervous he felt inside. No one liked combat. No one on the gunboat had been killed, but he was haunted by the countless dead bod-ies he'd seen in the surf and on the sand in the Marshall Islands. Japanese and American, it didn't matter once you were dead. All those men had families, he knew. He thought of his own family—his parents, two sis-ters, and a younger brother. If he died out here, how would they handle it? Overchuk didn't want to cause them any pain—especially his father. He was so close to him.

Overchuk's father emigrated from Russia in 1897, when he was sixteen years old. He made his way to the steel plants in Cleveland, Ohio, mar-ried, bought a three-bedroom house, raised a family. When his boy was big enough, Alex got him a job at the mill, too. It was grueling work, and young Overchuk knew he wasn't cut out for it. He hadn't made up his mind about what else to do.

The thing he loved best to do was dance—he learned his moves from Fred Astaire movies. He'd practice for hours. (Sometimes, he'd use a broom as a partner.) He had a dancer's body: long and lean. With short black hair, and a dimple in his chin, he looked the part. Overchuk wasn't sure he could make a living from dancing, but when he had a free night and a little cash he'd hit the nightspots in Cleveland—not to drink, but to dance. He loved swing music, and could do a mean Lindy Hop. Late at night, on the deck or when they were in their bunks, Overchuk told the other men tales of dance halls and honky-tonks, scouting the clubs in Cleveland for light-footed women. Once he singled her out, he'd sidle up close and grab her by her hand and swing her out onto the dance floor. The music just took them over, he'd say, smiling into the dark, and before she knew it, they were moving around like crazy. They'd often end up parked in a car, he said, in his favorite secluded spot along the Cuyahoga River, or in summer down along the edge of Lake Erie. Then the Japanese attacked, the war started, and everything changed.

Like so many of his shipmates, Overchuk was too young to join the military at the start of the fighting. Still, his father encouraged him to enlist. Old Alex Overchuk was a proud American. When World War I started, he wasn't an American citizen, but he'd enlisted in the U.S. Army infantry and fought in the trenches in France. Once home, he studied at night for the U.S. citizenship test. He finally took the pledge on November 1, 1930. He threw a big party at his house.

The new American instilled the same sense of patriotism in his son: America to them was a shining example for the rest of the world. Back in Russia, they were peasants, struggling for every scrap of food, generation after generation. There was no future there. But in America, everyone had a chance to succeed, as long as they worked hard and kept out of trouble.

When Overchuk enlisted, his father invited the whole neighborhood to the party. They packed the house, drank, and danced to Tommy Dorsey and Glenn Miller records. That unforgettable night, Overchuk danced the boogie-woogie with every girl on the block.

Overchuk smiled. If his father could see him here in uniform, ready for combat, he'd smile ear to ear. Whatever happened in the Mariana Islands, the sailor promised to make his father proud.

AT A CLUTTERED metal desk in the cramped radio shack, Max Ball was stunned but excited by the latest navy news broadcast: American forces had landed on the northern coast of France. They had encountered fierce resistance, but had established beachheads, thanks to massive air and naval support. There wasn't much more.

An invasion was expected, but this was huge: Allied troops on French soil! "I'll be damned," Ball said. Now, he wanted to make sure the men got the news right away.

As a radioman, Ball listened to the nightly navy broadcasts that summed up the day's latest war news. Midnight usually found his tall, skinny frame hunched over his desk, scribbling notes as the news came over the airwaves. He then typed up a one-page mimeograph newsletter that he'd pin on the ship's message board near the galley. It was their only way of keeping up with current events at sea.

The seamen craved information. They wanted to know how the war was going in Europe and the rest of the Pacific. Every detail could hold a clue to their most pressing question: When would the war end?

Ball listened to the rest of the broadcast, all of it reports from Europe: Rome had fallen to the Allies, Soviet troops were advancing. There was almost no news from the Pacific. Of course, Ball knew that would change in a few days when the U.S. Pacific fleet started bombing and shelling Saipan.

When the broadcast finished, Ball turned his attention to his notes. He wasn't a writer by trade, but he'd gotten pretty good at putting together the newsletter.

As much as Ball enjoyed writing, radio equipment had become his passion. He operated a bank of short- and long-range radios mounted on the bulkhead above his desk. Wearing headphones, he'd pull a plug, or jiggle one of the cords connecting the equipment to get the best reception. Sometimes, it was just a matter of turning a knob to the right position. He was fast and efficient, and the officers took notice. They praised his work, noting how quickly he deciphered messages and got them in their hands.

Before enlisting, Ball didn't know much about radios. But in training, he learned about wavelengths, frequencies, components. He broke down and rebuilt equipment. He knew that each radio was specifically calibrated to the right-sized antenna on the mast for proper bandwidth. As long as the mast was up, Ball was confident he could keep the radios going under any condition.

On the navy's big ships, they had several radiomen to operate their communications equipment. But on the 449, Ball was the only one. (A sailor on the 449 was training to become a radioman.) Ball monitored the COL-5225 transmitter and COL-46159 receiver. (The Collins Radio Company of Cedar Rapids, Iowa, built both pieces for the navy. The receiver had a frequency range of 1,600 to 12,000 kilocycles per second.) He listened to the SLR-12-B shortwave radio receiver that was hooked up to the ship's speaker system. (The crew used the radio to tune into Tokyo Rose's propaganda broadcasts from Japan.) He was responsible for monitoring Identification Friend or Foe (IFF), a device that sent a radar-coded signal to transponders on approaching U.S. and Allied planes. If Ball received a return signal, he knew the plane was friendly.

It was a lot of work, long hours, but Ball loved being a radioman.

Ball took a sip of an hours-old cup of coffee, then pulled a dictionary from a metal bookcase in the corner. He put together quick sentences in his head as he pulled a chair up to the desk and rolled a sheet of paper into the typewriter. Instead of writing a few short items like he normally did, tonight he decided to roll everything into one. Allied troops had landed on the French coast and were moving inland, strongly supported by naval and air forces. The Nazis took another hit with the fall of Rome. It was just a matter of time before General George Patton and his tanks would roll toward Germany. Hitler was on the run. The troops faced heavy enemy fire, but there was no word on casualties.

He glanced at the copy and smiled. It looked good. He strode over to the mimeograph machine. He wanted the newsletter to be on the bulletin board when the crew got up and headed for breakfast.

BOZARTH PEERED INTO galley storage lockers with Kepner and Rosenbloom, searching for cans of fruit, shortening, and flour. They were on a pie-making mission, and Rosenbloom said he'd seen the ingredients in there somewhere. They didn't know when they would have another chance to use the cooker, not with the 449 nearing Saipan.

They were fixing a pre-invasion banquet, a special meal complete with desserts. Once they were in combat, the four-burner oil stove in the galley would be turned off. It was too dangerous. The smoke from the stove escaped through an exhaust vent on the deck, making the gunboat a perfect target for the Japanese, especially at night. So it would be sandwiches. No one knew what would happen in the coming days, if any one of them would be hurt or lost or killed in the battle. This was a chance for everyone to sit down together and enjoy a proper feed, maybe for the last time.

This was a little tradition founded by Bozarth last time they'd headed into battle, just before the Marshall Islands campaign. Not only did he help make the desserts, he held a prayer service the night before the invasion. He was handy in the kitchen, and today he worked with the cooks to make something special.

When Bozarth was growing up, his father taught him how to turn flour, water, butter, and salt into bread, buns, cakes, and pies. His father loved apple pie, and his son watched dozens of times while the old man carefully shaped pie crust into a pan, then peeled and sliced apples into small pieces and mixed them in a bowl with white and brown sugar, lemon juice, nutmeg, and cinnamon. When the pie came out of the oven, it was perfect every time.

Bozarth knew all his father's recipes, but the gunboat galley rarely had the right ingredients. He improvised. The goodies were usually less than elegant, but no one ever complained. There was never a scrap left over. Today would be no different. There were no apples, but they'd turned up several cans of peaches. Everybody loved peach pie. Bozarth started in on the crusts.

Kepner and Rosenbloom pulled chopped meat from the freezer and decided on meat loaf and mashed potatoes with gravy, the same meal they'd served the night before the Marshall Islands invasion. It was good luck then.

Word spread among the crew about the feast, and aromas of roasting meat and caramelized fruit floated from the galley. The men often came to dinner straight from their duty stations, in dirty dungarees and greasy T-shirts. But this day, they headed into the galley with their faces washed and uniforms clean.

When everyone was seated, Bozarth stood up. The galley fell silent.

"Let us pray," the young sailor said. Three dozen heads bowed down.

"Lord God, in your mercy bless this food. Let it give us strength to fight when our bodies are weary," he prayed. "Keep us safe in the battle to come. Hear our prayers. Forgive our sins. Keep each one of us in your loving care, good father." He ended with a quote from the Book of Joshua 1:9: "Be strong and of a good courage; be not afraid, neither be thou dismayed: for the Lord thy God is with thee whithersoever thou goest."

11

"WE'RE JUST A few minutes out!" shouted the pilot over his shoulder. The officers lounging behind him unbuckled their belts and jumped to their feet. They crowded around him or pressed their faces near the windows to get a first view of the tiny patch of land below.

Surrounded by acres of Pacific Ocean, Iwo Jima was covered in green trees and foliage in some places, and stark, barren wilderness in others. Strangest of all was the steam—like something out of a creepy movie, columns of steam and smoke billowed up from the earth in spots all over the little island. Rearing up at its southernmost point was a volcanic mountain, belching black vapor. It looked like it was ready to blow.

The general muttered something no one could make out.

It was dispiriting, but it was no surprise. Everyone had read the reports on this rugged, harsh landscape. Reading reports was one thing, but seeing it in person was something breathtaking. It had all the makings of a real hellhole.

"Honorable sirs, please take your seats and buckle in," the pilot said.

Within a few minutes, the aircraft's wheels bounced onto the runway, engines screaming, skidding crazily and dodging pits. When the cabin doors opened, Lieutenant General Tadamichi Kuribayashi smoothed his uniform and shrugged his shoulders comfortably into the space between the sleeves. First Lieutenant Fujita Masayoshi scanned the general's uniform, and then nodded: Everything was in order.

General Kuribayashi bounded off the plane and moved toward the officers gathered to welcome him. Following a brief introduction, Kuribayashi set off for a marathon walk of the entire island. Masayoshi followed close and took notes.

Kuribayashi was here to make the Japanese positions impregnable. But he didn't have much time. He knew the Americans were coming, but he didn't know when.

Iwo Jima was only six hundred miles east of Tokyo. If the Americans took the island, U.S. bombers would be within easy reach of the entire Japanese mainland. Everyone in Japan was at risk.

The Japanese needed a strong commander to lead the demoralized garrison. The fifty-three-year-old Kuribayashi was the ideal choice. He was personally known by Emperor Michinomiya Hirohito. He had a thirty-year distinguished military career behind him. He had been a deputy attaché in Washington during the 1920s. He knew and respected the enemy.

"The United States is the last country in the world we should fight," he wrote to his wife just before the war began. "Its industrial potential is huge and fabulous, and the people are energetic and versatile."

Now he had to find a way to stop the American advance in the Pacific.

Kuribayashi walked up sunbaked roads with a line of panting officers trotting behind him. He stopped and watched two men hacking away at a bombed-out bunker, cutting into the volcanic rock with pickaxes, chisels, and hammers. The ground was hot beneath his shoes. The brutal sun, the lack of water, the sulfuric steam spurting out of the holes . . . it was a scene out of hell. And now he was in charge.

For two days, Kuribayashi traipsed the island, followed by officers. At one point, the general turned to speak to Masayoshi, but what he saw in the sky beyond the man's shoulders took his breath away. On the horizon, moving in fast, a flock of black-winged American fighter planes and dive-bombers was heading straight at them. The officers' heads turned to see. A siren wailed, men shouted, Kuribayashi scrambled into the half-finished bunker, jammed together with the island's top brass and the filthy excavators.

Outside, hundreds of American aircraft swarmed over the island. From end to end they strafed and bombed everything that stood upright: houses, shacks, bunkers, cars, trucks, motorcycles, radio towers, grounded aircraft.

The earth shook, the dust and steam and flying rock peppered their skin. Just when the men thought it might be over and they began to emerge from their gash in the earth, another wave of aircraft descended.

The racket was terrifying, deafening. A bright light, a whoosh of air, and suddenly nothing—Kuribayashi's hearing was gone; dirt, rocks, bits of trees and brush cascaded into the bunker.

This is the end, he thought. His family—he would never see them again. But his ears kept ringing . . . he was still alive. Adrenaline kept his thoughts sharp and focused. Masayoshi was still right there. The general realized that the lieutenant was standing over him, sheltering him with his body.

And suddenly the roaring faded, the men stopped shouting. They stood. Masayoshi pulled out his kerchief and dusted off the general's uniform.

That night, Kuribayashi wrote a candid letter to his wife and children. He told them about the "massive bomb" that had landed next to the bunker, and the huge explosion.

"I was convinced that the dugout, with me in it, would be blown to bits, but as luck would have it, I didn't even get a scratch. For the duration of the ferocious raid, the only thing I could do was wait in the dugout in a state of extreme anxiety, and pray," Kuribayashi wrote.

"I want to say goodbye now," he said. "I might not be so lucky next time. I could be killed anytime."

To his children he wrote, "Always do what your mother tells you. After I have gone, I want you to help your mother, treat her as the center of the family, and help each other so you can all live vigorous, positive lives."

But Kuribayashi didn't let his men know that he expected to die.

The following day, the general stood in the shadow of Mount Suribachi, staring out into the Pacific. Iwo Jima was much too vulnerable. He had to dramatically improve the island's defenses, fortify the Japanese positions, and get the soldiers properly trained, all before the Americans returned.

He'd have to start with the men, Kuribayashi told himself—they were demoralized. Once they recovered their belief in the cause, they could do anything, fight off any attack. The American planes would be back. But Iwo Jima was still Japanese territory, and the Japanese were a long way from finished.

— 12 —

AT DAYBREAK, THE gunboat flotilla advanced steadily across the sea. This was it: Invasion Morning, but Nash's gunboat was hundreds of miles from Saipan. The seven boats weren't creeping along shorelines spreading a spawn of frogmen. They were guarding transport ships loaded with the U.S. Army 27th Infantry Division. It wasn't romantic or exciting, but it was still risky. The transports were prime targets for Japanese aircraft.

The gun crews were at their general quarters, ready for anything, their eyes scanning the skies. The action, though, was far away to the west.

Saipan was the first U.S. assault on Japanese territory.

Saipan hadn't always been part of Japan, but in the previous half century the Japanese had transformed the little place into a key territory, with infrastructure built to support massive sugar plantations. It had its own power stations, paved roads, ports, schools, and airfields in the north and south. At least thirty thousand Japanese soldiers were stationed on Saipan, and the Japanese Imperial Fleet plied the waters offshore. And there was a wild card: Most of the island's thirty thousand civilians were Japanese settlers. No one could say if they would join the fight.

Japan's prime minister General Hideki Tojo had proclaimed that the United States would never take Saipan, but U.S. war strategy depended on it. Saipan was the first of a planned one-two-three assault on the Mariana

Islands. Once Saipan, Guam, and Tinian were conquered, Japan would be cut off from its resource-rich southern empire. The islands would become launchpads for attacks on Japan's home islands—the air force's new long-range B-29 Superfortress bombers could inflict punishing strikes on the homeland ahead of a full-on Allied invasion.

Nash and every other commander on the sea were briefed on what lay ahead. Saipan was going to be a bitch to overrun. It wasn't big, just five miles wide by twelve miles long. But the terrain was all cliffs and deep caves—perfect hiding spots for Japanese snipers, machine guns, and artillery—as well as steep hills covered in scrub trees and dense grass. Endless fields of sugarcane would make it difficult for ground troops to maneuver. To make matters worse, there were few beaches to land on.

The Americans had picked a four-mile stretch of sand along the southwestern edge of Saipan as the primary invasion area. This very day, two Marine divisions were set to land there simultaneously, establish a beachhead, then push northward across the island. Marine General Holland "Howlin' Mad" Smith had his orders. He was told to take the island in three days.

Nash wasn't sure about the time frame.

"It's not going to be so easy," he had told Herring. "They have some dreamers at headquarters. You can bet the people who put this together aren't anywhere near those beaches."

Herring agreed. He'd seen how hard the Japanese fought in the Marshalls. Tough as hell. It was a mistake to underestimate them.

For now, Nash and his crew would putter around in the Pacific, consigned to the sidelines.

Radio traffic kept them all glued to their mimeographed newsletters: Battleships, destroyers, and planes had punished the island for days with tens of thousands of shells. The bombardment was over, and thousands of Marines were headed ashore in amphibious landing craft. It sounded like U.S. troops were facing heavy resistance, taking lots of casualties.

The captain's feelings were mixed. His gunboat was supposed to be in there on that beach. Yesterday they'd have laid down covering fire for the underwater demolition teams, and then this morning they were going to join nearly two dozen gunboats on the first sweep of the landing beach.

The plan was scrapped at the last minute. Nash didn't know why. Somebody way above his pay grade made that decision. He swore out loud when the news came over, but now, hearing what was happening on the front lines, he wondered if it wasn't a blessing. A bland, boring sort of blessing.

So here he was on the bridge, staring at damn transports to his right and left. For now, they were sheepdogs herding troops to combat. And that's the way it would stay until they reached Saipan. They'd live to fight another day.

BANKO PEERED AT the shore from behind his 40mm gun, out on the bow. He didn't move a muscle. The rest of the gunners and their crews huddled behind their guns, trying not to breathe too loud. Machine guns chattered in the distant darkness. Mortars barked, and artillery shells thumped down somewhere deep on the island.

Banko hated the dark. Firing the big 40mm was hard enough in daylight, but at least you could see your target. Now you couldn't see a damn thing. Even the stars had taken cover.

They'd delivered the transports to Saipan. Now the gunboat was stuck fifty miles off the island's lower western beaches. They waited there for two days before receiving their orders: Garapan Harbor, patrolling close to shore. Garapan would be their area of operations until further notice.

It was shortly after midnight on June 18 when they finally rolled into the harbor. Cruisers and destroyers were putting on a brilliant light show—star shells arched high over the island and exploded with a tremendous flash, exposing the landscape. Each flash released a giant flare on a parachute, which drifted slowly back to earth, swinging back and forth like a silly afterthought. A few seconds later, one after another, another star shell went up.

The Marines wouldn't be outdone. They had flares, which only lasted a few seconds. Between the star shells and flares, Banko could see the outline of the shore—tops of the palm trees, jagged hills just beyond the beach. It was damn eerie, he thought.

They were lighting the way for the Americans on the island. For days, two Marine divisions and the army's 27th Infantry Division had been fighting for every inch of Saipan. By the end of the first day, more than two thousand Marines had been injured or killed. They'd managed to capture Aslito Airfield, but it was a long, bloody slog. General Smith's plan of taking Saipan in three days was a pipe dream.

There was no rest for anyone. American forces set up perimeters, but the Japanese poked at the edges, triggering firefights. There were no lulls in the action. No one slept.

The gunboat patrolled the harbor. Banko swallowed back a bad feeling. There were Japanese boats out there, moving men and supplies. Their drafts were shallow, they moved silently. They could launch an attack any time.

Keep alert, he told himself.

Dawn broke. Aircraft engines droned above the clouds. Banko looked up. Planes broke through the cloud cover and swooped down on the island. He froze—American, or Japanese? From some place starboard he could hear Hoffman whistling "Yankee Doodle Dandy." Americans! Every man on deck released a giant sigh. The planes vanished beyond the island, where daylight revealed night's gruesome harvest. The harbor was littered with twisted scraps of metal, all that remained of several Japanese ships and barges. Life jackets, uniforms, canteens, gasoline cans, boxes, crates, and a few dead men floated on the surface.

Banko wanted to turn his head, but couldn't. He kept the gun aimed at the shore. It was the only thing he could do.

ARTILLERY BELCHED AND thumped. Machine guns rattled somewhere on the shore. Nash felt someone tap him on the shoulder: Radioman Max Ball.

"Urgent message," he shouted. "It's LCI command."

During combat, Ball moved his Signal Corps transmitter-receiver from the radio shack to the bridge. It was critical the radioman stay near the skipper. Ball kept low, with headphones on, listening carefully to the special navy command channel. He relayed orders immediately to Nash, sometimes signaling him with a quick tug on the leg of his pants. The only thing Ball didn't like about the SCR-610 radio was the batteries. They were big and bulky—each one weighed fifteen pounds—and he had to wear them strapped inside a backpack. It was hard for him to move around. If he ever fell overboard, he'd sink straight to the bottom.

Ball told Nash that all the gunboat skippers were reporting to LCI-457 for a meeting. "They're sending a small boat to pick you up in a few minutes," he said.

Nash turned to Herring on the bridge. Herring was in charge of the Garapan Harbor patrol until he got back. "I'm not sure how long I'll be gone," Nash said to Herring as a small motorboat moved up alongside. "But it shouldn't be long."

Herring wished him luck, then turned his attention back to the harbor. Even though they were hugging the shore, they hadn't been in any firefights. But he knew the threat was there. He could hear it.

A few days earlier, right at dusk, Japanese planes had attacked a convoy anchored off Saipan—sixteen LSTs filled with troops and the ten gunboats that guarded them. The gunboats opened fire with their anti-aircraft guns as the torpedo planes swooped low. One of the planes dropped a torpedo. Instead of landing in the water, it slammed into the side of LCI-468, tearing a huge hole in the bow and killing thirteen sailors.

Nash came back with the latest news. LCI Group Eight Lieutenant Commander Theodore Blanchard was worried about barges. The Japanese were moving supplies and men to key positions on Saipan. Some of the barges were coming from the island of Tinian, only a few miles south. Blanchard warned that the invasion had a long way to go, and their role for now was breaking the barge-borne supply line.

The Marines were still fighting for Nafutan Point, a rocky peninsula on the far southern tip of the island. The Japanese were so sure the Americans would invade there that they'd built artillery defenses designed to fire on U.S. warships. But the Americans landed to the west, and the Japanese couldn't move their heavy artillery. Still, U.S. forces faced intense enemy fire as they moved up Nafutan Point's steep, craggy ridges.

Nash said their mission was still the same as before: Patrol the harbor. Stay alert, be prepared. Shit happens fast.

The gunboat veterans understood that. They didn't like the noise, the chaos, the uncertainty, but they knew what to expect. The new men, though, seemed a bit shaken. Down in the engine room, Holgate could hear the commotion above the diesel engines' pings and clangs. Sometimes he could feel the aftershock of explosions in the water or on the nearby land. But as long as the 449's guns were silent, he knew they were probably OK. At least that's what he told himself.

By the starboard's 40mm gun, Lemke was living off adrenaline and fear, just like the others who hadn't seen action. Hoffman was usually smiling and whistling, and it had reached a point that some of the guys groused and told him to knock it off. He'd laughed and ignored them. But today Hoffman was quiet. Standing back of Lemke, his lips were pursed so tight that he almost couldn't breathe.

AT NEARLY MIDNIGHT, the men on deck heard a fire alarm sound, then a massive blast lit up the darkness over the island: A Marine Corps ammo depot had exploded. Most of the gunboats in Group Eight went to help with the firefighting. When the crafts couldn't get close enough with their fire gear, the crews lowered the hoses and pumps into small boats and headed to shore. But the 449 wasn't ordered to the scene. Instead, the crew watched the fire from the top deck. Sidelined again.

Just after midnight Ball heard the call over a radio: "Shakers 345, 457, 346, and 438 proceed to Mutcho Point and prevent the escape of enemy barges from Garapan." Ball knew Shakers was the code name for the LCIs—and this was trouble.

Mutcho Point was a narrow strip of land in the middle of the island's western side that jutted out into the sea. It was close to their position on Garapan Bay. "Shit," he mumbled. It seemed that at Saipan, everything happened after dark. During the day, they were sightseers, but when the sun went down, "the work began," Ball recalled.

Word spread as their heading changed, but the order didn't come to move forward. Everyone was ready. The tension was palpable as Johnson and the other gunners searched the water for targets. The continuous roar and flash of explosions from the ammo dump only added to the stress.

Every slap of a wave against the hull of the gunboat could be a Japanese swimmer, and every reflection off the water could be a barge.

Ball listened closely for the order to head to Mutcho Point. A radioman on one of the other LCIs said he spotted at least three barges. From their vantage point on the top deck, Overchuk and the crew could hear a firefight. They were so close they could see tracers streaming back and forth between the gunboats and the barges. A destroyer fired a star shell to lighten the sky, and seconds later a massive explosion rocked the harbor. The destroyer had fired a five-inch shell into the fight, effectively blowing the barges out of the water. Pieces of boats and god-knows-what rained down from the sky and splashed into the water, soaking the crew up top with seawater. The tension suddenly broke, and the crew let out a collective cheer, as if they were rooting for the home team at Yankee Stadium. Moments later, they were brought back to reality. Air raid sirens. Ball shook his head. It was going to be another long night.

JUNIOR RAY HOLLOWELL rubbed sleep from his eyes. He'd managed to spend part of the night in his bunk, but the sleep was no good. It was too claustrophobic below. Hollowell needed space to breathe, so he went topside and found a little spot on the fantail where he could stretch. The sun was coming up. His shift started soon.

He was still trying to find his place on the gunboat. A year before, he was scratching for work around rural southern Oklahoma near the Texas border, trying to help out his family. His life was straight from the pages of *The Grapes of Wrath*—his father was a cotton farmer who'd lost his land to boll weevils, dust storms, and bankers. There was nothing left for his children to inherit. Junior Ray, the sixth of ten children, was a wiry, scrappy kid, quick with his fists. His parents thought some discipline would do him good, and wished him well when he turned eighteen and signed up for the navy. Six months later he was in Pearl Harbor, sent to serve on the 449 just before it left Pearl Harbor for Saipan.

He loaded ammunition on Johnson's gun. Him, a white man, toting ammo for a black boy! His daddy would have had a fit if he'd seen that. Oklahoma was one of the most segregated states in America, and Negroes who put themselves above a white man saw their homes and businesses torched and their young men hanged from trees. It wasn't that long ago the governor declared martial law to rein in the Ku Klux Klan.

Hollowell heard all about the Tulsa riots and lynchings while he came up, and he knew the Klan was still thriving in those border towns.

But Tulsa was a long way away from the Pacific. Hollowell had seen himself how good Johnson—or "R.L." as everyone called him, was with that gun, and the skipper didn't hold with any kind of ugly talk. Out here, Negroes and white men had to work together. Besides, after a while, the two of them got to talking. They got along. They both were from the same part of the country—Decatur, Texas, Johnson's hometown, was right down the road from Hollowell's home in Durant, Oklahoma.

Hollowell also made friends with Bozarth, another Oklahoma boy. They both came from hardworking families with lots of brothers and sisters. They had plenty of time to talk. One afternoon the week before they'd shared family pictures, and Hollowell noticed Bozarth's good-looking sister.

"You think she'd let me write to her?" Hollowell asked. Bozarth laughed.

"Maybe," he said. "Far as I know, she's dating a guy in Oklahoma City, but he ain't much. I'll ask her next time I write."

Hollowell mused over what he'd write to a girl he'd never met. She'd probably be religious like her brother, respectable. It didn't hurt she was such a looker. He'd have to ask her for a snapshot. He let himself hope.

Time for work. On the way to the 20mm gun Hollowell passed the radio shack. Nash was in there, pounding away on the ship's typewriter. Must be something important, the deckhand thought.

Nash always wrote his letters longhand. He rarely used a typewriter, but yes, this was important. The skipper had a bee in his bonnet.

When Nash had joined the Naval Reserve, he applied for national service life insurance. The Veterans Administration program provided up to $10,000 in life insurance to men heading into combat. It was a good deal, and many military families stood a good chance of collecting on the policy. On August 1, 1942, Nash duly mailed the application along with a $32.85 check for his premium. But on January 5, 1943, he received a letter saying his application was "defective." It had to be a mistake. Nash, ever the litigator, wrote three letters over a fifteen-month span asking why. He didn't get an answer.

Now he was really angry. Operation Forager was his second major campaign, and he knew more would follow, if he wasn't killed first. And that was the whole point: He'd paid the premium, and he wanted the insurance to help his parents if he wasn't there to help them grow old. He didn't have to join the navy. He gave up a thriving legal practice to help defend his country. But he couldn't get a damn answer from the VA about why he'd been rejected for life insurance. With his last letter, he'd asked the VA to at least refund his premium. Again, he didn't receive a response from the agency. So he began pecking at the keyboard.

"Your position in this matter, if, indeed you have taken any, is unknown to me due to the fact that you have neglected to acknowledge or answer any of my letters," he wrote. "If you are 15 months behind with your correspondence the situation is lamentable; if you have ignored my request for this period of time the situation is deplorable.

"The sum of money involved here is not significant. However, there is a matter of principle at stake," he said. He said the lack of response created a loss of faith in the government. And he wondered if other fighting men were having the same problems, adding that "this state of affairs is most distasteful to me . . . Your prompt reply to this letter will be only consistent with the demands of common courtesy and in fulfillment of an obligation every governmental agency owes to each citizen."

With that, he whipped the paper from the carriage. He signed his name at the bottom of the page, carefully folded the letter, and placed it in an envelope. He wasn't sure what would happen, but at least he'd gotten it off his chest.

YARBROUGH HEARD A faint voice in the fog. A man's voice, calling his name. He tried to ignore it, but it wouldn't go away. He opened his eyes. It was Johnson, standing over him.

"Lieutenant Yarbrough, it's time to get up, sir," he said.

He was still in a daze, but then Johnson's words registered. The lieutenant sat up in his bunk and yawned. He hadn't been sleeping much. Noise. Rotating shifts. Night patrols. No wonder he was dragging.

"Coffee's ready in the galley," the steward said.

Yarbrough nodded, then readied himself for his midnight to 4 a.m. shift. He pulled on his khaki pants and tan shirt, tied his brown shoes, and grabbed his kapok life jacket, helmet, binoculars, and a holster holding his .45-caliber pistol. He checked the magazine to make sure it had rounds, then placed it back in the holster. He headed to the galley.

On the way, he poked his head into the radio shack, where Ball was reading a magazine.

"Everything OK?" Yarbrough asked.

"Yes, sir, it's been quiet," he responded.

Yarbrough walked into the galley, where Johnson and Kepner, the cook, were bullshitting. Johnson and Kepner were part of the original crew, thick as thieves just because they spent so much time working together. Johnson started toward the coffeepot, but Yarbrough motioned for him to keep his seat. The lieutenant poured himself a cup, took a sip, and smiled. "That's a good cup of joe," he said.

"It's fresh for a change," Kepner said. "It's all downhill from here."

Yarbrough turned around and headed to the hatch leading to the well deck. When he got there, he pulled back the blackout curtain covering the opening. He unlatched the lock, walked outside, and closed the hatch behind him. The night air was cool, but the stars lit up the sky. In the distance, he could see flares shooting over the island. But there was only sporadic machine-gun fire. A good sign.

With the cup in his hand, Yarbrough trudged up a ladder to the gun deck, then another to the bridge. Lieutenant Duvall was glad to see his relief.

"Quiet the past four hours," Duvall said. "Flares over Saipan every few minutes, but that's about it."

"Good. Get some shut-eye, Bob," Yarbrough said.

Duvall bounded down the stairs to his bunk. The two sailors on the bridge still had another hour before their replacements would arrive. The seaman who was striking to become a radioman nodded under his headphones. He could barely keep his eyes open.

Yarbrough scanned the ship. He had a clear view of the sailors on topside. They were all peering out into the darkness, looking for the tiniest hint of trouble. A few minutes later, Yarbrough heard footsteps ascending the ladder. It was Johnson, carrying a plate of sandwiches and a flask of coffee.

"I thought you guys might like something," Johnson said to the men. He knew what it was like to pull the late night "dog watch." You needed energy to stay alert. Food and coffee always helped.

Johnson passed the plate to the striker, but he held up a hand, his eyes wide. "Urgent," he said, a little too loud. "Enemy aircraft approaching."

"Sound General Quarters," Yarbrough barked.

The young sailor reached down and flipped a switch, and the piercing air raid alarm screamed through speakers all over the gunboat. Within seconds, the ship was alive with sailors scurrying to their assigned stations. Johnson laid the plate on the steel deck, then raced down the ladder to his 20mm gun.

Yarbrough glanced at the gun deck and glimpsed Duvall, staggering into position in the pilothouse. He couldn't have gotten more than a few minutes of sleep.

Nash joined Yarbrough on the bridge, while Herring rushed down to the engine room to make sure everything was under control.

Then they waited, guns pointed to the sky. And waited.

No planes came.

Nearly an hour later the all clear came over. The crewmen grumbled and headed below; they were asleep before their heads hit horizontal.

Meanwhile, Yarbrough resumed his vigil. He picked up the flask and grinned at the weight of it. There was still plenty of coffee to help him get through the night.

THE WATER WAS emerald-green, calm, and inviting, perfect for diving. Yarbrough wanted to refresh his soul in the water.

Saipan was that kind of place. Coconut and papaya trees, coral reefs, picture-perfect ocean, fruit doves and exotic birdsong—it was a tropical paradise. Take away the guns and troops, add a few lounge chairs and hotels along the shore . . . it would be a perfect getaway.

But for now, the inviting little island was more death trap than tourist destination. Two weeks into the invasion, American troops were still fighting bitterly, with no end in sight. But Yarbrough was hopeful on that afternoon of June 28. The firefights in the distance didn't seem so threatening. The mortars and artillery were exploding in the hills, well beyond the beach, far from the gunboat.

He had a crazy idea, a good idea. What the hell? Yarbrough bounded into the wardroom, where Nash was dozing over a table layered in maps. When Nash looked up, Yarbrough didn't even stop to say "Hello, sir."

"We should organize a swimming party!" he blurted out.

Nash was puzzled. "Swimming? Now? Here?"

"Yes, sir!" Yarbrough said, remembering his manners. "The crew needs a break. They've been at battle stations around the clock. They're getting punchy, sir. And the water out there, well. You gotta see it. It's just perfect."

Nash's mind raced. They'd organized swimming parties before. Usually, a few of the men stood guard on deck with their M1s, looking for sharks, but they'd never had a swim in the war zone. It was unsafe. A battle was still raging on Saipan. A Japanese plane might appear out of nowhere. Hell, who knew what was in the water—mines, dead bodies? But Yarbrough was right. A break in the chaos would be good for the crew. Besides, he wanted to jump into that emerald-green water, too.

"Let's do it," Nash said.

Word spread fast. Quartermaster Second Class William Vollendorf steered the gunboat to a spot nominally out of range of Japanese guns and dropped the anchor. Soon as the movement stopped, someone shouted "Party!" Men stripped off shirts and pants, while on-duty sailors moved to the deck to watch.

Yarbrough stripped down to his shorts and climbed to the edge of the bridge. With the men cheering, he paused for a moment, then jumped high in the air. He bent his body in mid-flight, touched his toes, then straightened out before he hit the water without a splash. A perfect, Olympics-worthy jackknife. Yarbrough's body hit the water hard and cold, but the cold ran up his body like rejuvenation. He was a kid again, swimming in the Gulf of Mexico, his siblings and friends jumping in all around him, sometimes into him. He surfaced, and waved to the other sailors, who shouted and cheered. They began diving in from the deck, splashing and laughing, swimming around the gunboat, floating on their backs.

Bozarth was one of the first in.

Anytime anyone took a dip, Yarbrough and Bozarth were right there in the middle of them. They were known to sneak away for dips and races anytime their boat was anchored. Bozarth had learned to swim in lakes, but every time he felt the salt water against his skin, he was reminded of the few weeks he spent in San Diego just before he joined the 449. Good days, those. Maybe the best.

San Diego was where he'd met Elaine Butler. While he was waiting there for his orders, one afternoon Bozarth stepped into a local broom shop, for a little dose of home. Inside, behind the counter, sat a petite brunette, stitching a brush to a handle. Bozarth was usually shy around girls, but that day he walked right over and started gabbing about the only thing he knew they had in common: brooms. She said her name was Elaine. She smiled a pretty smile and listened while Bozarth chattered about Oklahoma and cornstalks. He wasn't the usual gruff, strutting sailor she'd learned to brush off. This boy was polite, with a warm smile and smooth skin. He looked too innocent for that navy-blue uniform and sailor cap, she thought.

Bozarth didn't know how long he would be in San Diego, so he asked Elaine if he could take her out that night.

She said no. It was Wednesday. She had to go to prayer meeting. That usually sent the sailors scurrying for the door. But instead, Elaine saw Bozarth's eyes light up.

"Can I go along with you?" he asked. She was a little flustered. Yes, she said, but first he had to meet her mother. When she got off work at 4 p.m., Bozarth was waiting on the corner. They took a bus to her house.

Mrs. Butler's husband had left her years earlier, and she was raising three children by herself. They sat down in the living room, and Bozarth told them about his family, his broom-maker dad, the reason why he went into the shop. He answered Mrs. Butler with "no, ma'am" and "yes, ma'am," and he didn't miss a beat when asked to say a blessing over their dinner.

Bozarth escorted Elaine to the Seventh-Day Adventist Church. They sat in the living room for most of the rest of the night, playing records and laughing.

For nearly two weeks, Bozarth spent every free moment with Elaine. Christmas came, and he feasted with her family. They took a day trip to Pacific Beach, where they walked along the busy main street and stopped in a soda shop for ice cream. They found a secluded spot in the dunes, and marked their place with a blanket. Then he grabbed her hand and they ran together, full speed, into the surf. They jumped into the waves, floated, embraced. When he thought they were alone enough, Bozarth pulled Elaine close to him and kissed her. He could taste the salt water on her lips.

New Year's Eve fell on a Friday night. Elaine was expected at the Watchnight Service, where the faithful welcomed the new year with hymns of praise and prayers for peace. But Bozarth's orders had arrived earlier that day. He had only a little time, just hours before he'd join the 449 and ship out to Pearl Harbor. Bozarth knew Elaine was serious when she ditched the church service to be with him.

Elaine was crushed. She knew it was coming—their romance had been such a whirlwind. She'd hoped maybe he'd be one of the lucky sailors who stayed in San Diego while everyone else shipped out. She had never felt this way about anyone, she said—he was kind and gentle, a good Christian man—he wouldn't hurt a soul. Yet here he was, going off to war, where he might have to kill to live. The paradox wasn't lost on her.

They headed to Pacific Beach, and stayed up all night talking about their lives. He felt a call on his life, he told her—the Lord wanted him to be a preacher like his grandfather, maybe plant a small church in Oklahoma. But it was really too early to think about things like that, not with the war. You couldn't plan too far ahead. They'd have to put it all in the hands of the Lord.

"When this war is over, I'm coming right back here and knocking at your door," he told Elaine. "You're the best thing I ever found. I want you setting the kitchen table for supper, with every room in the house full of joy and laughter." Suppertime was special at his house, he said. His family prayed then, and talked about their day, and sometimes prayed after, for what each one of them was facing down, or rejoicing over.

Elaine wanted nothing more than a little joy. She'd seen her fair share of heartbreak and disappointment. After her father abandoned them, her mother had to work odd jobs to make the rent. Elaine dropped out of high school to work in the broom shop. If everyone didn't pitch in, they would be out in the street.

Bozarth and Elaine held each other tight. It would be a long time before they'd see each other again. They took the first bus back to her house, and he walked her to her front door just as the sun rose. He brushed away a grain of sand and kissed her lips goodbye.

Elaine said she would write, but so far they hadn't exchanged many letters—neither of them was much for writing. Still, Bozarth thought about her every day, and prayed for her and her family. He thanked the Lord for sending her into his life.

As he swam off the coast of Saipan, his mind and heart were back at Pacific Beach. Every time he surfaced he smelled salt water, and thought of those lips, those kisses.

HOFFMAN SAT AT a greasy table in the mess deck, pen in hand, trying to write a letter to his parents. He didn't have much time, and he wasn't allowed to tell them anything: where he was, what he was doing, or who he was working with. All of it would be blacked out. What could he say to them? His shift started in just a few minutes. He needed to drop off this letter quickly in Yarbrough's box, if he was going to send anything. The gunboat was headed to the command ship for a mail run. They'd be there soon. If Hoffman didn't finish, he didn't know when he'd have another chance.

Hoffman was lucky at mail call. His family and friends sent him stacks of letters and cards, and he tried to reply to all of them, assuring everyone that he wasn't in harm's way. He lied. He felt a little guilty about that, but it was better if they didn't worry. What good would it do?

Hoffman had only been on the gunboat for five weeks, the busiest, most on-your-toes days of all his life. Just a couple of days after he reported to the 449 in late May, the gunboat was on its way to Saipan. Everything revolved around the mission, and the mission seemed to be focused on "stay sharp." "Keep alert!" So what if nothing ever happened, you had to be shitting bricks to keep these people happy.

Blow kept everyone on their tiptoes, with firefighting drills day and night. Gunnery teams practiced passing ammunition from the storage lockers, loading and unloading the big guns. It all seemed to be paying off. While they hadn't been in any firefights, they were ready and operating as a cohesive team. Still, Hoffman wondered what would happen if they actually came under fire. Would they panic? Stay calm? What if all this practice had worn-out the breeches of the guns?

Hoffman sighed, and turned his attention back to his letter. Holgate walked in, his dungarees streaked with black grease, his hands and fingernails permanently blackened. Working in the engine room was brutal, but Holgate didn't seem to mind. The engines fascinated him.

Holgate sat down next to his shipmate. "You on break?" Hoffman asked.

Holgate nodded. The black gang were regulars in the galley. No one stayed too long down in the engine room without coming up for fresh air. They sweated profusely, and had to get water or they'd pass out.

Outside in the distance, machine-gun fire and bombs exploded.

"Any news?" Holgate asked.

"Nope. We're in a mail run, though. Got anything to go?"

Holgate frowned. He hated mail call. The whole time he was in the navy, he'd never received a single letter. Holgate didn't say anything, but he felt jealous when Hoffman read letters aloud with the latest family news from Saint Louis.

Holgate knew those letters were a bright spot in Hoffman's life. In just a short span, they'd become close friends, a bond that could only have been forged in war. The two eighteen-year-olds stayed up late bullshitting in their room and topside, discovering they had a lot in common.

They both loved music, especially big bands. Hoffman was a Sinatra fan—he could whistle every tune, he knew all the words. Holgate could play piano by ear; his stepmother had a piano and all he had to do was listen to a song, and he could play it—classical and country music, even blues, jazz, gospel. Back home he built crystal radios, just to pick up broadcasts from stations all across the country.

Hoffman told him about his band in Saint Louis, how they played festivals. They talked about starting a group after the war, maybe recruit some of Hoffman's friends from the old neighborhood. Hoffman's parents were sending him a harmonica, so he could learn to play on board during their downtime. Holgate laughed. Between the whistling and the harmonica, Hoffman would drive everyone crazy.

It was during those late-night sessions that Hoffman and Holgate shared their secrets. Hoffman told Holgate that his parents didn't tell him he was adopted, that he had believed all those years that his stepfather was his biological father. "It still bothers me," he said.

As bad as that was, it was nothing compared to the crap Holgate had been through. One night on the way to Saipan, Holgate told Hoffman his story. He was the oldest of six children. His dad, Norman Ray Holgate, had owned a bar in Mountain Home, Idaho, a played-out stagecoach stop and mining town. When his mom found out the old man was having an affair with the cleaning lady, his dad took off, got a divorce, sold the bar, and headed to Terreboone, Oregon, to live on his parents' ranch. Meanwhile, Holgate's mother, Recelia, labored long hours as a waitress and a cook to support her children.

In 1939, when Holgate was twelve, his father showed up in Idaho, demanding that Holgate, his brother Walt, and his sister Maggi come with him to live in Oregon. He had just married his mistress and set up a repair shop. Holgate's mother couldn't afford a legal battle, so his father loaded the children into the car and pulled away. When Holgate looked back, he saw his distraught mother crying in the front yard. He never forgot that.

Holgate quickly learned that his father was still an asshole. Anything his children did was a call to discipline—arriving home late, or "looking at him the wrong way." He set up a special basement room where he worked them over with a thick leather belt, even little Maggi. "My brother tried to protect me," she recalled years later. "When my father accused me of something, he would take the blame. He would take the beating for me."

The violence escalated, and Holgate and Walt, his younger brother, enlisted in the navy the moment they were old enough. They got the hell out, and never looked back.

Hoffman listened to his friend's story in stunned silence. After all that, Holgate could easily have turned out to be a jerk. Instead, he was full of life, a guy who always had your back—full of fun and music. Hoffman wanted to do everything to keep him safe.

The gunboat engines dropped to B-flat and two-quarter time, a sign they were probably close to the command ship. Hoffman came up with an idea. If he hurried, he could get his letter to Yarbrough in time for the outgoing mail.

On the bottom of the paper, under a quick P.S., he asked his mother if she could correspond with Holgate—that his friend didn't receive any mail from home. He didn't go into the details, but said it would mean a lot to his buddy knowing that somebody on the home front cared about him.

He folded the letter, put it in its envelope, scrawled on the address. Hoffman didn't say a word to Holgate about his plan. He wanted it to be a surprise.

HERRING COULD SEE the ship in the distance, the USS *Kennebago*, a fleet oiler. He checked his watch. They'd be alongside in a few minutes. It would take a few hours for the oiler to pump 6,800 gallons of fuel and 1,750 gallons of freshwater aboard, before sending the 449 on its way.

The calendar said today was the Fourth of July, and Herring's mind was home in North Carolina—picnics, speeches, and fireworks. He'd spent his Independence Days at White Lake, where every cottage along the water proudly flew a U.S. flag.

His mother and brother and cousins were there at the lake with all his uncles and aunts—peach pies and potato salad, frankfurters and cole-slaw. Herring wasn't the only one thinking about home. The whole crew was homesick, wondering what their wives were roasting on the barbecue out back, imagining the feel of their girlfriends' embraces as the fire-works colored the sky over the town square.

Holidays could be depressing, but at least there weren't any cards on July 4th. Thanksgiving and Christmas were the worst, with cards and gifts from family and friends. It reminded the men of how much they missed their homes and loved ones, and that they might never see them again.

Back in January, everyone had said the Pacific War would be over by the end of 1944. The year was half over now, and here they were bogged down in Saipan . . . the "three-day conquest" was now nearly three weeks old, and American forces were still fighting. And Guam and Tinian still remained.

Herring cleared his mind. Maybe he'd make it home in time for the next Fourth of July. He smiled. July 4, 1945. If he did, he knew exactly what he'd do. After the cookout, he'd pull the old boat off the drydock and go sailing out over the lake. He'd stay out there all night long, all alone.

ON SAIPAN, THE morning of July 7, soldiers in the U.S. Army's 105th Infantry Regiment braced for a Japanese counterattack. What they didn't expect were four thousand Japanese soldiers with guns and bayonets charging and screaming in a last-ditch effort to break through the American lines.

More than a thousand American soldiers were killed or wounded in the suicide charge. But when it was over, the Americans had wiped out their Japanese attackers. The charge confirmed the commanders' worst fears: The Japanese would rather die than surrender. In nearly a month of carnage, Japan lost thirty thousand soldiers. The devastating defeat led to Tojo's resignation as prime minister.

Ball was alone in the radio shack, headphones on, noodling with a transmitter, trying to get a clear signal. He caught the tail end of a message: Night patrols suspended.

The battle of Saipan was over.

It wasn't a surprise, especially in the wake of that Japanese banzai charge.

When Nash walked into the radio room, Ball relayed the message.

Nash was subdued. Now that they had Saipan, troops would be headed to their next destination: Guam. He didn't know when they'd be pulling out of Saipan. All of Operation Forager's plans had been pushed back. The invasion of Guam had originally been scheduled for June 18. *June 18.* In retrospect, the commanders appeared to have been wildly optimistic. It was hard to believe they thought Saipan would be such a cakewalk.

Nash turned to Ball: Just because nighttime maneuvers had been suspended, the gunboat still had daytime patrols. Most of the Japanese troops were dead, but U.S. commanders were still concerned about potential pockets of soldiers hiding and fighting in caves.

The gunboats soon headed to Marpi Point, the northern tip of the island. When they left Garapan Harbor, the crew breathed a sigh of relief. They'd be anchored by nightfall. Maybe they could finally have a full night's sleep.

Marpi Point was a series of sheer, eight-hundred-foot-high cliffs overlooking the water, a spectacular piece of geography. Duvall peered through his binoculars to get a closer look. But what he saw choked the breath in his throat: Men, women, and children were lining up near the edge of the cliffs. To his horror, it looked like they were flowing fast down the sides . . . they were jumping, or being pushed. It couldn't be.

He shouted something unintelligible. Someone wailed from a gunboat nearby as other men glimpsed the same images and began shouting: "Don't jump!" An endless line of people, ready to die. In quick succession, the older children nudged the younger ones, then the mothers shoved the older children and the fathers pushed the mothers before jumping over the edge themselves. They fell screaming like dolls onto the jagged rocks below, hundreds of them sliced open, crushed, drowned. The water turned a sickening shade of red.

Tokyo had told the civilians time and again that if the Americans seized the island, they would torture, rape, and kill any survivors. Like the soldiers in that last-ditch banzai attack, the families chose death. There was little the Americans could do. As the gunboats drew near, the sailors used loudspeakers to appeal to the people not to jump. But nothing changed their minds. It was a gruesome scene, and it would go on for days, over and over . . .

Bruce Hallett tried to look away, but wherever he turned, he couldn't escape "the bodies of the women and children floating in the water." They were everywhere—thousands of men, women, and children bobbing like dead fish, Holgate recalled. Bozarth wept and prayed on his knees for the Lord's mercy on those poor souls. Most of the crew stood by and didn't say a word.

As darkness fell, the men returned below. No one slept that night. Not with the bodies of the dead thumping against the sides of the gunboat.

13

THIS WAS IT. No more rehearsals. The gunboat was heading into action. Every weapon was manned, and ammo passers were holding extra clips. Nash stood on the bridge, Vollendorf at the helm below matching the speed of LCI-441, the gunboat out front.

Underwater Demolition Team 6 was curled into several thirty-foot-long plywood boats (landing craft, personnel ramps, or LCPRs) motoring to a beach on the island of Guam. The men looked like they were headed to a swim meet, not a war zone. The so-called frogmen wore swim trunks, masks, and fins to protect their feet from poisonous coral. Their bodies were strapped with knives, demolition kits and fuses, and marking slates with waterproof pencils to create detailed maps, but little else. Their muscular hides shone with aluminum-based greasepaint tinted bluish-gray for camouflage and to protect their bodies from the cold water.

Each of their wooden landing craft carried an inflatable rubber boat to help them get supplies to shore and scoop up swimmers after the mission. They were quiet men, wiry and strong. They were incredibly important to the invasion. They blasted shipping channels through the coral reefs. They blew up obstacles that could disable the amphibious vehicles. They marked the water depths at the reefs as well as the best places to land on the beach. They did a shitload of reconnaissance work in a short time—and right now, they were doing it in broad daylight.

The teams created by Lieutenant Commander Draper Kauffman had proved their mettle on Saipan. They set charges, took measurements, and when they got back to the ship they spent the rest of the night drawing up detailed charts of what they'd seen. Their intelligence proved critical to the invasion.

This mission, Nash and other gunboats would hug the shore near Agat on the southwestern side of Guam. They were decoys, diversions— they would draw the Japanese fire while the frogmen sneaked ashore to do their work.

Nash was looking forward to the operation. He knew his men needed to put Saipan behind them, days of bloated disfigured corpses rising to the surface, bouncing like rubber balls, rotting in the sun. A few of the crews began shooting the corpses, and they sank like deflated balloons. But there were just too many of them, and every shot released a cloud of noxious gas. Within days, the stench and swarming black flies were overpowering. No one could eat, and many of the of the men had nightmares.

Guam gave the men something new to think about. They were on a tight schedule. The invasion was due in four days, set for July 21, when the 1st Provisional Marine Brigade would land bright and early on Agat beaches. The army's 77th Infantry Division would follow, landing a little north that afternoon, and the Marines' 3rd Division would launch their attack ten miles farther north, near Asan Point.

Nash's gunboat had just passed a line of destroyers, cruisers, and battleships, all bristling with guns, all pointed toward the little island. American aircraft filled the sky. But once the gunboats reached the shore, Nash knew they'd be on their own.

Nash peered at a crescent of sand a few hundred yards away, then glanced at his watch. It was 16:00. "There they go," Yarbrough sang out. The swimmers were sliding over the sides of their fast-moving crafts, slipping into the water like minnows. Meanwhile, the gunboats moved slowly along the edge of the reef that ran parallel to the shore.

The gunners held their fire. The barrels of the 40mm guns swiveled left and right seeking targets. Overchuk on the port-side 20mm gun looked down his gun sight searching for targets. His loader, Seaman First Class Leonard Sless, asked over and over: "See anything?"

Overchuk's answer was quick and to the point: "No." "No." "Not yet."

Across from him on the starboard side, Johnson manned his 20mm gun, but since his side was facing out to sea, he had nothing to do but wait for the 449 to complete its path along the reef. Once it turned in the opposite direction, it would be his turn.

Johnson felt the ship begin to decrease its forward motion, then begin a tight 180-degree turn. His loader, Junior Hollowell, full of adrenaline, yelled out: "Here we go, R.L.!" Johnson didn't respond, but he tightened his grip on his weapon and swiveled the 20mm, feeling the gun move sweetly in its carriage.

Johnson was now in position as the 449 moved slowly, covering its sector of the beach. But the Japanese held tight. They didn't want to reveal their hidden bunkers.

Without Japanese fire there was little to shoot for. Beyond the beach rose a wall of palm trees and a thick brush—bright spring green at the top, darker near the ground. There were pillboxes and emplacements in there, but they were damned if they could see anything.

Just over a mile inland, Mount Alifan towered over the beach. It was 770 feet high, with a Japanese command post on top. The seven gunboats were in plain sight, moving slowly up and down the reef at its feet. Back and forth, like crooks casing a joint.

Ball grabbed Nash: Message. Gunboats get in position now and wait. At 16:48, another order: Commence firing. The crew's guns raked the greenery beyond the beach, careful not to hit any of the teams. Some of the guns focused on the treetops, remembering what the Marines had seen at Guadalcanal: Japanese snipers lashed high in the palms, waiting, camouflaged by the thick evergreen leaves. The guns tore the jungle to ribbons, but nobody shot back.

The tops of the trees were gone, blown into air. Dirt flew in every direction. Four minutes later, the skipper called cease fire. The swimmers were finished. Regroup at the destroyer USS *Kane*. Next deployment: the same beach. Tonight, after dark.

Meanwhile, the gun crews prepared for the next mission. They only had maybe ninety minutes before dusk. Once darkness fell, Nash would enforce strict blackout. Smoking cigarettes would be prohibited. Even a flicker of light could be seen over a great distance.

On the 449, Blow moved quickly among the crew, keeping them focused, checking for any performance problems with the guns or other gear, making quick repairs. The crew took turns hitting the head. With the way things were going, they didn't know when they'd get another chance to go.

CLOUDS COVERED THE midnight sky. No stars. Nothing. It was so dark that Nash could barely make out the faces on the bridge: Yarbrough, Ball, and signalman Arthur Lewis. He could hear the men whispering below, but he couldn't see them. Every once in a while he'd hear a faint thump as a knee or shin collided with a pipe or bulkhead, followed by someone cursing under his breath.

They'd been there for hours. The demolition team had gone into the water ages ago, and the gunboats were told to stay in position along the beach and keep close watch of the shore. No one knew how long the swimmers would take. All they could do was wait.

Nash and Yarbrough peered through their binoculars looking for any sign of danger. Their eyes played tricks. Every bush became a sniper. Every sapling tree became a lunging soldier with a bayonet. Finally they heard noises. Dogs.

Seaman First Class Charles Hightower, an ammo loader on the port-side 40mm gun, leaned over to his buddy Ralph Owens. "Do you hear dogs barking?"

A quiet whisper came back: "Yeah."

Banko heard the dogs barking on the shore, and what sounded like people talking. It was a foreign language. Probably Japanese.

Meanwhile, the demolition team was busy examining the part of the reef closest to the sand, trying to decide whether it was going to be a problem for the landing crafts. If it was, they'd blow it up. But they couldn't see a damn thing.

"The darkness greatly reduced the effectiveness of the reconnaissance," a UDT 6 member wrote in an after-action report.

Suddenly the Japanese fired a star shell, then another, and the beach lit up like a Christmas tree. The swimmers' dark camouflage concealed them in the water, but on the reef and the white-sand beach, they stood out in stark contrast.

Yarbrough wheeled around to tell Nash: "There's someone on the beach." Nash saw the men, too. *Frogmen.* "Damn," he said.

Yarbrough told the gunners to keep watch for movement coming out of the jungle, but not to fire without orders. No one wanted to kill a member of the demolition team.

The wait was agony, but moments later the gunners got the word: "All gun stations open fire, repeat, all gun stations open fire."

The gunboats sprang to life, spitting yellow and orange flashes over the beach and into the trees. They lit up the sky, filled the air with an acrid, explosive stink. Bushes ignited, grass fires spread. Amid the chaos, the demolition team swam toward their LCPRs and safety.

"Cease fire!" the order came. Again, the Japanese didn't return rounds. But in the distance, Nash could hear small engines heading in their direction . . . the LCPRs! One of the boats pulled up port side to Nash's gunboat, and a voice shouted: "Hey, can some of the guys come on board?"

Nash ordered the crew to give them a hand. On deck, the swimmers began to change into clothes, chafing their skin to get warm. When everyone was ready, the gunboats and demolition teams received orders to return to the *Kane.*

The boats turned for deeper water, and ran into a heavy, driving rain. Because of the "very limited visibility" the LCIs "became disorganized from formation."

Nash couldn't see a damn thing. The gunboats switched on wake lights to try to keep a proper distance, but they switched them off quickly, afraid the Japanese would spot them, too. Helmsman Vollendorf lost sight of the boat ahead, and stopped the engine until he could get his bearings. The boat was suddenly rammed from behind by LCI-438.

Nash and the other officers rushed to the stern to see what had happened. The damage to the 449 was minimal, but it was a different story for LCI-438, which "suffered a hole in the bow about four feet above the waterline."

No one was injured on either gunboat, but it was an inauspicious way to end the operation. There was not much they could do. Within a few hours, the gunboats and the demolition teams would return to the beach. They were running out of time.

JOHNSON DIDN'T MOVE for two days. He sat behind his 20mm gun, surrounded by his crew, waiting for the order to fire. He fired hundreds of rounds into the jungle, until the order came to stop. It went on and on, endlessly. With the invasion so close, the demolition teams worked ceaselessly. They needed the gunboats there for protection.

In Saipan, the crew of the 449 had often gone a long time without sleep, but this was different. There were no rotating shifts. They weren't hunting phantom Japanese barges in the dark. This was never-ending, continuous. It seemed like the gunners fired their weapons every few minutes. The Japanese couldn't set one foot on the beach while the demolition teams were out there. The Japanese couldn't step one foot on the beach after the frogmen left, either. Military planners were worried the enemy might install new obstacles, or remove demolition charges the teams had set. There had to be a twenty-four-hour presence, gunboats shooting up the beaches every few minutes.

The crew was dragging. But nobody griped. Everyone knew the invasion was critical. This was why they were here.

America was on the verge of taking back Guam, a U.S. territory overrun by the Japanese at the start of the war. Guam was thirty-two miles long by ten miles wide, the largest island in the Marianas chain. And as on Saipan, the landscape was formidable: mountainous terrain with steep peaks, deep gorges, and thick jungles. Once again, there would be ample hiding places for Japanese guns, mines, and fighters. Nineteen thousand of them, according to U.S. Command.

Taking Guam would be symbolic as well as militarily important. It had been in U.S. hands since the end of the Spanish–American War in 1898. The navy established a base on Guam, and the captain served as both commander and governor of the island. Still, the navy only had a small presence there, and the federal government had rejected requests to build it up. When the

Japanese attacked on December 8, 1941, there were about 550 Marines and sailors on Guam, as well as two patrol boats, a minesweeper, and a freighter. The island held out for two days.

It was said the remaining islanders had hoped ever since for the Americans to return. Now they were getting close.

While the gunboats stood guard, the demolition teams had moved from their "sneak and peek" phase to "wham and scram"—they blew up anything that got in the way.

During the day, Nash and the other commanders watched in awe.

"With a large explosion that sent coral, debris and water several thousand feet into the air, the demolition team blew out several hundred yards of coral cribs on the southern beaches. As the explosion subsided . . . not a coral crib remained where only a few seconds ago they had been strung like beads in a necklace along the reef. It must be a discouraging sight for the enemy to see his carefully prepared beach obstacles so destroyed," one commander wrote in a report.

Meantime, the gunboats fired at everything that moved, and some things that didn't. The gun crews competed against one another, pointing out targets and then seeing who could destroy them first. They spotted the tower of a white church on a hill, an ideal Japanese observation post. Hallett and the other 40mm gun crews challenged one another to find which crew "could put fire directly through the windows." No one knew who won. The tower collapsed after just a few minutes.

Through it all, the Japanese shore batteries offered little resistance. The Japanese had learned not to expose their positions too early. They survived the pre-invasion bombardments by staying put in their heavily fortified positions, then attacking the troops when they landed.

It was critical to the U.S. admirals and generals to ensure the landings went as smoothly as possible. The demolition teams, the constant firing from the gunboats, the all-night shifts were all part of the run-up to the big invasion. So much was at stake.

CLARENCE KEPNER SHOOK his head, willing himself to stay awake. Coffee didn't work anymore. There was no chance of getting any sleep.

Not tonight. He took one last sip from the cup, pulled himself up from his chair, and grabbed a couple of tin mugs. Once again, water the ship.

Two deckhands hoisted water pitchers and followed him from the galley. The trio traveled the gunboat from bottom to top, rehydrating crewmen who'd been at their positions for days.

Down a ladder they clambered, into the bowels of the ship, where the black gang was living a troll-like existence. The men were shiny with grease, bilge water, oil, fuel, salt, and sweat. The noise was deafening, the stink was overpowering. Every time Kepner ventured into the pit, he wondered how the guys could take it.

The men were shirtless. Holgate and Casaletto, who could tell if there was anything wrong with the engines by the smallest shift in sound. Meredith Luckner and Alfred Fox surrounded Robert Carrell, who sat at the control board, glimpsing the pressure gauges and annunciator to see if there were any changes in speed. Kepner shouted at the men to get their attention. They couldn't hear him.

Eventually they stopped and stood up straight, happy to see new faces. They grabbed the cups, gulped the water. "Glad ya didn't forghettabout us, Kep!" Casaletto said. The others gave Kepner the thumbs-up sign, and the cook headed topside.

On deck, Kepner and the men shuffled their feet through hundreds of empty shell casings, trying their best not to slip and fall. Johnson and Hollowell sat on the well deck beside their 20mm gun. They could take a little break. They stayed at battle stations, but they were off the line: The 449 was broadside, parallel to the shore, with port side and forward guns ready to fire.

Johnson took a sip, then passed the cup to Hollowell, who emptied it in a single swallow. He thanked the cook, rested his chin on his chest, folded his hands across his life jacket, and closed his eyes.

The last few days were getting to the crew. Their hands shook from fatigue. They were having trouble keeping their eyes open. They couldn't even go to the head to relieve themselves—when they had to go, they pissed over the rails. After dark a few even dropped their pants, planted their asses over the rail, and defecated, telling the rest to not look their way for a minute.

Kepner knew the gun loaders were having a particularly tough time. They shifted, bent, and lifted the heavy cans of 20mm and 40mm ammunition, incredibly exhausting work.

Still, the gentle voice of Bozarth greeted Kepner at the bow gun.

"How ya doin', Kep?"

"Doing better than you, boy. Least I get to move around. Galley's never been so clean. One of these days we're going to make something on the stove again."

The men had been living on cold sandwiches. Hallett could barely hold the cup. He had been helping turn the wheel of their 40mm for hours. Their little crew was usually pretty lively, ribbing one another, trying to make Bozarth blush with particularly colorful cussing. But now they just focused on the water.

Kepner climbed to the starboard gun deck. He handed a cup to Gunner's Mate Third Class Howard Schoenleben, and asked if he had heard any news from his wife. Schoenleben had just learned he was going to be a father. He knew it was going to be a boy. It had to be.

"Ask Casaletto what his secret is. He's got tons of little boys at home," one of the men cracked. "He joined the navy so he could get a little peace and quiet!"

Everyone on the gun crew laughed—except Lemke. The conversation made him think of his own family. Little Mary was seven months old now, but he had never held her in his arms. He carried her photos in his wallet, and sometimes took them out for a look, or to show them to the other men. He'd miss her taking her first steps. He wondered if he would ever be there at all. Since Saipan, he had been thinking more about his baby. Lemke couldn't shake the images of the infants and toddlers tossed from Marpi Point, the tiny, blackened bodies floating in the water. He only hoped that the images would fade with time.

DESTROYERS, CRUISERS, AND battleships battered away at the island.

This was the gunboat's final day covering the demolition teams, but Nash couldn't tell anyone but the officers. The next morning, on these very beaches, ten thousand troops would swarm from inside amphibious landing crafts, onto the sand and onward into the jungle.

Nash didn't know what the 449 would do during the invasion, but he suspected they might not take part at all because he still hadn't been briefed.

Ball tapped Nash's shoulder—message from the command ship. Gunboats ordered to cease operations at the landing beach. Meet at the command ship at 17:15 for their next assignment.

The guns went silent. The gunboats peeled away from their up-and-down parade and lined up in formation. The demolition teams in their little boats buzzed among them. Commander Draper Kauffman had sent a message that morning: "You and your LCIs have done a great job. Our sincerest appreciation and thanks to all your LCIs from every man in the underwater demolition teams." It made the officers smile, but Nash knew it would take more than a few "attaboys" to get promoted.

He'd told the commanders he wanted more responsibility. It didn't matter that the gunboats earned praise for their pre-invasion action. The only way to move up was by accumulating more combat time.

They hadn't made it to the USS *Kane* before another call came in. The orders had changed. Gunboats to Saipan, to help set up the Tinian invasion. "Damn," Nash mumbled.

Lemke watched Guam disappear in the distance. Forget about the tropical paradise they'd seen on arrival. Now it looked like a typhoon had come ashore. Palms were bent and battered, uprooted and cut in half by their horizontal rain of steel.

Lemke knew they were damn lucky to escape with no casualties. Going in, they'd been ready for the worst—firefights, aerial attacks, rockets, torpedoes. But the Japanese held fire. As one fellow put it, the gunboats were like sitting ducks on a pond, but for some reason the hunters didn't shoot.

Maybe they were waiting for bigger prey.

14

A FEW DAYS of sweet sleep and resupply in Saipan, and they were ready for the next round. Orders arrived: LCI-449 would be in the first wave of gunboats covering the 4th Marine Division when they landed on the northwestern side of Tinian.

The island was only a few miles south of Saipan, but wasn't as big—twelve-and-a-half miles from the northern to the southern tip, and five miles at its beam. Tinian terrain was open and park-like, with groves of trees dotting the sprawling cane fields.

The American brass wanted to take Tinian just as much as they'd wanted Saipan. Its wide-open landscape would provide a perfect airfield for the new B-29 bomber, or Superfortress, as it was called. The Japanese Air Force used it as a fueling station, a stop-off to and from the empire. There already were several airstrips at Ushi Point on the northern tip, and an airfield at Gurguan Point on the southwestern side of the island.

And there were about nine thousand well-armed Japanese fighters there, too.

The all-too-familiar Pacific-island problem presented itself: Where to land U.S. troops? Tinian seemed to rise straight up from the sea. Its coastline was cliffs, from a few to a hundred feet high. The best spot was near Tinian Town to the southwest, where the coastline merged gently with the island terrain. The Japanese would probably place most of their garrison near those beaches.

The strategists came up with a plan.

They decided to fake an attack near Tinian Town to divert Japanese attention, while Marines landed on two narrow strips of white sand on the northwestern side of the island. The beaches were about a thousand yards apart and were dubbed, poetically, White I and White II.

The 449 was ordered to move close to the shore at White II and fire at Japanese positions. Unlike during their time in Guam, Nash knew the Japanese batteries would shoot back. Saipan had taken nearly a month to overrun, and from what Nash could tell from radio traffic, the fighting was just as fierce on Guam. Tinian would probably be more of the same.

Nash and his officers told the crew they'd be shipping out July 24. The night before, Kepner prepared the ritual pre-battle meat loaf and mashed potatoes dinner, and Bozarth made rolls and pies. When dinner was ready, the men sat quietly in the galley and bowed their heads while Bozarth prayed a blessing on the food, and petitioned the Almighty for safety and success in the battle to come. They ate quickly, then headed to their battle stations to check their equipment yet again.

WITH A COFFEE cup in one hand and a rag in the other, rocket-man Paul Vanderboom stared out the hatchway. It was raining squalls, threatening to ruin all his hard work.

Over the last twenty-four hours, Vanderboom and several deckhands had assembled 240 rockets. It was painstaking work, and over several hours they'd carefully racked each one in a specified slot in proper order, ten racks of 120 rockets. The mission called for two runs along the shore.

Just when everything was set, the sky opened up and the rain poured down. Storms usually provided a short and welcome relief from the tropical heat and humidity, but tonight the rain was a real pain in the ass. The electrical circuits on the rocket launchers didn't hold up well when exposed to water. Vanderboom would have to recheck them all, as soon as the rain stopped. This was the first time the gunboat had been ordered to use rockets in the Marianas, and Vanderboom wanted to make an impression.

He sipped down the sandy end of his coffee. The deckhands gathered around, rubbing their eyes and grousing. They all wanted to get finished, get some sleep. Vanderboom tucked a rag in his back pocket and wheeled around to retrieve dry towels and his circuit tester kit. There was no time to waste. In the distance, he could hear explosions; the navy's pre-invasion bombardment of Tinian.

At another hatchway, Blow waited, too. The boatswain needed to make sure ammunition was stocked in the right places. He watched the skies, knowing that once the rain passed he'd have several crewmen form a bucket-brigade sort of line and pass cases of ammunition from the lockers to the gun tubs.

Across the ship, most of the crew was up. Some, like Vanderboom and Blow, were hard at work, but several more were in their bunks, doubled over with sharp stomach pains. It wasn't the big dinner. It was anxiety and fear. The men tried not to think of death, but the sound of navy guns in the distance was a constant reminder that they'd soon head into the fire.

Vanderboom knew the key was to stay busy. When the rain finally passed, he emerged with several dry cloths in hand. He moved to the portside ramp, where banks of launchers were positioned to fire rockets at various elevations. One by one, Vanderboom and the deckhands moved down the racks, drying the electric contact points and all exposed wires. Vanderboom checked connections with his handheld circuit tester, ensuring there were no short circuits. He and his crew wiped and dried and tested each port-side launcher, then did each of the starboard ones. They were in perfect working order. Vanderboom glimpsed Nash on the bridge and gave him the thumbs-up sign. They were ready to join the other ships gathering for the invasion.

BANKO SAW THE outline of the island growing in the distance. They'd be there soon. Stretched out on the sea before him were hundreds of ships and amphibious crafts pushing in the same direction. Just a little closer and they'd be in range. They'd get the signal. Just wait.

On the bridge, Nash and Yarbrough stood in their accustomed spots. Ball sat on the floor, headphones on, listening to the traffic on the SCR-610. No one said a word, not anywhere on the ship.

Their gunboat was one of eight in Group Eight attacking White Beach II on the overcast, drizzly morning of July 24. These eight were the old battleaxes of the flotilla—they'd seen combat all through the Marshall Islands, Saipan, and Guam, and now Tinian, too.

Some of the ships and landing craft broke away and moved out to open water, but Nash knew they were the diversionary force, taking part in the feint invasion off Tinian Town.

Everything there was going as planned, according to the radio: The Japanese had fallen for the ruse. Their batteries had opened fire on landing crafts that seemed to be heading to the shore. But instead of landing on the beaches, the crafts turned to a rendezvous point just outside the shells' reach.

Meanwhile, at White Beach II, word finally came from above: Commence attack.

Nash's gunboat and LCIs 345, 346, 348, 438, 441, 454, and 457 lined up side by side, each spaced seventy-five yards apart from the next. They opened the throttles and sped for the beach.

As the gun captain on the bow's 40mm, Banko had a front-row view, waiting for word as the 449 moved closer and closer to the shore. "OK, you bastards, here we come!" he shouted into the wind. In front of him, Hallett and Bozarth and others on Banko's gun crew waited, water spraying in their faces.

Once the first shot was fired, they'd scramble to keep ammo flowing into the 40mm gun. To Hallett, the gunboat was like a race car on a straightaway. It was scary as hell, but exciting at the same time.

At 07:47, when the gunboat was seventeen hundred yards from shore, Yarbrough's voice sounded in all the gun stations: "All stations, open fire, repeat, open fire." In an instant the sides of the gunboat burst into action as the 20mm and 40mm gunners strafed Japanese bunkers along the beach.

Then Yarbrough shouted another order: "Take cover. Take cover."

The gun crews scrambled into the deckhouse. Vanderboom leaned over a console and pressed a button on a control box, launching a long string of rockets. It was a powerful feeling; as long as the button was depressed, the rockets kept firing. Flames shot out of the end of the missiles; the men had to leave their positions so they wouldn't be burned. Vanderboom blasted a stand of palm trees and brush beyond the beach, sheared off tree trunks, and set fire to ragged cane fields.

When Vanderboom was finished, Yarbrough barked out, "Battle stations! Go, go, go, go, go . . ." The men rushed to their stations as incoming Japanese rounds came clattering after the gunboat. Hallett could hear them pinging off the deck.

When the bow of the 449 was several hundred yards from the beach, the gunboats turned 180 degrees. They had to move away from the shore. At the helm of the gunboat, in the pilothouse, Vollendorf looked at the gauges, and then headed to a rendezvous point four miles away. Duvall checked the navigational equipment and relayed a message to the bridge: They were right on schedule. Once regrouped, they would make their second run, followed by waves of landing crafts behind them waiting to get to the beach. It was a complicated choreography, but everything was coordinated.

Meanwhile, Blow was running along the main deck, checking on the men. Beuckman grabbed him. "Anybody hit?" Blow shook his head no, then climbed a ladder to the gun deck to see if everything was working. All the gun crews gave him thumbs-up signs. In the fantail, he checked on the standby brigade, which had the responsibility of extinguishing fires. There were none. He peeked into the engine room, just to let the crew know all was well and the ship was headed back in. The rocket crews scurried to reload the racks.

Banko could feel the gunboat turn. He took a few deep breaths to stay calm. As the 449 started toward the island again, Banko glanced at the landing crafts behind them, ready to take Marines to the shore. He knew that after the 449's second run there would be a chaotic scene on the beach: Marines would jump out of landing crafts, swarming ashore, running straight into enemy fire, trying to secure a beachhead. The landing area would be alive with men and heavy equipment—four battalions of artillery and dozens of flame-throwing tanks rolling forward from the water.

The engines roared and the deck vibrated as the gunboat picked up speed. They were headed in for attack. Banko heard Yarbrough say: "Open fire."

A sailor on Banko's gun crew pressed the foot pedal to fire the weapon, while the gun captain directed Hallett and the others. They were aiming the 40mm at shapes and structures visible just beyond the beach. They didn't let up. Hallett and Bozarth and the others on his gun crew were bathed in sweat, trying to keep pace. They shouted in relief when ordered to take cover again.

Soon as they were safe, Vanderboom began firing the second round of rockets along with the other gunboats. The landscape beyond the beach was in flames. Smoke roiled the morning mist. The palm trees bent over sideways from the force of the explosive shocks.

Hightower, an ammo loader for the port-side 40mm gun, wondered how anyone could survive that barrage. Their boat's 40mm guns had just expended nearly 2,000 rounds, and Vanderboom had fired 173 rockets.

When the 449 was close to shore, Vollendorf turned the ship, heading to a new position. But the operation was far from over.

Their orders were to patrol the northwestern side of the island in formation with the other gunboats, to protect the flank. They traveled up to Ushi Point in the north, then five miles south to Fabius Hilo Point. Then back again, an endless loop. Hurry up. Wait.

RALPH OWENS WAS dead weary. He had been behind his 40mm gun for most of the night. Hightower, his loader, noticed that Owens was struggling to stay awake. The gunner let his burning eyes close, just long enough to feel his chin drop to his chest. Then he'd suddenly jerk his head up.

"You OK, ol' boy?" Hightower asked. Owens shrugged.

"What do you think Nina is doing?" Hightower asked. His thick Southern drawl made her name "Nay-nuh."

And Owens smiled for a moment. He talked nonstop about his girl-friend Nina, and he knew Hightower was just trying to keep him awake, harping on his favorite subject. The eighteen-year-olds had joined the ship the same day in August 1943, and had been bunkmates since. Hightower, a country boy from Russellville, Arkansas, was the "straight man." He'd ask a question and move out of the way while Owens rambled: How he was going to leave Prater, Virginia, behind, 'cause there was no way he was spending his life working down a coal mine like his father and brothers and all his relatives. Deer hunting in the thick woods along the snowy ridges, fishing in the cold streams. But no matter what came up, the subject always turned to Nina: She was the prettiest, sweetest girl in Buchanan County. Each conversation went the same way: "Boy, Hightower, I'm gonna marry that gal one of these days."

He meant it: He'd taped her eight-by-ten portrait on his wall. Nina was the first thing he saw in the morning and the last thing he saw at night.

As dark turned to morning on the gun deck, Owens ran out of words. Hightower understood. After the fear and excitement of the beach landing, they'd patrolled for the next twenty-two hours. The last few were the worst. The gunboat bounced around, ordered from one hot spot to another as they helped the Marines push back several Japanese counterattacks.

The Japanese liked to strike at night, so the invaders stopped their advance in late afternoon and set up a perimeter. They strung barbed wire along the front lines, placed machine guns in key positions. Mortar crews were assigned target areas. Artillery batteries in the rear knew the probable enemy approach routes.

All through the night the Japanese probed the front lines and mounted suicide attacks at different points along the perimeter. With each assault, the gunboats were called in to fire into the Japanese positions. The Marines held their line. Now, at daybreak, they were getting ready to resume their advance.

The gunboat headed south, toward the beaches, again. Hightower could hear sporadic machine-gun fire and a few mortars in the distance. The Marines were on the move, he thought. He glanced at Owens: He was awake now, alert.

But now Nash had new orders. Instead of staying in action, they were sent to tow a disabled LVT (landing vehicle tracked) from White Beach II to Saipan.

BUT IT KEPT right on, this hurry-and-wait nonstop tedium. The other gunboats in the flotilla stayed alongside Tinian, doing useful front-line jobs, but once the busted LVT was delivered, the 449 was stuck in Saipan, waiting.

When a call came from headquarters, Nash rushed to the radio shack, ready for a new assignment. But the news had nothing to do with the battle. Kepner's brother had been killed in action. The gunboat didn't have a chaplain on board, so Nash would have to break the news.

Since the ship had been commissioned in August 1943, more than one hundred men had served on the 449. Some had been rotated to bigger ships, replaced by young men with little or no experience. Many had brothers, uncles, fathers, even sisters serving in the military. But in all that time, no one on Nash's crew—or among their family members—had been killed or wounded in the war. The fact that the cook was one of his favorite people on board only made it more difficult.

Nash had Kepner summoned to the wardroom. He braced himself.

The cook arrived with a fresh cup of coffee. "Sit down," Nash told him.

He got straight to the point. "I'm very sorry to have to tell you this. Your brother, Henry, has been killed in action."

Kepner's face turned red, he clenched his jaw. "Are you sure?"

Nash nodded his head yes.

"How? When?"

Nash said he didn't know much. It had happened a few weeks earlier, but the news was just making it through the proper channels. Kepner's brother died July 13 as his unit was pushing toward the city of Saint-Lô in France. Battle of the Hedgerows.

Kepner knew his brother's unit, L Company, 320th Regiment, 35th Infantry Division, had been sent to France in the wake of the D-Day invasion. Just where, he didn't know. It had been a while since he heard from his brother. His parents kept him up to date. His parents . . .

"I'm sorry," Nash said. "My brother's over there, too."

Kepner didn't know what to say. He wanted to cry, but fought to hold back his tears. His parents—they had to be crushed. It couldn't be true.

The cook clutched the coffee mug and looked at his shoes. His younger brother Henry had grown up alongside him, running through the open fields or fishing along the banks, catching catfish and blues. They had two rivers to choose from in Cairo, Illinois, the Ohio and the Mississippi. It seemed that you could always find the boys there.

Clarence was the second oldest of six children, five boys and a girl. In the years following Pearl Harbor, the Kepner brothers would all join the U.S military. By 1944, Clarence's brother Andrew was a pharmacist's mate. Another brother, Albert, was in the army. And his baby brother, Robert, was a sergeant in the Army Air Corps. All were on the front lines.

Naturally, Keeley and Flora Kepner were worried about their sons. But if the nation's freedom was at stake because of those damn Nazis and Japs, they knew their boys would be in the fight. That's the way they were raised—church, family, sacrifice, duty.

When the war broke out, Kepner wanted to enlist right away. But first, he had to "tie up a few loose ends." He was thirty-one years old, divorced with an infant son. He was working as a truck driver, hauling new cars from a Detroit, Michigan, auto plant to Memphis, Tennessee. Not only was he supporting his boy, he was helping his parents.

By the summer of 1943, Kepner decided he couldn't wait any longer. If he was going to enlist, he'd have to do it now. He was getting too old. But first, he had something important to do. A few months earlier, Kepner had met a perky eighteen-year-old waitress at a roadside diner in Sikeston, Missouri: Ida Lee White. He'd call her every time he was in town. Soon, he was calling whenever he got the chance. After he enlisted in the navy, Kepner asked her to marry him. She said yes, and they tied the knot August 23, 1943. A few days later, Henry became the last Kepner brother to join the military.

The last time Kepner saw Henry was the night before he left to join Nash's ship. They celebrated with a few friends at a bar. They drank until dawn, told tall tales, sang stupid songs. When the sun came up the next morning, the brothers promised that when the war was over they'd grab the rest of the brothers and run off for a few days of nothing but fishing.

Kepner wiped away a tear.

"We can get you a leave, you can go home," Nash said. "Your family might need you."

Kepner thought for a minute, thought of his mother's tears, what his dad's face must look like. Henry would've been buried in France, anyway. Weeks ago.

"No thanks, sir," Kepner said. "I couldn't stand that. I think right now I just need to keep busy."

He left the wardroom. Word quickly spread. The men slipped into the galley when they could: Beuckman, Yarbrough, Duvall, Herring, Johnson, Blow, Casaletto, Overchuk, to offer condolences and sympathy. They shook his hand, a couple of them hugged him, but Kepner returned to his work right away. The attention was kindly meant, but too painful. He didn't want to dwell on the great lump of pain behind his heart. Get back to the stove. Get to work, cook. Focus on the next meal. That was the only way he'd get through this.

SIGNALMAN ARTHUR LEWIS glanced over his right shoulder, then his left. When he finished, he did it again. He was getting twitchy, he knew, but he couldn't take any chances. Lewis was used to perching like a crow on the bridge, turning flaps on a bright, blinking light to send messages to other ships. If the electrical system ever failed during battle, if the light went out, he'd grab a pair of flags and use them. He was right out there, an easy target.

It was always a risky job, and during Tinian, it was getting more dangerous. The shooters on the island were singling out gunboat signalmen. Lewis knew it probably had something to do with messages blasting from the ships' loudspeakers.

Most of the eighteen thousand people on Tinian were Japanese sharecroppers, brought over by the South Seas Development Company to work in the sugarcane fields. Commanders knew that "Japanese civilians had been saturated with propaganda to the effect that the Americans would subject them to the cruelest, vilest of tortures . . . This indoctrination had its consequences," according to a Marine report. "Loyal citizens" either committed suicide, or allowed the Japanese military to kill them, rather than face the prospect of American occupation.

U.S. commanders didn't want another Saipan-style civilian mass suicide, so before the invasion, planes dropped leaflets over Tinian, promising locals they'd be safe. American troops wouldn't harm them.

U.S. commanders were appalled by the Japanese military's manipulation of innocent civilians. They tried to counter it with leaflets "encouraging civilians to dissociate themselves from the military and come over to American lines."

The leaflets, called Japanese Surrender Tickets, were disseminated in three languages: Japanese, Korean, and English, and contained a "life-saving guarantee."

"The bearer of this card has the special right to be aided by the American forces," and according to international law, "we will give you fair treatment and will grant you sufficient clothing, food, and shelter as well as tobacco and medical treatment."

The rules for using the card were simple: "Raise both hands high above your head, and, holding nothing in your hands except this card, advance slowly toward the positions of the American troops. Don't crowd up; advance one by one."

There was a final warning: "Never approach American positions at night unless specifically invited to by radio broadcast."

While Japanese soldiers were encouraged to surrender, the leaflet's message was focused on civilians.

"They are lying to you. They tell you it is the duty of the soldier to die along with them. They told you such lies because they were thinking only of their own honor. You do not gain anything by dying. Do not sacrifice your valuable life to protect their honor. While there is life, there is hope," the leaflet said.

To reinforce the campaign, gunboats patrolled close to the shore, playing the message over and over.

Now the 449 and the others were charged with delivering the message.

Time was running out for the Japanese. The Tinian campaign was moving quickly. The Americans were on the verge of securing the island. Its rolling terrain was perfect for rapid-advancing infantry and tanks, and a new incendiary bomb helped them quickly clear the cane fields: a substance called napalm.

Thrown off by the feint invasion, the Japanese never managed to form a defensive line.

As the gunboat pushed along the northwestern edge of the island, they noticed how much had changed along the shores near White I and II. The Japanese gun emplacements that had peppered their decks a few days before were blackened concrete shells. The thick palms were shattered sticks. Americans controlled the coastline. The Japanese on Tinian were defeated, for all intents and purposes.

But Lewis, exposed, kept looking over his shoulder. Just to be safe.

HALLETT SQUINTED AT an object in the distance. The early morning sun flashed and sparkled on the water, but something was definitely there . . . Floating toward the gunboat was a raft. It looked like it was filled with debris. But he thought he saw something move, at the edge of the raft, a head bobbing up to catch a breath before ducking under water. Was he imagining? He wheeled around fast.

"You guys see that?" Hallett asked his crew.

"A raft," Bozarth said.

"Couldn't be," Banko said, shading his eyes, looking into the bright water. It was.

Banko turned around and signaled Yarbrough on the bridge: "Lieutenant. Take a look. Off the bow."

Yarbrough peered through his binoculars: Three men were clinging to the side of a raft covered with garbage. The crew had been warned about Japanese soldiers trying to escape from Tinian to Saipan on rafts, boats, anything that could float.

He alerted Nash, who rushed to the bridge. The men in the water began waving their arms over their heads, signaling they were trying to surrender. Nash ordered Vollendorf to move closer to the raft so they could pick them up. He spoke to the crew: Be alert. It could be a ploy.

Several deckhands stood at the edge of the bow, clutching their M1s as the raft drifted in close. Hallett stared. He had never seen a live Japanese soldier. He had only seen bodies, mannequins in uniforms with parts missing, distorted faces, bloated and floating. Hallett pushed away the memory. War was simple: Kill or be killed. Besides, it was the Japanese who started this damn thing, a war that reached from Asia to Europe. If Hallett had had his way, he'd be home, in college, going to dances, helping his father during the apple harvest with his three brothers and sister. Maybe Kepner's brother would still be alive.

After Pearl Harbor, Hallett saw all the caricatures of the Japanese in newspapers, magazines, and movies: They all had slanted eyes, buck teeth, yellow skin, and oversized ears. It was the way to demonize the enemy, making them less than human. The images were drilled in during basic training—commanders knew it would be easier for U.S. troops to kill ugly cartoon creatures.

But the men on the raft looked nothing like the caricatures. They looked worn out, scared, pathetic. They probably thought they were going to be shot, probably pissing their pants, wondering whether they'd ever see their kids again.

The gunboat pulled up to the raft. None of the Americans could speak Japanese, but Blow threw down a lifeline, and one at a time, the Japanese prisoners climbed the rope ladder to the gunboat. The Japanese barely had enough strength to make it. When they reached the top, Nash pointed to a spot near the bow where they could sit down in the shade, under the drawn guns of several crew members.

Meanwhile, Blow searched their raft, tossing debris to the side. Stowed beneath a stack of tree limbs in the rear of the raft was a sack of live grenades. Blow was stunned. Had they set out to blow up the ship? Or blow up themselves? He knew he would never find out why the men didn't use the grenades. He didn't want to take any chances that the grenades were rigged, so he dropped the sack into the sea. He clambered back onto the gunboat, which set a course for the prisoner camp on Saipan.

The crew looked at the men curiously: They were filthy, barefooted, their uniforms torn and creased. The seamen brought them food and water. They gobbled the sandwiches.

"They're in poor shape, the bastards," Seaman First Class Richard Holtby said out loud.

"They're the smart ones. They chose surrender over suicide," he recalled. When the war was over, they'd go home.

Holtby only wished he could say the same about his own chances.

JUST A WEEK after the fight began, General Harry Schmidt, commander of the 4th Marine Division, declared Tinian Island secure.

The Japanese had fought hard, but the Marines held their positions, and by August 1 the battle was over. But it wasn't time yet for rejoicing. U.S. troops were still bashing their slow way across Guam—another week or ten days would do it. Operation Forager was winding down. Nash wondered what was next for his gunboat. After the Marshall Islands campaign they'd done some mop-up duty: routine patrols, until they were sent back to Pearl Harbor to prepare for the new mission. They'd probably do the same again—this time around Tinian and maybe Saipan.

Wherever they were headed would be west, toward Japan.

15

NASH WROTE AS much truth as he could in his letters home to his parents. They hadn't heard from him in weeks. He didn't know how much they knew already about the Marianas campaign, or how much he was allowed to tell. So he wrote nothing about the battles, and the truth about the present.

"No excitement here," he wrote. "But we keep busy."

Now that the Mariana Islands were secured, there wasn't much for a gunboat to do but "grunt work": mail runs, towing, carrying repairmen from one ship to another. Nash took advantage of the lull to catch up on navy paperwork, letter-writing, and news from home. He'd fallen way behind. That's how it was during an invasion—you lived from one mission to the next, focused on getting the job done and getting out alive. Imminent death tends to focus the mind, he thought—the only radio broadcasts were the dedicated command channels, the only news was what came over the grapevine, from the Marines or other navy guys they ran across along the way. Now that the pressure was off, he didn't know what was going on in Europe or even other parts of the Pacific.

The radio had been too tied up to track the navy's daily newscasts. Ball hadn't put out a newsletter since just before Saipan. Mail delivery had been sporadic.

What Nash didn't know was that back home, the War in the Pacific was big news. Details of the invasions were splashed across the front pages of newspapers all over the country—details carefully vetted by the Office of War Information. Government control of the news was comprehensive. Stories accentuated the positive—nothing showed how dangerous it was for the men at the front. Still, readers had a general sense of the scope of the military operations, especially when newspapers published maps showing the daily progress. Ordinary Joes knew the geography of tiny atolls and remote fjords—their loved ones were fighting there, and newspapers and magazines did their best to illustrate strategy, wins, and losses.

They did a bang-up job on the Marianas, explaining that the remote islands were home to a "chain of bases from which American planes can strike at Japan's inner defenses."

One Associated Press story published on June 19, 1944, even mentioned LCIs:

> *While the ground forces slowly were fighting their way through strong defenses manned by an estimated 30,000 Japanese, the enemy made a desperate but futile attempt to land amphibious troops behind the U.S. lines south of Garapan. Armed landing crafts, probably LCI (Landing Craft Infantry) gunboats engaged the Japanese amphibious forces in an offshore battle and sank 13 troop filled barges, each of them capable of carrying 10 to 100 troops.*

Newspapers ran pages and pages of war coverage, detailing heroic tales of local men who won silver and bronze stars, picturing local women serving as military nurses, WAVES, and WACS. "Killed in Action" columns provided stark black-bordered photos and short biographies, somber reminders that the war touched just about every family in the United States.

Information came from other sources, too. Vivid radio broadcasts from the front lines brought the war into the nation's living rooms. Motion picture newsreels included dramatic footage of combat and uplifting stories about the war effort. And letters home were passed from hand to hand and read aloud in barbershops, church halls, dining rooms, and garages all over the country. Nash knew even this anodyne effort would make the rounds of his parents' circle.

He referred back to his mother's last letter. She'd asked how long the war would go on, how much longer till he could come home.

"Your guess as to how long the war will last is just as good as anyone's," Nash told her. "But it seems that most observers would agree that the internal troubles in Germany and Japan are very definite indications that their situation is critical. But who knows how long the critically ill can survive or how much damage they can inflict?"

HERRING STARED AT the cards in his hand, then glanced at the money in the middle of the table. Maybe ten bucks. Maybe more. He looked at the other players. Blow, Casaletto, and Ball were still in. Hightower and Owens were out. The faces of the remaining three were stoic. They were damn good poker players, but not as good as Herring.

Herring learned his best tricks back at Davidson College, during all-night marathons at their frat house. Herring almost always staggered off to class with his pockets full of nickels and quarters and crinkled dollar bills. The key was patience. Take a conservative approach early, assess your opponents' strengths, and in the end, attack.

"You in?" Ball asked.

"I'm in," said Herring, tossing another dollar on the table. But he wasn't finished. "I'll raise you a buck."

Blow, Ball, and Casaletto were in. Casaletto had two pair. So did Ball. Blow had three jacks. But when Herring laid down his cards, he had them beat: a straight.

"Thanks, fellas," he said, as he scooped up the money.

That was it. Game over. Herring had been cleaning up all night. Still, it was hard for the guys to be mad at him. He had that kind of personality. Herring was humble, warm, calm under fire. He was an officer, but he was one of the men.

"He was just a down-to-earth kind of good old boy," Hightower recalled.

Herring was the only officer on the ship so integrated with the enlisted men. Nash and Duvall liked to keep their distance. Yarbrough was friendly with the crew, but he didn't have Herring's outgoing personality.

When the gunboat sat at anchor, the officers often unfolded their canvas director's chairs and sat smoking on the gun deck, near the conning tower, writing letters or reading reports. Not Herring. He was in the mess deck playing poker, or rummy or canasta. He was in the radio shack bullshitting with Ball. He sat on the "top deck drinking coffee with us," Hightower recalled. He knew every crew member's name, where they were from. He loved listening to their stories as much as they liked telling them. It helped them all unwind.

Herring planned to enjoy the downtime as much as possible. They were safe, at least for a few days.

By early September 1944, Saipan, Guam, and Tinian were massive building sites. U.S. command was rebuilding the islands, constructing bases with roads, bridges, and airstrips that could handle the B-29 bombers. The gunboat was constantly ferrying construction workers and engineers to and from the islands.

Meantime, thousands of sailors and soldiers needed to blow off steam before the war heated up again. On shore, stores opened, and bars, ball fields, and other "places of entertainment."

The crew took field trips to Saipan to play other ships' crews in baseball and volleyball. It was like they were back in Pearl Harbor, except here the palm trees were all blown apart, and the mountains sometimes smoked. At night they shuffled to the destroyers to watch movies. When they came back, they stayed up talking, or playing cards.

Herring knew what he would do with his winnings. The next day he made a quick run to Saipan. He returned to the ship decked out in a long white bathrobe with silk lapels—a Noël Coward smoking jacket. He smiled at the snickers, and swept past the crew toward the radio shack. He looked in at Ball: "See what your money just bought me," he crowed.

Ball laughed out loud. Herring used his winnings to buy a damn bathrobe—and he was bragging about it! Only Herring could get away with it.

AS THE SUN crested over the navy ships in Saipan's Lao Lao Bay, Bozarth looked for a spot on the main deck of the gunboat.

He knew the ship was picking up the U.S. military–run radio network today, and one of the shows tonight was his favorite: *Your Hit Parade.* He had even scribbled a reminder in his scripture calendar: "Hit Parade. Tonight."

In Oklahoma, the whole family sat down on the couch and listened every week. It didn't always make it over the military network, and in the last two months the gunboat's radio receiver hadn't been tuned to entertainment.

With no new operation in sight, Bozarth was working hard to put the horrors behind him. He still had trouble sleeping. He dreamed of the mothers pushing their children off the cliff. In one dream the babies took wing and flew away before they hit the rocks . . . But then the 40mm gun chattered on the deck, and the little birds vanished. Bozarth woke up weeping.

Time and again, Bozarth closed his eyes and spoke to the Lord, seeking the peace that "passeth all understanding." Parents, and children . . . how could a mother do that, a father? It haunted him.

Hearing *Your Hit Parade* would do him good. For a half hour he could imagine himself back on the couch in Oklahoma, safe and sound. He could feel the comfort of that old routine.

The military understood that the soldier's life was "90 percent boredom interrupted by periods of sheer terror." If morale slipped, there could be a decline in combat efficiency. By early 1942, Hollywood stars like Bob Hope, Bing Crosby, and Frank Sinatra were performing live for troops overseas. But the front lines were way too dangerous for the entertainers; the last thing America needed was for the Germans or Japanese to shoot down a plane full of celebrities. So the military turned to radio.

The War Department created the Armed Forces Radio Service (AFRS) to provide music and entertainment programming for U.S. troops. Sometimes shows were transmitted by shortwave radio to frontline radio stations. But there were glitches: The shows could fade in and out, and the quality, with all the crackling and static, could be poor. That's why most of the time the programs were transferred to a V-disc—a twelve-inch, vinyl 78 rpm gramophone recording—and sent to the frontline stations. The

THE HEART OF HELL

only drawback was that the frontline stations would receive the discs a week or two after the original program aired in the United States.

The troops didn't care. They just wanted to hear the sounds from home. The military network obliged them, by carrying other shows that were specially created for the fighting units. Crosby, Sinatra, the Andrews Sisters, Judy Garland, Eddie Cantor, and all the big bands recorded special V-discs for sailors and soldiers.

On the gunboat, the crew often huddled around the record player in the mess deck and listened to music. The music could be piped through the PA speakers so sailors sitting on the decks at night could hear Sinatra or Crosby crooning another hit song, or sway to the rhythm of Glenn Miller, Benny Goodman, Tommy Dorsey, and Duke Ellington. Records were in short supply. That summer, someone played the bouncy Crosby hit "Swinging on a Star" so many times one of his shipmates tossed it overboard.

Bozarth found a spot near an ammo locker on the starboard side. He leaned back and looked up at the thousands of stars against the backdrop of the pitch-black sky. He'd asked Ball to turn on the speakers so they could hear the broadcast. Everyone on the gunboat was finding a nice spot, waiting for the music to start.

Bozarth smiled up at the stars when the cheerful theme music started, followed by a voice: "It's *Your Hit Parade*!" the announcer said, "broadcasting the most popular songs in America—especially for you men and women in the armed forces of the United States."

The songs weren't necessarily sung by the original artists. That night, Sinatra sang a few of the top tunes, including Louis Jordan's hit: "Is You Is or Is You Ain't My Baby."

Bozarth closed his eyes. He loved music. When he was at Elaine's house in San Diego, he'd noticed a Victrola in the kitchen hallway. It was an older model; the mahogany had scratches and was faded in some spots where her mother had polished the wood too hard. The needle was a little worn, too. He thumbed through her collection and stopped when he saw a familiar record: "Suppertime." It was an old gospel song, four-parts, like they sang in the Church of the Nazarene. "Come home, come home, it's suppertime, the shadows lengthen so fast. Come home, come home, it's suppertime, we're going home at last," it wailed . . . It made his heart ache from missing his daddy.

It was a house rule: Everyone stopped what they were doing and sat down to dinner as a family. It was the only time of day they could all talk to one another. Even though that got harder as his children grew up, Bozarth's dad still held on, still made his children know how precious they all were.

Far away in San Diego, Bozarth had played that record over and over, making himself terrifically homesick. He sighed. Some of his sisters and brothers were probably gathered around the kitchen table right now, Bozarth thought. He wondered where Elaine was tonight, what she was doing right now.

Of course, most of the countdown was love songs.

Up in his office, Nash was trying to finish a ton of paperwork. He'd turned down the speaker, but the program came in through the open windows and doors. And wouldn't you know, they played it: "I'll Be Seeing You." Pure sentimental nonsense, but oh, so lovely . . . a Dorothy Wallace kind of song. He wondered what she was doing tonight. She sometimes escorted entertainers to *Your Hit Parade*, and after the performance they went out on the town in a big group.

Nash hoped that wasn't the case.

He and Dorothy weren't officially an item, but he didn't want her rubbing shoulders with the likes of Sinatra, or any of the other Hollywood big shots. He was jealous. Stuck ten thousand miles from home, all alone with nothing but his thoughts. He had revisited their New York nights a thousand times in the last year.

A year, he thought. Damn. It was that long ago.

And this music didn't help. It was so sad, so full of longing. So apt: "I'll find you in the morning sun, and when the night is new, I'll be looking at the moon . . . But I'll be seeing you."

How many times did he stare at the moon, wondering if she was looking at it, too? It was just too much to take.

A few yards away, Bozarth felt the same way. He'd looked forward to the program all day, but when it finished, he didn't feel cheered up at all. The songs only made him feel more alone.

He headed to his bunk, to lay his burdens before the Lord.

IN SEPTEMBER, BETTY Jones wrote a letter to a man she'd never met—a sailor.

He was her cousin's friend's brother, and his name was Byron, of all things, Byron Yarbrough, a navy lieutenant stationed somewhere in the Pacific. Jane Yarbrough said her brother was warm and kind, but he didn't have a girlfriend and was feeling a little lonely. Betty's cousin Mary knew Byron, and vouched for him.

"You're just going to love him," she said.

Betty was dubious. She didn't know anything about this Byron Yarbrough except what they told her.

Jane added one more thing: A few girls had written to her brother before, but they'd stop writing after a letter or two. Poor Byron didn't have any luck with women, she said. He was always getting his heart broken.

If there was one thing Betty understood, it was heartbreak.

She stared through the branches of the towering magnolia tree outside her window. The year was almost over, and she was still in Cordele, still working for her father at the pharmacy, still trying to make her mother happy.

The days were getting shorter. Christmas would be here before long. Then winter.

Betty didn't want to feel down, but she couldn't help it. She was surrounded by family and friends, yet she was so lonely. She'd hear her mother's friends whisper, "Does Betty have a man?" "When is Betty going to get married?" She made believe she didn't hear them. The truth was, Betty wanted to get married, just like every other girl. She went out with men, but after a few dates, they'd stop calling. The fact was, the guys around here were boring. She just hadn't met the right one.

So Betty had taken down the lieutenant's address, but made no promises.

Her little radio was tuned to WSB in Atlanta; she was hoping to hear

Frank Sinatra or Dinah Shore. Instead, a reporter was reading the news—war, war, war. Allied forces were advancing toward Germany. In the Pacific, U.S. forces were moving from island to island on their way to an eventual showdown in Japan.

This poor boy, Betty thought. *In the Pacific, all alone. He might get killed out there. A letter from a girl might cheer him up.*

One letter. That's all. And it would be generic: Hello. How are you? Nothing more. And if he replied, she might write another one.

She was twenty-four, and single. She had gone to the Georgia State College for women and wanted to be a nurse.

Nothing exciting ever happened in town—with the exception of the great tornado in 1936, she wrote. During the spring of that year, a twister ripped through Cordele, killing thirty-three people and injuring hundreds. She recalled how horrible it was. As far as her family, she had two younger sisters and a younger brother, who was in the army. Her father was a pharmacist who owned his store. She worked there but had plans of getting out. Atlanta was her favorite city. She tried to get there when she could. But with the war, it was hard. There was so much rationing—gas and food. She said she liked movies—she went to them several times a week. She ended by saying she hoped he would write back.

It seemed stilted and stiff. She didn't know whether to send it. She didn't want to lead him on. She wasn't interested in a long-distance relationship. She didn't even know what he looked like, not that it mattered. All she wanted was a man who was smart and could laugh at the world.

It was late. Betty got up from the chair and left the letter on her desk. She'd make her decision in the morning.

NASH PUT ON the headphones, Ball handed him a microphone. "Headquarters," Ball said.

Group Eight Commander Theodore Blanchard wanted to see him. Be ready. They were sending a boat.

Nash had no idea why Blanchard wanted to see him. But that was never good. It usually meant you were being called on the carpet. He couldn't think of anything that had gone wrong. In his opinion, his crew was always prepared and performed very well in combat.

Before he left, he put Herring in charge. Herring wished him luck.

It didn't take long for Nash's boat to pull up to LCI-457, Group Eight's flagship.

When Nash got on board the 457, he was immediately taken to the commander's quarters. Nash snapped a salute and Blanchard told him to sit down. He wasn't going to waste any time. Blanchard said he was being promoted. The top brass had been impressed with Nash. Blanchard was, too. So Nash was going to replace him.

Nash sat there for a minute while it hit him. He would be in charge of Group Eight. Hundreds of men and officers. Excitement rippled up from the collar of his shirt and turned his face red. Finally, he was moving up!

He had really enjoyed his time on the 449, but he'd wanted more. This would mean more logistical planning, more paperwork, and more interaction with the high brass. Nash thanked Blanchard.

When Nash returned to the 449, he didn't say a word. He rushed to his cabin to finish the paperwork. He wrote his parents, but downplayed the promotion:

Today is my last day as "skipper" of the 449. Tomorrow I take over duties of Commander LCI Group 8. That means that instead of being a commanding officer of 1 ship, I will be a "flag" officer and have a number of LCI's under my command, each, including the flagship, with its own skipper. The result: less work; more responsibility and a possible spot promotion at a later date.

It also means that . . . I'll have to wait until I've been overseas for about 18 months before I have much chance of getting a leave. Who knows, perhaps it's all for the best?

Letters addressed to LCI 449 will reach me until I send the new address. No newspaper publicity concerning my new duty is warranted or desirable . . . Will write again soon.

It was another step on Nash's journey. He had pushed so hard to get appointed to the Naval Reserve. He only became skipper of the 449 when the man chosen failed the eye test. Now, an attorney from Saginaw, Michigan—not a U.S. Naval Academy officer—would be leading a squadron of gunboats. He was looking forward to the new challenge.

HERRING WAS STUNNED. Nash was going. And he was leaving Herring in charge.

Herring didn't know if he was ready. Yarbrough was executive officer, the next in line. He should have been first up for promotion.

Nash brushed that aside. Yarbrough was an excellent officer, but Herring was the right choice, he said. The two of them had equal experience—they'd both joined the Naval Reserves and gone through officer training. Both were smart college graduates who got along well with the crew. But Herring was a lifelong mariner, a natural sea captain, Nash said. That might make the difference if the gunboat got into trouble.

Nash said he'd break the news to Yarbrough. "Make no mistake," he told Herring: "You deserve it."

Herring left Nash's cabin, his heart heavy despite the good news. Nash had become a good friend, and he'd miss him. Herring had learned a lot from watching Nash: He was fair, decisive, and most importantly, always prepared. Nothing seemed to faze him.

Good leaders never lose their cool, Nash liked to say. That was something Herring promised to remember when he assumed command.

Herring decided to write his mother right away, to let her know. He knew she'd be touting that letter all over town, crowing about her boy. He hadn't given much time to letter-writing in the last few weeks. The last one was short. He'd begun with an apology, and reassurance:

We can't tell where we are, what we are doing or anything, but we have seen action not too long ago. Same old Fighting '49 came through again. There is nothing to worry about when the '49 is on the war path. Really the Navy, Army and the Marines are on the ball.

Herring knew it was a little pathetic, but his mother was his lifeline, his sounding board. Whenever anything happened, good or bad, he told her first. When he needed money, cigarettes (they were cheaper in North Carolina, where tobacco was king), or other items, she sent them on immediately. Ever since he enlisted he'd written her dozens of letters, sharing every detail, from the girls he dated in New York, to combat missions in the Pacific. His mother treasured his letters, and kept them for years afterward, tied in bundles, ordered by date.

In 1942, when he arrived in New York City for training, young Lieutenant Herring was overwhelmed by the sheer number of people in the streets. He'd traveled around North Carolina, and while at Davidson he'd hit the hotspots of Charlotte to hear the big bands, and he and his friends had thought that was the big time. Charlotte was the largest city in the state, with nearly 85,000 people. But in New York, there were nearly that many people within a few blocks of Penn Station.

Herring got off the train at 8 p.m. on August 15, 1942, with a few dozen recruits. He wrote the details in letters to his mom—how they bounded to a nearby subway and took a train to 116th Street and Broadway, and from there to Columbia University, their home for the next few months.

He roomed on the ninth floor of Fernwald Hall with a boy from Georgia: "Double decker beds but I got the bottom. Small rooms but better than the USS *Prairie State* anchored in the Hudson," he said, referring to a ship moored at a pier in the Hudson River, where less-fortunate officer trainees were sent to sleep. The training was tough, but Herring thrived on the activity. "Fun so far and not a chance to get homesick," he wrote home, "because there is so much doing."

Herring excelled. "They keep us busy all the time. We get up at 06:00, go to mess at 06:15. That sure is a pain, to get up and dress in 15 minutes. Also supposed to shave in that time. Hardly possible," he wrote.

After breakfast they had to "clean up the room . . . clean walls, make up beds, empty ash trays, and the like. It is just like Annapolis of 4 years in 4 months."

They ran down nine flights of stairs and drilled for two hours, had class and a study period, followed by more marching and more classes.

They got a break on the weekends. If they didn't screw up, they got liberty. Herring told his mother early on that he planned to take full advantage of his time in New York.

Herring was young, handsome, and single. He had no trouble finding dates or parties. When Columbia's sister school, Barnard College, held a dance, the young officers were invited.

Those were fun, he wrote, "but I still don't catch on to these Yankee customs."

In early September, he and some of his buddies attended the New York Giants–Eastern Army All-Star football game. There were sixty thousand people in the stands at the Polo Grounds: "More people than I have ever seen at one time."

Afterward, they dined on steaks and headed to a club to hear Harry James and his band. It seemed every weekend girls took him to some of the hottest nightspots in the city. One of Herring's college buddies visited, so Herring's date brought along a friend and they went to the swanky La Martinique, "where all the celebrities go," he wrote. But the girls got bored. Herring and his friend spent the whole night reminiscing about their glory days at Davidson.

He hit Broadway. He saw *Porgy and Bess* and *Arsenic and Old Lace*. On weekends the men partied all night in rented hotel rooms, living big while they could. The Hotel Astor was their favorite; the big bands played on the rooftop under the stars, with Manhattan spread out beneath them.

People in New York were friendly to the young officers. Some even opened up their homes to them. Three up-and-coming families one weekend invited Herring and five of his classmates to stay at their houses in South Orange, New Jersey. The young men were greeted at the train station, treated to a "buffet supper and party . . . They had us six dates for the party and supper," Herring wrote. On the table were "turkey, cheese, tomatoes, potato salad and whatnot. It was really good to get some good food," he said.

After dinner, they had coffee out on the lawn. They danced, they played bridge. "These people all have lots of money, so did the girls. Every one of the girls had their car and one had her station wagon, quite ritzy," he told his mother. The men and their dates went out to a club after, where they danced and took in a floor show. Herring talked to a pretty girl deep into the wee hours, bending her ear about Roseboro, sailing, and naval training, right up to her doorstep. Once there she moved closer, and gently placed her hand in his. He stopped talking for a moment—her blue eyes were shining in the soft October moonlight. They kissed then, under the stars.

At dawn, he sneaked into his hosts' house. He woke to breakfast: "fried eggs and bacon with rolls."

The young officers piled into the station wagon, and the girls drove them around town to see Thomas Edison's mansion and the other impressive estates. "I've never seen such elegant homes before," Herring told his mother. Another family hosted a luncheon: "a leg of lamb and eggplant."

Dusk saw the men off in Newark, where they caught the Hudson Line back to the city. "We had a wonderful time," Herring said. He saw the Jersey girl a few more times, but it was nothing serious.

Still, there were nights alone on deck when his mind would drift back to that October night in South Orange, and that girl's sweet kisses.

Herring graduated in December 1942. He shipped to Urbana, Illinois, to learn all about diesel engines and become an engineering officer. The new lieutenant junior grade was assigned to Nash's ship, the scrappy little gunboat where he'd now spent a long year.

So much had happened in that year—the Marshall Islands, the Marianas campaign—who knew how many more were ahead? He'd seen some success, and a lot of good luck. The Pacific War was a long way from over.

And now here he was, ready to embark on a new journey. A command. Maybe Herring would get through this, too. One thing Herring had learned about himself was that no matter how difficult the challenge, he could handle pressure. Pressure made him calm, it focused him. He could do this.

He knew it.

16

YEP, IT WAS a ship, but it wasn't much of one. Ensign Leo Bedell dropped his seabag on the dock, pulled a scrap of paper from his pocket, and looked up at the steep steel hull. Big white numbers were painted on the bow: 449. His new address. This was it.

Damn. Most ships have a name. This one had a number. After all that training, Bedell had expected at least a battleship, maybe even an aircraft carrier. Here he was, about to board a tin can. Nobody had asked him what he wanted, so he would have to deal with it.

Up the gangplank to the gunboat, over a sparkling clean deck to the deckhouse. He paused at the hatchway, hoisted the bag up onto his back, collected his thoughts. *Nothing to worry about*, he thought. *You got this.*

He walked to the wardroom and spotted two men talking inside the cramped space. "Lieutenant Herring?" Bedell asked, standing at attention.

A young man, blond, turned. Bars on his shoulders. Bedell had expected someone much older. This guy was his own age, maybe even younger.

"Ensign Bedell, sir, reporting for duty."

Herring grinned. "Welcome aboard. We've been waiting for you," he said. "Grab your bag, I'll show you your quarters and give you the tour."

Bedell followed Herring into one of the officers' quarters. Bedell would share a room with Byron Yarbrough, the ship's executive officer. Yarbrough was on shore, but would be back soon.

Bedell dropped his bag and again followed the skipper.

Into the galley to meet the cooks, then out to the gun decks to meet the seamen, forward and aft, up and down. Bedell smiled and returned their salutes. It was going to take a while to remember all their names, but once they were out to sea, there'd be plenty of time.

Bedell could tell Herring was genuinely excited to have him on board, and proud of his little ship. His enthusiasm was infectious. Like a museum docent, he explained all the gunboat's little details and nuances. But Herring's favorite part was coming up, he said: the engine room. Bedell was replacing him as the gunboat's engineering officer, so Herring wanted to introduce him personally to the crew. They descended into the belly of the boat. Bedell knew engine rooms were noisy and full of fumes, but he hadn't expected so much machinery and so many men crammed into a space the size of a closet. "You could only get a few guys in the engine room at a time," Bedell recalled. Even the cramped quarters didn't temper Herring's enthusiasm.

Bedell met Casaletto, the mechanic who could get things done "bang, bang, bang." Casaletto could "tear the engines down and have them back together again in a matter of minutes," the skipper bragged. Robert Carrell and Meredith Luckner had that same knack, but they couldn't shine without Holgate and the other black gang members. The men smiled at the praise.

"I won't say this up on deck where the others can hear, but I'll tell you here, the black gang is the heart of this ship," Herring said. "It's a hot, dirty, filthy job, but that's what it takes to keep the boat going."

When they returned to the officers' quarters, Herring told Bedell that the 449 had been stationed in Saipan since early August. He hadn't heard anything about the next campaign, and until word came; they were taking it easy. On shore, old army tents and Quonset huts served as stores, nightclubs, and taverns. The men played baseball against teams from the other ships, they went to movies over on the destroyers in the evening. It wasn't Pearl Harbor, but it wasn't bad, either.

Herring filled in Bedell about Operation Forager: endless nights at battle stations: "You could see how it got to the men," Herring said. Guam, covering demolition team recon missions. A little action on that first day at Tinian, a few patrols, some Japanese soldiers captured on a barge. But then the campaign was over—or so it seemed. Sometimes Japanese air raids happened at night, but the onshore anti-aircraft almost always got them. The Japanese Air Force was down to scraps these days, he said, at least around here.

Since U.S. commanders had declared victory on August 1, the gunboat was sent up and down the Tinian coast, occasionally firing into caves where Japanese snipers might be holding out.

They sometimes did tugboat duty, towing disabled ships, ferrying workers from one part of Saipan to the other. They did the mail runs, picking up mail from the shore and taking it around to other ships.

There were still Japanese holed up on these islands, Herring warned. You couldn't be too careful—there was still a war on, and the Japanese were getting desperate.

Bedell nodded. He followed closely the reports from other parts of the Pacific as well as Europe. Allied forces had liberated Paris, and were advancing toward Germany from the western and eastern fronts. In the Pacific, the Marines and the army were facing fierce resistance from the Japanese after landing on Peleliu in the Palau Islands, a key stepping stone in MacArthur's strategy to retake the Philippines.

Over a wardroom coffee, Bedell filled in his skipper about his background. He was from Akron, Ohio, went to John Carroll University, where he signed up for the navy's V-12 fast-track officer training program. After earning his engineering degree, he went straight into officer candidate school, then on to study naval engineering.

Herring's own story was similar. If it wasn't for the war, they'd probably both be building bridges and roads and sewer lines. Maybe they'd be in graduate school, or raising families. But for now, everyone's life was on hold. Some of the crew liked to talk about what they were going to do after the war. Herring listened, but didn't say anything. He wondered how anyone could make plans when they didn't know how long the war would go on, or whether any of them would be alive at the end.

It was a long trip from Pearl Harbor to Saipan. Herring told Bedell to unpack, rest up, and they'd talk later. When Herring left, Bedell sat for a moment. Herring seemed like a good guy, he thought. That was half the battle.

The cabin was tiny, really too small for two people. Yarbrough used the bottom bunk. The top one had a porthole where Bedell's feet would be . . . or his head. Bedell leaned back in the chair, took a deep breath, let himself feel tired. It was good to sit still.

Maybe Mary Jo will get the package today, he thought.

He stowed his things, and reviewed in his mind the joyful, impulsive thing he'd done in San Francisco, just before he left.

He had some money. He didn't know when he'd be home again. He'd wanted to show his girl how much she meant to him, even though she was still back home, even though he couldn't be there to do it in person . . . Bedell had walked into a jewelry store and bought a diamond ring. It didn't cost much. He went to the post office, and put the ring in a package with a note: "Will you marry me?"

He wrote her name on the outside: "Miss Mary Jo Costigan." He thought for a minute about adding "Bedell," but he didn't want to give it away.

She should have gotten it by now. He wished he could've seen her face when she opened it.

He knew it was nuts to ask her that way. What if she said no?

But she wouldn't. He knew she would be overjoyed, showing her little "rock" to all her friends. His parents would be happy—their families had been friends for years; they went to the same Catholic schools and same church, lived in the same neighborhood. He and Mary Jo didn't start dating until he began college, but once they did, he wondered why he hadn't asked her out earlier. Maybe it was because they were friends first.

He hadn't asked his parents about it. He thought a lot about his mom and dad lately. They'd given birth to a large family, and scrimped and saved to send their kids to private schools—even in the heart of the Great Depression, when Akron had an unemployment rate of 50 percent. It wasn't easy: There were nine Bedell brothers and sisters.

From the time he was little, his father lectured Leo: Education was the only way to get ahead. Without it, you would struggle. His father knew.

James Bedell was born Reno Bedelli in Brooklyn, the son of Italian immigrants. He hit the road at age fifteen, and during a stop in Oklahoma City, Bedelli realized that he had to do something about his name. There wasn't any more work for a "dago" than there was for a Jew or a Negro. So Reno Bedelli became James R. Bedell. The name change led to a job in a print shop, and eventually to Ethel Walker, the daughter of the landlady of the boardinghouse where he lived.

They married, and Leo was their firstborn. James took a job running a print shop at a rubber company, and eventually transferred to Akron, Ohio, the company headquarters.

Bedell's father was strict: The children went to parochial school, did their homework, then chores. But kids still must play: Leo was a daredevil. He once climbed to the top of the steel-girder bridge connecting Akron to Cuyahoga Falls, 150 feet up. The girls in the neighborhood were crazy about his piercing blue eyes, thick black hair, and mischievous smile. He was sarcastic, always cracking jokes, never taking himself too seriously. He pushed the limits; he said "sheesh" instead of "Jesus," but he wasn't afraid to "damn this, damn that," he recalled. But he said it in a good-natured way, shrugging his shoulders and laughing.

Bedell was a hard worker, determined to make something of his life. He did summer shifts in the tire factories and saved his wages for college. He and his brother Edward couldn't afford to live on campus at John Carroll University, so they hitchhiked back and forth, thirty miles each way, to get to classes. But Leo's savings ran out halfway through his junior year. He enrolled in the navy's V-12 program in the spring of 1943. The navy paid for Bedell to complete his education, and when he graduated, they sent him to Chicago for officer training, and to Harvard to study radar, electronics, and physics. He studied diesel engines at the General Motors Institute in Flint, Michigan. Finally he was deployed to the Pacific.

It was a grueling trip: a troop transport from San Francisco to Pearl Harbor, then a series of wave-hopper flights. There was no toilet on one of those, and he wrote home about having to "do his business" through a hatch in the floor. When he finally arrived in Saipan, his first impression was a "lingering odor of decomposition."

He only hoped that wasn't a scent of things to come.

And even before he could finish making up his bunk, the ship began to move.

"BEDELL, COME ON up here," Herring called down. "No need to start work yet. Just watch."

An urgent message had come over: Rendezvous with the destroyer USS *Downes* to pick up Marine snipers and take them to Marpo Point on the southeastern side of Tinian.

For days someone had been firing on U.S. personnel from a series of caves along the coastline. When troops checked the area, they couldn't find a thing. Now commanders were sending snipers from the 8th Regiment, 2nd Marine Division to try and pick off the shooters.

The Marines climbed a ladder into the 449 and gave Herring the coordinates. They were going to patrol an area between Marpo Point and Lalo Point at the southern tip of the island.

The Marines didn't say much, but they looked tough. They carried their M1903-A1 guns mounted with the Unertl 8x scope, Banko recalled.

When the boat reached Marpo Point, they worked in close to a reef and maneuvered slowly. At Lalo Point they turned around and headed north to Marpo again. Back and forth, watching and waiting.

A call came: sporadic fire from one of the caves. Now they knew the exact location. They arrived within minutes, and maneuvered into position to enable the Marine sharpshooters to fire into the cave. The ship's guns were manned—the cave was so close the gunners could see the narrow opening leading into the back.

"The 40mm can shoot right into that cave," Herring told the Marine officer.

The man didn't say a word. He held up a hand, as if to quiet the lieutenant.

"Look at the size of the door. The job requires more accuracy than you're ever going to get with a deck gun," the man said. "The opening is too small. You could never steady it enough."

So while the gunboat stayed in position, the snipers trained their sights on that sliver, waiting. But after a half hour, the gunman was still hidden. They had other caves to get to.

"Sir, if I may?" Herring said. "The bow gunner is a crack shot." The Marine nodded.

The word came down to Banko and he got his gun crew ready. Hallett helped move the big gun into position, pointing the barrel at the cave. The gunner turned to Banko. He sighted the opening. At 15:03, the order came to commence fire. They laid in a steady barrage, and each round seemed to go deeper and deeper into the cave, triggering explosions. At 15:12, the order came to stop.

The Marine officer looked at the smoking cave mouth. "I think the guy is dead now," he said, smiling. "That is a fine weapon. Let's get hunting, Lieutenant!"

For the rest of the day, LCI-449's 40mm guns took out caves while the Marine snipers stood down. The officer in charge filed a report later that week, expressing his "amazement at the accuracy of the shooting."

"Since other LCI (G)'s have had similar experiences, it is concluded that Army and Marine personnel have not appreciated the accuracy which can be attained by an experienced crew with a single-mount 40mm gun," he wrote.

Patrols continued for the next few days, and soon other flotilla gunboats were blowing up sniper caves along the coastlines. The island was too important to leave any behind.

On September 9, Herring's crew returned to the rugged stretch between Marpo Point and Lalo Point. This time, the Marines brought along three Japanese prisoners who used an "electric megaphone" to appeal to their fellow soldiers to give up. It seemed to be working.

"The purpose of our expedition was to get as close to the caves as possible so the interpreter could talk them into giving up," Banko recalled. They puttered along the shore with the megaphone, while dozens of people—old men, women, children—emerged from the caves with their hands above their heads. They were met by Marine patrols, who took the peaceful ones prisoner and killed the ones who refused to surrender.

As the gunboat worked its way around one rocky outcrop, they saw several people sitting on a gentle bluff outside a cave, about halfway down a sugarcane field. They were within shouting distance of the deck, and the interpreter started in on his spiel before the crew realized that these were not civilians. It was a group of soldiers, sitting in a circle.

"Without so much as a glance in the gunboat's direction, they all bowed to the center, and WHAMMO, blew themselves up with hand grenades," Banko recalled. Their bodies were ripped apart, and pieces of flesh, bone, and organs rained down on the decks, the shore, the water. It was horrific.

It was Bedell's introduction to the War in the Pacific.

As the day wore on, dozens of bodies appeared, floating on the current off Marpo Point. Like the people at Saipan, they had committed suicide rather than face American occupation.

"The bodies were floating everywhere; men, women, and children. It was almost impossible to miss them . . . [especially] being on the bow. It wasn't a pleasant sight," Banko recalled.

By nightfall, the crew was back off Saipan. They were sure that by now Tinian must be secure.

THE NEXT DAY, Bedell was still a little shaky. Bodies blown to pieces, and families floating dead in the water. This was horrible shit, and he'd only been here for a couple of days. What would happen next?

Yarbrough tried to ease Bedell's mind. With all the patrols, they really hadn't had a chance to talk.

"You OK?" Yarbrough asked.

"Yeah. But the skipper said things were pretty quiet."

Yarbrough laughed. "Things were pretty quiet, till you showed up!" he joked.

Some days are better than others, he explained. The military always shouts victory as soon as possible, even when there are still a lot of enemy hiding out. That's why you have to be careful. But Yarbrough assured Bedell the Tinian mopping-up was nothing like Saipan had been, when entire Japanese families jumped off cliffs right in front of them. "There might be a few bodies in the water today, but imagine thousands."

Bedell looked ill. Yarbrough knew he had to change the subject.

"The skipper says you're a Yankee," Yarbrough said.

Bedell laughed. "I don't know about a complete Yankee. I was born in Oklahoma."

They spent the night talking about home and family. Yarbrough said he was from Auburn, that he graduated college with a degree in agricultural engineering. His father was a doctor. He had a bunch of siblings, including a brother serving in Europe. He noted the one "luxury" he'd enjoyed for his entire time at sea: He'd had the room to himself.

"I'm going to have to get used to this," he said.

Bedell promised to be a good roommate, then shared his backstory with Yarbrough. He told him he'd sent his girlfriend an engagement ring in the mail.

"But what if the package gets lost in the mail? Then you're out a ring," Yarbrough said.

"Yeah, I took a chance," Bedell said, "but I wanted to surprise her. When you're in love, you don't always think straight."

Yarbrough shrugged. It had been a long time since he'd felt that way. He was going to change the subject, but a deckhand stuck his head in the door to announce the arrival of the mail boat.

"Gotta go," Yarbrough said. As well as censoring the sailors' outgoing letters, Yarbrough also distributed the incoming mail.

Topside, two big bags were waiting for him. The crew gathered around him, two and three deep. Yarbrough smiled. The job always made him feel like Santa Claus, even though the news he distributed wasn't always happy or welcome. He reached his hand in one bag, pulled out some letters, and started calling names: "Vanderboom!"

"Here!" and a hand reached out for the envelope.

"Lewis!"

"Right here, sir!"

"Holgate!" he called. No one responded. "Holgate!" Nothing.

Hoffman grabbed the letter. "He's downstairs. I'll give it to him," he said to Yarbrough.

By the time Yarbrough was finished, Hoffman had a few letters and packages of his own. He went back to quarters, and spotted Holgate lying on his bunk.

"Hey, you have a letter," he said.

Holgate looked puzzled. "Really?"

Hoffman handed it to his friend, but he already knew who it was from. It was postmarked Saint Louis.

Holgate opened the envelope and began reading.

"Dear Norman," it started.

It was from Hoffman's mother. She welcomed him to the family. She said "Junior" had told her all about their friendship, how they both liked music and sports, and after the war she hoped that Norman would visit and play the piano in their living room. They would have a concert.

If he needed anything from America, she would be happy to ship it. She would keep writing, she said, and he should write her, too. And she asked him for one favor: Please look after her son. Before the navy, her boy had never been outside Saint Louis. She was worried about him, worried about them both.

"Norman, you have a family in Saint Louis praying for your safe return," she wrote.

Holgate cradled the letter in his hands. No one had written to him since he left. Not a single person. He was touched by the act of kindness. Someone actually had taken the time to write, to say they cared about what happened to him. For a moment there was an awkward silence. Then, with tears in his eyes, Holgate looked Hoffman in the eyes.

"Thank you," he said.

Hoffman shrugged, but he didn't say a word. He didn't have to.

= 17 =

THE NAVY'S TOP brass strode into the big conference room at Naval Headquarters in San Francisco. Aides scurried around them, opening map cases and folders on the tabletop. Admiral Chester Nimitz took the leader's seat. It was time to plot the next steps in the slog toward Japan.

This was the navy, but this meeting focused on airplanes. General Curtis Lemay, commander of the U.S. Air Force 21st Bomber Command in the Marianas, needed the navy to provide more protection for the B-29 bomber: the Superfortress.

Boeing's new plane could fly 3,700 miles with 20,000 pounds of bombs aboard, and the new airfields on Saipan and Tinian were buzzing with bombers flying round-trips to mainland Japan.

Still, the targets were fifteen hundred miles from the base. The journey was fraught with enemy ground fire and planes, and too many American pilots were being forced down, crashing or ditching their bombers at sea. They weren't only losing pilots—there were nearly a dozen men aboard each plane, including a flight engineer, a bombardier, and a navigator.

The War in the Pacific depended on the strategic bombing missions—they were now taking out Japanese munitions and aircraft factories, shipyards and railways. The air force couldn't sustain the heavy losses for long.

They needed an emergency landing strip, a way station, somewhere closer to Japan.

Nimitz rolled open a map and showed the men what he had in mind.

For weeks he'd been studying the Bonin and Volcano islands, part of an archipelago south of Japan. One of these remote, mostly uninhabited islands would make a perfect way station, he said. Which one should it be?

Nimitz, the fifty-nine-year-old commander in chief of the Pacific Fleet, was a brilliant strategist and problem-solver. He was a team player who steadied those around him. He surrounded himself with the best and the brightest, and listened carefully before making decisions. He worked quietly, and more than once had run afoul of his flamboyant, hardheaded counterpart Douglas MacArthur.

Today he'd arrived prepared. A few days previous, Nimitz asked the Joint Chiefs of Staff for permission to "seize an island" in the archipelago.

In a one-line directive, the Joint Chiefs shot back: "Occupy one or more positions on the Bonin-Volcano Group."

The commanders studied maps, scrutinized the terrain, counted out contour lines. Consensus quickly formed around a flyspeck called Iwo Jima. It was 670 miles south of Tokyo, and its two airstrips sent up many of the airstrikes that were taking down so many Superfortresses. The air force had for months tried to destroy those airfields, but a seemingly endless supply of repairmen appeared as soon as the bombers flew away.

In the sixteenth century, Spanish ship captain Bernard de Torres wrote that Iwo Jima was a barren, windswept island of volcanic rock. There was little to attract European colonization. Iwo Jima remained largely uninhabited until the late 1880s when Japanese colonists arrived in small numbers to mine sulfur there.

It was a hardscrabble life. The water supply came from rain collected in concrete cisterns. There was no harbor. Supply ships had to anchor well out to sea and send in small boats tough enough to battle the unforgiving surf. Overwhelming and unescapable was the nauseating rotten-egg smell rising from the subterranean sulfur deposits.

The island was uninviting, but the commanders agreed: Iwo Jima was the place they were looking for.

By the end of the meeting, Nimitz had his target and the date of the invasion.

But he warned that only the top commanders would know the actual destination. If anyone asked, they'd say they were planning an amphibious assault on "Island X." The world would know the island's name soon enough.

— 18 —

MARY COOPER STARED out the window of the train. San Francisco was close. She could tell by the billboards and signs outside her window. The Union Pacific train drew closer to the city. Passengers stood, took parcels from the racks overhead, pulled on their jackets. Mary Cooper stayed in her seat, watching the billboards and suburbs roll past. She was nervous as a cat.

In just a few minutes she'd see Frederick again, feel his arms around her, fill her nose with his scent. They had a week, a whole week together in San Francisco. She tried to focus on the romance of it, the excitement of a new city. She was going to enjoy every moment, she wasn't going to think too much . . .

But at the end of the week her husband would go off into the Pacific, off to fight who-knows-where, for who-knows-how-long. Mary didn't know when she would see him again. She didn't want to think about that now. But it was all she could think about.

The war followed her everywhere. Daily headlines forever shouted about some new battle in Europe or the Pacific, with the lists of thousands of dead, injured, captured, missing. The war cast its shadow over the grocery stores, where meat, sugar, butter, and other food was rationed. Every time the radio played a Bing Crosby song, she missed her husband all the more.

Frederick and Mary were a striking couple. Mary was twenty-two, a petite brunette from North Manchester, Indiana. Frederick was a tall and muscular twenty-four-year-old with blond locks, the quiet son of the new pastor at the Congregational Christian Church. They'd met in Sunday school and fallen madly in love with each other.

Cooper graduated from college and took a job teaching in Iowa. He asked Mary to marry him.

The year 1942 was a blissful one for Mary. Fred Cooper excelled in the classroom, teaching science and English. He coached the basketball and football teams, and taught Sunday school, too. He loved teaching and working with young people.

When their baby girl was born, Fred fell in love all over again. They named the girl Rebecca. He loved his daughter and was always telling her so.

Even so, Fred Cooper also was wrestling with a personal crisis. So many young men, many of his students, were being drafted. It was just a matter of time before he was called up, too. Cooper had heard of a navy officer training program, and he knew he qualified. He talked to a recruiter, and enlisted March 11, 1944, even though the entire process gave him a very bad feeling. They let him stay home long enough to finish the school year.

He left for training at the end of June. He told Mary that he had to report to San Francisco on September 7, but he didn't have to leave for Pearl Harbor until September 15. Would she come out for a week to see him? His sister could keep the baby for them. Mary didn't hesitate.

When the train pulled into the station, Fred was waiting on the platform, decked out in his navy-blue officer's uniform and white dress cap. He looked so handsome! His face lit up when he saw Mary step off the train. They embraced so tightly, they didn't want to let go.

They walked a few blocks to the Hotel Saint Francis. They stepped inside and stopped in the glittering lobby. She was in awe of the black marble columns, chandeliers, wood-paneled walls, and a Magneta grandfather clock. The hotel billed itself as the "center of San Francisco life," located in the heart of the shopping and theater district.

They checked into the hotel, and the man took away Mary's bags. Fred took her around to the Mural Room, where in the evening they could dine and listen to orchestras play all the top tunes. The cocktail lounge, billed as "brilliant and ultramodern," mixed them drinks that made Mary's head spin.

They stepped into the elevator, and the boy took them up to almost the top floor. They were booked into the most expensive room: a queen-sized bed, and ten dollars a night! Mary pulled back the curtains, revealing a spectacular view over the city roofs. It was so alive, so vibrant, with tens of thousands of workers and sailors, restaurants, bars, and nightclubs. It was so new and exciting.

After Pearl Harbor was attacked, the Bay Area became a centerpiece of what President Roosevelt called "the arsenal of democracy." Shipyards went up almost overnight, fitted out to build the ships that would take the war to the Japanese. By September 1944, 244,000 people worked in the Bay Area shipyards.

Fred stood near her and pointed out the installations. There were nearly a dozen military bases clustered around them. Fort Funston stood at the ocean base of San Francisco, with gun emplacements facing the sea. Treasure Island in the bay housed the Naval Training Station. Warships roamed the bay, and Fort Mason, on San Francisco's northern waterfront, was the main port of embarkation for the Pacific War. That's where Fred would board his transport to Pearl Harbor.

Mary turned from the window. All she wanted to do was be here with Fred.

They threw themselves into the whirl of the city, walking the busy streets for hours, taking in the sights. San Francisco was open all night—people worked the swing shift and then partied through the graveyard shift until dawn. The Coopers went to the theater, and came back and had cocktails in the lounge.

They rode the cable cars, once even jumping on at the last minute. Out of breath, they held on to each other. And when the car started rolling down a steep hill, Mary threw her hands in the air and giggled as the wind blew back her hair.

They walked along Market Street, and held hands as they strolled along the pier, the Golden Gate Bridge in the distance. They went to Chinatown and trolled the little shops for souvenirs, then to Fisherman's Wharf for dinner. It was so much fun that they promised themselves that they'd be back after the war.

At night in the queen-sized bed they held each other. They'd stay up late, talking in the darkness. "You lived in the moment, then you would start thinking about things," Mary recalled later, her voice fading.

She tried so hard not to broach the subject. Not now. Not when they were having such a wonderful time.

On their last night together, they joined three of Cooper's buddies for dinner: William Corkins, Donald Cromer, and Julian Coghill. The four twenty-something officers had trained together in Plattsburg, New York: All their names began with "C," so they shared a room. They had become good friends, and were all ensigns shipping out the next day to Pearl Harbor.

After introducing their wives and dates, the couples ordered drinks. They swapped stories, laughed, and danced through the evening. They didn't talk much about the Pacific, the war, the men's training. They didn't want anything to ruin the night.

Mary and Fred laughed all the way back to the hotel, reveling in the good time they'd had. They didn't want it to end. They talked a little, and held each other. They had no idea when they would be together again.

Morning came. Cooper rose early. He didn't want to wake Mary, but she was up. He took a shower, shaved, and put on his uniform. It was time. He didn't want her to see him to the ship. It would be too painful. Better to say goodbye here. He hugged and kissed her, picked up his bag, and closed the door behind him.

Mary folded herself into the bed and let go of the great lump of pain she'd been carrying for days. It came from her in a deep, gut-wrenching cry, a pain she had never known. Then she heard the key in the door. She turned around and Fred was standing there, tears streaming down his face.

"I'll be home, darling," he said. "We'll start our lives all over again, without a war." He took a deep breath.

"I love you," he said, looking into her eyes.

"I love you."

Then he slowly turned around and left.

Mary lifted her suitcase and placed it on the bed. She had a train to catch. But as she packed, she had a sinking feeling in her stomach. She couldn't help but wonder whether she would ever see Fred again.

THE NEWS WAS bad. Herring didn't send someone else to look for Over-chuk. He went himself, and brought the sailor back to his office for a bit of privacy. The man was nervous. A summons to the commander's room almost never meant anything good.

"It's bad news from home, I'm afraid. No way to mince words. Your mother has passed away," Herring said.

Overchuk was stunned. He didn't know what to say. His stomach turned, it stung like someone had just punched him in the gut. He tried to say something but couldn't.

"I'm sorry, Overchuk," Herring said. "I can arrange for a stateside leave. You're due some time home anyway."

Overchuk could hear Herring talking, but he couldn't make out the words. He placed his head in his hands and sobbed.

Herring had lost his father, and he knew what new grief felt like: sharp, shooting pain that makes it hard to breathe. You just want to break down, lose your senses. Herring draped his arm over Overchuk's shoulders and called Yarbrough into the room.

"Take care of the paperwork," he told him. Overchuk was going home on leave.

Yarbrough nodded. He would take care of it.

Overchuk looked up at Herring. "Do you know what happened?"

Herring shook his head no. He handed the man a handkerchief.

Overchuk's mother, Margaret, was his rock. Anytime he needed money for anything, she always had it for him. When he needed someone to talk to, she was there. She would listen without judgment. She loved the arts, and encouraged his passion for dance and theater.

Always there, always encouraging. Now she was gone. She had just turned forty. She was so young. He didn't get to say goodbye. His younger sisters and brother. Their pain. And his father, dear God, he depended on her so much. She got up at all hours and packed his lunch before he left for the mill, and dinner was on the table when he walked in the door. She was from around Pittsburgh, a good Catholic, and went to mass every day. Always positive.

Overchuk knew he had to get up and head back to his room. He didn't want anyone to see him cry.

When he got to his bunk, he pulled his seabag from his locker and began packing.

Lemke came in. "Where are you going?"

"Home, Cliff."

"What's the matter?"

The words stuttered out. Speaking them made it so real. "My mom. She died," he said.

"Oh my God," Lemke said, stunned. "How?"

Overchuk shrugged his shoulders, then he turned to Lemke. "I want to go to the funeral, or at least visit the grave. My dad's going to need me, I think."

"Anything I could do?" Lemke asked.

Overchuk shook his head no. But then he looked at Lemke, and felt sorry to leave. He had become a sort of big brother to him. He laid a hand on Lemke's arm.

"Stay strong," he said. "It's a leave. I'll have to come back. Blow and the other guys are here for you, too. You just got to learn to relax. Don't take it all so hard."

Lemke sighed. "I'm sorry."

"When I get back, we'll go out," Overchuk promised. "Grab a few guys. Have a few beers."

It was strange. This was one of the worst moments of Overchuk's life, but still here he was looking out for a friend. Lemke would remember that on the days when life on the gunboat really got to him.

THEY ALL REPORTED at the same time in early October. When Cooper, Corkins, and Cromer got to Saipan, they discovered they were all assigned to LCI-449. Their friend, Coghill, however, was told to report to another gunboat.

The men were disappointed. They had gone through training together and thought they had a chance to land on the same ship. Coghill told them not to worry. At least they were all in the same flotilla. They'd still see each other now and then.

Then the three officers boarded, and a deckhand escorted them to the wardroom.

The men saluted the skipper, but he told them to relax, sit down.

Herring was a bit dismayed. These ensigns looked years older than him. When Herring asked them about their backgrounds, he found out they were "ninety-day wonders"—officers with only three months of training, rushed out to the field. None had any combat experience.

When Herring was a midshipman, he trained for nearly a year before he was assigned to a ship. But with all the new landing craft and casualties, the navy had to fill the gaps quickly. Herring welcomed the men aboard, saying that LCI-449 had one of the best crews in Group Eight, they were a team, they got along. Any questions?

Cromer had one: Would they be staying in Saipan or headed to another mission?

"Good question," Herring said. "I wish I had an answer. For now, we're stationed in Saipan indefinitely. No word yet on where we're headed next. Soon as I know, I'll tell you."

Herring showed them around the gunboat. He hoped their additional years would translate to maturity. He didn't have a lot of time to train them before the next operation.

HERRING COULDN'T SLEEP. He had a lot on his mind. Being the skipper was harder than he'd imagined. Dealing with the crew was not a problem—the guys were the fun part. The paperwork, though, was a pain in the ass, and there was no shirking it. If he didn't sign off on every requisition, every request, they wouldn't have meat or socks or mops, and the men couldn't be promoted or disciplined, or go on leave. Everything landed on his desk.

The three new officers were a clear sign, though, that the navy was getting ready for a new campaign. Commanders didn't add officers unless they knew they'd be needed.

Cooper, Corkins, and Cromer seemed like nice guys. He only hoped they were as good as Bedell.

The new kid had fit in perfectly, a hard worker with a sharp sense of humor. They got along well, even though they were from different parts of the country. They both were outgoing and smart; they could gab for hours about any subject.

It was near midnight. Herring got up from his bunk and sat down at his desk. He hadn't written his mother for a while; he was too busy filling in forms.

So Herring lifted his pen:

"Dear Mother: Sorry I haven't written lately, but it's the same old story, nothing to write about. I have been pretty busy explaining things to the three new officers aboard. Still can't figure everything out."

He said the new officers were "older than I am, and it feels funny as the devil to give them orders. They think being on a ship is swell . . . All are married and have kids, so the married men have us outnumbered now," he said.

He wrote about a successful requisition: "We got Pepsi-Cola on board . . . so we have a feast with Pepsi-Cola every night about nine o'clock. I'm keeping a lookout for any of the hometown boys. Sure would love to run into some of them," he said.

He said he knew his mom would start thinking about Christmas soon.

"You just wouldn't let one go by without trying to get me something even if I told you not to," he said. But if she wanted to do something for him, he asked that she take his Davidson College ring to "Miss Ellis, the woman in the jewelry store in Fayetteville, and have her send it to the factory for a new stone. I'd rather have that than anything."

Then he considered what he might do after the war: "Haven't done anything in so long, that it will feel funny to have to go to work again," he said.

Then he stopped. He was rambling. He wrapped up the letter.

"Guess that's all for now . . . Love to all. Geddie."

She didn't need to know anything else.

YARBROUGH RUSHED TO the deck. Another mail call. Now that they were out of combat, the mail was coming in quickly, four or five bags every day. It was a zoo with the men crowding around him, shouting and complaining if they didn't get a letter.

After parceling it out, Yarbrough retreated to his quarters with a few letters of his own. He looked over the envelopes before opening any, lining them up chronologically, according to the dates they were mailed. He knew all the postmarks except one—Cordele, Georgia. He didn't know anyone from there. Bedell had just gone to dinner with the other officers. He'd join them later. He pulled his chair up to his desk and used a letter opener to carefully slice open the top of the mystery envelope. Three pages. Whoever wrote it had impeccable handwriting—the letters were flowing, decorative, like calligraphy. Feminine.

It was from a woman named Betty Jones, a friend of his sister Jane. Betty said Jane had told her all about him, that he was probably lonely, that it must be difficult being in the Pacific so far from home. She admired that he was serving the country. She described her life, her schooling, her work in her dad's pharmacy . . . all the men gone into the military, or working in factories producing guns, bullets, trucks, and planes for the military. Her brother Russ was in the army and her sisters were in town. Cordele, she wrote, was a sleepy Southern town. Nothing much went on, she was living a dull life. She ended by asking Yarbrough to write back. She hoped to hear from him soon.

An ordinary enough letter, Yarbrough thought, but his heart was racing. He could tell she was sweet. An educated Southern girl who worked in her father's pharmacy. A good family, a friend of a friend. He wondered what she looked like.

Yarbrough was too shy to go on blind dates, but this time he didn't have to talk to a live girl. All he had to do was write. He pulled out paper and pen, started writing, then stopped. He couldn't think of anything to say. He realized he was analyzing each word. Finally, he decided to just get on with it.

"Dear Betty: I have started this letter three times so far, and each time I wasn't satisfied with what I said so here goes again. What I want to say is this. I was very much impressed by your nice letter, and I wish that I could begin to impress you as much in turn. It is very sweet of you to write to me, and I will try my best to return the favor," he said.

He told her about his life: "I've been overseas since January 6, 1944 and I have been on this ship since August 25, 1943." He said he loved sports—anything from the Southeastern Conference and his old college, the Alabama Polytechnic Institute. His family had been sending him the sports pages from newspapers back home.

Then he addressed her self-doubts: "Betty I think you are anything but dull, and your handwriting is as pretty + neat as it can be. You will think so too as you see this scratching of mine. Can you read it? Really, I don't see how you found so much to write about. I am happy for the pleasure of corresponding with you."

He asked her to send her picture.

"I am most curious to see what you look like . . . so that means I want a snapshot," he said.

Then he asked her to write back: "If I don't get a letter from you, I will be one sad sailor . . . There is nothing that lifts morale like mail call. Well, Betty I will be looking for a letter from you when mail call comes around, so don't forget, until next time. Sincerely, Byron."

He sat there for a moment, wondering if he should mail it. Finally, he grabbed an envelope, copied her address. He was going to do it. He had nothing to lose.

19

GENERAL KURIBAYASHI EMERGED from the bomb shelter and squinted into the late afternoon sunshine. Smoke billowed skyward from everywhere the bombs had dropped. Dust filtered down. The general turned and scrambled up a short trail. Up there he could get a better view.

He'd lost a lot of weight, his skin was pale, his clothes hung off his frame. The climb made him pant a little. Kuribayashi scanned the airfield below. Seven more aircraft were scattered over the tarmac, smashed like toys. The airfield itself was punctured with massive craters. The bombed-out buildings they'd worked all week to reconstruct were simply gone.

The fires would just have to burn. There wasn't water enough to fight them.

Kuribayashi was a man of action, an aggressor. He hated standing still while the enemy rolled over him, but there was nothing to be done about these daily air strikes. He and his men would just have to take it. The frustration used to make him angry to the point of nausea, but today he was pensive.

It was time to write that letter home to his son.

As the sun went low, Kuribayashi returned to his bunker, washed his face and hands, and prepared paper and ink. He didn't know if it would ever arrive, but he'd been composing the letter for days now. It was getting tougher for anyone or anything to leave the island. He would give it a try.

"We're getting air raids every day," he began. "These days it's usually one or two planes in the night, and about twenty in the daytime. Our airstrips and our defense positions are damaged every time. As far as the eye can see, trees and plants are wiped out, and the ground is all turned over—a pitiful scene.

"People in the mainland cannot imagine what it's like. When I imagine what Tokyo would look like if it were bombed, I see burned-out desert with dead bodies lying everywhere. I'm desperate to stop them carrying out air raids on Tokyo," he said.

The general glanced over what he had written and reimagined the scene. He picked up his pen, dabbed it in ink, and wrote, "What a pity that I have to bring the curtain down on my life in a place like this."

Kuribayashi had worked ceaselessly since he arrived in June 1944, charged with fortifying the defensive positions on Iwo Jima. He had studied every inch of the island, and the enemy's strategy and tactics. He'd come to this startling conclusion: Traditional defensive tactics wouldn't work against the Americans.

When U.S. fighting forces landed on a beach, the Japanese attacked them, hoping to push them into the sea. But Kuribayashi could see a better way to win: Dig in. Build an intricate network of tunnels in which to move, and hide guns, set up ambushes. Iwo Jima might appear to be a sun-blasted desert to the casual observer, but with time and labor, even with fire raining down from the sky outside, the island was being transformed into an impenetrable underground fortress.

Bombers and geology were not the general's only obstacles. His own officers had proved a major problem when he first arrived—they were old soldiers, set in their ways, dedicated to time-honored tactics. Even in the wake of devastating defeats in Saipan, Guam, and Tinian, his officers insisted on meeting the Americans on the beaches with gun emplacements and infantry. They slowed progress of the tunnel projects, questioned his orders, sent messages home that were less than supportive. Until Major Yoshitaka Horie came on the scene.

The envoy from Tokyo arrived at Iwo Jima on August 10, and soon seated himself at Kuribayashi's table. The general poured whiskey and vented his frustrations.

"My staff here are all graduates of the special course of the Army War College. I am unable to rely on them," he said. "They are slow in every action, and I can't help being impatient with them."

Horie listened in silence, swirling his glass of whiskey, and then spoke in parable: At Iwo Jima, "there are many old men helping to unload and reload the ships, working after midnight. Some of them are bent over at the back. It may be inevitable that they prefer taking it easy," he said.

The following day, several of these "bent old men," high-ranking army and navy commanders, arrived at Kuribayashi's headquarters for a defense meeting. One of them suggested building more pillboxes with hundreds of machine guns around the main airfield.

Horie immediately spoke up. "Would you please tell me exactly how the shoreline pillboxes at Tarawa were effective? A frontal defense against hundreds of the enemy naval guns and aircraft is out of the question. The past battle lessons we have received from Saipan, Guam, and Tinian have taught us clearly that there are no alternatives to sniping at enemy troops from hidden caves. It will be child's play if we attempted to use the pill-boxes with 25mm machine guns against the enemy's naval gunfire."

The envoy was only a major, but he had the ear of the high command. The commanders sat in silence.

"I agree with Major Horie," Kuribayashi said.

The meeting adjourned without an agreement on the weaponry and pillboxes the navy wanted. It was a stalemate, army vs. navy.

Kuribayashi slept on it, and the following morning he and Horie reconvened.

"Major Horie, regarding the problem of the pillboxes, your opinion is right from the viewpoint of tactics," he said. "But the resources the navy could bring here are also important. Particularly dynamite and cement are very valuable for what we are doing here on this island. Three hundred 25mm machine guns are also important. What do you think about the following plan? We could build some pillboxes using 50 percent of the navy's resources and use the rest for the army."

Horie agreed. A new meeting was called and the compromise offered:

Kuribayashi would build 165 pillboxes, and use the remaining materials for fortification projects throughout the island.

Horie returned to the mainland with Kuribayashi's wish list: Younger officers to replace the older, slower commanders. Weapons, ammunition, and explosives. Better shipping, and better escorts—too many supply ships had been lost to American aircraft and submarines.

Kuribayashi smiled as he thought of the energy younger officers would bring to the defenders of Iwo Jima. Horie had showed up at the right time, and delivered on his promises.

The new officers were all thirty years younger than their predecessors, and the old men were happy to escape the onerous duty station. The officers arrived along with stepped-up provisions of ammunition, arms, and dynamite. Kuribayashi finally felt able to achieve something.

Now, nearly two months later, in the middle of October, Kuribayashi's plans were coming together. The pillboxes were finished, and the other provisions had been used to turn every cave, crevice, and fissure into a defensive position, each one with a good field of fire.

There was still much to achieve.

The following morning, Kuribayashi traversed the island, inspecting the progress. As he approached a defensive position, the men jumped to attention and stood in silence.

Kuribayashi put them at ease and ordered them back to work. As the men began to swing their pickaxes and thrust their shovels into the ground, the general approached a young recruit whose bare chest was wet with sweat and smeared with dust.

The general pulled out a pack of cigarettes—cigarettes sent to him as a gift from the emperor. He stretched out his hand to offer one to the soldier. The young man, shocked, glanced over at his lieutenant as if to inquire, "What do I do?" The lieutenant was just as surprised. Kuribyashi chuckled. "Go ahead, take one."

The soldier beamed, bowed, and accepted a light from the general. The men stared, watching as the filthy young man shared a smoke with his rather dusty senior officer. This did not happen in the highly stratified Japanese military. Acts of kindness from high-ranking officers were unheard of.

Kuribayashi knew that that simple gesture had won the hearts of his soldiers, and they'd follow him to the death. The scene played out all over the island, time and again as work parties took a break to share the emperor's cigarettes with their general.

This devotion was helping create a defensive masterpiece. Much had been accomplished in the last four months. Iwo Jima was now honey-combed with tunnels that grew deeper and longer with each passing day. Kuribayashi knew the American air raids would continue, but he no longer worried about them. His weapons, supplies, and men were safely hidden under the hard volcanic rock in thousands of positions all across the island. For now.

It was a strange feeling. He knew that each day without an invasion meant he'd be able to exact a higher tally of American casualties. But he also knew how the story would end. He and all these men would die here.

Kuribayashi had already said his goodbyes to his family. A few weeks earlier, in a letter to his nine-year-old daughter, Takako, the general had said he wasn't coming home. "This war is a really big war now, so I really don't know whether I'll be able to make it home safely or not. If I can't make it back, I'll be most sorry for you, Takako. But you make sure and do what Mommy tells you, and grow up fast to be a big, strong girl. If you do that, it will make Daddy feel a whole lot better, too," he said.

To his nineteen-year-old son, Taro, he wrote, "Tokyo is not experiencing air raids now, but if the island that I am now defending ends up getting captured by the enemy, then [Tokyo] is sure to start being bombed around the clock. (Just as the place I'm now in started getting raids after the capture of Saipan.) The enemy counterattack is becoming fiercer and fiercer recently. It's only a matter of time before they come and attack the place where I am. When that happens, if we can't hold out, the next stage will be air raids on Tokyo. The awfulness, damage and chaos of air raids are inexpressible and beyond imagination of people living peaceful lives in Tokyo.

"You must understand that when there is an air raid the most important thing for you to do is to stop whatever you're doing, get together at the house, and do your utmost to protect your mother by any and every means. Even if the school has some rule about what you should do, you need to think that our house could be burned down or you might die, and you'll see there's no reason for you to blindly obey any school rules," he said.

It was a letter of passion and frustration, too. Kuribayashi poured his heart into the words, willing his spirit to help his son take his place at home if the worst happened, to somehow protect the people he loved most.

He didn't know that his fears already were reality. U.S. planes based in the Marianas were already dropping bombs on Tokyo.

Kuribayashi's vision of desolation, ruin, and death would prove prophetic.

20

BASEBALLS HIT GLOVE leather with a satisfying pop, back and forth, back and forth. The men hardly had to even look at the ball. Hollowell's mouth was running nonstop, talking about anything that came to his mind—he rattled through the plot of last night's movie. Johnson had been there, too; he'd seen the same film from the seat next to Hollowell, but he didn't mind the chatter. It was a welcome diversion.

The tropical sun pounded down on the makeshift ball field, an expanse of green near Tanapag Harbor on the western side of Saipan. They'd rolled up in two jeeps loaded down with baseball gloves, bats, and balls, and whooped it up with their shipmates. While Johnson played catch with Hollowell, Blow and Bedell hit a few balls to the other men.

It was hard to believe this was the same Saipan they'd fought for in June. In a few short months, the place had changed from a bombed-out major base in the Japanese Empire to a United States territory, replete with new roads, Quonset huts, and bathing beaches. American bombers were launching strikes deep into Japan from Saipan airfields, but the island was more oasis than way station. There was an officers' club along the beach, where Herring and his buddies could hang out and sip gin rickeys. There were other clubs, too, set up in old tents or Quonset huts, where Marines, soldiers, and seamen drank Schlitz or Schenley's Black Label. Military shops were opening where they could buy American goodies, and the men could explore the island, climb up into the groves and pick fruit from the trees that survived.

It wasn't completely safe. Every once in a while a Japanese sniper would turn up in a remote cave, and planes from the Bonin Islands occasionally appeared out of nowhere. Still, a man could relax and unwind on Saipan. It was getting better every day.

The crew of LCI-449 didn't know how much longer they'd be there, so they squeezed every bit of fun out of their stay. Baseball was a favorite way to relax. The crew had played a few teams from other gunboats, but they mostly just liked to throw the ball around.

Even in practice, some players stood out. Johnson, with his background as a semi-pro ballplayer, could do it all. During one game against another gunboat, the opposing team stopped pitching to him after he hit two long home runs. The irony wasn't lost on Johnson—he was on a white team competing against white players, something he'd never see at home. Back in his days with the Decatur Cats, his team would sit in the stands and watch barnstorming major leaguers play against local teams. The Cats had challenged the white teams to a game a few times, but someone always made an excuse. It never happened. It couldn't.

Still, Johnson's teammates always walked away feeling confident that they could hold their own against the white players. They'd prove it, too, if they had the chance.

Maybe the war would change that. Maybe when they all got home, they'd get that chance, Johnson told Hollowell. "It's just plain stupid, the way it is now," Hollowell said.

Hollowell was devoted to Johnson. "He was honest and protective. There's nothing he wouldn't do for you," Hollowell recalled.

They knew their friendship could never have happened at home in Oklahoma or Texas. But out in the Pacific, the sailors had bonded over a 20mm gun. During long nights on duty, Hollowell chattered and rambled, trying to keep Johnson alert. They knew all about each other's many sisters and brothers. They'd played ball on the same fields, eaten at the same backwoods barbecue stands. They'd both worked similar menial jobs to keep food on the table through the Depression.

Some of the men on the boat didn't speak to Johnson. They pretended not to notice when he was around. But the white kid from Oklahoma always asked him how he was doing, always offered him a cookie or a stick of gum when his family sent a package, didn't mind sitting with him when they went to the movies. He treated Johnson like any other guy.

Johnson didn't open up to many people, but he did with Hollowell.

That day, on the field in Saipan, tossing a baseball, Hollowell told everybody he couldn't wait to get back home, to go and see Johnson play for the Decatur Cats. He might be the only white person in the stands, but he didn't care. Nothing was going to stop him.

CORKINS LEANED BACK in a chair in the radio shack, relaxing. He had been on the gunboat for two weeks now, and was getting used to the routine. As the gunnery officer, his job was to keep the commander in contact with gun crews during firefights. He kept inventory of supplies, too, and that part was just like his old job at the meat-packing company. He had to be organized to be a salesman, and keeping track of things was one of Corkins's strengths.

So far, the transition from trainee to sailor was an easy one. It helped that Cooper and Cromer were there. The three C's were roommates once again on the gunboat, and all the other officers had made them feel welcome. Corkins took a shine to Bedell, another Ohio guy—Bedell was from Akron, and Corkins from Cincinnati.

Bedell was a diehard Cleveland Indians fan, while Corkins closely followed the Cincinnati Reds. They were united in their passion for Ohio State University football. October was the heart of college football season, and Corkins and Bedell scrounged for any bit of sports news they could find. It was so frustrating, Corkins thought. If they were in Ohio, they'd be listening to the games this afternoon. Hell, if Corkins was in Ohio, he could get tickets: He graduated from Ohio State in 1937. The last Corkins and Bedell heard, Ohio State had won its first two games of the season and were playing at the University of Wisconsin.

Corkins considered playing with the shortwave till he picked up a signal from the Columbus station. But that would get him in trouble, especially if Ball walked in. Ball hated people messing with *his* radios. And trouble was the last thing Corkins wanted.

There was nothing else to do but write another letter. The mail went out in the morning, and he owed a letter to his sister and her little boy, whom he called "Champ."

"I am aboard a Landing Craft Infantry that has been converted into a gun boat. It has been in on 3 invasions, but at the present we've been idle as hell in the harbor," he wrote.

He played up what little action there was. "There are some Japs hiding out within gunshot of the ship," he said, but most had been rooted out.

He was getting along with everyone on his boat, he said.

"I've never met a finer bunch of fellows than aboard this ship. We're lucky to start out under them. There are 4 regular [officers] and we 3 new ones. We do little work now but are learning everything about operating the ship. Our job is to go in with the pre-invasion demolition boys and then with the Marine invaders. We lay down a heavy barrage to force the Japs under cover and away from their own heavy and light guns. Sounds interesting if we ever get to see action," he said.

Corkins wanted to be in combat, the reason the twenty-nine-year-old father of two enlisted in the navy. All men between the ages of eighteen and forty-five were subject to military service. Nearing thirty with a family to support, there was a good chance Corkins could have sat out the war. But Corkins was restless. He was always looking for new challenges. And this was his latest, a tiny gunboat in the Pacific. It was a far cry from his childhood home in Ohio.

Corkins grew up in a big house in Cincinnati. His father was a successful businessman, who founded a chemical company that specialized in soap, disinfectant, and pesticides. But Corkins wasn't fond of urban areas.

As a child, he'd spend long days exploring the fields on his grandfather's farm, watching birds and animals, collecting arrowheads. He planned to become a farmer. At Ohio State University, Corkins majored in agriculture. During an interview on the student-run radio station in 1934, as a freshman, he explained why. He had spent the previous six summers on a farm in rural Ohio, working to earn his "board and lodging." It was backbreaking, but "when the work is done, there are so many things to do that are fun, and which a city boy cannot do. Swimming after a hot summer's day's work is only one of the pleasures," he said.

He said he knew trying to make a living as a farmer would be difficult, but he wouldn't let that deter him because the lifestyle had built-in advantages: "I believe that on the farm one can still have a warm house, three square meals a day, and a friendly environment in which to live."

That feeling never waned. But during college, he got sidetracked. He fell in love with Dorothy Ottenfeld, an attractive Ohio State student. After he graduated, they got married, had two children, and he took a job selling farm products.

He still held out hope that someday he would own a farm. But now he was sitting in the radio shack, which was "as hot as Hades," trying to finish a letter. So he ended with a message to his nephew: "Tell Champ I'll try to get him a souvenir of some sort."

In his room down the hall from the radio shack, Duvall was writing another letter to his wife, Evelyn. He didn't have much time for correspondence during the Marianas campaign. He was still catching up, trying to answer all the letters from his family and friends. But every chance he could, Duvall wrote his wife. He wanted her to know how much he missed her.

In a few weeks, they'd be celebrating their first wedding anniversary. Just thinking about it broke his heart. He was stuck in the middle of the Pacific. It had been so long since they were in each other's arms. At night, he dreamed of her, the long walks on campus, the sweet kisses. He wanted the dreams to last, but they never did.

He knew Evelyn was trying to keep busy. She had landed a job as assistant general manager at Golden Dreams, a food packaging company in Ashland, Kentucky, only thirty miles north of her parents in Louisa, Kentucky. He encouraged her, writing that she was probably the "top general manager" at the company. He couldn't share any details of the battles, what he saw. Even if he could, he wouldn't. She didn't need to know. And after the war, he'd try to forget, move on with their lives. "What a wonderful day it will be when we can continue our happiness together," he wrote.

In his bunk, Bozarth was writing to his grandfather. He had finished opening his mail, and found out his sister Evelyn was engaged. He was happy for her and wished he could be there for the wedding. Hollowell was pestering him again, asking whether one of Bozarth's sisters could write him. Bozarth hadn't gotten around to asking. Now he could cross Evelyn off the list.

He said he hoped his grandfather was doing well and said the weather had been gloomy. "We've been having a little rough weather here lately. It's a good thing we weren't at sea . . . It rains often here, several times in a day."

He assured his grandfather that Evelyn's future husband was a "swell fellow."

"The fellow she is engaged to is a sailor I know him well . . . They are to be married after the war. Everybody is sure doing good back home. As long as they're getting along OK, I can be happy although I am alone, a long way from home," he said.

Bozarth got bunches of letters from home, but he didn't get anything from the one he wanted to hear from the most: Elaine. He didn't know why she didn't write. But it didn't change his plans: He was going to see her after the war.

He glanced at his grandfather's letter, and the other mail on his bunk. He told the old man he had to answer other letters and promised that he would visit him when he got back. He folded the letter into its envelope and moved to the next. Staying busy was the only way to hang on.

HOFFMAN'S HARMONICA, A gift from his mom, was driving everyone crazy. Soon as it arrived he started right away, blowing into the holes on the mouthpiece. He thought since he played the accordion and the piano, he'd get the hang of the harmonica quickly, but it didn't work out that way. So he practiced day and night, playing blues scales and individual notes. He tried his best to bend notes like he was playing on some back porch in the Mississippi Delta.

He got the knack soon enough. Sometimes, the crew could hear Hoffman playing on the fantail in the middle of the night. The officers told him he couldn't play while he was on guard duty. But Holgate knew nothing could stop his friend when he was determined. Holgate would hear the faint tones, a lonesome bluesman in the middle of the night.

But it was starting to get on Holgate's nerves. One afternoon, after a particularly excruciating rendition of "Comin' Through the Rye," Hoffman went off to the head and left the harmonica on his bunk. Holgate grabbed it, stuffed it in his pocket, and walked out onto the deck. He was about to slip it into the water, but he stopped himself. He couldn't. Not after everything Hoffman had done for him.

Over the last few weeks, he had received several letters from Hoffman's mother, Mary. The letters were so upbeat, filled with the latest family news. She asked how he was doing, and if he needed anything. She always ended by reminding Holgate that he was one of the family. She was the sweetest woman he had ever known, Holgate thought. When the war ended, he promised that he would find a way to thank her for her kindness.

Annoying as it was, the harmonica had come from Mary Hoffman. He couldn't throw her gift into the ocean.

Hoffman appeared again. "Hey, did you see my harmonica?" he asked.

Holgate paused for a moment. "Um, yeah. I got it." He handed Hoffman the instrument. "I was just bringing it to you. You leave it laying around, it's going to end up in the drink."

Hoffman wasn't buying it. "Don't tell me you're like the rest of the guys?"

"No. I love to hear you play."

Hoffman looked at the harmonica, then put it in his pocket.

Something was wrong. "You OK?" Holgate asked.

Hoffman shrugged. "Not sure."

"What's the matter?"

He hesitated for a moment, then blurted it out: "I don't know if I'm going to make it."

Holgate was puzzled. "What?"

"I don't think I'm going to make it. I'm not going to make it back."

Holgate knew his friend was depressed. He felt pretty bad himself sometimes. "A lot of combat soldiers and sailors get that feeling," Holgate told him. "You wouldn't be normal if you didn't think that way some-times. Just throw it out of your mind."

Hoffman was silent. This wasn't just some passing mood. It was some-thing more lasting. He'd told his best friend Ollie Berger the same thing, just before he left Saint Louis for boot camp.

Holgate thought the adoption thing was bothering Hoffman again, so Holgate reminded his friend about their postwar plan: After the war, they were going to form a band. They'd travel the country, play in the bars and dance halls. Everything was going to be good.

"Don't play sad tunes, man. It's bringing you down," Holgate said.

Hoffman managed a weak smile, then pulled the harmonica from his pocket. He held it with both hands, lifted it to his mouth, and blew the first plaintive notes of "Knoxville Girl."

Blues. Holgate didn't say a word. He wasn't going to stop him. He just stood there and listened.

BETTY JONES SAW the letter on the tray, as soon as she stepped through the front door. It had her name on it and an overseas postmark, but it wasn't her brother's handwriting.

Betty opened the letter and smiled. It was from Byron. She hadn't thought he'd write back, but she'd let herself hope. And there was his name, at the bottom of a three-page letter. She bounded up the stairs to her room, closed the door, and sat on her bed.

She read it closely. It was a sweet letter, one filled with clues about his personality. He encouraged Betty to write more to her brother Russ, but hinted that he loved to get mail, too.

"I know how much those letters mean to him. They are just like pay day or weekends when you are in school, only much dearer," he said.

He asked her to send her picture: "I am most curious to see what you look like . . ." While she was insecure about her looks, she decided to do it. She wanted to get that out of the way now before anything serious devel-oped. Not that she wanted to start a long-distance relationship with a man she'd never met. But his words were revealing. He seemed shy, lonely. She could identify with his loneliness. What was the harm of sending a picture?

Betty got up from her bed and rummaged through her desk drawer. She had a few snapshots in there, somewhere. No luck. So she began searching a box in her closet filled with mementoes, and sure enough, she found a few portrait shots. She went back to her desk and began writing Byron another letter. She shared the latest news in her life: She had just received two wedding invitations, and that meant buying new clothes and gifts. It was hard to keep track of her social calendar, she wrote.

She enjoyed sports, and her beloved Georgia Bulldogs had just lost to Louisiana State University, 15–7. Then she went into more details about her family, her father's drugstore.

When she started the letter, she didn't think she'd have much to say. But within minutes, she had already written five pages.

She stopped. Betty didn't want Byron to think she was a chatterbox. So she folded the letter around the photos in the envelope, and left it on her desk. She'd mail it in the morning. She got up and turned on her radio. A band played "Blue Moon." It was almost too silly, she thought.

She read his letter one more time. It was strange, but Betty hadn't thought about Byron before she opened his letter, but now she couldn't stop. What did he look like? she wondered . . . It would be too forward to ask for a photo. Not that it mattered. The only thing she cared about was whether he was kind, someone who loved to laugh and believed in romance. It was way too early to know if Byron was the one.

WITH A PAINT scraper in his right hand, Hightower chipped a section of the gun deck near the port-side 40mm gun. A few days earlier, one of the officers had noticed a little rust near the weapon. So he asked Ralph Owens, the gun captain on the port-side gun, to take care of it. Owens grimaced—"busywork," he groused. Too much idle time. "They're always trying to find something for us to do," Owens said.

But Hightower came to his friend's rescue. He volunteered to remove the rust and repaint the area. No big deal, right? But now, in the sweltering heat, he was having second thoughts.

Hightower was used to hot days—he grew up in Russellville, Arkansas, a railroad town near the Arkansas River, where temperatures in August would routinely hit the upper nineties. But it was nothing like this, not with the humidity. It always felt like you just stepped out of a shower. Nothing you could do about it.

He placed the scraper on the deck and jumped to his feet. He needed a short break. Hightower walked to the edge of the gun deck, hoping to catch a breeze. But the air was still. Nothing. The sailor was about to return to work, when he glimpsed Ensign Cooper, who had just climbed the ladder to the gun deck. As the officer on duty, Cooper was responsible for doling out the day's work assignments. He walked toward Hightower, who noticed that Cooper was carrying a round tin can in his hands.

"How are you doing, Hightower?"

"Fine, sir," he said.

Cooper lifted the top of the tin can and pulled out a piece of hard candy. "My wife sent these. Pretty good. Do you want some?"

"Sure, sir," he said. Hightower grabbed several pieces and stuffed all but one in his pocket. "Thank you, sir," he said.

Cooper smiled as he put the lid back on the can, then turned and faced the sea.

"You OK, sir?" Hightower asked.

Cooper nodded his head yes.

But Hightower didn't believe him. He removed the wrapper and tossed a piece of candy in his mouth. Hightower didn't know much about Cooper. He only knew he was a teacher from Iowa, and he might have a family. Cooper was a quiet guy. Didn't say much, even when he was around his friends Corkins and Cromer.

"You have anybody back home?" Cooper asked.

"Um, my mother and father, a brother . . ."

"No," Cooper interrupted. "A wife? Girlfriend?"

Yes, a girlfriend, Hightower said. He had wanted to marry her before he left for boot camp, but her father wouldn't let him because she was too young—she was sixteen. "She's waiting for me, sir."

Cooper looked at Hightower. "How old are you?"

"Eighteen."

Cooper smiled. He recalled when he was that age. He was in college, had just met Mary. He was so shy. It didn't help that she was so pretty.

They'd drive around in his father's car some nights without talking. But when a Bing Crosby song played on the radio, he'd sing along. Then, feeling more comfortable, Cooper would open up to her. Every time Cooper heard the song "Where the Blue of the Night Meets the Gold of the Day," he was taken back in time to his father's car, driving along a rural Indiana road guided by the stars. In those days, Cooper was an optimist, something he learned from his father, a pastor. That's one reason why he went into teaching—you encourage people, give back to the community. But lately, Cooper was focusing more and more on the negative, and he didn't like it.

"What about you, sir? Do you have someone?" Hightower asked.

"Yes . . . I'm married and have a daughter. Rebecca."

"It must be tough, sir."

Cooper nodded and started talking. He missed them dreadfully. He was always thinking about them. And lately, he'd started worrying what would happen to them if he was killed in combat. It kept him up at night.

Hightower didn't know how to respond. He thought about that, too. He loved his girlfriend, his family—especially his father, who worked so hard to make ends meet. He was a carpenter and part-time farmer. When he closed his eyes, Hightower could see the old man cutting down pine trees on hot afternoons like today, struggling to haul the timber back to his little workshop to make furniture. But Hightower said he didn't obsess about getting killed in combat, because if you did, it would consume you, drive you nuts.

Another thing, Hightower said. He knew it could get chaotic in combat. But in the confusion, he could always count on Owens to look out for him. And Hightower would do the same. In fact, despite differences with some of the guys, including the Chicago boys, who called the Southerners hillbillies, they all "pulled together in battle." They protected one another. So why think about what would happen in a firefight? As long as your buddy had your back, that was one less thing to worry about, right?

Instead, Hightower said he kept busy. It helped keep his mind off the other stuff. That's why he volunteered for extra work on the gunboat.

That's why he liked to hang out with the guys. That's why he stayed up late playing cards and talking about baseball, girls.

"That's why I don't mind Owens talking about Nina all the time. It's his way of getting through the day," he said.

What he did mind was that Owens would go "a long time without taking a bath," he joked.

Cooper laughed. "Thanks, Hightower," he said.

Hightower watched as Cooper, clutching the tin can, turned and headed to the ladder leading to the well deck.

What Hightower realized that afternoon was that while Cooper was an officer, he had the same fears as the enlisted men. Cooper just had to clear his head and everything would be all right.

BAKING IN THE sun on the other side of the gunboat, Hallett and Banko were still working on their 40mm gun.

They spent most of the afternoon examining and cleaning the weapon. They hadn't been ordered to do it, but it didn't matter. The men knew that keeping the 40mm in top condition was important. You never knew when you'd have to use it.

By late afternoon, they stopped and sat on the well deck. They used rags hanging from the back pockets of their dungarees to wipe the sweat from their brows.

"There's gotta be a better way to make a living," Banko quipped.

Hallett smiled. "Yeah. Picking apples."

They laughed.

After spending so much time together—first on LCI-455, now the 449—they knew everything about each other's life. They read their letters out loud. They knew when the other was down, and the right words to say to cheer him up.

Hallett had been talking about apples for weeks. Banko knew why: He had received a letter from his parents about the family orchard. With the Hallett boys in the military and a shortage of labor, they barely had enough help this season for the apple harvest.

Banko knew this was Hallett's favorite time of the year at home. He had heard him talk about it so many times: The weather was crisp in Wenatchee, the trees in the Hallett orchard were filled with bright red apples.

Emery Hallett and his wife Inez didn't have to ask their four boys and a girl to work in the orchard: They volunteered. In late August through early November, the siblings would spend part of their mornings and afternoons working side by side with field hands. They'd reach up and pick the low-hanging fruit and use ladders to pluck the rest. The view was spectacular: The Hallett orchard was in the shadow of the Central Cascades Mountain Range.

No matter where you went, the town was awash in red. Wenatchee dubbed itself the "Apple Capital of the World." The state's annual Apple Blossom Festival was held in town. Images of apples were on signs, billboards, and letterheads. There were football games, parades, and large outdoor parties lit by bonfires.

"What I wouldn't do to be back there now," said Hallett.

"Yup," Banko said. "I'd even help, for some apple cider."

"Forget apple cider. Only the hard stuff," Hallett joked.

Banko smiled. With the lull in the action, it was hard for him to believe he was in the middle of a war. When he closed his eyes, he could see his home, the front yard, his mother in the kitchen preparing dinner. He could recall that morning in his father's gas station, reading the "Sunday funnies," when he heard a man's voice interrupt the music on the radio: Pearl Harbor had been attacked. Banko didn't know what to make of it, until he saw the distress on his father's face. The old man had served in World War I, on the front lines in France. With three sons nearing draft age, he knew they'd eventually serve.

So much had happened in Banko's life since that morning. His brothers enlisted. And when it was his turn, he believed he would be an officer. When that fell through, he wanted to at least serve on a battleship or destroyer. But when he reported for duty, he couldn't believe he was assigned to a "little vessel." He turned to the baby-faced sailor boarding the ship with him and expressed his disappointment. "This thing doesn't look capable of going more than a few miles offshore, let alone several thousand miles in the open sea."

"Ain't that the truth," said the sailor with a big grin.

Banko introduced himself, and the other crewman said his name was Bruce Hallett.

When they boarded, they decided to bunk in the same quarters. Now, here they were, nearly eighteen months later, hardened combat veterans. It had been nearly two months since they last saw action. They knew they'd embark on another campaign—the Japanese weren't going to surrender anytime soon. Yet the mood on the gunboat was relaxed, thanks to the skipper.

Herring set the tone. He was easygoing, as long as you did your job. If you didn't, he'd let you know in private. But there was something else. When the gunboat wasn't in training, or when Herring didn't have to meet with officers on other ships, he loved to wear khaki pants and a white T-shirt. On those days, with his short hair and binoculars, Herring looked more like a Boy Scout troop leader on a field trip than the captain of a ship. The other officers took his cue. Yarbrough and some of the new officers would walk around in T-shirts, or without shirts at all.

A few days earlier, Corkins had snapped a picture of Herring, Yarbrough, Bedell, and Cooper on the bridge. Herring was standing, while Yarbrough, Bedell, and Cooper sat on top of the metal wall encircling the bridge, their feet dangling in the air. Herring and Bedell wore T-shirts; Yarbrough and Cooper were bare-chested. They looked so young, teenagers hanging out in a neighborhood.

Unlike Nash, Herring wasn't a stickler about dress code on the 449. He knew there were more important things to worry about than uniforms. When they were on mail runs, the crew would see the sarcastic looks on the faces of the sailors on the navy's big ships. Those sailors already looked down on the gunboats, derisively calling them the "Waterbug Navy," because of the way the small boats darted across the water.

Herring suspected the gunboats were treated differently when it came to requisitions. They were always last on the list. He couldn't remember the last time Duvall was able to procure ice cream for the crew.

But Herring knew that his men were as good as any sailors in the damn navy. Yes, the gunboats' crews were young, and none of the LCIs got the press coverage. They didn't share the limelight or carry the cachet of battleships, aircraft carriers. But even if they didn't get the respect, gunboats were a critical part of the navy. They were helping win the War in the Pacific. And in the end, that's all that really mattered. Not the accolades.

Herring reminded his crew of that every day.

That's why Hallett and Banko and the rest of his men worked so hard. There was no slacking off.

Hallett and Banko jumped up, then turned their attention back to the 40mm. They wanted to inspect the weapon one more time before they headed to the galley for dinner.

= 21 =

HUDDLED OVER HIS typewriter, Ball was pounding out the latest news for the crew. He hadn't had much time to do it during the Marianas campaign. But now he was back in his daily routine: listening and condensing the navy's nighttime broadcasts to a one-page newsletter.

Tonight's newscast had nothing to do with the war. It was about the presidential election: Franklin Delano Roosevelt had been elected to an unprecedented fourth term in office. No surprise.

For most of the crew, Roosevelt was the only president they had ever known. He had been in office since 1933, guiding the nation through some of its darkest hours: the Depression and now World War II.

As he was banging away, Blow and Casaletto walked inside the radio shack and made themselves at home.

"You busy?" Casaletto said.

Ball stopped typing and stared at Casaletto.

"A little," said Ball, a bit annoyed.

"I'm getting together a little card game. Want in?"

Ball said yes, but he had to finish the newsletter first.

"Can't you do it later?"

Ball shook his head no. He was going to be too tired in a few hours. Plus, everyone would want to know that Roosevelt had been reelected.

Casaletto grinned. It would have been news if Republican presidential candidate Thomas E. Dewey had won.

Blow agreed. Plus, it was real late and they had a couple of sailors waiting in the mess deck. "Just wrap it up."

Ball waved them off. "I'll be there in a little bit."

They got up, but before they left, Casaletto turned to Ball. "You want to be a reporter when you get out?"

No, but no matter what you do, you can't slack off, he told Casaletto.

When they left, Ball turned his attention back to the typewriter. Maybe they were right. Maybe it wasn't big news. Still, he kept thinking about everything Roosevelt had done for the country over the years.

Roosevelt had given hope to so many people struggling to get back on their feet in the wake of the Wall Street stock market crash in 1929. So many families across America had to fend for themselves when they lost their jobs, their homes.

Hell, Ball saw friends and neighbors down on their luck. He couldn't think of anyone on the gunboat who wasn't hurt by the Depression, except for maybe a couple of the officers. Now there were federal programs to help the poor, the elderly, like Social Security. Many people were working, optimistic about the nation's economy.

And what if Roosevelt hadn't been around when the Japanese hit Pearl Harbor? Ball didn't want to think about it.

When Ball finished typing, he pulled the paper from the carriage and rushed to the mimeograph machine. He wanted the men to know about Roosevelt's reelection when they headed to the galley for breakfast.

BOZARTH WAS EXCITED at the news—he wouldn't spend his whole hitch loading guns. The navy was sending him for the next two weeks to baking school, aboard the USS *Kenneth Whiting*. Bozarth already knew the fundamentals of baking, but now he'd have real training. He'd soon be proficient enough to make all kinds of pies, pastries, cakes, and rolls, even bread.

At that point, maybe they'd pull him from the gun crew and reassign him to the kitchen. Bozarth liked the camaraderie of the gun team.

Banko and Hallett were swell guys who always looked out for him, and over time they'd all become like brothers, or at least cousins. Blow had become a protective figure. He was all bluster and noise in the daytime, but in the quiet of the night shift, when no one was around, the tough guy bowed his head and prayed with Bozarth.

Bozarth hadn't complained about loading ammo. He worked hard, he got the job done. But lately, with the campaign wound up and some time to think, he'd let Kepner put the bug in his ear.

The cook knew how much Bozarth liked to bake. He told Bozarth that he was pretty good at what he knew, but there was a lot more he could learn. The *Kenneth Whiting* had an advanced program, and if he went, Kepner promised Bozarth he'd find a way to get him into the galley. He'd put in a good word with Herring.

When Bozarth asked to take the training, Herring didn't hesitate. He contacted the *Whiting* brass and discovered he could send two sailors to the program. He asked Kepner if anyone else showed potential. Yes, Kepner said: Charles Vogel. Since he came aboard with Lemke in May, Vogel had spent much of his free time in the galley, watching Kepner and Rosenbloom prepare meals, taking notes. He even studied the navy's cookbook, a "summary of the principles of cookery, menu planning and a comprehensive collection of recipes based on the new knowledge of nutrition."

The book suggested weekly menus for all the seasons, and recipes based on the latest science:

> *Active men need large amounts of energy, 3,000 to 4,500 calories per day. In a well-balanced diet it is estimated that approximately 10 to 15 percent of the calories should be derived from protein; 55 to 70 percent from carbohydrates, and 20 to 30 percent from fat. It is evident therefore that although protein is useful as an energy producing food as well as its muscle building foundation, the majority of energy is derived from carbohydrates such as starches, and sugars and fat. Best sources: fats and oils; flour (bread, cake, pastry), spaghetti, macaroni, rice and other cereals; sugar and syrups.*

Vogel had even memorized many of the recipes. Now he and Bozarth were going to learn how to put them to use.

Bozarth knew that cookbook, too, but he focused on the cakes and pastries. The gunboat didn't carry many of the ingredients, but he wanted to try making cream puffs and éclairs and the chocolate malted milk cream icing to spread atop a yellow cake. The *Kenneth Whiting* must have all the ingredients, he presumed, otherwise they wouldn't include the recipes in the cookbook.

He wanted to learn enough to produce a real four-star feast on special occasions. With Thanksgiving and Christmas coming up, he could try out his skills. And before their next mission, wherever or whenever that happened, he wanted his friends to have a feast they'd remember for the rest of their lives.

THE LETTERS CAME fast and furious. Yarbrough got one at every mail call, sometimes two. As soon as he read them, he'd answer, sometimes within minutes.

Bedell laughed at his enthusiasm. "Slow down. You never met her," he said.

Yarbrough ignored him. It was easy for Bedell to dispense advice—a guy who'd mailed an engagement ring to his girlfriend! (She wrote a letter back saying, "yes.") Yarbrough liked Bedell, but sometimes he missed his privacy. Especially when he was writing.

Bedell could sense when Yarbrough was getting a little tense, so he'd head to the deck to see if there was a card game going on, or to hear Hoffman's latest harmonica tune. Still, he gently teased his friend, joking about when "Betty and Byron were going to get married."

"How do you know these snaps are really her? Maybe they're her friend," Bedell said.

But Bedell always knew when he was close to the edge by the expression on Yarbrough's face: He would glare at him, bite his lower lip. Then Bedell would break the mood by laughing. "OK. I'm leaving. Sheesh."

Yarbrough read and reread Betty's letters, and kept them neatly ordered in a drawer in his desk. In just a few weeks they'd exchanged nearly a dozen, each one revealing a bit more of their lives. When he got her picture, he was thrilled. She was so pretty, even better-looking than he'd imagined: "I think the picture of you is quite nice, and I think I can say, without hesitation, that you are very nice looking," he wrote. "I wish you could know how much a simple thing like a picture means to me. I don't guess it can be described, at least, not by me.

"You know, it's funny how two people can write to each other and become acquainted. It's also just as funny how or why they enjoy it. I guess it is because of the thought and spirit behind the gesture that makes it a go. What do you think?"

He described the air raids, and the anti-aircraft guns' great accuracy. "It is certainly a sight to see one of those Jap planes explode after being hit, especially if he still has his bomb load," he wrote. "They make a big orange-red glow, and then a few seconds after, you hear the noise of the explosion."

In one letter, he described the staff. "We have seven officers aboard, four are married and three are single. Three of the married officers have children. One of the single officers is engaged to be married and the other two, the skipper and myself, are as free as the wind," he said.

In another letter, he asked her for more pictures. "I wonder if sometime in your leisure, you could have another one made, and send it to me, so that I can get a better idea of your looks. If you sent me a whole bushel basket of them, you wouldn't hear a single peep, except of gratitude. That's about all these guys do out here, is flash their girl's picture in your face, and of course you'd like to have something to flash back at them," he wrote.

In one, Yarbrough wrote that he loved sports and was glad that she did, too.

"My roommate got a sports page from his girl, so I didn't miss out on the scores. He gets a sports page every week, so you really don't have to send one, unless you get some pleasure from it. I wouldn't want to deprive you of any pleasure you might get from doing things for another," he wrote.

He added that his "roommate was from Akron, Ohio, and he thinks no football teams can compare with those of the Midwest. Well, I can give him a little argument on that score, and I usually do. I constantly remind him of the four bowl teams that the SE Conference had in 1942. That slows him a little."

In her last letter, Betty had asked Yarbrough what kind of music he liked and more details about his family. He said he liked big band music. They had just gotten some "V-disc records and I'm having a good time trying to learn all the new songs. They sound sort of funny at first, but then they get better with each playing. I like Glenn Miller's 'Poinciana' and 'Fellow on a Furlough.' Do you like popular music?"

He told her he didn't smoke—not since he was ten, when his dad caught him and "gave me a whipping." He said he was a social drinker. "You know it is hard these days to find associations that are not delvers in whiskey," adding that that was one of the reasons he left his fraternity. He said his fourteen-year-old brother, Clarke, was the only sibling still at home. "He has just started dating girls and going to dances, too. Am I old? Whew!"

When Betty disclosed that she had some freckles, he said he didn't mind. "I like freckles, used to have some, wish I still did."

As he sat in his little steel room he couldn't believe how lucky he was. This pretty girl, from a good Southern family, was writing regularly to him, like they were a real couple. She wanted to know everything about his life. It felt so good to get her letters, to carry around her "snap." He felt like he was really one of the guys. He finally belonged, and he owed it to Betty Jones.

THE GALLEY WAS fragrant with roasting turkey, garlic, onions, celery, and sage. Bozarth and Vogel, fresh from their two-week stint at bakery school, pulled pies, cakes, and dinner rolls from the oven. It was November 23, Thanksgiving, and the gunboat was alive with holiday spirit.

This was a combination Thanksgiving feast and goodbye bash. Casaletto, the father of many children and butt of many jokes, was heading back stateside. The navy was building so many ships for the War in the Pacific, they needed veteran mechanics to sprinkle in with the greenhorns. The battle-hardened LCI corps was being raided to fill the gaps.

Casaletto was a perfect choice. He'd been with the ship since the beginning. Nash, Herring, and the other officers sang his praises; there was nothing he couldn't fix. And they were going to miss his big personality.

When Blow found out Casaletto was going, he was depressed as hell. So was Ball. What were they going to do without him? Blow took it really hard. Whenever he felt a little down, Casaletto was there. He didn't have to pretend to be a tough guy with him. He could be himself. Blow could talk about his mom. His girlfriend, how much he missed her.

"You crazy bastard," Blow said. "I can't believe you're leaving."

Casaletto told Blow it was for the best. Nothing had changed at home. At least now, he'd get to see why his kids weren't writing. He'd face the problem head-on. No excuses.

"You know what you guys mean to me. We'll always be brothers," he said.

But the transfer also meant something else: The military was throwing all its resources into an all-out push to Japan. The end was in sight. "Sooner or later, we're going to invade Japan, right?" Casaletto said.

No one really wanted to think about that. An invasion would be a suicide mission. But if an invasion was required, the navy was going to need more grizzled veterans on the new ships. No one would be surprised if Blow and some of the others on the 449 were transferred, too. Their paths might just cross again. Imagine that, Blow, Casaletto, and Ball hanging out in some juke joint in New York, San Diego, San Francisco. It could happen.

As the men gathered in the mess deck for the meal, Casaletto rushed to his room and pulled an autograph book from his locker. He had been keeping it for just such an occasion. Inside he'd carefully inscribed information about all the operations, where they had been, the dates. But it also had a section for sailors to sign their names, write their addresses, and leave a message.

Casaletto passed the book around the galley, and the men crowded around to sign. Beuckman wrote, "Hope we meet again." Bozarth wrote a simple "Good luck," and Arthur Lewis wished him "Best of all luck possible." Duvall's was a little sarcastic: "Good luck with the first five kids."

But Casaletto loved it. The laughter, food, and great company were the perfect way to end his deployment on the 449.

22

THE ROOM WAS crowded, the hour was late, but the officers were not sleeping. Corkins, Cooper, and Cromer just couldn't shake the blues.

They smoked. They took turns telling what they'd done the previous Christmas: a drive to Granny's house, the search for the perfect Christmas tree, midnight church, wrapping gifts into the wee hours. Not this year.

They'd all been strong young men on the rise, college-educated Midwesterners, sons of pastors, farmers, small businessmen, ready to take their places in the working world. They'd followed all the rules, married nice girls. Corkins had two young sons, Cooper a little girl, and Cromer planned to start a family soon. They were interrupted men, ripped from their comfortable middle-class rhythm and planted together on a tin-can boat in the far-away Pacific.

They missed their old lives in a terrible way. They were bored to tears, waiting for action, but secretly thankful they'd not seen much violence. They dreaded what they knew must be coming.

So far, the gunboat sat at anchor, or went on mail runs. They'd fire on caves now and then, up the coast. Japanese bombers occasionally swooped down to strafe U.S. positions or drop bombs. There was no guessing when the planes would appear. The men had spent a few nights at battle stations, but mostly they waited. They learned the minutiae of the gunboat and the navy, and wondered when the war would come and find them. They couldn't stay in Saipan forever.

Corkins summed up his feelings in a letter to his sister:

"I'll bet lots of fellows in the States who are working hard, long hours feel conscious of not being in the service, and yet, being in the service, I'm conscious of doing practically no work! I think Navy officers do less work than anyone in the world. I can rationalize a little by saying that when we are asked to work, the job is all important and probably carries more responsibility than people dream of."

While they weren't involved in any combat operations, "we probably will be later on," he said. He warmed to the writing, and described life on the boat.

"A lot of our time is occupied in getting fuel, water, dry provisions, fresh provisions, GSK supplies (ship supplies) etc. Being anchored out in a harbor there are no taxis or buses or streetcars. Every 2 hours (usually 3) there is a little LCVP small boat who acts as a taxi and makes the round of all ships to take you into the beach. To get from one ship to another (maybe just 100 yards away at anchor) can take 3 or 4 hours, catching the small boat, going into the beach, catching the next small boat out to your destination!

"I have a lot of letters to answer so will close. Tell Mom for crying out loud not to worry. It will be some time before we see any action, and even then her Billy Boy won't be making any landings (which is where most casualties occur). We're comparatively safe on our little ship out in the water."

Corkins wasn't sure that was true. There was always danger. That's why they were up so late. It wasn't only about missing their families, not being home for Christmas. They were thinking about not making it home at all.

They made a pact that night, just in case: If any one or two of them were killed in combat, whoever survived would contact the bereaved families and personally tell them what had happened. They all agreed.

Cooper and Cromer finally hit the sack. Corkins, though, decided to stay up. He walked outside on the well deck and moved to the bow. He knew he should be glad that nothing much was going on. They were safe for the time being. And the recent success of his beloved Ohio State Buckeyes should have given him a boost. The day after Thanksgiving, they beat

Michigan in the last game of the year, 18–14, to finish the season 8–0, 6–0 in the Big Ten. The Buckeyes finished second in the national polls, right behind Army.

But something bothered him. All that talk of death . . . he thought about his sons and wife, imagined their lives without him. They needed him. When he was a boy, his father was always there. He taught Corkins how to hunt for arrowheads and flints out in the fields. Their house was filled with music—his mother and sister played piano, and Corkins could bang out tunes himself. His parents' love and attention gave him the foundation to be successful at Ohio State, an A student, president of his fraternity, member of the student senate.

His boys deserved the same kind of stable home, Corkins thought. He was on the right track to provide that for them. But this business, this war . . . it was out of his hands. Something bad was going to happen, he felt, and there was nothing he could do to stop it. He went back to the room. Cooper and Cromer were sleeping. He tried to sleep, too.

IN ANOTHER BUNK in a crowded room below, Lemke imagined what his baby daughter might feel like in his arms. He'd cuddled some babies in his day, but he'd never held his own. When he got home she wouldn't know him. His wife would be a stranger, too. They'd only been together for a few months before he enlisted. Her letters were filled with the mundane: money, paying bills, diapers. It's not that he didn't want to hear it. It was just that out here, life was simple: Be smart. Follow orders. Stay alive. You couldn't think about anything else. If you did, you'd drive yourself crazy. You'd be vulnerable. And in the next air raid, or combat mission, you'd be dead.

Lemke wanted to get the hell out of the Pacific, but he dreaded the thought of going home.

It would be a big adjustment. He'd have to find a job, a place to live . . . he would have to learn how to be a husband and a father. He'd have to settle down, for the rest of his life. He'd been in the navy for a couple of years, he was thousands of miles from home, but he didn't feel like he'd seen the world at all. And once he got home, well. It would all be over for him.

Maybe he'd stop in at Park Falls first and see his dad. If anyone understood him, it was Fred Lemke. He knew what war was. His letters were always filled with good news: Don't worry about us here. Take care of yourself. Be safe, son.

Now surrounded by all this Christmas, he couldn't help but wax nostalgic. He remembered the snowy Christmas of 1936, when Park Falls first decked the streets with electric Christmas lights. Families walked through the fresh snow, and the gentle glow of the lights created a magical scene. They strolled Main Street, stopping to admire the displays in the storefront windows. At home they lit a candle in the window, a signal to the carolers.

The children were allowed to stay up late. His mom stirred hot chocolate on the stove, and when the carolers rang their doorbell, Fred Lemke was there waiting, with his children gathered round the doorstep. They always asked for "Silent Night" and "Hark the Herald Angels Sing." The kids shivered in the draft, and held their parents' hands while the music warmed the cold night air.

The choir then crowded into the kitchen for hot drinks, popcorn balls, and good wishes. Lemke felt warmed by the memory.

There never was much money, but Fred Lemke always made sure there was a decorated tree with a few presents underneath. Fred had seen firsthand the brutality of war. The very least he could do was celebrate the good in the world, make sure his family experienced the season's love and hope. He knew that without hope, there was no reason to live.

Standing on the deck, Lemke understood why his father went all-out for the holidays. It made sense. So Lemke decided not to let this holiday season get him down. He was going to make the best of it. If he was lucky enough to be home the following Christmas, he'd pull out all the stops. There'd be no reason for him not to.

NASH KNEW SOMETHING big was up. His boss, Commander Michael "Mad Mike" Malanaphy, had called a meeting to discuss a new military operation. The Philippines, probably . . . that was the logical guess. He was ready to go, wherever it was. Nash was thankful he'd had nearly three months to get acclimated to his new job.

Now a lieutenant commander, Nash was responsible for LCI Group Eight—twelve gunboats, five hundred men, and millions of dollars of government equipment. He had pushed for more responsibility, and now Nash had the authority he'd craved. He had no regrets.

He was busier than he'd ever been in his life, and enjoying the major perquisite that came with leadership: manpower. He had a staff. He issued orders, and they made it happen.

But he felt the weight, too. Many of the men had never been tested in battle. But the crews had also suffered casualties, injuries, leaves. He had to keep them all sharp, keep them trained, fueled, and stocked and ready to roll when the call came.

Nash knew Malanaphy would accept no excuses. Malanaphy was the commander of Flotilla Three, three dozen gunboats divided into three LCI groups: Seven, Eight, and Nine. The forty-five-year-old commander was a hard-charging, tough-as-nails navy vet with nearly twenty-five years of experience. Malanaphy's philosophy was simple: no obstacles, just challenges. He could call on you anytime.

When Nash was skipper on LCI-449, he'd bounced ideas off Herring. On the LCI-457, he had been doing the same with its skipper, Lieutenant Junior Grade Jerome O'Dowd. Although Nash was older, they had a lot in common. They were both from the Midwest, and O'Dowd, who'd graduated from Notre Dame in 1941, wanted to be an attorney. Both were sticklers for protocol. When Nash asked O'Dowd to take care of something, it was as good as done.

Still, Nash missed Herring's affable, easygoing manner, and those late-night bull sessions. He had checked in a few times to see how Herring was doing as skipper. They'd ended every conversation the same: When this mess was over, they'd go sailing.

Nash didn't see that happening anytime soon. He was under no illusions the Japanese would surrender, and if there was an invasion, they would be on the front lines.

Still, Nash didn't want to worry his family. In letters home he tried to downplay the dangers. He stuck with the day-to-day of life on a ship:

"My new quarters are much larger than the old, somewhat cooler and all in all, more comfortable. As before, I have a good 'sack' complete with inner spring mattress and a light for reading. My predecessor had things well organized so most matters are routine," said Nash. He harkened back to his sailing days with one complaint his parents would understand: "I don't get to conn the ship now, but guess I won't forget how."

He missed Saginaw, he said, mostly the change of seasons.

"One disadvantage of the climate here is that . . . we don't have the seasons in the normal sense. At present it is hot, when it isn't raining. The good cool October Michigan nights would seem most pleasant for a change."

He pined for the comforts of home, especially "a tub (bath) with plenty of hot water, and a cold glass of milk," he wrote. "Wouldn't want you to think that I don't keep clean or get enough to eat. It's just that fresh water must be conserved and that there are few cows and no pasteurization plants in this part of the world."

With Christmas so close, he wanted them to know he was well. He'd seen a few movies, including *Gaslight*, a thriller starring Ingrid Bergman. "Things are much the same as usual," he assured them.

"If I were home I would probably be getting ready to begin my Christmas shopping . . . There is very little here on which to spend money," he wrote.

He wished his parents a Merry Christmas, adding that he didn't want a thing. He only had one wish: "Will be looking forward to a white Christmas, Saginaw, namely, in 1945."

BETTY JONES SCRAMBLED to get ready. There was so much to do, running from one Christmas party to the next. The tree was up, decked with colorful lights. The front porch was wrapped in red ribbons; a wreath greeted people at the door. Betty was happier than she had been in a very long time.

Almost every other day, she'd open her mailbox and find another letter from Byron. And when she did, she'd rush to her desk and respond. Their letters were getting longer as they shared more of the intimate details of their lives. She'd never enjoyed correspondence so much.

Her mother didn't know what to make of it: Betty was talking about Byron so much you'd think he lived down the street. She didn't complain about working late at the pharmacy, and she did all her chores without being asked. She sang along to songs on the radio, and stared off into the distance at odd moments. It almost seemed like she was in love.

At night she re-read the letters while the radio played romantic songs. Sometimes she'd close her eyes, and she was there.

He wrote there'd been more air raids than usual, but she shouldn't worry.

"The other morning about nine, we had a 'Flash Red,' (radio code for General Quarters.) A Jap plane came in at about 5,000 feet, and it happened that one of our P38's was soaring around up about 10,000 feet. Well, when the P-38 got the word on the Flash Red, he came tearing down out of the sky, right on top of the Jap and got him with the first burst. Then in about five minutes, there came a 'Flash White' over the radio (All clear.) That's it. It was the first daylight raid that we have had, and I don't mind those kind at all," he wrote.

He complimented her for "catching on quick" to "naval terminology," which she began sprinkling in her letters.

"I will try to keep you informed from time to time on the different terms. Here's a rather humorous one some of the crew have been using rather frequently. When they see a good-looking girl in the movies, they speak of her as 'some lash-up,' or 'wotta lash-up.' In the Navy, to lash something, is to tie it together. Do you get the idea?"

"I'm Asiatic: Navy for 'crazy' . . . 'Lagoon Happy' is another term with the same significance."

They both liked dancing, but nothing too wild. "I'm very much like you," he wrote. "I have never learned to 'jitterbug' and I like slow, sweet tunes to dance by. I was always crazy to learn to 'jit' but I like the sweet music best of all." But he said he liked swing: he rattled off three songs he'd just heard on the gunboat that he really liked: "I'm Alone with You" by Jimmie Lunceford, "I'll Remember April" by Charlie Spivak, and "All of Me" by Count Basie. "The last one is an old tune, but an especially good arrangement," Yarbrough said.

He warned Betty there might be times when he couldn't write so much because of his duties.

"Betty, I suppose you will have to be patient with me," he wrote. "I will write as often as I can, but there will be times when I won't be able to mail the letters. I hope you understand."

Betty wasn't worried. So far, Byron's letters had been arriving on a regular basis. Sometimes, though, she could see his pessimistic side slip into his sentences.

"I am getting along so well lately, that I am looking for some sort of a letdown. You know how people have their ups and downs and I'm no exception. Well, I have been up lately, but I guess things are looking up all over the world lately, at least they seem to be temporarily. Can you understand this nonsense? I have just read over it, and I almost wish I hadn't put it down. I guess it's time for me to sign off when I get to writing stuff like that. Don't judge me too harshly."

Betty didn't. She knew what he meant. Feeling so good was bittersweet at times, when you knew it all might end in heartbreak.

Likewise, Betty disclosed to Byron that friends and family teased her for still being single, that she was in danger of becoming a spinster.

Byron told her not to worry. "I think those people are just jealous of your good sense. They know that you can catch somebody just by wiggling your little finger if you wanted to," he wrote.

She smiled when she read that line. Byron was so wonderful, understanding. But in his last letter, he hinted at something disturbing. "Things are pretty quiet here lately. We haven't had an air raid for some time now. We still have our card games and Pepsi Colas at night, although the Pepsis have run short of late. Something big is coming up before very long, and if it comes, I probably won't be able to write you for a while."

He didn't elaborate, but all the signs were there: new supply ships arriving daily in Saipan, the sudden increase in meetings between the skippers of the gunboats and commanders.

He didn't want Betty to worry, but she could tell he was going through one of his "down periods."

"The way I feel right now, I wouldn't give you a nickel for this life. I suppose in peace time the Navy wouldn't be so bad. What I don't like is being away from your people so long."

Betty's heart melted. She wished she could be there with him, hold him, tell him that everything was going to be OK. Instead, she did the next best thing. She started writing another letter. Hopefully that would cheer him up.

THE MENU WAS mimeographed and distributed over the boat: roast turkey and chicken, English peas (canned), mashed potatoes, plum pudding, sliced bread with butter, canned peaches, and two kinds of cake: fruitcake and a yellow cake with green-and-red frosting. The desserts boasted fresh fruit for flavoring, thanks to Beuckman. While picking up hospital supplies on shore, he'd detoured through the woods and picked lemons the size of grapefruits.

It seemed like half the U.S. Navy was docked in Saipan, and that added to the excitement. Signalmen on all the ships in the harbor spelled out "Merry Christmas" with blinker lights and flags. The base exchange sold fat cigars, and some of the crew were planning to break out theirs after dinner.

Herring was in the Christmas spirit, too, dressed in his formal whites, slapping the sailors on their backs, promising this would be their last Christmas away from home. Underneath the jolly surface he was worried. The new operation was going to start soon, after the first of the year. He was putting it out of his mind today. No worries. Not on Christmas.

It was time to get moving; everybody felt it. He'd had to step up discipline when crew members straggled back to the gunboat after curfew. Food went missing from the galley, and Herring ordered an inspection of all seamen's quarters. The missing items turned up in Arthur Guajardo's locker. The young sailor had reported to the gunboat only a few weeks earlier. His disciplinary hearing found him guilty of theft, and he was taken by Cromer and Yarbrough to the brig on the USS *Fulton* to stay until a court-martial could convene. On other ships the men were reporting for duty while intoxicated, coming back from liberty unable to stand up. A few nights earlier, when they were moored beside a larger ship, Herring and Yarbrough were awakened in the middle of the night by drunken shouts. A sailor on the boat beside them screamed, then fell overboard. The drunk fought off his rescuers, shouting that he wanted to stay in the water.

In their quarters, Corkins, Cooper, and Cromer were dressing up for the holiday feast, but they all felt a little worse for wear. They'd been up all night celebrating Christmas, decorating a little tree that Dotty Corkins had shipped them, admiring Billy Corkins's crayon-colored paper Santa. Their bunks were hung with cards sent from home. They'd placed all their wrapped gifts under the tree, and at midnight they opened them, mostly tins of cookies, cakes, and candy. They passed around the goodies, then sang a few Christmas songs before giving up and having "a bull session that lasted far into the morning."

Talking kept the loneliness at bay. They didn't want to feel depressed, but they couldn't help imagining the family waking up on Christmas morning without them. Little Rebecca Cooper was too young to care, but Corkins knew once his boys got up, they'd be leaping around like broncos. They were old enough to know that Christmas morning meant toys. He smiled when he thought about it.

He had expressed his thoughts in an earlier letter to his sister, Jane:

"You know darn well I wish all of you the happiest Christmas and New Year's you ever had, and just wish I were home to enjoy it too. But I am willing to be out here if I can be home for the rest of the Christmas's and won't have to be away again," he wrote.

He told her not to worry.

"I'm really in no more danger here than thousands of other fellows, and I won't feel in danger until we actually get in on an invasion," he said.

Like the other officers, he had a hunch that they'd be in action soon. After the feast, he intended to drag Cooper and Cromer over to the officers' club on the beach. Drinks were on the house today, and everyone knew there would be a "tremendous drunken mob on the scene."

Corkins looked forward to going, he didn't think he would drink that much. "My taste for anything alcoholic is down to nil. Had one glass of beer in the last month and didn't even relish it. Don't know what is the matter," he wrote.

YARBROUGH WAS IN the room puffing on a huge stogie when Bedell walked in. He'd just returned from the officers' club, feeling good after a few drinks.

Above: Ensign William Corkins was nearing thirty with a family to support when he enlisted in the Navy in 1944. He wrote vivid letters to his family about his adventures in the Pacific while he was on LCI-449.

WILLIAM CORKINS FAMILY COLLECTION

Left: Ensign Donald Cromer poses at his family farm in Indiana before departing for the Pacific, where he would join LCI-449. DENNIS BLOCKER COLLECTION

Private Fred Lemke sits on the hood of his ambulance in France, 1918. Lemke was a U.S. Army ambulance driver during World War I. But decades later, Fred Lemke would try to discourage his son, Clifford, from joining the U.S. Navy in World War II to spare him from the horrors of war. DENNIS BLOCKER COLLECTION

Above left: Ensign Frederick Cooper in his official Navy photograph. Just a few months before this picture was taken in 1944, the twenty-four-year-old Cooper was a high school history teacher and coach.

MARY AND REBECCA COOPER COLLECTION

Above right: Ensign Frederick Cooper and his wife, Mary, in happier times. The photo was taken in Orange City, Iowa, 1944.

MARY AND REBECCA COOPER COLLECTION

Left: Gunner's Mate Third Class Charles "Chuck" Banko was a teenager minding the family store in East Selah, Washington, when he heard a bulletin over the radio: Pearl Harbor was attacked by the Japanese. Banko enlisted after graduating high school and became best friends with another Washington native: Seaman First Class Bruce Hallet.

CHARLES BANKO FAMILY COLLECTION

Above left: Looking toward the gun deck of LCI-449, Gunner's Mate Third Class Hillman Ryan straddles the bow's 40mm gun, while officers mingle on the top of the bridge. The photo was taken during the Marianas Island campaign in 1944.

DENNIS BLOCKER COLLECTION

Above right: Seaman Second Class Robert Minnick of Akron, Ohio. One of the youngest members of the crew, Minnick turned down an offer to play minor league baseball to enlist in the U.S. Navy. He joined LCI-449 a few weeks before Iwo Jima.

ROBERT MINNICK FAMILY COLLECTION

Right: Gunner's Mate Third Class Howard Schoenleben, a tough kid from Chicago, Illinois, was already a combat veteran by the time LCI-449 reached Iwo Jima. Just before the last campaign, he received a letter on the gunboat that changed his life.

HOWARD SCHOENLEBEN COLLECTION

Steward's Mate Ralphal Johnson (left) and Gunner's Mate Third Class Ralph Owens (right) pose with a big catch. Johnson was the crew's only African-American sailor.

DENNIS BLOCKER COLLECTION

Seaman First Class Lareto Paglia was a promising student at the Maryland Institute College of Art when he decided to enlist in the U.S. Navy. He joined LCI-449 just days before Iwo Jima.

LARETO PAGLIA FAMILY COLLECTION

View of the gun deck and pilot house of LCI-449.

DENNIS BLOCKER COLLECTION

View from LCI-474 at Iwo Jima on February 17, 1945. Within two hours, LCI-474 would rest on the ocean floor. From foreground to background are LCI-474, 438, 449, 441 and 457.

LCI-449 and LCI-80 enter floating dry dock ABSD-6 at Guam, late 1945. In the months following the Iwo Jima mission, the new crew aboard LCI-449 would often find blood-tinged pools of water on the decks after storms.

Above left: Photographer's Mate Harry Leo McGrath in North Bend, Washington, where he helped his relatives run a family restaurant and hotel. An avid photographer, he had been in several battles before landing on LCI-449 at Iwo Jima.

HARRY LEO McGRATH FAMILY COLLECTION

Above right: Ensign Leo Bedell poses in front of the pilot house on LCI-449. The youngest officer on the ship, he would mature in a hurry at Iwo Jima.

LEO BEDELL FAMILY COLLECTION

Right: Crew of LCI-449 poses with a large barracuda caught in the Marianas Islands in 1944. (Sitting, left to right: William Hudson, Leonard Sless, and Hillman Ryan. Sailors, kneeling, unidentified.)

DENNIS BLOCKER COLLECTION

Officers of LCI-449 on the bridge. (Left to right) Lieutenant Junior Grade Rufus Geddie Herring, the gunboat's captain, Lieutenant Junior Grade Byron Yarbrough, Ensign Leo Bedell, and Ensign Frederick Cooper. The picture was taken in the Marianas Islands in January, 1945.

Ralph Owens (left) and Hillman Ryan on the port-side 40mm gun aboard LCI-449.

Right: Electrician's Mate Paul Vanderboom of Fond du Lac, Wisconsin, a veteran of the Marshall and Marianas campaigns, would find his courage tested at Iwo Jima. DENNIS BLOCKER COLLECTION

Below left: Pharmacist's Mate Henry Beuckman was the oldest member of the crew. As the gunboat's only medic, he was overwhelmed by the number of casualties at Iwo Jima.
HENRY BEUCKMAN FAMILY COLLECTION

Below right: Ralph Owens hailed from Prater, Virginia, and looked forward to marrying his fiancée, Nina, at the end of the war. DENNIS BLOCKER COLLECTION

Above left: Seaman First Class Bruce Hallett, a native of Wenatchee, Washington, tried to enlist in the U.S. Navy when he was seventeen years old, but his parents stopped him. When he turned eighteen, he joined and saw combat in the Marshall and Marianas islands.

BRUCE HALLETT FAMILY COLLECTION

Above right: Lieutenant Junior Grade Rufus Geddie Herring of Roseboro, North Carolina, as an original member of the gunboat. Beloved by the crew, he was the ship's captain at Iwo Jima and proved his mettle under fire.   NATIONAL ARCHIVES

Left: Lieutenant Junior Grade Robert Duvall of Frankfort, Kentucky, at home in Frankfort, Kentucky. He was a newlywed when he joined the crew just before the Marshall Islands campaign.

ROBERT DUVALL FAMILY COLLECTION

Seaman First Class Charles Hightower grew up in Russellville, Arkansas. By the time he turned nineteen, he had been in several major campaigns.

Seaman First Class John Overchuk loved the nightlife in Cleveland, Ohio. He was an excellent dancer, sometimes practicing with a broom. He was one of the leaders on the gunboat.

Seaman First Class Lawrence Bozarth was a man of faith. At night, he'd read his bible, and was usually joined by some of the men on the crew.

LAWRENCE BOZARTH FAMILY COLLECTION

Willard Nash was the first captain of LCI-449. An attorney, he was in his early thirties when he gave up his legal practice in Saginaw, Michigan, to enlist in the U.S. Navy.

WILLARD V. NASH FAMILY COLLECTION

Dorothy Wallace, a New York writer and publicist for CBS and *Life* magazine, worked with many of the big recording and movies stars during World War II, including singer Frank Sinatra. But it was a naval officer, Willard Nash, who would capture her heart.

WILLARD V. NASH FAMILY COLLECTION

Above left: Seaman First Class Clifford Lemke was too young to enlist when the Japanese bombed Pearl Harbor on December 7, 1941. But when he was old enough, he joined the U.S. Navy, leaving behind his pregnant wife in Wisconsin.

DENNIS BLOCKER COLLECTION

Above right: View from the gun deck of LCI-449. The 40mm gun on the bow is visible though the weapon is cover by a tarp.

DENNIS BLOCKER COLLECTION

Right: Seaman First Class Anthony Serine of Pennsylvania (left) and Seaman First Class Charles Hightower of Arkansas, were two combat-tested veterans on the gunboat.

CHARLES HIGHTOWER FAMILY COLLECTION

LCI-449 is lashed to the USS *Terror* as the sailors from the minesweeper evacuate the wounded from the gunboat on February 17, 1945.

Aerial view of Iwo Jima just before the invasion clearly shows the beaches (to the right of Mount Suribachi) where LCI-449 and other gunboats on the reconnaissance mission would meet their fate on February 17, 1945.

Above left: Betty Jones dreamed of leaving her home in rural Cordele, Georgia, to go to nursing school. But while working at her father's pharmacy she began writing to one of the officers on LCI-449. The decision would set the course for the rest of her life.

NANCY DUPREE COLLECTION

Above right: Three members of the original crew of LCI-449. (Left to right) Coxswain Samuel Anthony, Boatswain Mate Second Class Frank Blow, and Quartermaster William Vollendorf.

DENNIS BLOCKER COLLECTION

Right: Boatswain Mate Second Class Frank Blow was a natural leader. His decisive action at Iwo Jima saved lives on the gunboat.

DENNIS BLOCKER COLLECTION

Above: View from the gun deck of LCI-449 between the two 40mm guns facing the bow.

DENNIS BLOCKER COLLECTION

Left: LCI-449 in dry dock as it gets ready for action at Iwo Jima.

DENNIS BLOCKER COLLECTION

Right: Lieutenant Junior Grade Byron Yarbrough was the gunboat's executive officer. Raised in a prominent Auburn, Alabama, family, Yarbrough was a well-respected leader who took part in some of the bloodiest campaigns of the war.

NANCY DUPREE COLLECTION

Below left: Clarence Kepner was the gunboat's main cook. His four brothers all enlisted in the military after Pearl Harbor, and one was killed in Europe in the summer of 1944.

CLARENCE KEPNER FAMILY COLLECTION

Below right: Seaman First Class Clifford Lemke with his young wife, Eleanor, in Baraboo, Wisconsin.

DENNIS BLOCKER COLLECTION

"You know you're going to get sick, right?" Bedell said. "You're not supposed to inhale it."

Yarbrough smiled. "I won't get sick," he wheezed.

"Yeah, you will. You don't smoke cigarettes. You're not used to it."

Maybe Bedell was right. Yarbrough felt a little dizzy, and there was an awful hot-pepper taste in his mouth, like a platoon of Marines had stomped through. Yarbrough wanted to kick back and relax. His parents and family and friends had all sent him cards and presents, and the chow had been the best he'd eaten in a long time. The radio broadcast an Armed Forces Network Christmas carol program, and the boys on deck sang along to "The First Noel."

Yarbrough was filled with Christmas spirit. It didn't hurt that he was falling in love.

It was a little weird, feeling so strongly about someone you'd never seen in the flesh, but Yarbrough felt like he knew Betty just as well as any of these guys knew their sweethearts. She was sweet and decent and kind. She understood him and his insecurities. They liked the same music and movies. She was perfect. Yes, he didn't really know what she looked like. Still, he'd gaze at her snapshot over and over, and he could find nothing wrong with her looks.

Bedell sat curled in his bunk, scribbling a letter of his own.

"O Night Divine" suddenly stopped dead, right at the big final climax. A siren screamed. Air raid.

"Damn them," said Bedell, rolling off the top bunk.

Men scrambled to their battle stations, scanned the darkening skies, and waited for instructions. Anti-aircraft guns went poom-poom in the distance. Then were silent. A few minutes later, they received the signal: all clear.

Most of the ship went to quarters and off to sleep, but Japanese planes returned two more times in the night, rousting them from sleep and out to their battle stations to simply wait a half hour for the all clear. The men groused and cursed beneath a banner proclaiming "Peace On Earth."

THE NEWS HAD just come from Nash: The gunboats would leave Saipan on January 4, move north to Guam for two weeks of training and resupplies, then head west toward a new amphibious invasion, a really big one. The gunboats would play a major role. That's about all he knew.

This would be Herring's first combat mission as skipper. He had only two officers on board with combat experience. To make matters worse, he had just gotten word he was losing another key crewman. Ball was being transferred stateside to join a new ship under construction, just like Casaletto had a few weeks earlier. Ball would leave in twenty-four hours, on New Year's Day.

The military brass learned a costly lesson on D-Day in Europe, when too many of the landing troops were untested. Sowing a few combat-seasoned veterans in with the recruits would keep them all moving forward, lessen the panic, confusion, and losses. They needed to press every advantage, if and when Americans invaded Japan.

Military planners had been writing statistics, refiguring the numbers, trying to calculate how many Americans would be killed and wounded in each phase of the action. Predictions varied widely. It all depended on how the Japanese civilians resisted the invasion. That was the big unknown. If they resisted like the Japanese on Saipan, the Allies were looking at more than a million casualties. But nobody knew for sure. It was all guesswork, based on earlier battles.

When Herring told Ball to pack his bags, the radioman greeted the news with a whoop of joy. Stateside!

Herring said he wished Ball the best, and would miss him. He was the best damn radioman in the navy. Ball smiled, snapped a salute, then turned and left the cabin. On his way to his locker he realized this meant goodbye to Blow and all these guys, the people who'd shared his life so closely for so many months. Ball had been on the gunboat since the beginning, and he'd likely never see it, or the guys, ever again.

Like they'd done at Christmas, all the men on the ship talked about New Year's Eve, and how it was done back home. Some were hoping to make it to shore, to see the year out with some drinks.

Ball told Blow his good news—the last night of 1944 would also be his last night on the gunboat.

Blow tried to be happy for him, but Ball could tell he was depressed. It was tough to take. Blow had lost Casaletto, and now Ball. Who next? A bunch of guys had been transferred just before the Marianas campaign, too. Some of the old crew were still here: Beuckman, Vollendorf, Vanderboom, Johnson, Kepner, Lewis. But there were so many new men now, he didn't know all of their names. More were set to come in the next few weeks.

Blow opened his locker and plunged his hand deep beneath the rolled-up laundry. He grabbed a big bottle: Scotch.

Ball smiled. It had become a tradition: Good or bad news, they'd pass around a bottle.

"This is good stuff. At midnight, if there's no alert, let's break this open," Blow said.

"I'll be here," Ball promised.

The sun set, the gunboat fell quiet. Bedell was at the officers' club with "the C men." Yarbrough didn't go to shore. He didn't drink, and he was scheduled for the late-night shift. He stayed in his quarters, writing to his girl. Just a short letter. He had others to write.

He told Betty he'd received a letter from his mother and it made him miss home. She'd described all the Christmas preparations, gift wrapping, pie baking, tree trimming, all the things of "Christmases of the past at home." He'd asked his father to write to him, but he didn't. "He is getting so old and I love him so much, that I forgive him anyway," Yarbrough wrote. "Just wait until you meet him, and you'll see what I mean."

He described what his sisters and brother did over the holidays. He encouraged her to tell him more stories of her family.

Then he got serious. "There is quite a bit of activity here, although it's nothing I can write about. But something is coming off in the not too distant future," he said.

Up on the bow, Bozarth had a spectacular view of the harbor. Midnight drew closer, and the ships started shooting rocket flares into the sky, red, green, blue, and yellow. The signalmen climbed up onto their towers and blinked their lights into the night, spelling out "Happy New Year." Voices whooped and shouted across the water. It was like the Fourth of July. As usual, some of the crew asked him to go ashore, but he, like Yarbrough, took the midnight shift so they could go out and have fun.

He didn't feel like celebrating all that much. His mind was on Elaine, the wonderful New Year's Eve they'd shared exactly a year ago, the beach, the embraces, the way the hours passed so fast. He'd been so excited to think they could be a couple, maybe even get married someday. He still held out hope.

For now, there was nothing to do but enjoy the fireworks. Soon it would be January 1, 1945, a whole new year. And maybe, with God's help, the war would end, and they could all go home and get on with their lives.

PART THREE

ISLAND X

23

HERRING CLIMBED THE ladder to the bridge and felt the ship moving under him, turning, picking up speed. Though it was early, his shirt was already soaked through. The heat had kept him awake. He'd drop off for a little while, but then a tide of salty sweat seeped under his eyelashes and stung him awake again. It wasn't just heat, he knew. He was anxious.

They were headed for Guam, that much he knew. After months of "hurry up and wait," they'd head out for "God-knows-where." Herring, Yarbrough, and Duvall had spent many empty hours looking for clues in the maps and directives. They finally gave up. There were just too many islands and atolls out there. And in the end it didn't matter if their guess was right or not. They wouldn't know where they were going until the brass hats were ready to tell them. After days of paperwork and guesswork, supplies and schedules and practice drills, they'd go, ready or not.

The gunboat left Tanapag Harbor behind. Herring let his mind ramble once again over all the possible invasion scenarios. He kept hearing Nash's words: Be prepared. But that was hard to do when you didn't have all the information.

The uncertainty was wearing on Yarbrough, too. The new officers peppered him with questions. This was the first invasion for most of them. Yarbrough understood their angst, so he tried his best to ease their fears.

Bedell asked about what happened in the engine room during combat. The crew down there said the blasts of the big deck guns reverberated all the way down to the keel, but the men inside the boat usually had no idea what was happening topside. Bedell asked if he should worry. How would they know?

Yarbrough just told Bedell what he already knew: During combat, the engine room was in almost constant contact with the pilothouse and the bridge. Bedell's job was not only making sure the engines were running, but to keep close contact with the officers above and the crew below.

"You'll know what's going on," Yarbrough said "You'll be on the horn. Blow will be moving all over the boat, reporting to you and me and everyone else. He reports to you first. You'll know what's happening better than anybody."

"But what if things get so busy topside that nobody has time to come down and check on the engine room?" Bedell asked.

"That'll mean the ship's in big trouble," Yarbrough quipped.

That was not the answer Bedell wanted to hear.

FRED WALTON WAS a California boy. He lounged his long, tanned frame against the wall of the well deck, shirt off, face to the sun. He was six-foot-three, 190 pounds, blond hair—a lizard in the sun. He didn't know where Guam was, but what the hell. He was ready for adventure.

He'd only been on board a few weeks, but his easygoing optimism was an easy fit. When others complained about the heat, food, or loneliness, he grinned and told them, "It's not so bad.

"It could be raining," he'd say. "It could be a lot worse."

It's not as if he'd seen a lot of suffering himself. Walton was eighteen, handsome, the youngest boy in a big loving family. He had a good-looking girlfriend waiting for him back home in Pasadena.

Walton's two older brothers were in the service. His half brother, William Schade, was in the army, and had fought in the brutal Aleutian Islands campaign. His other brother, Bill Walton, was getting ready to graduate the U.S. Naval Academy in Annapolis, Maryland, and would probably be assigned to the Pacific. Fred Walton had felt he couldn't stay home if his two brothers were out there fighting.

When Fred said he was enlisting in the navy, Schade was beside himself. In 1943 he'd been in the middle of several fierce attacks that wrested two tiny Alaskan islands back from Japanese invaders. Thousands of American boys died there, or went home with parts missing. Schade felt he had to protect his younger brother from the horror.

So he wrote to his mother.

"Mother, if you let Fred go in this war I will never forgive you," Schade wrote. "There is no need for one of his age. Take it from me. I know. His going to school is much more important to the country. Anytime we can't lick the Japs without boys of his age, well, something is wrong. Please make him stay in school."

His parents agreed. They begged Fred to go to college, to stay out of the military at least until his draft number was called. He dismissed them with a wave of his hand. "Don't worry," he said. "Things always work out for me. You know that."

Walton was a good student, athletic and popular throughout high school. As a teenager, his talent for mimicry landed him a part-time job at nearby Walt Disney Studios as a voice extra for Donald Duck cartoons. He still had friends at John Muir High. In November 1944, he sent a letter to the football coach, asking him to read it to the team before their big game with arch rival South Pasadena.

"We are all buddies fighting for the same cause whether it be on a battlefield or on a gridiron—that cause—Victory . . . I feel like I know each and every one of you. So fellas, while you are in school, love it, learn to appreciate it and make the best of it," he wrote.

The Muir High–South Pasadena match was Southern California's version of the "Army-Navy game," he wrote, a "grudge battle built up through many years of competition."

"Win it! And with it the right to say your team is City Champs!" he said.

And then there was Betzi. Betzi Smith, the prettiest girl in the graduating class . . . she sent him pictures, letters, and poetry.

Walton's path to LCI-449 was filled with good fortune. He was sent for basic training the summer of 1944 to San Diego, near enough to home for his parents to visit him on weekends. Walton shipped out for Pearl Harbor in September aboard another LCI, and lingered in Hawaii for a few months before joining Herring's crew.

Along the way, Walton took in the sights and sounds, all of which he chronicled for his parents.

"Boy you would die laughing at some of the things these guys do out here to amuse themselves," Walton said about the crew of the 449. "Some guys get yo-yos and go around all day playing with it like a kid. Even some of the old boys on the ship going around going—beranggg, beranggg—with the yo-yos (ha ha). You ought to see all the pin-up girls on the bulkheads of movie stars—Yo! Boy it makes a guy think of home (yummmm!), ha ha! Oh by the way Yo is a new expression used by us salts. It's just a way of expressing yourself when something excites a guy!"

He carried around a pocket-sized book where he wrote down his thoughts. He said he had enlisted because he would do anything for "Old Glory." Besides, being in the navy "makes a man of you."

The crew liked being around the fun-loving kid. His hair was too long for regulations, but he still couldn't quite raise a mustache. "I haven't had a haircut since I left Pearl, but I don't care," he wrote his mother. "A guy can be sloppy out here and it doesn't hurt his pride because there is no one to see him."

The only thing Walton didn't enjoy was being away from his girl.

In a letter to his parents a few days earlier, he'd told them he was excited about receiving two letters from Betzi.

"Oh wonderful day," he said. "She is so wonderful and I love her very much. One of her letters sounds very encouraging. Sounds like maybe she sort of loves me, I hope. Also she sent me two snapshots of herself. Boy she is beautiful. She was wearing a bathing suit, Woo! Woo! What a figure . . . Ha Ha! I'm a bad boy," he wrote.

In the same letter, he reminded them of his upcoming birthday: February 6. "By the time you receive this letter I will be 19. Getting old," he said.

"I am healthy and well," he reassured them, "thinking of you constantly and loving you both."

THE GUNBOAT PULLED into the dock at Apra Harbor, Guam. From his perch on deck Lemke scanned the port. There by the portage, waiting to board, was a big man with a familiar face: Overchuk! He'd been away since September, so long that Lemke thought he might've been reassigned.

Lemke had missed his friend in the months since. He kept to himself, did his job, played cards with the guys. Most of the time he blended into the background.

He was glad to see his friend was back—he needed to tell someone about his nerves. Lemke felt tense all the time. Some nights he didn't sleep, he was afraid to close his eyes, his dreams were haunted by images of dead bodies floating on the water. Sometimes, he'd jump up from his bunk, disoriented, unable to remember where he was.

Back when the dreams started, Overchuk was there. He'd always been there. He knew, and didn't tell anyone else. "Stop thinking about it," Overchuk told him. "It's over now. In the past. You're gonna be fine." His simple words had a soothing effect.

But that was months ago. Lemke wondered whether he could still lean on Overchuk, who would still be grieving for his mother. Lemke couldn't imagine what it would be like to lose a parent, especially his father.

Lemke knew now his father had done the right thing when he stopped him from enlisting just after Pearl Harbor. The Marianas campaign had given him an idea of what his father might have gone through in World War I, and why those nights spent reading the newspaper at the kitchen table got the old man so angry. Lemke didn't regret enlisting. The nation's freedom was at stake, and every man had to do his part. But even though he'd suffered no physical harm, Lemke knew the things he'd seen had injured him inside. He would never forget, hard as he tried. Maybe with time.

Overchuk stomped up the steps and boarded the 449. The sailors mobbed him, shook his hand, slapped him on the back, peppered him with questions about the States. What was it like, being back home in Cleveland?

Overchuk shrugged. "It's the same, but different," he told them. He hadn't been home since early 1943, but the city was still steeped in patriotism. Storefronts were covered in war bonds posters, and newspapers were still filled with stories from the front. But Overchuk could sense that the mood was changing.

Two years earlier, there had still been uncertainty about the war. No one doubted America would be victorious, but the burning question was "How long can this go on?"

Nowadays he saw widespread optimism that war could be wrapped up by the end of 1945. The Allies in Europe were on the outskirts of Germany. The Pacific was a slog, but U.S. forces were making slow, steady progress toward Japan. The Axis powers were on the run. It was just a matter of time before U.S. forces surrounded the Japanese mainland.

The newspapers at home let themselves imagine life without war: How would the war change the world's geography, economy, and politics? What would happen when all the veterans returned home? Would there be enough jobs and housing for them all?

Overchuk thought it was silly to think that far ahead. He knew the War in the Pacific wouldn't end in 1945—not if American forces had to invade Japan. Even with flags flying from every home, many of the families living inside were weary of war. So many men had been killed. So many families were praying for loved ones to return intact. They couldn't keep it up forever.

As Overchuk headed to his quarters, he caught up to Lemke near the deckhouse. "Glad to have you back," Lemke said. "I saved your bunk for you."

Overchuk smiled. "It's good to see you," he said.

They walked into their room, and as Overchuk unpacked his seabag, Lemke gave him a quick update. The gunboat hadn't seen any action since he'd gone, except for a few air raids. They were on a new mission, but nobody knew where. Casaletto and Ball and a few other sailors had gone, and replacements had arrived, including three officers. More seamen were expected to join the gunboat before they left Guam.

Overchuk sat on his bunk. He didn't like the idea of heading into combat, but staying busy was the best thing for him right now. If he had too much free time, his mind inevitably re-ran details of his mother's death and scenes from his visit.

His mother had collapsed as she was dictating a letter intended for Overchuk to a family friend. She was taken to the hospital, where she faded in and out of consciousness for four days. Just before she died, Margaret Overchuk asked a patient in the next bed to relay a message to her husband: She had hidden a diamond ring and some money in the house, just in case the banks failed like they did during the Depression. The hospital called Alex Overchuk, but his wife died minutes before he got there. The patient disclosed Margaret Overchuk's last words.

By the time John Overchuk arrived from the Pacific, his mother had already been buried. But his family took pictures of the funeral to show him, including his mother's still, pale form. As Overchuk looked at the pictures, his father, a tough steelworker, began breaking down in tears. If Overchuk didn't stay busy now, he'd cry, too.

GUAM WAS A tropical shopping district, and Corkins and Cooper were tourists, scouring the markets for souvenirs and trinkets for the folks back home.

They'd been ashore for only a few hours, and they were in no hurry to get back to the ship. They ambled along narrow dirt roads lined with coconut groves and banana plants with broad, green leaves and long bunches of fruit hanging low. Vendors hawked papayas, guavas, and vegetables from little stands made from wooden crates. Other merchants peddled bracelets and necklaces crafted from seashells and pearls.

The officers were welcomed everywhere they went. The Chamorros, the island natives, felt at home with Americans—Guam had been an American base before the Japanese invaded in December 1941.

"This is the life, huh?" Corkins said.

"I have to keep reminding myself I'm not on vacation," Cooper said.

Just six months earlier, the island was in Japanese hands. American forces spent nearly three weeks liberating Guam, and casualties were high on both sides: More than 18,000 Japanese were killed, and nearly 7,800 Americans were killed or wounded.

Since then, the U.S. military had been rebuilding the piers, docks, and facilities. As the locals emerged from hiding, the truth came out, too: stories of Japanese atrocities circulated freely.

During their short occupation the Japanese or their agents had tortured or murdered hundreds of people. They beheaded American prisoners of war, killed a Jesuit priest, and raped and tortured countless Chamorros.

The Japanese not only terrorized the people, they forced the Chamorros to learn their language, customs, and songs. But the Chamorros always believed the Americans would return, and they wrote their own ditty that they'd secretly sing in their homes: "My dear Uncle Sam, won't you please, come back to Guam . . ."

And when the Americans did, the troops were treated like royalty. Corkins and Cooper enjoyed the full benefit of their welcome.

Corkins bought his wife, Dotty, a simple pearl bracelet. He didn't have to haggle. It was just a few bucks—pearls held together by a strand—and he knew it would cost ten times that amount at home. He kept his eyes open, searching for a souvenir for his nephew, Champ. His sister Jane's kid was always sending him coloring-book pictures. Corkins's section of wall was papered with them, a collection of scribbly cartoon characters and nature scenes. He wanted something special for the little guy.

In a letter to his sister, Corkins asked the boy what he wanted: "Champ, if there is anything you would like to have from out here, write me and let me know. Some things I can get for souvenirs, but other things like Jap pistols and swords and flags are hard to get now. But maybe if you have something in mind I might be able to find it sometime."

He hadn't heard back yet, but he knew the kid probably wanted something flashy. He felt a wave of frustration roll over him—he longed to pick up the phone, dial his sister's number, and ask her himself. Imagine, calling his own sons, just hearing their voices!

The time away was getting harder for Corkins. He missed his family, and secretly wondered if he'd made the right decision. He'd wanted so much to be part of the action, to get out there and fight . . . but he hadn't counted on the loneliness. His early letters to family and friends were filled with optimism and tales of adventure. But lately, he was dispensing wisdom to family members like he was a wise old man in Shangri-La.

In a letter to his sister, Corkins said he was happy she was enjoying her new job, but "don't neglect your home life any. If the occasion ever arises where you are taken from it, you'll certainly regret it. Just one quiet evening at home, listening to my records, watching Dotty and the kids, and maybe pitching a little woo, would seem like heaven now," he said.

He didn't want to think about home. Not now, on this beautiful day, in this lovely place. Corkins threw himself into chattering, talking about what it felt like to become a father. Cooper strode alongside, nodding, wondering if it felt any different when the baby was a boy. The two friends were as opposite as they were close. Corkins could talk for hours on any subject—sports, history, politics, family. But Cooper was more reflective. He didn't say much, but when he did, it carried some weight. Like the time he stopped Corkins from going on a bombing run.

While they were on Saipan, Corkins visited an airfield and toured a B-29 bomber. The damn thing was impressive. The pilot gave him the dimensions: 99 feet long, with a wingspan of 141 feet. Four engines with a maximum speed of 357 miles an hour. Its big belly could carry up to 20,000 pounds of bombs. Corkins was so excited he asked if he could tag along on the next bombing mission over Japan. The pilot said "sure thing."

Corkins was over the moon. He told Cooper all about the plane and the pilot and the mission, and was a little miffed when his friend told him not to go.

"If the plane gets shot down and you get killed, your family won't collect on your life insurance. It's an unauthorized mission. Not worth the risk," Cooper told him.

Corkins thought about it. His friend was right. He swallowed his enthusiasm and passed on the flight.

Corkins knew he was fortunate. He had two people in the navy he trusted: Cooper and Cromer. They were roommates in training and shipmates on the gunboat. At night, they were like friends on a sleepover, sometimes talking until dawn, forgetting they were in the middle of a war in the middle of an ocean.

When mail arrived, they often read portions of their letters aloud, sharing intimate details of their lives. The men could share among themselves the things they couldn't tell their wives, siblings, or friends: They were scared. They didn't know if they'd ever see home again. In the privacy of their room on the 449, everyone understood the fear. It was safe to talk about it there.

Only once did Cooper let his true feelings slip to his wife. In a recent letter to Mary, he asked: "Will I ever see my 25th birthday?" In retrospect, he knew he should have crossed out the line, or crumpled up the letter and tossed it away.

He didn't want to do anything to scare her. He could tell she was trying to stay upbeat. She said they were doing well. His sister and the neighbors were helping with Rebecca. Everyone was pitching in. Please don't worry about us, she'd written. But how could he not worry?

Corkins noticed that his friend seemed a little distant. "You OK?"

"Yes. Just thinking of my little girl. I'm all right."

"Just making sure," Corkins said, as they turned into another little marketplace.

Cooper stopped at a jewelry stand when something caught his eye. He gently picked up a mother-of-pearl necklace from the little display. It was just what he'd been looking for.

"Damn, that's nice," Corkins said.

It was more than nice, it was stunning. Cooper imagined the long strand of pearls around Mary's neck. It was elegant, simple. It didn't matter what the necklace cost, he was going to buy it.

Cooper pulled out his wallet and handed the man twenty dollars, while Corkins examined the shiny white pearls with flecks of pink.

"How are you going to get it to her?"

"I'm going to mail it."

"You're going to take that chance?"

"Sure. If Bedell could mail an engagement ring, I can certainly mail a necklace."

Corkins laughed. "Sure. It makes sense."

It was getting late, but the men walked farther inland down a dirt road to a village of thatched-roof huts. A group of locals gathered at the foot of a coconut palm tree.

The people greeted the officers. Corkins asked what was going on.

"We're making tuba," one of them said. "Just watch."

A nimble old man shimmied up the tree trunk. He didn't cut anything down—he pulled together several of the flowering branches and bundled them in a bunch. He cut off the leafy end of the bundle and hung a bamboo pitcher under the cut end. Moments later, a white juice began to drain slowly into the "tuba," about a gallon a day, the villager said. Leave it alone long enough, and you'd have coconut-sap wine. It kept fresh for about three days. They all kept a jug in their huts.

The villager offered a swig to Corkins, who shrugged and lifted the jug. "What the hell," he said. "It's an adventure!" He took a long sip, scrunched his face, and swallowed it down. "Damn," he shouted. It tasted like corn mash before it's run through a still. He handed the jug to Cooper, who had the same reaction. The villagers laughed and clapped.

Corkins and Cooper could have thanked the villagers and headed back to the ship, but they decided to stay. The villagers brought out fish, bananas, and mangoes, and the people danced and sang as they passed around the tuba jug.

The sun was setting over the harbor, and the two officers looked at each other and grinned. The more they drank, they more they forgot. It was the perfect way to end the day.

BEDELL ROLLED OVER and opened his eyes. Yarbrough was at the desk in his familiar position, white stationery in front of him, pen in hand.

Bedell privately called that his "Betty-Letter Pose," but wasn't going to tease his friend or hurt his feelings. Still, Bedell was concerned about how deeply involved Yarbrough was, emotionally. How much could these letters really tell him about Betty? The guy was heading for heartbreak, but Bedell wasn't going to interfere. No advice unless asked, was his new rule. And the only advice Yarbrough was asking for these days was what kind of present he should buy her.

Bedell told him that a lot of the crewmen were picking up nice necklaces and bracelets from the natives. He'd go over shopping with him if he wanted. Yarbrough had already bought a collection of shells so Betty could make her own necklace. But he'd like it if Bedell went with him to get the rest of the chain and clasps. First, though, he wanted to finish this letter.

Bedell sighed. OK, he said. He'd close his eyes and wait.

In her last letter, Betty had asked Yarbrough if he liked the new Bing Crosby song: "The Day After Forever." He smiled. The lyrics reflected the way he felt about her: He knew that he wold be thinking of her "all day tomorrow" and whispering her name the day after forever.

"I have that record and I'm crazy about it. I have memorized the words, and I sing it in the shower," Yarbrough said.

And instead of surprising Betty, he told her about "the perfect gift" he was planning to send.

"In this particular area there are some very lovely shells, from which very lovely necklaces are made. I have heard them called Lao and Bugi. They are large, and some get as large as an egg. I have some smaller shells which are called Chigai . . . The larger shells range in color from yellow to dark brown, and the small ones are nearly every color. They all have a shine or gloss much like mother of pearl," Yarbrough wrote.

"I have seen the necklaces on sale out here + they range in price from $15 to $30. I imagine they would cost a pretty penny back in the States. It is very simple to make such a necklace, and at practically no cost."

He said he was sending the shells with instructions to make the necklace.

Then Yarbrough turned serious. Betty had asked for him to send a photo of himself. At first, he was reluctant—what if she didn't like what she saw? But in his last letter he had enclosed a couple of official Navy snapshots. He hesitated for a moment, but then asked her if she had gotten the pictures.

"You haven't spoken of them, so I just wondered," he said.

He stopped for a moment. In four months, she had become the focal point in his life. A letter from Betty was the bright spot of his day. Her writing was so vivid: She brought to life the small town of Cordele, the gossip, the fads, the petty irritations and joys. The fact that she was devoting so much time to writing only boosted his morale. Writing letters was hard work. They took time and energy. There was something special about her—and he wanted to tell her. No holding back.

"Betty, I must say that I am very impressed with you, probably more than you seem to be with me. I do think you can tell a great deal about a person by that person's letters, and it holds true, too. In censoring the crew's mail, I find out some things about their character that I probably wouldn't discover ordinarily. I wish you could know how much I am wishing for the time when I can meet you in person," he wrote.

"You know, I never had a girl that I could actually share confidences with, and somehow I feel that you are understanding enough to fill that place. That's how much you impress me—and just through letters, too. My only hope is, that you don't find me less attractive when we actually meet, until we do meet. Betty, I am going to express myself just as I feel, and I hope you will feel free to do the same," he said.

He was getting ready to sign off, but he wanted to answer a question she had raised in her last letter. She feared her letters were boring.

"You are just about to be reprimanded. You shouldn't say that your letters are dull because that is a gross misstatement. Your letters are more interesting than a Readers Digest and I demand more of them," he said.

Then he asked her for a favor: Would she write him every day? He knew it might be an imposition, but it would show him she was just as serious as he was. They didn't have to be long letters. Just a note.

He was finished. But before he folded the letter, at the bottom of the last page, he wrote for the first time: "Love, Byron."

He hoped she would notice.

HERRING HAD HIS orders. Nash had told him this was the big one, the biggest. Herring called his officers together in the wardroom to give them the news. Nash wasn't bullshitting.

One by one, Yarbrough, Duvall, Bedell, Corkins, Cooper, Cromer, Beuckman ambled in and sat down. Herring didn't waste time.

First, a week of repairs. The 449 would moor in Apra Harbor alongside the USS *Luzon*, a repair ship with teams of mechanics adroit at patching up crafts, getting them battle-ready. They'd get the same total tune-up they'd had in Pearl Harbor: electrical system, engines, propellers, pipes, guns.

After the repairs, another location—the staging area for the invasion.

The room was quiet. The men's faces were tense. There was nothing Herring could say to ease their fears.

"If the seamen ask, tell them the truth," Herring said. "Most of them already know we're getting ready for a new campaign. We didn't come all this way for a nice holiday cruise."

When the meeting was over, the officers went back to their quarters.

Corkins sat on his bunk. "Looks like we're in for the rough stuff," he said.

Cooper and Cromer sat silently. The men did not look at one another.

Before Corkins enlisted, he read everything he could find about the war. He watched the newsreels in the movie theater, sometimes staying after the feature to catch the news again before the second show started. They showed all the noise and smoke, but you never saw any blood. The same was true with the war movies themselves: Someone might die heroically, but you didn't see any blood and guts. Newsreels were heavily censored. And the movies? Well, it was Hollywood. In a war, people die, often in horrible, messy ways. From chatting with the sailors on board, from hearing them cry out in their sleep during the night shifts, Corkins knew the images of violence and sudden death stayed with you, crept into your thoughts, haunted your dreams.

They were fitting up the ship for combat. It was just a matter of time before they knew where the battle would be. What mattered was their assignment, their mission, what job they'd be doing during the invasion. Support, front lines, recon? That made all the difference.

The engine changed pitch, and the gunboat moved across the harbor. When it drew alongside the *Luzon*, the crew knew something was up.

Banko and Hallett turned to each other.

"What do you think?" Hallett asked.

Banko stood there nervously, stroking his long red beard. "Your guess is as good as mine," he said.

But they both knew. Everybody knew. But no one was ready to talk about it.

BEDELL WAS FRAZZLED after two weeks of keeping track of people. Once he got these nine new men aboard, he intended to relax a little.

The sailors looked up from their seats in the small boat alongside, taking in the steep, freshly painted sides of what would be their new home. Bedell needed to get them aboard quickly and get them situated. They were on a tight schedule.

The 449 would pull out of Guam in a few hours and join a great convoy of ships headed 850 miles southwest to the Ulithi Atoll in the Caroline Islands.

The ship was in great shape. Every piece of equipment had been checked and rechecked, oiled and machined by the *Luzon's* repair gangs. Meantime, the gunboat crew chipped off the latest paint and primed the steel for a new paint job: a camouflage of green, brown, tan, and black intended to blend them in with island vegetation and beaches. The white ID numbers on the bow were painted bigger, so other boats could identify them from a distance. The gunboats now stood out among the fleet of gray ships, like mallards in a domestic duck pond.

The ship was stocked with food and fresh water. Once the new sailors boarded, it would be set to go.

Bedell watched them climb up the gangway. They were kids, even more boyish than the last batch. Clearly, none of them had ever seen combat.

He greeted the men, told them "at ease," and waved to Blow to join him as nine seabags dropped simultaneously onto the deck. Usually, they'd escort them up to meet the skipper, but there was no time for that now. Bedell told the men they'd depart in an hour with other LCIs in Group Eight. They'd be spending most of their time on drills in the next few days, including gunnery practice. Get settled, he told them.

Blow stepped up and took the new men down to their quarters. Bedell headed to the wardroom, where Herring was briefing some of the officers on what was coming up. Work and drill schedules were going to be important.

On the way to Ulithi they'd have gunnery drills and tactical maneuvers with the other gunboats. At some point, Herring would meet with his commanders and discuss the operation in more detail. He would get the gunboat's assignment, the logistics. Only then would he share the information with the officers and, later, the crew.

They'd have a lot to do in a short time, but they'd be prepared for the battle when it happened, Herring told them.

Yarbrough, Duvall, and Beuckman had been through this before, so they'd get the new officers up to speed with all the pre-invasion exercises. Like Nash before him, and like all the other commanders heading into the fight, Herring wondered how the new sailors would respond to the mayhem of battle.

Blow wondered the same thing. He'd escorted the men to their bunks and talked briefly with them. Only a couple of them had even been on a boat before they enlisted. He had no idea how they'd act under fire. That was always the real test. He'd seen so many sailors who could bullshit about staying cool when enemy bombs were exploding around them. They were the ones who cowered at the first sign of trouble.

Of the nine who reported on board, one sailor stood out: Robert Raymond Minnick. He was a quiet eighteen-year-old, a tall, skinny kid who looked about fourteen. Minnick was an outstanding baseball player in Akron, Ohio. Someone told Blow that Minnick was so good that the Cleveland Indians had offered him a minor-league contract, but he turned it down to enlist. Blow was impressed.

After the men unpacked their seabags, Blow asked Minnick to take a walk with him topside. Bedell joined them, and they learned about the new kid.

Minnick was from Ohio. His dad abandoned his family before he was born. His mother remarried. He had four siblings.

"What's this I hear about you and baseball?" Blow asked. Minnick's face lit up.

He had been playing on the sandlots since he was little, from sunup to sundown. He played shortstop, and during his senior year in high school, a Cleveland Indians scout asked if he'd consider playing for one of their farm teams. But after talking to his family, he turned it down.

"How could you pass that up?" Blow asked.

"Because it wouldn't be right, playing ball when all my friends are getting drafted, or enlisting. I figure I'll get another chance after the war, if I'm still any good."

Blow and Bedell didn't know what to say. There was always a chance Minnick would return unscathed. But why take the risk when you had that kind of talent?

At that moment, Bedell knew he'd do everything to protect that kid. As a Cleveland Indians fan, it was the least he could do.

24

FELLOW FLOTILLA GUNBOATS chugged in formation fore and aft, with the sun glinting bright on the quiet sea between. Yarbrough smiled at the powerful picture they made, and was happy his anxiety hadn't dampened his appreciation for a pretty scene. They were a day out of Guam, getting close to Ulithi Atoll. Soon he'd know the plans, and know what they'd be facing. The unknown was the hardest thing of all, the waiting . . . the not-knowing was weighing on everyone.

The new officers kept asking questions: What was it like in combat? How close would they get to shore? Would they be in danger? Which position on the deck was the most risky?

All the new crew were doing that. Minnick ended up in the same quarters with Overchuk, who took him under his wing when he discovered the kid was from Akron. Along with Lemke and their other bunkmates, they stayed up late playing cards and talking. During one late-night conversation, Minnick turned deadly serious.

"How is it when you go into combat . . . and firing?" he asked.

Overchuk told a few vivid tales of Saipan, Guam, and Tinian—the endless night patrols, the deafening clatter and boom of the guns, the bodies floating in the water. "Well, it got a little hot and heavy, you know," he said. "But don't worry about it. You'll be OK."

But Overchuk could see Minnick's face was pale, his heart was probably racing. He wished he hadn't said anything to the kid.

Yarbrough tried to be careful, too. He'd probably told Bedell too much, but they were roommates and they spent a lot of time together. He knew Bedell could handle it. But with the other new officers, he wasn't sure. He didn't want to scare them. There was really no way to describe the sheer terror of battle, knowing that your life could end in the next second, the exhilaration and exhaustion.

Herring joined Yarbrough on the bridge. He peered through his binoculars at something that looked like a city in the middle of the ocean. Hundreds of battleships, carriers, cruisers, destroyers, oilers, transports, and supply ships were spread out across the horizon.

Herring turned to Yarbrough. "Take a look."

Yarbrough lifted his binoculars to his eyes. He was struck speechless.

They'd heard the navy was building a large base somewhere in the Pacific, a launching point for the eventual invasion of Japan. But as they drew closer, the sheer number of ships was something beyond their imagination. It was impressive and scary at the same time.

Standing by the deckhouse, Blow stared at the ships in the distance. He quickly turned to Bedell and asked: "I hope they're not all going our way." Bedell knew what Blow meant: If the ships were all taking part in the next campaign, it was going to be one massive invasion.

What they didn't know was that this was a different kind of navy base—a moveable shipyard.

Ulithi was a typical volcanic atoll with coral, white sand, and palm trees. Three dozen tiny islands surrounded a twenty-mile-long, ten-mile-wide lagoon with depths of up to a hundred feet—perfect for anchoring big ships.

After the U.S. Navy took control in September 1944, military planners began developing four of the islands. In just a few months, the navy built a small boat pier, a shop for maintaining and repairing landing crafts, and an airstrip for flying in air freight, supplies, men, and mail. They also created a recreation area on one of the islands.

Most remarkable were the floating dry docks with a mobile ship-repair service that employed thousands of fitters, welders, engineers, and electricians. As U.S. forces advanced toward Japan, the floating dry docks and mobile unit could move with them. Admiral Nimitz had called the mobile service force his "secret weapon" because it created repair facilities thousands of miles away from the nearest actual navy port.

The gunboat navigated Mugai Channel on the way to Berth 484, where they would stay for the night. The men lined the decks, fascinated by the sight of it all, the massive scale of what was to come.

ALL THE STOREFRONTS were shut tight for the night. If Betty Jones had had her way, she would have left hours earlier. She knew there was another letter from Byron waiting for her at home, and the expectation gave her a titillating little flutter. Every letter contained some new detail about her dashing navy officer, new clues about his feelings.

She knew her letters were lifting his spirits the same way. He told her so. In his last letter, he said he was keeping busy, keeping his chin up. "The minute you become idle, you start thinking about how long you've been out here, or how much you'd like to be at home, or you get to thinking about somebody you would particularly like to see. That's when old brother despair comes around," he said—her letters were a godsend.

Byron said Betty was good-looking, and he was always requesting pictures of her to show his shipmates. The thought gave Betty a much-needed lift. Every girl wants to be pretty!

"You should have more pictures made of yourself, as pretty as you are, because they are a source of pleasure to others, even if you don't know them," Byron wrote. "The one I have of you is in a picture folder of mine, and if it was not enclosed in a cellophane case, I know it would be worn through. I certainly do have a good time with that picture because other people don't know if you are my wife or what, and I don't always tell them. I hope you don't mind."

(Wife! He'd said wife!) No, Betty didn't mind. It's what she wanted. Everybody in Betty's inner circle knew about the pen-pal relationship, and some were even teasing her. At her bridge club they called Yarbrough "Betty's man." She just laughed. It was flattering. Betty certainly felt like his girl; he was always showering her with compliments. She was sure the new letter waiting at home had more words of admiration.

When she reached home, she grabbed the letter from the foyer table and bounded up the steps to her room. Door closed, radio set to soft music, Betty sat on her bed and read.

The beginning was typical Byron, formal, but jocular: "To have the privilege of writing to a nice girl like you, and to get such nice responsive letters in return, is something I've always dreamed of, but I never thought it would actually happen. I don't need to see you to see how nice you are. Your character is conveyed fully in your letters . . . I am so grateful for the gracious manner with which you have accepted me, as a friend + confidant."

Then he revealed the truth about his past love life—he'd never had one to speak of.

"I have always more or less steered clear of just one girl or a 'steady' as they call them at home. But now I am beginning to see what I am missing. I guess every 'guy' has to have his 'gal' to make things complete," he said.

Betty's heart started to melt. Byron talked more about his family— that there was a big age difference between his oldest brother, Pete, who was forty-four, and his youngest brother, Clarke, who was fourteen. He said he was glad Betty was close with her family. "I wish, sometimes, that our family were closer," he confessed.

He ended by saying he can "hardly wait for mail-call each day to see if I have one postmarked Cordele." And he ended the same way he'd started signing the others: "Love, Byron."

It was that sign-off, the word *love*, that was really getting to her. It had been so long since she'd felt like this about anyone. Everyone had been asking her for years when she was going to get married. Now there was hope. She even allowed herself to ask: What if it really works out with Byron? Maybe it was better letting a courtship develop slowly through letters than to be set up on a blind date. That way, it's not superficial, it's not all based on looks.

The only thing separating them now was the war. The news heading into early February was positive. Allied forces were in Germany now, and

U.S. troops in the Pacific were wrapping up the Philippines. Betty followed every detail. Surely, it would be over soon. She tried not to think about the danger. It was better to stay positive, listen to happy love songs on the radio. It would be spring soon, and time for the flowers to bloom, time for Cordele to come alive.

Betty moved over to her desk and sat thinking for a moment on what to say. In her last letter, she'd told Byron what the bridge club girls were saying. Now she was wondering if she'd done the right thing:

"I hope you haven't gotten the wrong idea about my letter . . . in which I told you the girls here in my bridge club were now calling you 'Betty's Man.' I've wondered ever since what sort of person you must think I am. I'd like to explain that Cordele is more or less the worst place in the world for pairing people off. When I was in high school if you had a date with a boy one time, you were then considered that boy's girl, and everyone else laid hands off," she said.

"Nowadays it doesn't matter so much, but it has been so long since people could pair me off with any one that when they found out I was writing to a Navy man that was all they needed. I've been worried for fear you would think me a very forward person. I'm not really, but it does make me feel very proud to know that the girls have all the fun they want to by calling you 'my man' so if you will take it for a while I won't tell them any different," she said.

She filled the letter with the mundane. Her mother was asking her to do more chores around the house because they were having trouble finding help. A family friend, a lawyer, seemed to quietly taunt her for being single. She detailed his latest slights and clumsy attempts at matchmaking: "I guess I'm fuming, but I have to make up my own mind about things and not have them shoved at me as he always has done," she wrote. "I'm glad now that I haven't found anyone, because if I were an old married gal, I couldn't write to you or you to me, could I? Or could you?"

Betty stopped and smiled. She'd save more for other letters. They had plenty of time. So she signed off:

"For now—Byron good night and sweet dreams and keep thinking of me because you're always on my mind. Please have the Navy hurry and send you home: Devotedly, Betty."

Much as Byron's use of "love" excited her, Betty wasn't ready to write that herself. She couldn't let him think her overly forward. She knew he could read it clearly enough, between the lines.

She folded the letter to the sound of violins, followed by Frank Sinatra's smooth baritone. She stopped. "When Your Lover Has Gone" was one of her favorite numbers, a torch song with melancholy lyrics: "When you're alone . . . the magic moonlight dies."

But tonight, Betty didn't feel sad at all. No, she was hopeful. When Byron returned, they'd be together. She was sure of it.

AN URGENT MESSAGE came for Banko: Herring wanted to see him in the wardroom.

"What did I do now?" he asked Hallett.

Hallett shrugged. "You seem like an A student to me," he said. "Not a lot of trouble around here to get into."

Banko was damned if he could remember doing anything wrong. He'd been on board since May, and he hadn't gotten into any trouble. It wasn't like his time on the other gunboat. Then, by his own admission, he was a troublemaker. He was always fighting with the boatswain, coming back late from liberty. He'd behaved himself here, but bad news travels. When you have a bad reputation, you're the first one they blame when something goes wrong.

"Wish me luck," Banko said.

"It's probably nothing," Hallett told him.

Banko shook his head as he walked to the deckhouse. He was only nineteen, but with his thick, bushy red beard and lines on his face, he looked like he was in his early thirties. As the gun captain on the bow, he could see trouble ahead. And he'd earned the reputation as being calm under fire. But now, as he knocked on the wardroom door, he was worried about why Herring wanted to see him.

"Come in," Herring said.

When Banko walked inside, he snapped a salute. But he could tell by Herring's smile that he wasn't in trouble.

"Sit down," Herring said.

Banko sat at the table, then Herring asked him a question: "How old are you, Banko?"

"I'm nineteen, sir," Banko said, puzzled.

"You look like you're thirty," Herring said. "Should've got some sunglasses when you were ashore. You've been squinting into the sun. Your skin's all dark. You're getting crow's-feet, you know?"

"I never was pretty," Banko said, relaxing a little.

"How long have you been growing that beard?"

Banko looked puzzled. "Umm, I'm not sure. Going on a year. I know it's not regulation."

"I didn't have any problem with it before, but now I want you to shave it," Herring said. "Keep it shaved."

Banko felt the fringe of fur along his jaw.

"Why now?"

"Well, we're going into action again, on an island much closer to Japan. Don't know where yet. But we have to be ready for anything, including gas. You wouldn't be able to put on a gas mask over your beard," he said.

Banko sat up straight. He was relieved: He wasn't being disciplined. He was intrigued—they had orders.

"I'll do it now, sir."

Banko stood, threw a salute, and bounded to his room. He picked up his shaving bag and a pair of scissors from his little sewing kit, and went to the head. He peered into the mirror. This was going to hurt.

But he took a deep breath, scissored off the worst of the scraggly hair, then lathered his face with shaving cream. A half hour later he was done: just a few cuts where the blade nicked him. He looked years younger.

The rest of the day was a series of pranks as he made his way unrecognized around the 449. No one had ever seen him without a beard. "They didn't know who the hell I was," Banko recalled. He made believe he was a new sailor just transferred aboard. When he walked over to a seat by the 40mm gun, Bozarth told him the gun tub was "off-limits to unauthorized personnel."

"It's me," Banko said, giggling like a little girl.

Bozarth stared at his face, then shook his head. "Banko?"

"That's right, sailor!"

"Wow! You look so different!" Bozarth cried. "You look . . . better!"

He knew he did. Banko decided he liked the clean-shaven look. Maybe it would help keep him out of trouble.

FROM THE BRIDGE, Herring could see the flotilla gunboats scattered along one side, the crafts carrying the demolition teams on the other. They were all headed in the same direction: a beach on Losiep, one of nearly three dozen tiny islands in the Ulithi Atoll.

The 449 was finally in action, even if it was only a rehearsal.

After a week of relative idleness in Ulithi, Herring was glad to get the men in movement. There were new men aboard all the gunboats, and plenty more among the frogmen. They had two days to work on the desert island, learning to coordinate ships, guns, and demolition teams into a choreographed fighting unit.

On the first day everything had gone as planned. Gunboats and the demolition teams' LCPRs moved in formation toward the shore. The gunboats, backed by booming destroyers in the distance, simulated firing their weapons. The frogmen rolled off their moving crafts and disappeared into the turquoise water, then emerged on the beach.

They were going to do the same maneuvers today. This time, however, they'd use live fire.

It was the best way to get the newcomers used to the sounds of war, Herring told his officers. The noise of combat—shells and mortars exploding, machine-gun fire—could rattle even the most grizzled veteran. The key was staying focused, keeping on with your work even as your heart pounded and the guns roared.

The entire group had to work as a team, he said. If one person on a gun crew panicked, that weapon could be rendered useless. He reminded them that the gunboats were the fist, the muscle. If the frogmen got into trouble, the gunboats would have to move in for the rescue.

Herring planned to watch the officers and crew closely as the guns blasted the island. When the gunboats were about two thousand yards from shore, Yarbrough stepped over to Herring. "They're starting," he said simply. Thump! came a thunder from the destroyers well behind them.

Herring braced himself. An odd silence filled the air as missiles passed overhead, then Boom! The bombs exploded on the ground beyond the beach. The gunboats picked up speed. So did the crafts carrying the frogmen. As they drew closer to the shore, the order came down and Yarbrough told the gunners "go." The 20mm and 40mm guns on every LCI suddenly leapt to life.

On the gun deck Cooper, Corkins, and Cromer watched the display. They'd heard weapons fired in boot camp, but this was another world, a ship in motion, the engines roaring, the guns so near and loud and continual, aftershocks rattling the deck underfoot and piercing their eardrums.

As the gunboats maneuvered back and forth along the shore, the demolition teams blew up obstacles and reefs. The only thing missing was Japanese soldiers and incoming rounds.

After eight hours of fireworks and war games, the flotilla headed back to Mugai Channel. Yarbrough found himself alone with the skipper, and asked him if he knew yet where they were headed, what they'd be doing. Herring said no, but there would soon be a big powwow to tell all the commanders at once. Action was only days away.

"You gotta assume we'll keep doing what we've been doing, what we did in Guam, what we just spent two days practicing," Herring speculated. "It's a specialized skill, covering the demolition teams. Otherwise, why would we all be here doing these exercises?"

The exercises got everyone's attention. Suddenly all the ships anchored everywhere, all the noise and racket and radio traffic, it all added up: Something big was happening. Cooper and Cromer chattered obsessively about the mission, while Corkins sat, strangely silent. Bedell walked and tried to change the subject, but that's all they would talk about. Cromer kept trying to make light of it all, talking about his biggest fear: "Getting hit and getting his balls knocked off," Bedell recalled. "He talked about it all the time. You just had to laugh."

When Bedell laughed, so would the others. Of all the things that could happen, that's what worried Cromer most? But Cromer had a point: The fear of the unknown scared the hell out of them.

When the others went topside, Corkins decided to write to his sister,

Jane. He'd already let his wife know that they were headed into action. He wanted to make sure his sister knew, too, but he wanted to keep the fact from their mother, who already was worrying herself sick. They all had to get their stories straight.

"Mom thinks we will go back to our original island and be stationed there for the duration, so I am going to write her that that is probably what we will do. Now I told Dotty I was going to do that, so you sort of hold the story up, too, and then maybe she won't worry so much," he wrote.

Corkins then wrote about Ulithi. No matter where he was in the Pacific, he told Jane about the landscape. This was one of the most impressive places he had been with the navy, he said.

"This is a pretty spot down here. The immense lagoon is formed by this ring of atolls, and they are nothing but long, narrow islands, composed of sand and palm trees and native huts. The natives have all been moved to another island so we see none of them. I don't know if I told you in my last letter, but we are seeing history made here. Today the ships in this harbor, right under my eyes, compose the largest collection of warships ever accumulated at one point in the history of the world! The roster reads like a Who's Who."

But then he stopped writing. He felt scared, and he didn't want that to creep into his letter. He didn't want to scare Jane.

The cabin forward was full of fragrant smoke. It was Yarbrough's twenty-fifth birthday, and he and Bedell were celebrating with cigars. They lit them up, but put them out after just a couple of puffs—too much smoke might stink up the place. They'd smoke the rest later. Bedell lounged on his bunk.

Yarbrough assumed his "Betty-Letter Pose," and started on another one. Bedell couldn't believe how many Yarbrough and Betty had exchanged. In the last month alone, Yarbrough had received nearly two dozen. He was surprised Yarbrough didn't have writer's cramp.

Meantime, Yarbrough was having trouble getting started. In her last letter, Betty had told him she loved his picture. That was a relief. But she still hadn't responded to his request about writing to him every day. That, he thought, would prove she was serious, that he was more than just a pen pal. Then he could take the next step in their relationship. Maybe she still hadn't received that letter, or her response was in the mail. Waiting was the toughest part.

The morning mail had brought him two letters from Betty. In one, she asked for advice about joining the WAVES. She'd heard a rumor that women might be drafted, and wanted to know what she should do. Yarbrough wanted to make sure she didn't enlist.

"Betty, when sister wrote me about you, she described you thusly. 'Byron, she is one of the most completely natural people I have ever met.' That characteristic has been displayed in your letters to me. I, for one, would like to see you keep that quality. Betty, here is what I'm trying to say: This is a big mean old world when you get away from the ones you love. So many people are just 'out for number one.' That is they are self-ish and greedy and unscrupulous. There are a whole lot of people in our armed forces who are supposed to be fighting the war. Instead, they are trying to beat Uncle Sam out of something. I am afraid you will see a lot of this, if you join the service. I have seen women in the service out here, and believe me, it is no place for women. In the meantime, if anybody asks you what you are doing for the war effort, just tell them 'I am keep-ing up the morale of a Navy Lieutenant in the Pacific' + believe me, you are."

Then he told Betty he lived to read her letters.

"Betty, you have an uncanny way of saying just what I want to hear in your letters, and so when I see one of your letters on my desk, I just take a 'time out' period and enjoy myself. You seem to be able to read my thoughts, if that is possible. Anyway I like it."

Then he once again told her how he felt about her.

"If I ever hurt you Betty, I assure you, it would hurt me worse. I am afraid to tell you how much I really do like you. Honestly, you are in my every thought and in my conversation a great deal of time," he wrote.

Then he made a birthday request. He wanted Betty to send him a five-by-seven photo of her from the "shoulders up, tinted, full face to sit on my desk and look at me while I write to its owner. That would be the answer to my fondest dreams."

Yarbrough read the line to Bedell.

Bedell rolled his eyes. "Sheesh, just ask her to marry you! What the hell are you waiting for?"

Yarbrough grinned. Not yet. Soon. Real soon.

IN THE DARKNESS before dawn, Seaman First Class Lareto "Larry" Paglia stood at the edge of the deck as his gunboat pulled closer to the other ship in the harbor. He squinted at the big white numbers on the bow: 449. His new home.

Paglia was anxious and sad. He was joining a new gunboat days before an invasion. Not a good thought. Just months earlier, he was in Pearl Harbor with LCI-1061. He felt comfortable on the gunboat. He was part of the original crew that sailed the boat in May 1944 from Bay City, Michigan, where it was built, down the Mississippi River to the Gulf of Mexico, through the Panama Canal to the Pacific Ocean, all the way to San Diego.

During liberty, they went to movies and nightspots. During one weekend pass, they visited Los Angeles, where they jumped from nightclub to nightclub, catching Count Basie in one spot and the Jimmy Dorsey Orchestra in another. They went to the Hollywood Canteen, where they spotted actress Bette Davis, and tried to pick up actresses. "You should have seen some of the swell looking girls," Paglia wrote his sister.

The fun continued when they reached Hawaii. During the day, the crew patrolled the islands, and at night they hit the bars. At times, it seemed more like a vacation than war.

So when his skipper told him about his transfer in November 1944, he was crushed. The captain said all the details were being worked out, but he would ride along on the destroyer USS *Radford* to a navy base in the Ulithi Atoll, where he would join another gunboat.

It was hard not to think about the combat to come. It didn't help when they pulled into Ulithi and saw hundreds of fighting ships.

This wasn't a place for an aspiring artist.

Only eighteen, Paglia was enrolled at the Maryland Institute College of Art, one of the most prestigious art schools in the country. The Baltimore native dabbled in different mediums, but it was his work in charcoal that captured the school's attention.

He dropped out of college after one semester to fight in a war that had been such a big part of his life. So many older men in his neighborhood had joined the military. So many had died. Now that he was old enough to enlist, he couldn't have lived with himself if he'd stayed in school.

After arriving in Ulithi, Paglia was transferred temporarily to the LCI-81. He took part in the invasion of Fais Island, a Japanese communication station about forty miles east of Ulithi. It wasn't much of a battle. The "defenders" turned out to be a handful of hungry Japanese soldiers hiding in a cave.

Paglia knew he'd been lucky as hell up until now, and he'd face more than a few Japanese on the next mission. He didn't forget the dozens of damaged ships he'd seen in Pearl Harbor, listing at anchor, waiting for space in the dry docks so they could be repaired. They had been pockmarked and blown apart by Japanese strafing runs or big coastal guns. Just thinking about those ships increased his anxiety.

Now here he was, on the last leg of the journey.

The deck guard on the 449 granted permission for Paglia to board. He jumped about a foot between the decks of the two ships. Paglia dropped his bag and took a moment to collect his thoughts, nervous about meeting the crew and his assignment as a radioman-in-training, a striker.

Blow, though, quickly greeted the new sailor. "Welcome aboard," he said to Paglia. He introduced himself, and told Paglia he'd take him to meet the skipper, and then escort him belowdecks so he could grab a bunk and put away his things.

Paglia nodded and stepped up behind Blow. Then a voice came from the deck behind him: "Paglia, is that you?"

He turned around and recognized the face. "Freddy!"

It was Walton. The two sailors ran to each other, embraced, and slapped each other on the back.

"You're a sight for sore eyes," Paglia said.

Walton and Paglia had served together on LCI-1061 and had become good friends. They drank countless beers under the stars in Pearl Harbor. The boys looked different, but had the same outgoing personalities. Walton was the typical Southern California teenager—tall, tan, and blond. Paglia was handsome, too, but handsome like a street kid from the East Coast:

barrel-chested, thick black hair, and a glossy mustache. They both loved to talk, especially about girls, even though Walton always eventually steered the conversation back to Betzi.

Walton never tired of watching Paglia paint watercolor landscapes of Hawaiian beaches, but his talent was also a great lure to young ladies. Sometimes on liberty, he'd set up his easel and art supplies at a spot along the beach. Whenever ladies gathered around to watch, he'd hit them with the line "How would you like me to paint your picture?" Walton and Paglia were a formidable team where picking up girls was concerned.

Blow turned to Walton. "I'll give you fellows a few minutes to catch up."

Walton was so excited to see his old buddy. "This is the best ship I have been on, Larry. The officers are great and the fellas are swell."

He added that the ship had been in combat all through the Marshalls and Marianas and that the crew was battle-tested.

Paglia frowned. "Do you know where we're going?"

"Nope. But the fellas are all telling me not to worry. We're shoving off in a couple of days."

"That's not long," Paglia said.

"Long enough to get your paints out. The sunsets here are spectacular," Walton said.

But as Paglia stood there, remembering all those damaged ships in Pearl Harbor, all he could do was fret. He couldn't paint when he felt like this.

"No, I don't think so," Paglia said. "I'm leaving them packed up, I think, till after the invasion."

25

THE GUNBOAT PULLED alongside the USS *Estes*, an amphibious command ship. The deck officer lowered an accommodation ladder, a portable flight of steps with a platform at the bottom. Herring and the other gunboat skippers scrambled up behind Stanley Hudgins, captain of the LCI-471. When Hudgins reached the top, he saluted the deck officer. "Request permission to come aboard."

"Permission granted," the man said.

Hudgins turned and saluted the U.S. flag. An officer assigned to shepherd the gunboat captains to the big meeting stood stiffly by while the men assembled on deck. Herring saw sailors scurrying from one workstation to the next. The *Estes* was huge, with several decks. It would be easy to get lost.

The *Estes* was a floating command post with all the latest communications equipment. The ship was nearly three times the length and width of Herring's gunboat—459 feet long and 63 feet wide, with a radar station, four towering masts, and rooms large enough for commanders to gather and plot out the next step in the war.

It also was the home of Rear Admiral William H. P. "Spike" Blandy, a tough-as-nails commander who had earned a reputation for getting things done. The fifty-four-year-old Blandy had graduated first in his class from the U.S. Naval Academy in 1913. He had worked his way up, taking part in the occupation of Veracruz, Mexico, in 1914, and then serving on the battleship *Florida* during World War I. Blandy specialized in navy gunnery and ordnance, working in the late 1920s in the navy's Bureau of Ordnance gun section. In 1941, as the youngest rear admiral, he was appointed chief of the Bureau of Ordnance, where he served until 1943. He was instrumental in developing and adapting the Swedish Bofors 40mm and the Swiss Oerlikon 20mm anti-aircraft weapons. He had been at Normandy for D-Day, taken part in Marine landings across the central Pacific, and had a new title: commander, Group 1, Amphibious Force, Pacific Fleet.

Now Blandy was taking on even more.

With the Island X campaign, Blandy had become the first commander to coordinate all pre-invasion amphibious operations in a central Pacific mission.

His Task Force 52 would oversee naval gunfire in pre-invasion bombardments, minesweeping, underwater demolitions, and air support. It was Blandy's job to make sure the Japanese guns were knocked out and beaches were softened up before the Marines landed.

His command included battleships, destroyers, cruisers, auxiliary craft, and the LCIs in Flotilla Three.

Blandy and his staff had spent months plotting every detail of an invasion plan: from sailing schedules, target lists, and tactical formations right down to bandages, plasma, toilet paper, shoelaces, and cooking oil. The invasion plan was several thousand pages long. It ran through various battle scenarios and dozens of possible outcomes. Every page was stamped "Top Secret."

Today, Herring would finally learn what came next.

He followed the other officers down a maze of long hallways and stairwells connecting the decks. They stopped at the end of a long hall, where the sound of a crowd came from behind a closed door. Burly Marines with M1 rifles stood guard outside.

The *Estes* officer stopped. The Marines checked each of their names against a guest list—it was like attending a society ball, Herring thought to himself, but instead of debutantes in ball gowns, the stars were admirals in bright white uniforms.

A look around showed Herring that the briefing room was really the officers' mess deck, obviously the only room on the ship large enough to hold everyone. The place was packed, with maybe a few hundred people— it was part briefing, part social event, the air hazy with the smoke of dozens of cigarettes. Officers and aides huddled in groups, catching up. Gray-haired admirals and commanders embraced and slapped one another on the back, asked after moms and dads, wives and kids.

Meanwhile, maps and folders were spread out on the rows of eight-foot-long rectangular folding tables where the officers would sit during the briefing. The walls were as drab as the room—gray, with pipes and ductwork running along the ceiling. It was hot and stuffy. Fans swirled the stale air. Some of the portholes were open to help with circulation.

Blandy was talking with Michael "Mad Mike" Malanaphy, the commander of Flotilla Three. Herring spotted Draper Kauffman, the hero frogman, and Captain B. Hall "Red" Hanlon, the commander of the underwater demolition teams, as well as Rear Admirals B. J. Rodgers and Calvin Durgin, officers he'd heard about for years. He was here in the same room with them, sharing secret plans for a massive invasion.

It was intimidating. It was easy to feel out of place. Herring wasn't the only one cowed by the company.

"I had never before seen such a collection of brass hats," recalled Jerome O'Dowd, captain of LCI-457.

Herring felt a tap on the shoulder. "How are you, Geddie?" asked Nash, smiling.

Herring hadn't seen Nash for months. He felt himself grin. "It's really good to see you," he said.

They made small talk: Nash asked about the crew. Herring said everything was going smoothly. Then he asked if Nash had ever heard any more from that girl he was writing to in New York.

Nash grinned. They had been corresponding, but not as much now, since everything was so busy. Nash thought about Dorothy all the time. He hadn't seen her for a year and a half, the last time he was home. Still, he thought more about her every day. Nash felt himself getting older. He wanted to fall in love, settle down, raise a family.

Before the war, he didn't think much about those things. He parents, siblings, career, and of course, sailing kept him busy. But now he had been thinking more about his own mortality, and what he might leave behind once his life was over. If he came out of this alive, he wanted to share his life with someone. He didn't know if Dorothy was the one, but he knew when he got back he'd call her and see what developed.

A microphone squeaked, and Herring and Nash turned their attention to the front of the room. An officer was at the podium. They were getting ready.

"Take care, Geddie. I'm sure we'll talk later," said Nash, before turning to join Malanaphy and other officers in the front.

Herring turned and sat with the other gunboat commanders in the rear of the room. He took a deep breath as the officer at the podium began talking about the mission.

"The island is called Iwo Jima," the man said. "Japanese for Sulfur Island. But don't let the name fool you—it is a vital target. It's only 670 miles from Tokyo. It has airfields with B-29 capability—useful for aircraft returning from bombing raids. Intelligence says more than 20,000 Japanese army and navy troops presently occupy Iwo Jima."

A sort of sigh went up from the assembly. Twenty thousand!

The attack plan called for U.S. military to bomb the island by air and sea for three days, then send in three Marine divisions to land on the beaches.

Other officers covered additional details, focusing on the terrain. The island was mostly barren, with volcanic ash, steaming sulfur pits, and caves. And on the southern tip of the island was Mount Suribachi, an imposing fortress. It was 550 feet high, a dormant volcano that gave the Japanese a perfect view of the entire island.

As Herring glanced at the maps, he quickly realized that Iwo Jima was a rotten place to try and overrun. The landing crafts would be clear and easy targets. And when the troops made it to shore, they could get bogged down in the soft, dark soil.

Then the first briefing officer returned to the podium. He disclosed more disturbing details: U.S. military intelligence had identified a staggering number of priority targets that had to be destroyed during the pre-invasion bombardment.

Targets were divided into three priorities:

Priority A: Installations that threated ships, planes, and underwater demolition teams.

Priority B: Emplacements that threated the landing force in the ship-to-shore movement, including blockhouses, covered artillery, pillboxes, and command posts.

Priority C: Positions that threatened the troops after the landing, including caves near the beaches.

Military planners said there were 724 Priority A and B targets, and possibly hundreds more Priority C objectives. No one could say how many hidden traps Marines might encounter during the invasion.

Planners had divided the island into numbered squares, and assigned each to a specific ship. Targets were numbered and indexed with specific information. The master target list would be maintained aboard the *Estes* and continually updated throughout the bombardment. When a target was destroyed, it would be crossed off the list.

The navy would use its big guns armed with armor-piercing and high-capacity ammunition "to wreck the greatest possible number of enemy defenses at a given time."

The briefing officer addressed the plans for February 17, two days before the scheduled landing.

"Where are the LCI gunboat captains?" he asked. Herring and the other gunboat skippers raised their hands. Most were in the back of the room, sitting with Herring. "That morning, you will move in and provide cover for the underwater demolition teams." He paused for a moment and looked around the room. "And where are my commanders for UDT 12, 13, 14, and 15?"

As he called their unit's name, the officers raised their hands. The gunboat skippers and the UDT commanders glanced at one another, as the briefing officer continued.

"It is vital that the gunboats stay in there as long as the swimmers are in the water. We are assigning UDT officers and observers to each LCI as liaisons to ensure cohesion," he said.

That was critical.

He said the four teams would swim to beaches on the southeastern side of Iwo Jima. On the maps, each beach had been divided into seven

500-yard sectors: Green, Red 1 and 2, Yellow 1 and 2, Blue 1 and 2. Herring's gunboat was assigned to Yellow Beach 2, right in the middle.

Once the frogmen were finished, the LCIs would form up again on February 19 and go in with the first wave of Marines. They were on the front end of the great invasion. Herring felt a lump forming in his throat.

He knew all about the dangers of combat. He'd seen action in four major campaigns. This had the potential to be the worst ever. The fight could take weeks. Conditions would be harsh: His men would get little sleep, tethered to their battle stations.

When the briefing officers finished, Blandy strode to the microphone. He was confident but blunt. The battle would be brutal, he promised. The Japanese had been digging holes on Iwo Jima for months, and they were tough sons of bitches. The Americans would pound the island to powder in the pre-invasion bombardment, he said, and that would go a long way toward softening up the enemy.

Iwo Jima would be "a tough nut to crack," he warned. He wished them all the best.

The briefing was over. Malanaphy called together the gunboat skippers for another few hours, to hand down specific battle plans and assignments.

WORN OUT AS Herring felt, he called a meeting with his officers as soon as he returned to the 449.

Malanaphy, Nash, and the other flotilla officers had done nothing to ease his mind. The gunboats were now on a nonstop schedule of rehearsals, gunnery practice, and coordinating drills with the demolition teams. They'd return to Saipan and Tinian for two days of exercises . . . nine days to get ready.

He knew the next days would be long and stressful, and he wanted his officers to know what they'd be facing. When they entered the wardroom, Herring didn't greet them with his usual levity. Today, his face was stern.

Herring wasted no time. He told them about their part in the Iwo Jima mission: two days of recon, protecting the frogmen along the beaches.

Then, the invasion. Going in with the Marines, blasting the beaches for hours, just like they did at Tinian. The schedule would be tight. Over the next day, he'd get them all the timelines, radio codes, and other details they needed to memorize.

No one said a word.

Herring could feel the tension. The new guys looked perfectly terrified.

"A busy schedule is common before an invasion," Herring said, trying to focus on the present. "We've done this before. We know how," he told them, trying to lighten up the mood a bit.

"Brief your men. Be honest with the men about the mission. But just for security's sake, don't mention the name of the objective until I give the green light."

The meeting seemed to be ending. The men rose from their seats. "There's one other thing," Herring said. The officers stopped and turned their attention once again to the skipper.

"Encourage the men to get their affairs in order. They need to write letters home now, while they have the chance. Because soon as we get under way, they're going to be cut off from the world."

THE NEWS FILTERED down to the crew: Blow heard about the mission, and told Banko, who spread the word to Hallett and others on the gun crews. Soon, everyone knew: They were leaving in the morning for Saipan, for rehearsals in advance of an invasion. The fact that they were leaving for a new mission was no surprise. When they'd left Guam, the sailors knew they'd soon be in action. Now they had details:

February 9: LCIs of Group 8 depart Ulithi Atoll for Saipan
February 10: En route to Saipan
February 11: Arrive in Saipan, gunnery practice
February 12: Practice run on beach off west side of Tinian
February 13: Practice run on beach off west side of Tinian with live fire;
    Depart for invasion

Reality began to set in. This was their last night in Ulithi. As the sun set over the islands, there was not much left to do. So the men huddled in their bunks, or slipped away to quiet corners of the gunboat with pens and paper in hand. They wanted to at least warn their loved ones they might not be getting letters for a while.

Alone in his room, Corkins still had more than a dozen letters to answer. His wife, parents, sister, and friends sent so many it was hard to keep up, but he loved their letters. They were his lifeline, a way to keep up with everything at home. He'd spend all night answering them if he had to.

Corkins was excited and scared at the same time. He had spent so many days in Cincinnati reading stories of the war, wishing he was on the front line. Now he was about to get his wish. On the other hand, he'd give anything to be home, just for a few minutes, to hug his wife and children, his parents, his sister, Jane.

He'd write his sister and her family first. She had shared some good news: Her husband, Howard, had just been promoted at work. (He worked for the public library.) Corkins congratulated Howard, but offered some advice: The promotion won't mean a thing if it cuts into family time.

"I hope it is a stepping-stone, at that, to even bigger and higher things. More than good luck and congratulations, though, I wish you happiness. If you have that in your work, then even ditch digging can be an honorable profession. And without it, any job is just a job and robs you and your family of the life and fullness of it that is rightfully yours," Corkins said.

"That is one of the reasons I am out here. I guess married life did not take the itch out of my feet, and I knew the rest of my life would always be wondering, wondering, if I hadn't come out to find out for myself. Sometimes those itching feet are more of a curse than a blessing, but I guess I am stuck with them for the rest of my life," he said.

He felt the urge to reveal more: "I didn't expect to run this into two pages, but I guess I might as well." Corkins began reflecting on his life, the good times, old friends he hadn't thought of in years. When he closed his eyes, he could see their faces. He could see himself, too, as a teenager, running and laughing, going to parties, having fun before life became complicated.

"Say hello to Vera Strecker for me whenever you see her. I still think of her as Vera Todd. And whenever I think of her I think of a masquerade party she had one time, and I believe I was in high school, too. I wore the Scotch outfit Mom bought me from Scotland, and during the party we played a game where the girls had to walk the fellows wheelbarrow down the stair. The damn kilt kept slipping up on me, and all I had on underneath was a pair of jockey shorts. Never more embarrassed in my life, I believe. I remember feeling sorry for girls who had to wear skirts. But oh boy! Leave me at them now!" he said.

Corkins recalled another costume party, dressing like a gypsy girl, wearing high heels. There was a girl there, too, that he couldn't forget: Marie Oehlrich.

"We played a kissing game and I was again girl shy, and when Marie was supposed to kiss me, I ran out. She ran after me and caught me because of those damn high heel shoes. I wasn't so sorry after that that I wore them. Whatever happened to her, anyway? I remember her daddy as being something of a contractor. Seems to me she was a very voluptuous girl in her young days, wasn't she?"

Corkins paused for a moment to collect his thoughts: "From the theme this letter has taken you can see the state I am in. It's a damn easy state to drop into, too, and not so easy to get out of. But right now that is the least of my worries, I guess," he said.

When he finished, he carefully folded the letter and placed it in an envelope. Then he grabbed a blank piece of stationery and turned his attention to his parents. Corkins said he knew about Howard's promotion.

"I hope his new job works out swell, that he makes a lot of money, and goes on to better positions and more money. But mostly I wish for them happiness, for without that their work or income won't mean a thing. They should appreciate their life that allows them to be together, and I know they do," he said.

He urged his mother not to worry about him, adding that the landscape in the Pacific was stunning.

"You would sure like the beautiful sunsets here, Mom. Living here on this ship in this harbor is like living under an immense blue bowl, upside down, which is the sky. This is a storm center, so there are always storms visible and always a big patch of bright blue sky. You can see the horizon in any direction you look, too, or no hills to hide any part of the sky. Just water and ships and little low islands, few and far apart, and outside of them is the deep, blue ocean, stretching for thousands of miles in every direction," he said.

Then he warned that his correspondence might be sporadic, but they shouldn't worry. Then he ended his letter a little differently. Instead of signing his name, he wrote: "The best of luck to both of you."

Meanwhile, Walton was topside, near the 40mm gun on the bow. He could tell by the look on some of the veterans' faces that they were headed into some deep shit. Usually at this time of night the deck was filled with sailors playing cards and gabbing while they listened to music played over the PA system. Tonight, though, it was quiet. Too quiet. This was the first time Walton was nervous. He wanted to talk to Paglia about it, but stopped. Everybody in the place was scribbling away, writing home while they could. He'd already written to Betzi earlier in the day. Might as well write to Mom, he thought. His mom didn't seem to mind him rattling on about how homesick he felt, even though he was doing fine. Walton filled all his letters with optimism. "Mom have you seen Betz lately? If so, how is she? Gee she sure is a wonderful girl and I love her more than anything in the world. Of course my mom comes first. She's my favorite gal," he wrote.

He wanted to marry Betzi when he got home, he said. "I'm quite sure she will be ready to say yes, don't you?"

Walton took her snapshot from his wallet and stared at her image. He closed his eyes and let himself remember her kisses. He opened his eyes, picked up the pen. "No girl can kiss the way Betzi kissed me," he wrote. Just thinking about her was helping him cope. "You know out here, if a guy didn't have anyone to come home to, like his folks and his girl . . . I think he would go nuts!"

He just knew Betzi was waiting for him, even though he hadn't received a letter from her in a month.

"Mom darling, don't you go worrying about me now. I'm all right and in good health and happy . . . What more could you ask?"

He urged his mother to "be in happy spirits . . . and before you know it I will be home! I am in happy spirits. Of course, I'm lonesome for you and Dad and Betz, etc. But I figure it doesn't do any good to be droopy and down and out, because I have to be out here, so I might as well make the best of it!"

From the forward deck came the sound of Hoffman's harmonica. He was pretty good, Walton thought. He played "Shenandoah," a sad old folk song, then "Old Rugged Cross" and "Amazing Grace." Enough to make you cry. Bozarth must be up there, Walton thought.

Walton read over his letter to his mother, then decided to "add an extra note and tell you about something that has been on my mind for quite a while."

He said he appreciated everything she and his father did for him, for always loving him, sticking by him even when he got into trouble. "You and Dad were so wonderful to me and gave me just about anything I wanted," he said, adding that he'd "changed a lot."

"Now I understand and appreciate all that you have done, and some-day I will repay you both in full! Maybe not in money . . . but more than that, being a good citizen, a good husband and father and working hard and being kind!!"

And he made a promise: No matter what happened in the war, he'd always stay cheerful. He'd never become a bitter old salt. "I mean every word of it!! I'll love you always, your son, Freddy."

Walton placed the letter on his bunk, then reached into his back pocket and pulled out his wallet. He removed the snapshot of Betzi, gently rubbed his finger over her face, wondering when he'd see her again. And as much as he tried, he couldn't help but feel blue.

HERRING AND THE officers leaned over the table, staring at the scattered charts and grainy black-and-white reconnaissance photographs they'd been staring at for days. Here were all the long-awaited details of the invasion. No one knew what to say anymore.

This was nothing like the Marianas. Those were tropical islands with white sand, palm trees, and thick jungles. Iwo Jima was an ugly, barren chunk of volcanic rock with a towering mountain overlooking the landing beaches.

The Marines, dear God, the poor bastards. They'd have to go over every square foot of the place, root out all the Japanese dug in all the way up Mount Suribachi with bullets and mortars hailing down on them. "Heavy casualties anticipated," the summary read. They're going to die by the dozen, Herring thought. The Marines would take the brunt of this battle.

But Herring didn't want to downplay the gunboats' role in the invasion, either. What if the Japanese guns opened up when they were up against the shore covering the demolition teams, or protecting the Marines landing on the beach? What if a dive-bombing Japanese plane strafed the deck? Anything could happen. The officers had been going over the plans for days now. And that's why they were going over them again.

On the way to Saipan the gunners had practiced, firing at balloons released from another gunboat. At Saipan, there were meetings, coordinating with other skippers, other boats. Then they traveled in formation to Tinian with the rest of Group Eight.

Now back in Saipan, back in the wardroom with the officers, back with the battle plans.

Herring could see that his officers were getting tired. They still had more work ahead. At dawn, they'd return to Tinian for two days of practice runs to the beaches with hundreds of other ships and amphibious crafts. After that, Iwo Jima.

This was the last night to get letters in the mail before the invasion, Herring told the officers. Once they left Saipan in the morning, there would be no more mail until after the battle. The officers passed the word to the sailors, and picked up their own pens.

Some hurried to finish letters they had started earlier in the week, while others scrambled to write new ones.

Seaman First Class Leroy Young knew he had to fire a quick note to his fiancée Evelyn Moon. They had been going out for years. Young enlisted in 1943, and Evelyn promised to wait for him. Young was nervous about this mission. He didn't want her to worry, but she needed to know how much he loved her, just in case something happened.

"My Dearest Darling: This is the first chance I've had to write for a few days so I better drop a line." He told her that he had a slight head-ache, but it was getting better. But he didn't have time for the mundane. He got down to business.

"You don't know how much I miss you honey, words can't explain it at all. I just can't wait to be near you but there isn't anything I can do about it. Oh why do they have wars? I love you dearest and until we can be together I'll wait with high hopes . . . I love you so much it hurts."

At the other end of the gunboat, Bozarth wrote to his sister. He was going to ask for a favor, so he eased into it: "Well Mary I haven't heard from you for some time now," Bozarth wrote. "I've been waiting, hoping I would get a letter from you so I could answer it, but I haven't so I decided to write you anyway."

He wanted to ease into it. So first, he asked her about new songs on the radio. They used to spend hours listening and talking about music. "I haven't heard a new song in so long it's not even funny. So set me on the right track and tell me some of the new songs."

Then he told her about Hollowell—he wanted her to write to his lonely friend.

"Another friend of mine said he was going to write you tonight. He has been wanting to write you for a long time. You see, he is from Okla-homa, too. His name is Hollowell. I hope you don't mind my calling him by his last name, but it just wouldn't sound right if I called him by his given name," he said.

"I know you will answer his letter so I won't ask you to. You know I'm really a lucky guy even if I am out here. Do you know why? Well one of the reasons is that I've really got some swell sisters."

Then he changed gears, saying he'd received a letter and a picture out of the blue from a girl who used to work with Evelyn at a depart-ment store. He suspected his sister had something to do with it.

"I'm glad to receive a letter from anybody whether I know them or not. It just helps your morale to get a lot of mail," he said.

That was so true. Letters from family and friends had helped him get through the dark times. It would help him again.

As Bozarth was folding the letter, he spotted Hollowell. "Did you write her?"

"Yeah," he said sheepishly. "I didn't have much to say. I just told her about myself, you know . . . Do you think she'll write back?"

"If I know Mary, she will," Bozarth said.

Hollowell sat down next to his friend. "Thanks," he said.

"Do me a favor," Bozarth said. "If anything happens to me, make sure you tell my family."

Hollowell was puzzled. "What do you mean?"

"Seriously. If anything happens, just let my family know that I'm gone home. And that someday we'll see each other again."

"Come on! Nothing is going to happen," Hollowell assured him. But he could tell that Bozarth was serious. "Yeah, I'll tell them."

"And one more thing," he said.

"Yeah?"

"Make sure Elaine knows. I'll give you her address."

Hollowell didn't want to argue. If anyone on the 449 was going to make it, it would be Bozarth. He was the most devout person he had ever met, and that included all those revival preachers traveling the dusty back roads of Oklahoma. But for tonight, he'd make Bozarth happy.

"Sure. I'll tell her," he said.

They stopped talking. They stared at the stars stretched across the sky.

BEDELL KNEW WHEN Yarbrough was troubled. He'd go all quiet and stare into space, deep in thought. And Yarbrough had been in a trance since Herring announced that tomorrow was the final mail call.

Yarbrough had been sitting at his desk with a blank piece of paper in front of him, but he hadn't written a word. He hadn't said a word. The only noise was the flickering ping of the fluorescent tube on the ceiling.

Finally, Bedell cleared his throat. "You OK?" he asked.

Yarbrough nodded his head up and down. "Yes."

"Anything you want to talk about?"

"No. I just have to take care of a few things," he said.

Bedell jumped out of his bunk. He knew Yarbrough needed some time alone. "All right. I'm going to head to the bridge. You need something, though, come get me."

Bedell was a good friend, Yarbrough thought. He listened when he rambled on about Betty. He offered sage advice. But even Yarbrough knew it was time to act. He couldn't deny it any longer: He was in love with Betty Jones.

Earlier in the day, he'd opened her latest letter. And there it was: a promise to write him every day.

Now there was no turning back. He was going to take the next step.

He started writing.

Betty had asked where he had been in the Pacific. He told her. The words flowed.

"In accordance with censorship regulations I can now tell you a little bit of my past experiences. We were in on the invasion of the Mariana Islands and their subsequent capture. We took part in all three of the operations, Saipan, Guam, and Tinian. We were at Saipan on Christmas and New Year's. Of course, I can't go into all the details of our operations, but perhaps you read about the use of LCI's in the 'Mop-up' work, transporting of interpreters, and cleaning Japs out of caves etc . . . We had a part in those type of operations. Just so you will know some of the places I have been, and some of the action I took part in. I promise you this: I will have a lot to tell you when I see you in person."

Then he opened up. Life aboard the gunboat had been hell, he said. Not only did he worry about combat, but his room was just a few feet from the galley and the clanging of pots and pans made it hard to get any sleep. The drone of the generators was nonstop, and he was so close to the radio shack that he could hear the chatter from other gunboats and ships in the sector.

Despite all the hardships, he was happy now. She was in his life, and now she had agreed to write him every day, just like they were an old married couple.

"Betty, I am happy now. I have been waiting for you to make that decision, and somehow I knew you would. You are that sort of girl. I am speaking of your decision to write me daily. I wish you could know how good that makes me feel. If I don't get anything but Hello and Love, that's all I want," he said.

There was no holding back—he wanted her to know that she was the one, that they had a bright future together.

"Betty, why don't you and I have an understanding? I have never had an understanding with any girl before, but I have heard and read about it, and I like the sound of it. Let's have it understood that you are my girl and I am your boy, guy, beau, 'Man', or whatever it is. They really don't have a nice sounding possessive for a man, do they? But when a guy speaks of 'my girl.' That is something really nice. I am your guy, if you want me, and I want to be yours . . . So, you can tell your bridge club whatever you like now, and it will be so."

Then he said he wanted their relationship to take the next step, he wanted to be more than boyfriend and girlfriend. He said every guy has to have a girl to make things complete. And he wanted her to be with him forever.

"Betty, nothing would make me happier than to have you meet me at the train when I come home," he said, adding that he was going to write his parents and tell them about their relationship. His sister already knew. Heck, she was responsible. But now it was time for the rest of the family. He didn't have much time to write tonight, but he didn't tell her why.

"Well my girl, I will stop for this time. I just want you to know that in the meantime, I'll be thinking of you . . . Love, Byron."

He let out a huge sigh, and realized he was smiling.

He began another letter, this one to his parents. It was time to tell them about Betty.

"I have spoken of Betty Jones a few times in my letters, but I think I had better tell you just how well things are going now. We have been writing to each other regularly since we started back in October. I don't know why, but we seem to have a great deal in common and our relationship has developed rapidly. Indeed, it has developed so rapidly, that I want to warn you about it, before anything embarrassing can happen," he said.

"Our relationship has developed to this extent: I received a letter from her this week, in which she states that she is going to write me daily. For my part, I have asked her to be my girl, which might seem absurd, but she accepts it, and so do I. We both think it strange that we should become fond of each other merely by writing each other, but each admits that it is so," he said.

"I have asked Betty several times in my letters to go over and visit sister and get acquainted with you folks, so don't be too surprised if she does one of these days. I have also asked her to be present, if I should ever get a leave and come home. I don't know if sister knows how well we are getting along, so be sure and tell her."

Then he asked them for a favor, just to show how serious he was about their relationship: "I would like very much to send Betty something nice as a surprise to her. Could you help me out on that proposition?"

He hoped his parents would do it, maybe buy her a ring. He'd pay them back. Yarbrough didn't know how they'd react. His father would probably be skeptical. He was a practical man—you didn't marry someone you never met. Yarbrough knew his father might try to dissuade him.

But at this point, Yarbrough didn't care what his father, or anyone else, thought of his relationship with Betty. He had spent his life trying to please his father, trying so hard to make him proud. That's why he joined the navy in the first place. He'd heard his father preach time and again about doing the right thing: Don't smoke or drink. Serve your country. Be honest.

Yarbrough did everything his father asked. He was a good son. But after all these years of being alone, he just wanted a relationship. Betty's words comforted him. Betty's letters gave him hope. Betty's love gave him the strength to keep fighting, the will to survive.

So that night, in his room, his mind was made up: When he got home, when he finally jumped off that train in Auburn, Alabama, he was going to ask Betty to marry him.

AT DAWN, A small boat pulled next to the 449 and picked up several bags of mail, then dropped off a few sacks, too. Word spread quickly and the men gathered near the deckhouse, waiting for Yarbrough.

Yarbrough emerged from the building, looked at the crowd, and grinned. "I've never been so popular!" he quipped to Bedell.

Yarbrough wasted no time. They'd have to leave soon. He reached into the bag, pulled a handful of letters at a time, and started calling names.

A few seconds after Yarbrough slipped Howard Schoenleben a letter, he heard him scream: "It's a boy! It's a boy!"

Then he started running around the deck, zigzagging back and forth, holding the letter over his head until Blow grabbed him. "Hey, what's going on?" Blow said.

Schoenleben was so breathless, he could barely get the words out. "I have a son!"

Blow grabbed the letter and started reading. Then he shouted so everyone could hear: "Hey, Howie's got a son!"

All of the men congratulated Schoenleben, slapping him on the back. The other members of the Chicago Three, Trotter and Tominac, gave him a bear hug.

Blow read the letter out loud. Schoenleben's wife had given birth two weeks earlier, but was unable to get a message to him, so she decided to write a letter. She named the baby Howard Schoenleben Jr. Mother and baby were healthy and well.

Herring congratulated Schoenleben and promised to find a way to get him a pass home after the battle.

"I'm the luckiest guy, Skipper," he said to Herring.

Schoenleben stood on the deck, dreaming of home, making plans for his newborn boy. He'd buy a house with a big backyard where they could play catch. They'd get a dog. He'd take the kid to Chicago Cubs games, they'd root for the Chicago Bears.

Bring on the Japs, he thought—the future was bright, now that he had a son.

THE SAILORS WERE in their battle stations. One more practice run, this one with live fire.

From the bridge Herring could see the beaches on the western side of

Tinian, as well as the other LCIs in the flotilla lining up in formation. Herring's gunboat was third in line, with Nash's ship leading the way.

Herring had done all he could to prepare his men for the invasion. He reviewed the plans with his officers. The crew's gunners were prepped on the invasion targets. They had practiced with the demolition teams.

As ready as they were, Herring still had some worries. They were heading into battle with inexperienced officers. There were newcomers in some of the gunboat's key positions. His radioman was Paglia, a kid with no battle experience. In combat, you depended on your radio operator completely. Ball was one of the best. He had become Nash's trusted adviser, and assumed the same role when Herring took over. Ball even put out a newsletter and, on good nights, could find radio broadcasts from the States.

Herring knew he'd have to lean on the veterans: Blow, Vollendorf, Vanderboom. But most of all, he was depending on Yarbrough. He knew Yarbrough had been stung when Nash passed him over and made Herring the skipper—the job was rightfully Yarbrough's. But Yarbrough never complained. He was the first one to congratulate Herring.

Yarbrough was cool under the pressure of battle. It was his voice the men heard when time came to fire, and his voice that called them off. And in between, Yarbrough worked his ass off. How many nights did he stay up late censoring the men's correspondence just so every letter went out the following day? How many nights did Yarbrough volunteer to take the late shift, standing on the bridge from midnight to 04:00, just so others could get some sleep, or go out and have fun? Yarbrough was essential, Herring thought. He was the glue that held the gunboat together. After this mission, he'd put the word out, and make sure Yarbrough got the promotion he deserved.

When Herring got the signal, the gunboat followed the others toward the beach. Yarbrough's voice came over, and like clockwork, the men on the gun decks scrambled into the deckhouse. Vanderboom pushed the button, the rockets launched, and a thicket of palm trees exploded just beyond the white sand. Gun crews hurried back to their stations, and fired at the targets along the beach.

Everything went according to plan. The 449 and its counterparts then headed back to Tanapag Harbor for refueling and provisions.

As the gunboat moored alongside the fleet oiler, Herring glanced at his watch. It was 15:00. In three hours, they'd be leaving for Iwo Jima. All the planning, all the practice was over. The next time they fired their weapons, it would be for real.

AN URGENT MESSAGE arrived just before they pulled out: Another sailor was joining the ship. A navy photographer. Instead of a gun, he'd carry a camera bag.

A photographer on an LCI? That was a first, Herring thought. Photographers were usually reserved for the big ships: destroyers, cruisers, aircraft carriers. In the Pacific, photographers went in on landing crafts after beachheads were established. They not only snapped stills, but movies, too.

Herring knew navy photographers played an important role. They helped document battles. Many of the images, all of them cleared by headquarters, appeared in newspapers or newsreels. But as he waited, it just made Herring wonder more about the invasion. He knew commanders were expecting a bloody campaign, that was a given. But for a navy photographer to be aboard an LCI? What did it mean?

Herring told his officers about the new addition, and told them to send the man to the wardroom when he arrived.

But before he got a chance to go, Blow spotted the boat. "Hey, Skip. He's here."

Herring waited. Moments later, a gangly teenager with several camera bags dangling from his neck come on board. He saluted Herring, then introduced himself: Photographer's Mate Third Class Harry Leo McGrath, assigned to shoot stills and movies of the entire Iwo Jima campaign, from start to finish. "Everything from the pre-invasion to the invasion," he said.

Herring invited him to the wardroom, where they would talk in private. McGrath followed Herring into the deckhouse and wardroom. Herring closed the door and told McGrath to take a seat.

The eighteen-year-old removed the straps from around his neck and placed the camera bags carefully on the floor. Herring asked him about the assignment. What exactly was he looking for? McGrath said he wanted realistic shots of the men. He promised not to get in the way. "It'll be like I'm not even here." And McGrath said he was particularly interested in the frogmen—he had heard all about their exploits and this was his first time to see them in action.

Herring asked him about his background. McGrath said he was from North Bend, Washington, just outside Seattle. His family owned a hotel, and he had been into photography since he was a kid. He'd set up a darkroom at the hotel, and earned extra money snapping landscape shots and portraits of the guests. He said when he enlisted he told the recruiter he was eager to put his hobby to work.

"Have you been in combat?"

"Yes," McGrath said, "the Marianas."

He had watched as Marines fought in hand-to-hand combat there. He snapped pictures as U.S. troops used flamethrowers and grenades to force Japanese soldiers out of caves and into the open. He shot footage as shrapnel and mortars ripped into American men advancing on the islands.

Herring was impressed. At least this was one newcomer who had experience.

THE GALLEY WAS busy. Kepner stirred the pots on the stoves, while Bozarth and Vogel mixed ingredients in batters. Johnson was there, too, stirring away at a bowl filled with heavy cream, vanilla extract, and condensed milk to make ice cream. They'd started preparing earlier in the day, and now the counters were filled with food in various stages of development. Kepner wanted this to be a Christmas-like feast, a special dinner they'd all remember. It would be their last hot meal for a while.

The gunboat would be in action the next morning, February 17, protecting frogmen as they blew up obstacles and gathered critical information for the landing. The men would live on sandwiches and snacks until the operation ended. It might be weeks before the stoves were lit up again.

Earlier in the day, the sailors had been told what their officers already knew: In a couple of days, the Marines would invade Iwo Jima. The island's name didn't mean a damn thing. It was just another stop on a long, bloody road to the Japanese mainland.

Somehow, though, the announcement laid a strange mood on the ship.

When the gunboat left Tinian for Iwo Jima on February 13, Kepner and Beuckman had stayed up late, drinking coffee. Beuckman said he had a bad feeling. "Clarence, I can't explain it," he said. "We've been pretty lucky so far. But sometimes, your luck runs out."

Kepner understood. He knew men were killed in wars. But until his brother's death, Kepner had believed that it only happened to other families. Now he knew death could come from anywhere, anytime. No family was immune.

As he put together the menu for the pre-invasion dinner, he decided to forgo the usual meat loaf. Tonight it was roasted chicken, mashed potatoes, canned peas and corn, pickle relish, olives, celery, bread and butter, and biscuits. He'd brew up coffee and tea, and they'd drink Pepsi-Cola. And for this dinner, they'd break out the beer, two cans for each sailor.

For dessert, Bozarth and Vogel would bake cherry, pumpkin, and apple pies, and plum pudding with sauce. In fact, they were baking extra pies and breads so the men could snack for days. After dinner, Beuckman would go to the locker in his dispensary and pull out the cigars.

Just before 16:00, Kepner took a step back and gazed at the food. It was quite a spread. He thought of other feasts before other battles, and hoped their good luck would hold, that they'd escape. No casualties. Maybe this would be the last pre-invasion dinner. Maybe after this invasion, the Japanese would come to their senses and surrender. As unlikely as it seemed, Kepner prayed every night for the war to end.

After his brother was killed, people said that time would heal his pain. But six months later, it was still there, a wound that never healed. When he heard a song or a phrase that reminded him of his brother, the scab would open and he'd start bleeding again. This war had to end. Too many people were feeling this way, just how he felt. It couldn't go on.

But on this night, he'd try not to think about it. He would stay positive: "OK, fellas, we're ready!" he shouted.

The sailors were ready, too. They filed into the galley, filled their trays with food, and carried them to the tables on the mess deck. Noise filled the crowded room as the men squeezed into seats. Some sat on the floor. But no one touched his plate. Not yet. Not until Bozarth said the prayer.

When everyone was seated, Bozarth moved from behind the counter, untying his apron, and stood in the center of the mess deck. He looked over the assembled men, then bowed his head. Other heads bowed, eyes closed, across the room. Many hands made the sign of the cross. Overchuk clutched his rosary beads. Bozarth stood quiet for a moment. Prayer came easy to him, but today he struggled. This wasn't just him talking to the Lord. He wanted the right words to comfort his fellow sailors.

He took a deep breath.

"Dear father, we gather here in your name, we bow before you to praise you for your providence, and to ask for your protection and strength," Bozarth said, enunciating each word carefully. As the scripture tells us, he said, we shall "be strong and of a good courage, fear not, nor be afraid of them. For the Lord, thy God, will not fail thee." He raised his hands toward the men. "We believe your words, Father, and into your hands we commend our spirits." A sigh went up as the men received the blessing. Bozarth folded his hands again.

"Thank you, too, Father, for this food, which we are about to receive from thy bounty, and for the friendship of the men gathered here, these warriors, my friends, my brothers . . ." His voice cracked just a little, but it gained strength as he wound up the prayer. "I ask for your continued grace, blessing, and divine protection for my nation, my family, my shipmates, and myself. I ask this in the name of our Savior, the Lord Jesus Christ. Amen."

Everyone in unison quietly said, "Amen."

Then the men took up knives and forks and dug into the feast. Beer cans hissed open. A few of the men thanked Bozarth for the prayer. A couple moments later, they heard a voice over the public address speaker: It was Vanderboom. He said he was dedicating the first song to Bozarth, for all his hard work and spiritual guidance.

A few second later, music streamed out of the speakers, and Bozarth beamed when he heard the opening strains of the gospel song "Blow Your

Trumpet, Gabriel." The tune was one of Bozarth's favorites—he had played it so many times on the ship's record player that everyone knew the words by heart. He'd sing along with the song, rocking back and forth like he was in a black church in the Deep South. Tonight was no different, and all the men sang along, shouting the chorus: "So blow your trumpet, Gabriel. Blow your trumpet louder."

The men laughed and talked as they ate and listened to music. They went up for seconds and thirds. They grabbed Vogel's rolls and biscuits, extra slices of Bozarth's pies, and scoops of Johnson's vanilla ice cream. They smoked cigarette after cigarette, sang the latest Bing Crosby song, "Don't Fence Me In," and Overchuk grabbed a mop, leapt up, and danced on the table to Tommy Dorsey's "Boogie Woogie." The men landed extra cans of beer, tossed them around. The noise was so loud that Herring and the officers left the wardroom and joined the sailors. McGrath took out his camera and began snapping frames.

Recalled Seaman First Class Bill Wilcox: "It was a party. No one thought about Iwo Jima. We tried to put everything out of our minds."

And for a few hours that night, they did. No one discussed the mission, Iwo Jima, the war. For a few hours, they were at peace.

ALL THE DISHES were washed and put away, the tables wiped down, the ovens cleaned. Kepner stored the last few pots, then covered the pies, bread, and other baked goodies. He reached over the ovens and turned them off at the mains.

In the wardroom, Herring was going over a few last-minute items with the officers. In the morning, two observers would join the crew, he said. The one from Underwater Demolition Team 14 would relay instructions to the frogmen in Yellow Sector 2. The Marine observer would call in additional fire if needed.

Herring told them to look after McGrath—they didn't want anything to happen to him. It was the big ships that got all the publicity. This was a chance for the gunboats to show the world what they could do.

"We'll be famous," Cromer joked.

"Not if you get your balls shot off," Bedell said. They all laughed.

After they left the wardroom, Herring sat there ruminating. He knew they were ready. Everything would go as planned, he thought. The operation with the frogmen was just a reconnaissance mission. They had done it before and had encountered little Japanese resistance.

It was the main invasion that really had him worried, and the fact that his men would once again be tethered to their battle stations, living for days, maybe weeks, with little or no sleep. They'd be facing Japanese kamikaze pilots and big coastal guns. They'd be within range of mortars, and even machine-gun and small-arms fire. Someone was going to get hit, he knew.

Even though he'd been through this before, Herring realized he never got used to it. He let his mind wander for a moment to North Carolina, his mother and brother, sailing on White Lake. He recalled those glorious nights in New York, when he was a young officer in training, exploring the wonders of the city with the war so far away, in newspapers and newsreels. Now it was his whole world, like it had been for the last year. Herring promised himself that if he made it back home, he would live a simple, peaceful life. He'd like to have children, he thought. He'd read them stories every night, before they went to bed, the stories behind the constellations in the night sky. Herring realized he missed seeing children, hearing young voices. When had he last spoken to a child?

With dinner finished, most of the men were in no hurry to go to their bunks. A few had taken their second beers topside and were sitting under the stars. They all wanted to keep the party going, but as night went on the men noticed a chill in the air. It was cool for a change, not hot and sweaty.

Wilcox noticed the change as he pulled guard duty with Schoenleben. This would be Wilcox's first battle, and as they walked the decks he asked Schoenleben what to expect. Schoenleben would usually answer a question with a wisecrack, then ask Trotter or Tominac to help him come up with more. But tonight he was quiet, preoccupied with something. Wilcox thought maybe Schoenleben hadn't heard the question, or was ignoring him.

But as they approached the quarterdeck, Schoenleben turned to Wilcox. His face was filled with fear. "I don't want to die," he said.

Wilcox was stunned. He didn't know what to say.

"I want to hold my boy, and I don't think I'm going to get the chance . . . I don't want to think about dying. But that's all I can think about."

Wilcox gave him a pat on the back, told him everybody was scared, too, told him that Bozarth had blessed them, that they'd be OK. But Schoenleben didn't say another word for the rest of his shift.

Fear and foreboding walked the ship that night.

Holgate and Hoffman were topside, finishing off beers and shooting the breeze. They were only supposed to have two, but they bartered with some of the non-drinkers on board. They ended up with a few extra cans. The alcohol loosened their tongues.

Hoffman said he just wanted the war to be over. He kept thinking about home, playing music, wondering if he'd lost his chops out here without any practice. He couldn't get his mind off his parents and friends.

"I keep hoping the war will end, because maybe it's like a race, you know? Because the longer I'm out here, the shorter my time is. I stay out here long enough, I won't ever make it home," Hoffman said. "I don't think I'm going to make it."

Holgate shook his head. "Come on. You thought that before, and here we are. Nothing is going to happen."

"I know it, Norm. I'm not going to make it."

"That's ridiculous."

"No, it's not."

Holgate had to cheer up his friend, get him out of his funk. He talked about the end of the war, said he'd go home with Hoffman, meet his folks, maybe even start his life over in Saint Louis. There was nothing for him in Oregon anyway.

"You can't die, you know. You gotta introduce me to your mom, and Ollie Berger, and that girl whose picture you got in your wallet!"

Hoffman managed a weak smile. Holgate was like a brother. Nine months ago, they were strangers, but they'd become close friends, sharing their gossip and secrets. Hoffman wanted to believe that this was just another mission. Maybe Norm was right, they'd get through it. He prayed they would, even though he still couldn't shake the bad feeling.

Neither could Overchuk, who was lying down a few yards away in his bunk.

"That was some party, right?" Overchuk said to Lemke, stretched out in the bed above him.

"Yeah. Wish we had more beer."

Overchuk laughed. "I don't think they wanted us to get drunk, just to have a good time."

That night, Overchuk repeated the same stories Lemke had heard a dozen times before. After the war, Overchuk was thinking about becoming a dancer. Maybe he'd head to Broadway, he joked. But he was certain of one thing: "No way I'm going back to the mills," he said.

Lemke didn't think that far ahead. If he was lucky enough to stay alive, he'd head back to a wife he barely knew and a daughter he had never held in his arms. It had been so long since he had seen his parents, his sister, Park Falls. What he wouldn't give just to sit in the back row of the Rex Theater once more . . . What he wouldn't give to turn back the clock, watch his father read the paper, his mother prepare dinner in the kitchen, his uncles and aunts show up for Sunday lunch.

"We better try to get some sleep," Overchuk said.

But Lemke already knew that was impossible.

So did Johnson. He rarely, if ever, revealed his feelings. Hollowell was one of the few who knew him at all. They sat outside for a while that night. Hollowell tried not to talk about the invasion, but it was hard not to. They were ready, he said. They were a good team.

"Well, R.L., we'll be in the thick of things," he said.

Johnson nodded. "Nothing we can't handle."

"Right."

"I wish I had a chance to talk to my parents, though, before the shooting starts," Johnson said. "Just to hear their voices one last time, just in case. You never know what could happen."

Hollowell understood. Yes, they practiced. They went through endless exercises. Still, anything could happen. And while Johnson didn't talk much, Hollowell knew he loved his parents, his siblings, that he wished they could see him as a gunner. They'd be so proud.

"Nothing's going to happen. You'll tell them everything," Hollowell said.

For some reason, Hollowell wasn't having any premonitions like the other sailors. Poor old Ralph Owens was in his bunk holding his girlfriend's eight-by-ten photo in his hands and repeating the same letters over and over: "N-I-N-A."

It was driving his buddy Hightower crazy.

"Hightower, I'm going to marry that sweet little thing one of these days," Owens said.

"I know."

Then Owens sat up in the bunk and stared at Hightower. He felt a desperate urge to tell the truth, tell his friend his darkest fear: "Make sure that you tell Nina. Tell her what happened."

Hightower was puzzled. "Tell her what?"

"Just tell her what happened. I want her to know."

Hightower didn't know what to say. He had never seen his friend so upset and he wasn't going to push him. Not now. After the outburst, Owens rested his head on his mattress, closed his eyes, and fell asleep clutching the picture of his girlfriend.

In his room, Bedell wished he could sleep. Yarbrough was taking a shift on the bridge, and Bedell was alone—and he didn't like it. Even though he had dispensed advice to the newcomers—he'd told Minnick earlier that night that everyone gets scared before battle—Bedell didn't know what to expect. He got up, left his room, and went to see if Corkins was still up.

Just as he expected, Corkins, Cooper, and Cromer were awake, sitting in their bunks, gloomy as a funeral wake.

Bedell thought he'd try to cheer them up. "Why the long faces?" Bedell joked.

At first, they were hesitant to say a word. Then Cooper shook his head. "I'm going to get killed," he said, matter-of-factly.

Before Bedell had a chance to respond, Corkins blurted: "I'm going to get killed, too."

Bedell was shocked. He'd heard Cooper talk about it before, but not Corkins. "No one is going to get killed. Has the ship ever been hit?"

Cooper said, "No."

"But there's always a first time," Corkins said.

"Why are you talking like that? You shouldn't talk like that or think of things like that," Bedell said.

"No, that's the way it's going to be," Cooper said.

"Sheesh . . . Nobody can read the future. Knock it off, guys," Bedell snapped.

But they couldn't. They were resigned to the fact that they were going to die. Although Bedell knew there was probably nothing he could say to make them feel better, he tried again. He repeated what the veterans had told him: While the gunboat had been in heavy action, they hadn't lost a sailor. Not one.

"This is a lucky boat. It's going to be the same," Bedell said.

"Can you guarantee that?" Corkins asked.

Bedell knew he couldn't.

So just before dawn on Saturday, February 17, Bedell left their room, praying that Corkins was wrong.

AS THE SUN began to rise on Iwo Jima, families in the United States, eight thousand miles away, were getting ready for sleep.

In Iowa, Mary Cooper had just put Rebecca in the crib. Sitting in her living room, she looked at the wonderful necklace her husband had sent from the Pacific. She had saved every letter, read them over and over. She was worried about the tone of the last few. She was especially worried when he asked if he would ever turn twenty-five. His birthday was in a few weeks, March 2. She tried to dismiss the comment, telling herself that he'd make it back safely.

But his letters were dark. He had changed so much in a year, and she wondered if he would ever be the same. She walked over to the radio and tuned in to the news. She wanted to hear the latest from the Pacific, but then she decided against it. She'd turn it on in the morning. Right now, she was too tired to stay up.

That night, Betty Jones was in her usual spot: at her desk, radio on, writing another letter. It was dark, the wind whistling outside her window. But she was filled with hope. She was Byron's girl. They really were a couple. They really were . . .

"Sometimes I have to pinch myself to be sure it really is true that I'm writing and hearing from you. You seem to be a perfectly swell person from your letters, and I wonder quite often if I'm going to be able to stand it till you get home, and I can really see you. I guess I'll have to bide my time on that item tho', but I will be glad when that letter comes saying, 'Be on your way to Auburn gal, the prodigal is on his way.' That is, you are a prodigal."

As she sat there, she reflected about their relationship.

"I'll have to confess, Byron, that when I first started writing you I was a little dubious. Naturally, since I know very little about you, only what Jane and Mary had told me, I wasn't quite sure how I would like it. Letter writing heretofore has been mental strain and torture for me; therefore, I did very little of it. But the more I heard from you, the more I began to enjoy writing you, and now, if I miss a day, I feel as tho' I've missed the best part of the day—my talk with you. You really must, if I may say so, Byron, feel flattered because you are the first person in all of my life that I have ever written to with any regularity."

Then she heard a lovely song, Dinah Shore and Frank Sinatra singing a duet, "My Romance." She loved the line "My romance doesn't need a thing but you." That summed up their relationship.

Her mother had told her she was foolish—you couldn't fall in love via letters. She knew that some of her friends were probably making snide comments behind her back. But none of that mattered. She knew in her heart that Byron was the one. They'd spend the rest of their lives together. Of that, she was sure.

"Oh, we really have a lot to catch up on when you get home—about twenty-five years of knowing each other. I really feel like I have known you fully that long. Byron, I hope you remember that I'm thinking about you all of the time and praying for your safety . . . For now, Byron, my love. Betty."

She carefully folded the letter, then stared out her window. Maybe, if everything went right, he'd be home by the time the azaleas bloomed.

= 26 =

IT WAS NO use trying to sleep. Lemke stepped outside onto the fantail and made fists inside his pockets to keep warm. The gunboat was bathed in dark silence, but in an hour's time they'd be near Iwo Jima.

Lemke shivered. He touched the steel deck rail to make sure it really was as cold as he thought, that it wasn't just his nerves. There in the bottom of one pocket was a bit of paper. A dollar bill, forgotten; he hadn't worn the coat for weeks. Lemke tried to convince himself it was a good sign, that everything was going to be fine. But this morning he wasn't buying it. They were going on a reconnaissance mission, the front line of the front line.

Lemke wasn't the only man waiting for daybreak up on deck. Banko leaned against the rail near the front of the ship, his face to the wind. The ocean hissed as it passed the bow. He was glad he'd pulled on an extra shirt. Someone said the temperature had dropped thirty degrees overnight.

The horizon turned pink. Hallett emerged with John Flook, a new seaman first class who'd just joined the ship in November. They joined Banko at the rail. This was Flook's first invasion.

"You smell that?" Banko said.

"Yup," Hallett replied. "It's starting to smell a little like Saipan."

Flook was puzzled. He had been to Saipan, but he didn't remember it smelling like this. This was like the pungent smell of sulfur, rotten eggs.

Banko turned to Flook and explained: "The Marines killed so many Japs they couldn't bury them fast enough. Couldn't get bulldozers onto the beaches to bury them, so the bodies just laid there in the open, getting ripe in the sun. You could smell them out at sea."

They didn't mention the thousands of bodies that had crowded the water all around them—entire families that had chosen to die rather than suffer an American occupation.

Then Hallett interjected. "Some of the fellas put cigarette butts in their noses to help with the stench. It was awful."

Terrified, Flook didn't say another word. If it smelled this bad already, where the hell were they going?

Herring was up on the bridge, waiting for his officers. He knew the roster by heart, but looked it over anyway.

Cooper: 40mm gun on the bow, relaying orders to the gun crew.

Corkins: the pair of 40mm guns on the gun deck.

Cromer: relay orders to the crews manning the pair of 20mm guns aft.

Bedell: engine room and damage control brigade.

Duvall: pilothouse and course marking.

Yarbrough: coordinate communication between the officers.

Herring just had to keep everything running smoothly. No glitches. No problems. The last thing he wanted to do was radio his commanders that the 449 was in trouble.

The officers reported in. The engines were humming. The gun crews were ready.

Herring was pleased. Whatever happened next, they'd be ready.

LIEUTENANT LEE YATES got his assignment, and he wasn't happy. He was part of the reconnaissance mission, but not as a frogman. Instead, he was stationed on a gunboat, an observer. This was not what he'd signed up for.

He went straight to Underwater Demolition Team 14's commanding officer Bruce Onderdonk, but he couldn't be swayed. Neither could Executive Officer Chuck Emery. They went through this every time these assignments were made.

We have to have observers, they told him. The frogmen had to have one of their own to oversee the action on Yellow Beach 2. He had to make sure the shells fired from navy ships didn't land too close to the teams. Every gunboat on the mission would have both a UDT and Marine reconnaissance observer, looking out for their own.

"We need you, Yates," Onderdonk told him.

He knew that, but he didn't like it. Being an observer was like his old position before he became a frogman: "beachmaster." Yates liked to say that being a beachmaster was like being a traffic cop: He'd stay on the shore and direct arrivals and departures of amphibious ships for days during invasions, often under heavy enemy fire. He left because he was ready for a new challenge. Hell, it was a challenge just finding out about the frogmen.

Through the grapevine, he'd heard bits and pieces about the navy's elite underwater demolition teams. Frogmen were athletes who took part in daring reconnaissance missions. Yates didn't know much more. Neither did any of the officers on his old ship, the USS *Winged Arrow*. So Yates wrote directly to Draper Kauffman, the navy commander who created the program. It took months, but in September 1944, right after the Marianas campaign, Yates got a letter: Kauffman was giving him a tryout. He'd train at their school in Fort Pierce, Florida.

He was ready. Yates was a star athlete in high school and college. He was a center, and a damn good one. At six feet, two hundred pounds with thick arms and big hands that wrapped around the laces, he could snap the ball with precision and knock opposing defensive linemen on their asses. At Central High School in Nashville, Yates made the All-City Team in his senior year. Then he went thirty-five miles down the road to Middle Tennessee Teachers College (now Mid-Tennessee State University) in Murfreesboro, Tennessee, where he picked up where he'd left off in high school.

During his four years, Yates played on the baseball, basketball, and football teams. He received a Little All-America Team honorable mention in his senior year. (The Little All-America team was for schools in the smaller conferences.) And after graduating in 1940 with a teaching degree, he received offers to try out with the Detroit Lions and the Cleveland

Rams in the National Football League. The fledgling league needed offensive linemen, and pro scouts saw his potential. But Yates decided to become a high school teacher and coach. Along the way, he got married, had a son, and enlisted in 1942 after his younger brother joined the navy.

The training to become a frogman was grueling. It was six weeks of physical challenges. Hell Week, at the very start, was the worst. That's when they "separated the men from the boys." It was seven days of nonstop physical conditioning, with only few breaks for sleep and food. Four miles swimming in rough surf. Swimming in the surf at night, with heavy loads on their backs. Ten-mile runs with obstacle courses. Hand-to-hand combat training. Some of the guys dropped out, but the twenty-six-year-old Yates had never quit anything in his life. He loved the camaraderie. Hell Week survivors shared a tremendous esprit de corps. So many of the candidates were just like him: ambitious and young, bored with serving in routine units. They wanted to join the elite forces, and they felt confident they could meet the challenge.

They swam endlessly, they learned judo, they learned which snakes and sharks were dangerous. And they learned everything about explosives: different types and properties, how to set charges to blow up obstacles underwater or on a beach.

He worked hard, pushing his body to the limit. His muscles ached, muscles everywhere, even behind his ears. Just when he thought it would get a little easier, it didn't. But he made it. He had only been on one mission, in the Philippines, before this one.

Now, after all his training and expectation, Yates wanted to be in the action. But he was stuck on the sidelines, on a damn gunboat.

He watched for sunup on the deck of the USS *Bull*. At some point he would board a boat that would take him to an LCI.

A scout from the Marine Reconnaissance Unit, Corporal Edward Brockmeyer, leaned against the rail beside Yates and introduced himself. They'd both been assigned to the same gunboat: the 449. Brockmeyer was a little upset, too. He'd wanted to go in with the first wave of Marines, but they needed a Marine observer aboard the gunboat. He'd drawn the short straw.

The two men talked in low voices. Like Yates, the twenty-two-year-old

Brockmeyer had been in combat across the Pacific, and joined the Marines recon unit because he wanted to play a bigger role in the war.

In fact, Brockmeyer was a certified war hero already. During the invasion of Saipan, he and a buddy, Warren Somerville, spotted a pillbox full of enemy soldiers mowing down Marines. Brockmeyer grabbed a jerry can of gasoline, and while his friend covered him, he bolted to the pillbox. Somehow he made it without being shot, climbed on top of the concrete box, and poured the gasoline into a ventilation duct. Then Brockmeyer lit a match, igniting the vapors.

As the Japanese bolted from the burning bunker, Somerville and Brockmeyer mowed them down. Brockmeyer was later awarded the Silver Star. The newspaper in his hometown in Maryland even wrote up his story. But Brockmeyer was no glory hound.

During a battle in Palermo, Sicily, in July 1943, his brother Robert had been killed by a dive-bombing German plane. His death fueled Brockmeyer's rage. He volunteered for training that would sharpen his skills: scout training, sniper training, combat swimming, and then recon.

Ed Brockmeyer was ready for Iwo Jima. He was even looking forward to it. He was a well-honed arrow, waiting for the bowman to release him.

Yates told the Marine about the LCIs. He'd seen the same gunboat group during the invasion of Tinian. None of them was hit. It seemed like the Japs left them alone, focusing instead on the big ships: destroyers, battleships, aircraft carriers.

Brockmeyer said he had been at Tinian, too, but he didn't elaborate. Some Marines enjoyed trading war stories and adventures, but tall tales didn't interest Brockmeyer. He was focused on the hunt, the next target.

Yates saw himself in the young man. Maybe in the future, they'd work together in the battlefield, not just as observers. Brockmeyer said he'd like that.

AS THE FIRST rays of daylight fell on the water, Vollendorf steered the ship into position. This was it, Herring thought: 07:00, clear, sunny, perfect weather for the mission. The gunboats in Flotilla Three, Group Eight lined up in formation and took the straight path twenty miles north to

Iwo Jima. They'd be there by 09:30, and in position an hour later for the assault.

Herring knew the fleet's movements were closely choreographed. Every ship—gunboat, battleship, destroyer—had to be in the right place at the right time to ensure that each phase of the pre-invasion operation did not interfere with the next.

Herring felt calm. Everything was going smoothly. Minesweepers were clearing shipping lanes close to the island, trying to detect explosive devices that could disable landing craft. Radio traffic was positive. No waves of Japanese planes. Not yet. Those would probably come later, Herring thought. The Japanese were getting desperate. Tokyo military leaders had been ordering more kamikaze attacks.

Before very long Herring spotted the outline of Mount Suribachi on the horizon. It was unmistakable after the countless hours he'd spent studying reconnaissance photos. He worried they'd be easy targets when they passed under the cliffs of Suribachi, but there was no way to avoid moving in its shadow to get to the island's southeastern beaches.

Herring once again turned his thoughts back to the mission, the memos, the planning sessions. Seven of the gunboats—457, 441, 449, 438, 474, 450, and 473—would provide "intensive close-in fire" for the demolition teams' daylight reconnaissance mission on the eastern beaches. The fire would focus on "neutralization" of areas "behind the landing beaches . . . while the UDTs are operating." Five gunboats would be held in reserve, in case ships on the firing line had to be replaced.

With the 449 on course, most of the crew went topside to watch the fleet bombard the island. The noise grew louder as they moved closer. The battleships fired fourteen-inch shells, while the cruisers launched eight-inch shells and the destroyers blasted the island with five-inch shells. Walls of white-and-black smoke rose up and formed thunderheads in the sky above.

The newcomers had never seen this kind of firepower. Even the veterans were stunned by the intensity. It seemed that all the ships they'd seen crowded into Ulithi were there, firing all at once.

McGrath bounded to the bridge, trying to find the right angle, the right spot, for the perfect photograph. He smelled opportunity there among the awesome fear—maybe a wire service would pick up one of his shots and it would end up on the front pages of all the newspapers. McGrath knew the dangers—he had been on the front lines before. There was always a chance he could get wounded, or even killed. But the risk was worth it. He was a witness to history, a chronicler of heroes, and his portfolio was already strong, maybe good enough to help him land a job after the war at *Time* or *Life*.

Overchuk, sandwiched between Beuckman and Hightower, turned around and noticed the photographer on the bridge. He gave him the thumbs-up sign.

"You gonna make us famous!" Overchuk shouted.

McGrath smiled. "I'll do what I can," he said.

McGrath already had photos of just about everyone on board. Everybody wanted the photographer to snap his picture, and McGrath always obliged, snapping away. And with every picture, he'd write down the sailor's name, just in case the photographs were published. There was always that chance.

Herring watched his men heading to their battle positions, getting ready. They didn't need orders.

Cooper plugged the wire on the headset under his helmet into a jack by the ammunition locker near the bow. He tested it, to make sure the officers on the bridge could hear him.

"Bridge, this is Cooper on the number one gun, how do you copy?"

"Fred, I hear you loud and clear," said Yarbrough on the other end of the line. Cooper wheeled around and waved to Yarbrough to signal it was working.

Yarbrough started through another series of checks. He had to make sure every part of the ship, from the pilothouse to the engine room, could communicate with the bridge.

Everything was working. So Yarbrough turned to Herring and gave him the thumbs-up sign.

They drew closer to Iwo Jima and the smiles faded. Mount Suribachi was no longer an image in a grainy black-and-white reconnaissance photograph, or a silhouette in the distance. It was an imposing, forbidding mass of rock, a fortress with hellish vapors rising from the hot volcanic soil.

It's like a Frankenstein movie, Overchuk thought.

Men on the other gunboats that morning felt the same. Seaman First Class Larry Hermes, over on LCI-471, saw "a barren rock, an ugly-looking thing." Onderdonk saw "the ominous-looking island with steam spouting here and there. I was reminded of Dante's *Inferno*."

There was no going back. The column of gunboats maintained its course. Overchuk headed to his station, the port-side 20mm gun. He slapped Hightower on the back.

"Well, here we go," Overchuk said.

"Yup. See you later, ol' boy," Hightower said.

One last thing, Overchuk thought: Where's Lemke? He bounded to the starboard 40mm gun and there he was, putting his arms through his life vest.

"Hey, Lemke. Good luck," Overchuk said.

Lemke grinned a rueful grin. "You, too. And remember, John, don't shoot till you see the whites of their eyes!" Lemke laughed, and his gun crew laughed, too, breaking the tension. For a moment, Lemke forgot just how terrified he was.

By the deckhouse, Holgate said goodbye to Hoffman. "We're going to get through this. Stay positive," he said, laying a hand on his friend's shoulder.

"I will," Hoffman said.

"You got a good crew," Holgate said.

Hoffman knew that. Schoenleben was the gunner. Leroy Young and Lemke were on his team. They were fast, efficient, battle-tested. "You're right. There's no better gun crew anywhere."

Holgate knew it was time. "Listen, I better get below. See you later."

"Later," Hoffman said, quietly.

Holgate walked past Walton and Paglia. The two handsome boys watched the bombardment on the gun deck and said not a word. Walton saw why his brother didn't want him to enlist. He was trying to protect him. But his brother wasn't here now.

"You'll have to paint this someday, when this is over," he told Paglia. "Sit on a beach and paint it."

"A nice, quiet beach," Paglia said.

Paglia looked into the thundering, stinking island, the rolling smoke and shrieking, flashing shells, then slipped into the pilothouse. The little steel room felt claustrophobic, crowded with equipment and four men. Vollendorf was at the helm; Duvall, as communications officer, stood behind Vollendorf. Richard Holtby stood at the engine-order telegraph, ready to relay directions down to the black gang.

It was dark inside, the portholes around the conning tower were covered with metal for protection from shrapnel. A single red light cast an eerie glow in the murk. Poor visibility, no ventilation, and the stink of four sweating men.

The saving grace was the time Paglia would spend up on the bridge with his SCR-610 radio pack on his back, relaying messages to Herring. But the more he thought about it, the more Paglia realized that he'd be in even more danger up there. At least in the pilothouse there was a thin shield of metal. On the bridge, there was no protection at all.

Paglia stopped his mind with busyness. Overnight he'd memorized the code names for all the LCIs and other ships taking part in their piece of the invasion. The code name for 449 was Mullet 9. The 457, Nash's gunboat, was called Rumpus 7. The 438 was Spike 8. The 474 was called Swami 4. Down the list he went, wondering whose job it was to come up with these things.

Even the tiny crafts carrying the demolition teams onto the beach were given code names. LCIs were called Pigeons. Destroyers were Seahawks. Commanding officers of the UDTs were called Tuffy to be followed by the unit number. It was somewhat comical listening to the radio traffic as Mullet 9 chatted with Rumpus 7, trying to get in touch with Tuffy 14.

Down in the well deck, Johnson was checking all the movements of his 20mm before loading the first round. He leaned right to make sure the lever located just above his right-hand grip was set to the "safe" position. He asked Hollowell to harness him in. He turned sharply from side to side, making sure the pivot movement of the gun was smooth. Satisfied, he squatted down to see if the 20mm would point skyward. Then he stood up on his tiptoes to make sure the gun pointed right down. It all checked out. Hollowell stood over Johnson, watching the checks, chattering about the pineapple cakes and cherry pies lined up in the galley.

"You hungry? Boy, I'm hungry. Can't you smell 'em? It's going to be a while before we eat anything . . ." He rambled. All he had to do was walk inside the deckhouse, right behind them, and grab one, he said. No one would know.

Johnson knew Hollowell wasn't going to steal a snack. He was just trying to lighten the mood, but right now Johnson wanted to get focused on the targets. There would be plenty of time for pie and jokes after the mission.

On the bow, Bozarth lowered his head and prayed in the gun tub, out of sight of the others. Hallett looked over at him, then turned his attention back to his gun. Banko, the gun captain, was once again going over important points with Flook.

"The extractor is going to eject the empty case through the housing here and will hit the case deflector here, spilling it onto the deck," Banko said, pointing to different parts of the gun. "One of your jobs is to make sure the casings don't pile up under the gun. Also, watch your footing. I don't want you falling down and getting hurt on these casings. They're going to be rolling around everywhere."

He could tell Flook was scared. But he had to make sure he got it right—he had to keep drilling it into his head.

"Oh, and remember, when they first come out they're hot as hell, so put on those gloves when you need to push casings out of the way. You got it?" Banko said.

Flook nodded.

Banko caught sight of Hallett. "Man, that guy is green," they silently agreed.

Meanwhile, on the fantail, Beuckman and Bedell were giving last-minute instructions to the standby brigade. They were green, too, mostly men who had joined the 449 in the last few weeks. They had little or no combat experience among them.

Beuckman was being a hard-ass. "If we get hit and we have casualties, I'll go forward and see the extent of injuries. You men are not to leave the fantail unless instructed to do so. Understand?" he barked.

The men meekly nodded.

"If we take casualties, I am going to depend on you men to help me. I'm the only medical person aboard ship so do your duty and do what you are told when I tell you. Got it?"

Again, the men nodded.

Beuckman looked over at Kepner and yelled out, "Well, old man, here we go again. Let's hope our luck holds."

Kepner laughed. "Who you calling old man, Grandpa?"

The men on the fantail laughed just a bit too loud.

THE LINE OF gunboats closed in on a line of destroyers, cruisers, and battleships near Iwo Jima. A thunderous roar almost deafened them all. The USS *Pensacola*, an American cruiser, was hit by Japanese guns. Moments later, another explosion rocked the cruiser, and this one sent shock waves across the sea in all directions. The *Pensacola* was firing back, but it was still being slammed, over and over. The ship turned and pulled away from the island, her decks afire.

At that moment, everyone on the 449, even the veterans, knew this was real. They'd just seen Americans killed, probably. There had to be casualties: The ship was hit six times in just a couple of minutes. Now everyone's adrenaline was in overdrive.

Let's get in there, Hallett thought. *Let's just get this over with.*

But it was like they were moving in slow motion.

Their formation reached the southern tip of the island, and the shadow of Mount Suribachi draped itself across the column. Banko looked up at the crag and expected big guns to open fire, just like they'd done with the *Pensacola*. Hallett craned his neck, looking for any signs of life on the desolate island. It was nothing but rocks . . . and that horrific odor. Overchuk, on the port-side 20mm gun, had a ringside view. But like Hallett, he saw nothing but rocks, bushes, and black sandy terraces. Once they were past Mount Suribachi, Banko felt a little relieved. Maybe they'd be safe—it would be like the other reconnaissance missions, where the Japanese ignored the little gunboats.

The ships continued north until they were parallel to the eastern beaches. They made a ninety-degree turn to port, until all of their bows were facing the shore. All they had to do was move forward, about thirty-five hundred yards, and they'd run straight into the beach. But they weren't going anywhere. Not yet. They waited there while a line of destroyers slowly moved into their assigned positions, about five hundred yards in front of them. The gunboats stayed in position, engines idling, waiting for the order to attack.

Herring could see Yellow Beach 2 directly in front of him. He glanced across the decks, at the men in their battle stations. It was *his* responsibility to keep these men alive. He could do this, he knew. Still, he closed his eyes for a moment and asked God for strength and courage.

Signalman Arthur Lewis shouted to Herring: The observers were approaching the gunboat in a LCPR. Herring turned around in time to see a fast-moving LCPR swoop in beside the gunboat's fantail. In a matter of seconds, two men jumped aboard the 449, and the zippy little craft disappeared again. The movement was impressive. Herring could see that one of them was obviously a navy officer, and the other, judging by his camouflage apparel, was a Marine. Herring welcomed them aboard.

Yates and Brockmeyer quickly staked out their places on the crowded bridge. Besides Herring and Yarbrough, Lewis and McGrath were there.

Yates twisted the straps on his binoculars. This mission was going to be a bitch. The water was cold, fifty-nine degrees. Anything below sixty could reduce a swimmer's strength and endurance. Yates clenched his teeth, remembering the ache of too-cold water on hard-swimming muscles . . . but he wished to God he was in the water, on the beach, not on the bridge of the 449.

No one knew just how many obstacles and mines they'd have to blow up. He'd read the memos: "Be prepared to clear all mines and obstacles discovered during the reconnaissance." But today, his job was a little easier: He'd be responsible for coordinating Team 14's activities with the 449, including keeping watch for any swimmers that might need help. Swimmers were told to wave their arms if they were in trouble. If Yates spotted one, he'd call in the nearest craft to rescue the frogman. His binoculars would be critical, constantly scanning the water. He wouldn't be able to leave the bridge at all. He was stuck there.

By ten-thirty, every commander had binoculars trained on the gunboats and demolition teams heading toward the beach on Iwo Jima. Admiral Blandy was on the bridge of the *Estes*, watching. Captain B. Hall "Red" Hanlon, commander of the underwater demolition teams, was aboard the destroyer USS *Gilmer*, monitoring the radio traffic. Captain Malanaphy was ready on LCI-627, planning to sail from position to position to observe and issue orders. And Draper Kauffman, never one to stand on the sidelines, had just jumped aboard the LCI-438—the gunboat in the dead center of the line. From there he'd have the best vantage point on the entire operation.

The crafts carrying the frogmen were getting ready to drop their men in the water. On the ship's communication system, Paglia, in the pilot-house, relayed a message to Yarbrough from the command ship: The mine-sweepers had just finished up.

Inside the pilothouse, Holtby had just moved the brass handles of the engine-order telegraph to *Stand By*, alerting the engine room that they were about to receive orders.

All eyes were on the 457, Nash's command ship, waiting for the signal flag to go up, ordering the gunboats to advance. Moments later, Herring and the other gunboat captains spotted the flag. It was time. Holtby moved the arrows on the engine-order telegraph to *Half Ahead*. Down in the engine room, the indicator arrows cranked, buzzed, and went to *Half Ahead*.

With Vollendorf at the helm, the 449 moved forward. Up on the bow, Banko yelled out: "Here we go!" It was a war cry, his way of letting everyone know his gun crew was ready to fight.

Up ahead, Banko could see they were quickly approaching the line of destroyers. He glimpsed the fast boats of UDT 14 as they zipped past both sides of the 449. The little boats did not slow, and the silver backs of the frogmen, one by one, peeled away and slipped into the water like so many fish swimming to shore.

At the same time, the gunboats jolted through the line of destroyers and raced toward the beach. There was nothing between them and the Japanese now but a stretch of water. With the wind in his face, Banko watched as the shore rose up nearer: 1,900 yards, 1,800 yards, 1,700 yards . . .

Something in the water caught Banko's eye. He squinted and then recognized them: They were buoys, spherical-shaped, with an eighteen-inch-high pyramidal antenna **on top** of each one. Banko knew buoys were used to mark targets, but **as far as** he knew, the navy hadn't dropped any in these waters.

Then it hit him: The buoys were range finders. Not for the U.S. Navy, but for the Japanese.

Banko's heart raced. He had to tell an officer, fast, before it was too late.

27

SEAMAN FIRST CLASS Koizumi Tadayoshi could see history unfolding in the water below Mount Suribachi, but it couldn't see him. The horizon was dotted with American ships, dozens and dozens of them. This had to be the American invasion, he thought. They'd waited for months for this. Tadayoshi and his gun crew were ready.

The Americans were sticking to their usual playbook. For two days, the big U.S. ships had been pounding the island with large-caliber shells, keeping their distance, hoping for a lucky shot. But this morning, something new was happening. A line of smaller boats was advancing to the beaches on the eastern side of Iwo Jima, right below them, clear targets. Through his gun sights Tadayoshi could see men crouching on the decks. The bigger ships coming up from behind were loaded with invaders. They had to be.

Tadayoshi could not know this was only a recon mission, that the real invasion was still days away. This looked, to him, like the real thing.

Tadayoshi informed his officer. He then sat behind his 25mm gun and waited. His mouth was dry. His hands were wet.

His job was important to Japan, he knew. His family was in grave danger. Every Japanese man, woman, and child was in danger, and Iwo Jima was what stood between them and American savagery. The high command even wrote an Iwo Jima song to encourage them; they'd broadcast it over the island channel every night for the past week, and on Radio

Tokyo at home. The lyrics said Iwo Jima guarded the "gateway to our empire," and that the "brave men" on the island had been chosen to protect the emperor. They had endured "sickness, hardship, filthy water," but they would keep working together until "the hated Anglo-Saxons, lie before us in the dust."

Do not fire, Tadayoshi told himself. *Do not. No matter how clear the target.* Everyone on the mountain was under strict orders to not open fire, orders straight from General Kuribayashi himself. They'd worked long and hard to conceal most of their fortified positions, especially on the high ground. They couldn't reveal their positions before the American troops landed.

It was not like nobody ever shot a gun. Early in the morning, some of the coastal guns hidden along the beach sometimes opened fired on American ships moving along the shoreline. But the fire was just a reminder, a minor irritant to their routine patrols. It stopped as soon as it began.

But this was different. These ships were coming from the high seas, in coordinated ranks and rows. These had to be invading troops.

Kuribayashi received the urgent message in his underground bunker: The American invasion was under way. The general jumped on the command radio to alert his troops. "All shout banzai for the emperor. I have the utmost confidence that you will all do your best. I pray for a heroic fight," he said in his broadcast.

Men rushed through the intricate network of tunnels and trenches to man their camouflaged guns.

Kuribayashi knew how much Iwo Jima meant to Tokyo. If Iwo Jima fell, the entire nation would be vulnerable to even more devastating air attacks by American B-29 bombers. In a letter to his wife Yoshi, on January 21, 1945, Kuribayashi said that by now, there were probably close to 150 B-29s based on Saipan.

"By around April, that number will be 240 or 250, and by year-end it's likely to rise to about 500 planes, meaning that there will be that many more air raids than now. On top of that, if the island I'm on gets captured, there'll be an increase of several hundred enemy planes, and the air raids on the homeland will be many times more savage than now," he predicted.

Kuribayashi had struggled hard to prepare Iwo Jima, not only against the barren geography, but against a military hierarchy dedicated to its tried, traditional tactics. His strategy flew in the face of convention. Throughout the war, when Americans invaded a Japanese-held island, the Japanese simply defended the beaches and strove to drive American troops back into the water. If that failed, the soldiers would launch banzai attacks, figuring it was better to die a hero than to surrender.

Kuribayashi took a different approach. He knew he couldn't stop this invasion at the beach. The Americans had too much firepower. Instead, he'd built an intricate network of caves and tunnels that could withstand naval and air attacks. He brought in engineers to design the underground fortifications, and they'd worked for months, turning Iwo Jima into a labyrinth of mutually supporting bunkers, gun emplacements, and blockhouses that took advantage of the terrain.

The fortifications were strong, and they were all but invisible. The gun ports blended into the rugged surfaces and gaps in the mountainsides, and nests of artillery and machine guns crouched unseen in the rocks, caves, and sand. They'd built 750 defensive positions, and linked them together with nearly fifteen thousand yards of tunnels.

So once the invaders landed, America would quickly realize that Iwo Jima was a death trap, engineered to kill its soldiers on an industrial scale.

Tokyo initially rejected Kuribayashi's strategy, but their minds changed as the war went on and their options narrowed. The general worked tirelessly with planners, his fighting men traded guns for picks and shovels and stayed in fighting form by toiling in rat-infested tunnels. They'd created an invisible fortress, a defensive masterpiece.

Kuribayashi's command post was the jewel in the crown. It was a series of concrete-reinforced caves seventy-five feet underground on the northwestern side of the island, connected by five hundred feet of tunnels. The openings were hidden between two small hills, visible only if you knew just where to look.

The general was known for his morale-building work among the men. He gave each a copy of what he called "Courageous Battle Vows," an apocalyptic call to the "defense of this island . . . We shall grasp bombs, charge enemy tanks, and destroy them. Each man will make it his duty to kill ten of the enemy before dying."

Perhaps his theory would be tested today, he thought.

But as more information arrived about the U.S. ships, the information did not spell "invasion." The force was too small. There should be hundreds of amphibious crafts carrying troops and equipment, but this was a small force, not worth them tipping their hand.

His men should hold their fire after all, he thought. He didn't want them to give away their secret positions. He reached for the radio.

But in the distance he heard the familiar thump of artillery fire. Telltale puffs of smoke rose from high on Mount Suribachi. It had started anyway. The dam had burst.

28

BANKO TOOK A few steps toward Cooper, but stopped when he heard a collision—metal smashing into metal, like a car accident. A geyser of water shot high in the air, spraying the deck and soaking Banko right to the skin.

Wiping the seawater from his eyes, Banko quickly turned left, toward the racket. The 441 had just been hit. Smoke belched from the hull. His nose prickled with the sickening stench of cordite. Japanese artillery. The Japs were firing on the gunboats!

"*Holy shit*," he said out loud. The ocean erupted all around the gunboats as shells landed forward, alongside, way too close.

Forget the buoys, Banko thought. He wheeled around and scrambled back to his 40mm gun, shouting to his gun crew: "Get ready!"

"Open fire!" came the order from Herring. The LCIs came alive, throwing bright metal back at the enemy positions on the shore. The frogmen were still in the water, advancing toward the beach. The gunboats still moved slowly forward into the boiling fight. Shells of every size rained down and exploded, water and metal clattered onto the steel decks. Voices yelled and bellowed.

The bridge throbbed with noise, smoke, and anxiety. "Prepare to fire the rockets," Herring shouted at Vanderboom.

Vanderboom didn't hear him, so Herring leaned in closer. He tugged on Vanderboom's life jacket, then yelled into the mate's right ear: "Paul, prepare to fire. Just wait for my order." Vanderboom nodded and started hitting his switches. He had 120 rockets racked and ready to fly.

It was 10:55.

Below, the gun crews frantically loaded and reloaded as the guns spun and chattered. Shell casings rolled and bounced across the deck. A member of Banko's gun crew, Seaman First Class William Hildebrand, was midway on the metal ladder connecting the well deck to the bow, helping pass ammunition from the storage locker to the loaders. He glanced at the sky, and noticed something strange. Something was missing—an element that had been with them during all the rehearsals.

"Hey," he shouted to Seaman David Fletcher, who stood just below him. "Where the hell are all the planes?"

Then Hildebrand's world went black.

A tremendous explosion rocked the gunboat, followed by a spectacular orange wall of flames.

A Japanese mortar had struck the bow, just a few feet from the 40mm ammunition locker.

On the bridge, Herring felt a terrible blast of hot air, followed by a massive shock wave that nearly knocked him to the floor. A familiar noise surrounded the little steel cabin below, a noise like hail pelting the windows during a Carolina thunderstorm. But Herring knew this wasn't hail. It was shrapnel, razor-sharp metal, slicing into the bulkhead, deck, and pilothouse.

Herring regained his footing and quickly tried to assess the damage. On the bridge everyone was still standing. No one was injured. Thick black smoke blocked any view of the bow. The shrapnel probably had perforated the pilothouse, but he didn't have time to check. Not yet. The ship was on fire.

He turned to Yarbrough, but his executive officer was already in action, leaning over the edge of the bridge shouting to Bedell and the standby brigade. "Fire on the bow! Fire on the bow!" Yarbrough bellowed. Finally, Bedell gave him the thumbs-up sign.

The men leapt into action, grabbing fire hoses and running forward to douse the flames. Herring turned his attention back to Vanderboom. "Fire the rockets!" he shouted.

With one finger on the power button, Vanderboom pushed the fire selector knob. Nothing happened. Vanderboom was already rattled by the hit, and now the rockets wouldn't fire. He repeated the steps. Again, nothing.

Vanderboom was frantic. "The explosion," he cried, "it must have cut the wiring to the launchers. It's got to be something simple." He talked fast, and his mind raced even faster, tracing every step and junction where things might've gone wrong. "Just a minute, Skipper, I can fix it!"

Herring felt a little sorry for the fellow; he asked if Vanderboom needed help. Vanderboom shook his head no. The only thing he really needed was a little luck.

Hallett came to on the bow deck. He scrambled to get up, but fell down again. He let himself lie still a minute and tried to remember what had happened. He'd been adjusting the height of the 40mm gun on the bow, making sure it was in the proper position. He'd glanced at Bozarth, who was soaking wet, holding a clip of 40mm ammunition in both hands. Bozarth had grinned at Hallett, an act of bravado. And just then, Hallett felt a flash of intense heat, and a heavy blow to his back. The blast tossed Hallett a few feet forward. He landed on his face. The impact shattered his nose.

Hallett was groggy, but realized he had to get away from the fire. The flames were moving closer to the forward magazine, an ammo storage room below the bow. If that caught fire, the whole front of the ship would go up. Hallett pressed himself against the deck and crawled to the most forward point of the ship, the prow. Smoke billowed all around him. He coughed and gagged violently as he gasped for fresh air.

The pain was getting sharper: It wasn't just his nose that hurt now. His face and hands were severely burned, his body was riddled with bits of metal. His right leg throbbed, a piece of shrapnel was buried in the back of his knee. When he glanced down, he saw a huge tear in his pants just above his right hipbone, "with a big chunk of hamburger meat hanging out."

"My God, I've been hit," he screamed. He didn't think anyone could hear him, not with all the noise.

Hallett had crawled as far as he could. Hugging the deck, he could hear Japanese shells exploding around him. The fire was so intense he could feel the metal on the deck starting to melt. He didn't know what had happened to his friends, if they were alive or dead. All he knew was that he needed a medic. Taking deep breaths, he whispered a prayer as he prepared to die. It was the only prayer he could remember.

> *Now I lay me down to sleep,*
> *I pray the Lord my soul to keep.*
> *If I should die before I wake,*
> *I pray the Lord*
> *My soul to take.*

BY THE STARBOARD 20mm gun, Hollowell picked himself up. He had been reloading the gun while Johnson fired nonstop at targets along the beach. The next thing he knew, Hollowell woke up facedown on the metal, feeling like he'd been sucker punched in the gut.

He stood up, stunned. Bodies were strewn like dolls on the well deck.

Then he heard Johnson's voice. Johnson was down on the deck next to the gun. He'd been blown out of his harness. The skin of his right cheek was sliced open, exposing nerves, tissue, and shattered teeth. His right arm was laid open to the bone and tendons. His uniform was black with blood.

Johnson was crying in pain. A weak sort of "help me" came from his broken mouth.

Hollowell stood there, petrified for a moment, but then felt himself fall to his knees at Johnson's side. "Breathe deep. Relax. I'm here. You're going to be OK, I promise."

Johnson knew it was bullshit. "I'm dying, Junior," he said, struggling to talk. With each word, blood from Johnson's mouth speckled Hollowell's face and life jacket.

"No, you're not. Listen, I'm going to get some first aid stuff. And then I'm coming back for you. I'm coming back with help. You're going to be OK. Just hang on, OK?"

Johnson reached up and, with his left hand, pulled Hollowell closer. "You gonna be back, right?"

"Yes. I promise. Swear to God," Hollowell said.

Johnson released Hollowell and closed his eyes. Hollowell bolted into the deckhouse. He had to find Beuckman.

A few feet away, Overchuk lay motionless on the gun deck. He'd been strapped into his 20mm, but for some reason the gun wouldn't work. He'd screamed to Seaman First Class Leonard Sless to help him get out of the harness.

"Here we are in battle and my damn weapon won't fire! It's gotta be a spring," Overchuk told Sless. As soon as he was free, Overchuk sprinted to the deckhouse. Just before he stepped inside he heard a roar like a tidal wave, and felt a bolt of pain shoot up from his ankle. The next thing he knew he was flat on the ground. He tried crawling, but couldn't move. The pain was intense. He screamed. He lost consciousness.

Charles Hightower was very near, still at his station by the port-side 40mm gun. When the mortar hit the bow, he saw a leg fly over his head and land about ten feet behind him. He saw a sailor blown overboard. The world shifted into slow motion.

First, Hightower checked to see if his gun crew was OK. Then he shouted as loud as he could, "Man overboard! Man overboard!" He leaned over the side of the gun deck and saw the sailor floating facedown in the water. He kept his eye trained on him as the waves splashed against the hull. The face bobbed up with a wave. It was Ensign Cooper.

"Oh, shit. Hang in there!" he screamed at Cooper.

Hightower's mind raced. The guy was half conscious, probably half drowned already. He had to save him. Hightower quickly grabbed a life ring from the railing, and following procedures learned over endless practice sessions, he held the ring in his right hand and fifty feet of rope in the other. He took a deep breath. He only had one shot to get it right. Using all his strength, he tossed the ring as far as he could. It landed near Cooper. All the officer had to do was reach out and grab it. Hightower would pull him in. But Cooper wasn't moving.

"Grab on, Ensign Cooper! Wake up! Take the ring. Look right! Take the damn ring!" he screamed.

Again, Cooper didn't respond. The current caught his body and pulled it farther from the boat. Hightower ran along the railing, shouting for

Cooper to wake up, grab the ring. But finally Hightower gave up. Cooper was dead. Hightower saw his body drift out to sea. Damn it, he'd done everything he could. Cooper had become a friend, ever since that day on the gun deck when the officer opened up. Hightower knew all about Cooper's life, his young wife and baby daughter. His fear of dying in combat. Hightower wanted to cry for a minute.

Instead, he wheeled around and ran back to his position.

"Who was it?" said his friend Ralph Owens, the gunner on the 40mm.

"Cooper."

"Did you see anyone else?" Owens asked anxiously. He pretended not to see Hightower's eyes.

Hightower knew what he meant. Cooper had been forward, up at the bow with Hallett, Banko, Bozarth, and several other sailors. But Hightower was so focused on trying to save Cooper he hadn't looked for the others. It was so hard to see any damn thing with all the smoke. "No," he told Owens. "I don't know where the hell any of them are."

Hightower suddenly could feel Minnick standing behind him near the ammunition locker. Minnick was trembling. Hightower knew he had to say something to calm down the kid. "We're still OK. Just keep passing the ammo, man. We'll be all right. Just keep it coming. Don't stop," he said.

BANKO OPENED HIS eyes, but nothing seemed to make sense. He took a quick sort of inventory.

He was upside down, his right leg stuck in the top rung of the ladder connecting the bow to the well deck. He'd been blown off the gun platform. His helmet was gone. His life jacket was shredded, his shirt wasn't much better. Something smelled terrible, and his right shoulder hurt like hell.

He worked his fingers through his clothing and found the wound, a deep laceration. Blood. His fingers were burned.

He had to get out of there. He twisted and wriggled his right leg free, and a few seconds later he dropped bodily into the well deck, landing on his back. He heard himself scream. He blacked out for a second, then scrambled to his feet. He gave his head a good shake to clear his vision. He took a deep breath, stood up straight, and looked at the deck around him.

I am dead, he thought, *and this is Hell.*

Smoke belched from a gaping hole in the deck. A six-foot crater yawned in the spot where Cooper and Seaman Flook had been standing a minute ago. The crew that had been there, the men? The men were gone. Their bodies were everywhere, reduced to bits, hanks, gobs, spatters. Banko was revolted, but felt oddly numb at the same time. He knew someone needed to put out that fire, or they all were going to die. It was just next to the forward magazine.

Banko stumbled toward the deckhouse to get help, marveling at the noise and racket and shouting around him, wondering why he was still standing up. Something disturbing caught his eye. There, near the hole in the deck, were the charred, headless remains of a sailor.

Banko wondered vaguely who it was. He didn't have time to find out. He had to get Bedell and the standby brigade onto that fire. That was the only way to save the ship.

Three steps later, Banko stopped. There was the small black water hose right there, the one the gun crew used to wash off the deck, clean out buckets, and do laundry. It was nothing more than a little garden hose, but it was what he had. He turned around and headed back to the bow. Each step was suddenly excruciating, like a thousand sharp needles traveling up from his legs into his lower back. Smoke stung his eyes. His skin burned. But he reached the spool bolted to the bulkhead near the bow ladder. He unraveled the hose, turned on the faucet, and cooled his blistered palms. With a steady stream of water pouring out of the nozzle, Banko made his way up the rungs again, this time stopping to tug on the hose when it caught on the railing. He reached the top of the ladder. He felt the waves of heat licking at his face, irritating his burns. He pointed the little garden hose at the flaming hole and sprayed, sprayed, sprayed. As long as he was alive, he wasn't going to give up.

BY THE DECKHOUSE, Overchuk opened his eyes. He was in the same spot where he had collapsed: sprawled on the well deck, left ear pressed against the floor, facing the door he'd been reaching to open. He blinked several times, then noticed blood dripping down the bulkhead. But it was more than blood. It appeared to be a man's face, an eyebrow and an ear with skin attached, all in one big piece.

Overchuk panicked. "Oh, shit. Is that my face?" He reached up and touched his mouth, nose, eyes. He quickly realized he was safe. But then the relief was replaced by anger. Yes, he was alive. But somebody else, somebody he knew, was dead. Deader than dead.

Overchuk tried to push himself up, but he couldn't stand. A piece of shrapnel was embedded in his ankle, stuck fast in the thick leather of his boot. That was the only thing that saved his foot. Now all he had to do was shake the shrapnel off and he'd be able to walk. Other guys were obviously a lot worse off.

He turned toward the bow. Johnson was there, a few feet away. Half his face had been shot off. Smoke poured from the bow. Ammunition was starting to explode, sending everyone ducking for cover. He felt a little dizzy. He smiled for a minute. It was a little like the Fourth of July, when the fireworks got out of hand. He thought he might faint again, but then Sless appeared, struggling to stay on his feet.

Sless grasped his stomach. Blood spilled onto the deck between his fingers. His face was ashen. "Help me, please," he begged. One of Sless's feet slid out from under him. Overchuk saw why.

The deck was like the killing floor at a slaughterhouse, slippery with body parts, entrails, and blood. Overchuk was stunned, but he had to help Sless. He pulled himself up, took a step toward his friend. He spotted Charles Vogel out of the corner of his eye. The man was wandering wide-eyed and stunned. "Vogel, go get help!" Overchuk yelled. "Swifty's hurt!"

Vogel said, "Yessir." He turned slowly and hung onto the rail, stepping carefully. He was shut down almost entirely, but now he had orders to follow. He moved slowly, but in the right direction.

Meanwhile, Bedell, Beuckman, and Blow and the standby brigade were making their way forward through the deckhouse, running down the long corridor to the well deck. In the semi-dark they could smell the pies and bread laid out for later. Inside the covered corridor the yeasty, fruity aroma still held sway over the stench of cordite, blood, and sulfur. Just before they reached the well deck door, Hollowell burst through from the other side. He was scorched, bloody, and rambling about Johnson, something about wounds and blood, hands and teeth and fire.

Beuckman assured Hollowell they were headed to the scene, they'd take care of Johnson. They didn't have time to stop. They had to reach the water hoses and put out the fire. They'd move the wounded to safety. "Calm down . . . Come with us. We need your help," Beuckman told Hollowell.

Kepner, too, was headed to the bow, but he took a different route. He grabbed a big wire litter from the fantail and climbed the ladder to the gun deck. As he ran past the pilothouse, Walton tried to stop him. "It's bad over there," he warned. "It's really bad."

Kepner kept going, but he stopped at the ladder leading down to the well deck. All he could see there was smoke, flames, and bodies. Jesus God, it was worse than he'd imagined.

The Japs kept firing shells, shells, shells. The frogmen were taking their blessed time, Kepner thought. The gunboats had done enough. It was about time to get the hell out of here. And this was just reconnaissance. The invasion, the real fight, wasn't for another two days.

29

THE SMELL HIT Bedell as soon as he stepped through the door to the well deck, a metallic coppery odor of blood and death. Bodies were sprawled everywhere under a roiling cloud of smoke. Bedell froze, wondering where to start. "Leo, get the fire under control, and I'll start taking care of the wounded," Beuckman said.

Bedell nodded, then turned to the standby brigade. He told them to grab the fire hoses from the reels mounted on the bulkheads, then start attacking the flames. They'd practiced this dozens of times, under much better conditions. As the sailors fanned out across the bloody deck, their feet slipped and slid from under them, their shoes bogged down in muck that made a horrible sucking sound as they moved.

Directly above them, Corkins could see that the gunboat was in big trouble. The 40mm gun on the bow was knocked out, as well as Johnson's 20mm gun. But that wasn't what worried him most. From his elevated position on the gun deck, Corkins could see geysers of water rising from the water all around them. Japanese shells—big, heavy artillery shells—were closing in on the 449. Other gunboats were taking hits. The Japanese artillery was fast, furious, and beautifully camouflaged. The radio traffic said the news wasn't good. Casualties. Shouting. A guy was screaming somewhere not too far away; Corkins could hear him through the radio and in real life, too.

The gunboat continued its forward motion; they were less than a thousand yards from the beach, and closing in. They were in perfect range of the Japanese big guns. Corkins could do nothing but try to keep his 40mm crews focused on the shore and the targets. Maybe they'd get a stroke of good luck real soon, maybe the destroyers and battleships behind them would knock out the Japanese guns.

Corkins shouted instructions to his men over his headset. Someone was coming up the ladder. It was Vogel, carrying the news about the injuries and fire. Vogel yelled something, but Corkins only saw his lips moving, he couldn't hear a word, not with his headset on. Not with all the 40mm fire so near. Corkins couldn't leave his position. Vogel would have to come right by the pilothouse and shout it into his ear.

BEUCKMAN MOVED TOWARD Johnson, who was just a few feet away. The medic tripped over something on the deck, almost fell, righted himself just in time. It was someone's head, the face too charred to recognize. Beuckman fought down his revulsion. Keep going, he told himself. Keep going. Concentrate on the ones who can still be saved.

Beuckman knelt down on the bloody deck beside Johnson. "All right, R.L., let's get you taken care of. Just hold still," he said.

Beuckman reached into his medical bag and pulled out gauze bandages. Without any hesitation, he began pushing the hanging scraps of Johnson's face back together. Each time he put a piece of flesh back in place, Beuckman would wrap a bandage over it, pressing firmly to help Johnson's platelets clot off the tiny capillaries and veins that were oozing the life-sustaining blood. The process seemed time-consuming, but it was over in a matter of seconds. As he was looping a bandage roll around Johnson's head to keep pressure on the wound, Beuckman told the steward's mate he would survive.

"I know you're in a lot of pain, R.L., but I can't give you any morphine. You've lost so much blood, I'm afraid the morphine would kill you," Beuckman said. He encouraged Johnson not to talk because every time he moved his mouth, it opened up his clots. "You'll just bleed again."

Johnson closed his eyes and slowly nodded his head that he understood. As Beuckman prepared to put a splint on Johnson's mangled arm, something huge exploded directly above him. The force slammed Beuck-man to the deck.

Another Japanese mortar had just crashed into the 449. This one struck the gun deck, between the two 40mm guns, just below the bridge.

It was 10:57.

THE SECOND SHELL exploded just as Overchuk managed to get on his feet. The aftershock sent him tumbling to the deck again. As he looked up, Overchuk could see a hole punched into the bulkhead above him, with flames shooting out. Suddenly, a wave of blood spilled over the edge and ran down the wall. He knew he had to move. Each 40mm had an ammunition locker. If that fire spread, the ship could blow up. They still hadn't contained the fire on the bow.

Overchuk jumped to his feet, but he was wobbly. He was ready to head to the fantail, the only place that hadn't been hit, when he saw a figure staggering toward him through the smoke. It was Schoenleben.

"Jesus Christ, John, I'm hungry," Schoenleben said.

Overchuk was stunned. Of all things to say at a time like this!

When Schoenleben turned, Overchuk saw that part of Schoenleben's left shoulder was gone. His left arm was missing. He could see inside his friend's body. His organs were visible behind his ribcage. Schoenleben was in shock, walking around in a daze. Schoenleben is doomed, Overchuk thought. A whole team of surgeons couldn't save him.

Chaos was taking hold. Two hits in two minutes. It was all so quick. Now both the bow and the gun deck were on fire. Fear gripped the crew. Everywhere they scrambled were bodies, twitching in pain, screaming for help, while others lay motionless and silent.

Vogel had reached the top of the ladder leading to the gun deck, trying to find officers to warn about casualties on the bow. He had taken one step toward Corkins when the mortar slammed into the gun deck. He never made it. A shard of metal caught Vogel just above the eye-brows. As his body pitched forward, his skull opened and spilled its contents onto the deck. Shrapnel pierced Corkins's body, abdomen, and skull. The explosive heat melted his headset wires into his scalp.

From his high perch Herring scanned the destruction below. Smoke was belching from the gunboat. Massive casualties. Yarbrough jumped on the microphone, trying to reach Corkins below. "Bill, are you there? Do you copy?" He leaned over the edge and peeked down to the gun deck. Corkins was slumped against the pilothouse. "Come on, Bill, respond."

Herring glanced down at Corkins's punctured body. He turned to Yarbrough. "He's gone," Herring said. "He's dead."

Yarbrough glanced at the bow, but could not see any of the men who had been up there fighting the fire, treating the wounded. Where were they? Where was Cooper?

ON THE WELL deck, Beuckman was just getting back on his feet. He knew the second blast was probably as bad as the first. He glimpsed Hollowell and Overchuk standing near the deckhouse.

"Junior. Overchuk. Come here," he shouted. The men carefully trudged through the blood to Beuckman. He wasted no time. "Get Johnson and Sless to the mess deck," he barked. "That'll be our casualty collection point. Lay them on the tabletops. Take care of them the best you can. I will be there in a little while. I need to get up top," he said. Hollowell stood impassive, staring at the flaming gun deck. Beuckman flushed with anger. If they were going to save lives, they had to pay attention, listen to orders.

"Junior! I need you. You got this?" Beuckman snapped.

Hollowell jumped to attention. He had never seen Beuckman lose his temper. "Yes. I got it," he said. Beuckman glanced around the gunboat for more casualties. A pair of shoes stuck out over the top of the ladder leading to the gun deck, toes pointing downward—someone was face-down up there. Beuckman started up the ladder, edgy about what he might find. There might be someone alive, he told himself.

He reached the top, turned over the body: Vogel. Beuckman felt nauseated, not so much by the gruesome sight, but because of the terrible loss. Vogel was a kind soul. He'd enjoyed his baking school training, and was always handing out samples of his pies and bread to the guys. He'd talked about opening up a bakery of his own in Indianapolis. Some of his work was just below them, on the galley countertop. How would his family handle this news?

A crackling noise snatched Beuckman back to the present. On the port side of the gun deck, sitting in the trainer's seat of the 40mm gun, was William Tominac, a tough street kid from Chicago. He was dead. His body was on fire. Tominac's skin turned an awful dark reddish brown, and the flames spread the horrifying stench of burning hair and flesh.

Tominac was beyond saving. Beuckman heard someone call his name. It was Kepner, on the ground, in a pool of blood.

Kepner had been in the wrong place at the wrong time. He had taken the top route when he'd headed to the bow to help with the injured. As he passed the starboard 40mm, the Japanese mortar hit the gun deck. Shrapnel sliced into his legs. One leg was held on by a piece of flesh. The other was folded at an unnatural angle.

"Looks bad, don't it?" Kepner said, weakly.

Beuckman was stunned. Kepner was his closest friend on the 449. How many nights had they stayed up late, in the galley, sipping coffee and talking about their families? They were both in their thirties. They didn't have to enlist, but they had wanted to serve. And here was Kepner, for all his patriotism, bleeding to death. Still, Beuckman couldn't let his emotions get in the way.

"I'm not going to lie to you, you are probably going to lose both legs. But you will survive. I promise."

Kepner laughed. "Promise, huh?"

As Beuckman worked to apply tourniquets to both thighs above the wounds, he could hear the screams of the wounded and dying. For the first time, he felt overwhelmed. There was no help for it—he was the only pharmacist's mate on board the ship. All he could do was keep going and hope he didn't run out of bandages, sulfa, and morphine.

Beuckman stared into Kepner's eyes. "Hang in there, buddy. I'll be back." And just like that, Beuckman disappeared.

ON THE BOW, Banko was still spraying a stream of water through a garden hose into the gaping hole where his gun crew once stood. The second blast had knocked him down, but he got right back up. He had to get the fire under control.

Banko felt someone pat him on the shoulder. It was Blow. "You need to be treated," Blow said.

Banko shook his head. "No, I'm staying."

Blow grabbed the hose. "Like hell you are. Look at you."

Banko knew his wounds had to be bad. He could tell by the look on Blow's face. Suddenly, Banko realized he could barely stand up.

And deliverance stepped up in the form of Bedell, who told them he had just turned on a sprinkler system to flood the forward magazine. Hopefully, the water would cool the ammunition and prevent a massive explosion.

"There's too much to deal with right now. We can't fight all these fires, so we're just going to have to write off the ammunition up here," Bedell said.

Blow agreed, then turned his attention back to Banko. "Head to the mess deck," he said. "That's an order."

Banko didn't have the strength to fight. He turned and headed toward the deckhouse.

Hightower was gathering his wits. Seconds earlier, he had been passing ammunition, shouting words of encouragement to Owens, who was blasting Japanese positions on the beach. Then, without warning, a blast of hot air from the explosion knocked Hightower on his ass.

He jumped right up, and examined his body to make sure he wasn't hit. There were slivers of shrapnel in his pants, he was going to have some bruises, but he had escaped without injury.

But there on the rail was Gunner's Mate Third Class Amos Reagan, a member of his gun crew, unconscious and dangling over the side of the ship. Reagan's life jacket was on fire. The vest was snagged on a small hook on the railing. It was the only thing that kept Reagan from being blown into the ocean.

Hightower dragged Reagan back onto the ship, then patted out the flames. Reagan was in bad shape; his face and upper torso were terribly burned. A couple of shipmates quickly appeared and carried him below.

The burned smell was awful, and Hightower snorted and spit, trying to get it out of his nose. When he glanced at the 40mm gun, he saw Tominac's body engulfed in flames. Beyond that ghastly vision, slumped against the back of the gun, was his buddy, Owens.

Hightower bounded to his friend, wrapped his arms around Owens's waist, and tried lifting him. "I got you. Hang in there, buddy," he whispered in his ear. But Hightower could only take a few steps. The deck was just too slippery to get traction. So Hightower called out to Minnick, another member of his gun crew.

"Bob, where are you? Help me with Ralph!" he shouted.

No one responded. Hightower gently lowered Owens's body, then wheeled around angrily, looking for Minnick. But his anger disappeared quickly when he spotted him. He was lying facedown. His body was cut in half at the waist. His organs spilled onto the deck.

Hightower froze. He didn't know whether to run or cry. He wanted to pray, but he couldn't utter a word. This kid was going to be a baseball star. This was the teenager who'd postponed a major-league baseball career to serve his country. Now here he was, cut open like an animal in a butcher shop. Hightower shook. He turned his attention back to Owens.

He again lifted his friend to his feet. But this time, Hightower half dragged, half carried him, struggling to keep his balance. When he reached the conning tower, Hightower stopped. He couldn't take another step—he couldn't get Owens below by himself. So once again, he lowered Owens, leaning his body against the bulkhead near the pilothouse. Then Hightower dropped to the deck beside his friend.

He began desperately searching for a wound so he could try to stem the flow of blood. But after he opened his friend's jacket, he knew there was nothing he could do. There was a gaping hole in his left side. Hightower began sobbing. He held Owens as if he were a child, held him in close and hugged him.

"Tell them," Owens muttered and paused, before taking a deep, labored breath. Hightower pressed his ear up against Owens's face. "Tell them what happened to me, tell them what happened here . . . Tell my mom. Tell Nina. Please tell Nina. I love her."

"I will, ol' boy, I will . . . I promise. Why, you're going to be all right," he said.

There was no hope. "I told you. I'm not going to make it," he whispered. "I think I'm tired . . . I think I'll go to sleep."

Hightower wouldn't hear of it. "You're gonna be fine, you're gonna be fine, you hear me?"

But Owens didn't answer. He had lost consciousness. Hightower shook him, but couldn't get a response.

With tears streaming down his face, Hightower screamed: "Please, someone, help me!"

Beuckman came running over, saw blood pouring off Hightower's right hand that was still wrapped around Owens waist. He bent down and stared into Hightower's face. "Charles, wiggle your fingers."

So he did. But then Hightower snapped: "That's not my blood, I haven't been hit."

Beuckman quickly examined Owens, but he didn't have good news.

"He's not gonna make it, Hightower . . . I'm sorry, there's nothing I can do."

Hightower already knew that. So he sat there, cradling Owens, the two of them surrounded by death, sitting on a deck awash with the blood of their shipmates. At that moment, Hightower stared blankly at Mount Suribachi. He could see the massive explosions, American artillery hitting targets on Iwo Jima. But at that moment, he felt nothing. He was empty, done with this war. He just sat there, gazing at the mountain, hoping he, too, would die.

NEARBY, WALTON WAS uneasy. This was real. People were dying all around him. Moments earlier, Signalman Carl Park had been giving him some instructions, but the great white light of the second mortar sent chunks of steel into Park's lower body. Park was unconscious on the deck, bleeding profusely, his left leg severed. Walton had been standing right next to Park, but he didn't receive a scratch. He didn't know how, not with all the pieces of metal slamming into the gunboat. Park must've gotten his share.

This wasn't supposed to be happening. The guys had assured Walton not to worry about the reconnaissance mission, that the Japanese never fired on LCIs. Walton's only job was to help Lewis raise flags, or signal the other ships with a flickering light, and then only if they got in trouble. But now, he was treating casualties, wracking his brains to remember the first-aid basics he'd learned so long ago in boot camp.

Walton kneeled beside Park and set a tourniquet above the deep wound. But Park never opened his eyes. He was barely moving. Walton could see Park's neck pulsate with each heartbeat, so he knew he was alive. Still, from the look of the deck around them, Park had lost a lot of blood. Walton felt so helpless. He wanted to do more, but he had to stay at his post, wait for orders. He could hear his pulse pounding in his ears. He knew Paglia was just behind him, in the pilothouse. He wondered if Paglia was just as scared as he was.

On the bridge, Herring knew the mission had gone to hell. In less than two minutes, the 449 had been hit twice. All of his 40mm and two of his 20mm guns were knocked out of commission. He couldn't fire his rockets. Casualties were piling up all around him. The radio traffic told him that all of the gunboats were in the same position.

Despite the explosions, Herring remained calm. He had Yarbrough check with the engine room, pilothouse. He wanted to know right away about the damage. He planned to talk to Bedell, to get an update on the fires. Even though the mission had gone sideways, he felt it was important to continue. They had to get those demolition teams onto the beach and back again. There was no way he was going to pull back. Herring turned to Yates. He said they'd stay on the line as long as possible. Maybe Vanderboom would get the launchers fixed.

Brockmeyer, the Marine observer, had stayed on the bridge long enough. He told Yates and Herring that he was going to help Beuckman. There were just too many casualties, and he knew some first aid. Yates said he'd join him once he was sure the frogmen on his team had made it to the beach.

So Brockmeyer bounded down the ladder connecting the bridge to the gun deck. He quickly moved from body to body, checking vital signs, looking to see who was still alive. As he bent down to check the condition of one sailor, he glimpsed someone walking slowly in his direction. It was Banko, and he looked like hell. Even though he was seriously wounded, Banko had climbed the ladder to the gun deck to see if he could help.

Banko could barely stand. Brockmeyer knew he had to get him below. Brockmeyer jumped to his feet. He wrapped his right arm around Banko's waist, then draped Banko's left arm over his shoulder. He carefully led Banko aft of the pilothouse, to a ladder leading to the fantail. Along the way, they passed the lifeless body of Glenn Trotter.

And there was Hightower, cradling Owens's head. Even though Banko was seriously wounded, he reached down to check Owens's condition. When he did, Hightower snapped, "Leave him alone!"

They left them all there, made it down the ladder. Brockmeyer eased Banko to the deck. Then he reached into a satchel and grabbed some dressings.

"Where have you been hit?" he asked Banko.

"Right here, my right shoulder, that's the worst one."

Brockmeyer pulled out his knife and cut away some of the uniform that was sticking into the wound. "I'm not going to lie. This is going to hurt," he said, before sprinkling sulfa powder into the opening and covering it with a gauze dressing. Banko closed his eyes and clenched his teeth. No matter how much pain he was in, Banko didn't want to look weak in front of that Marine.

"You'll be OK for now, long as you don't move. I'll check on you later." Brockmeyer scrambled up the ladder to the gun deck to look for more survivors. A few seconds later, Banko passed out.

LEMKE COULDN'T BELIEVE his luck. When the second Japanese shell hit the 449, he was standing behind the 40mm gun on the starboard side of the gunboat. The explosion wiped out the men all around him, but Lemke was uninjured. He only had a few sprays of blood and tiny pieces of flesh on his uniform.

Still, Lemke was paralyzed by fear.

Just a few feet from him lay Kepner and Park, both seriously wounded. Leroy Young, a pointer on the right side of the 40mm gun, was slumped in his seat, his body perforated. Beuckman ordered Lemke to help the others start moving the wounded below, to the mess deck. If no orders had come, Lemke knew he'd probably just stand there for the rest of the war.

McGrath, the photographer, had seen this kind of carnage before, but it was on land, spread out over the ground, usually Marines. These guys, these sailors, occupied so much less space. They seemed heaped on one another, and the living tracked the blood of the dead across the decks. The blood showed bright on their white shirts. Taking pictures was his job, but it seemed wrong to take photos of the dead sailors. He had brought the camera up to his face a few times, but he just couldn't do it. He wrestled with propriety, and finally convinced himself that these men's families should know what had happened to them.

So nervously, with shaking hands, he snapped a picture of the bow with the thick smoke in the foreground, Iwo Jima in the background. He removed the negative, placed it in his satchel, then wound the next film onto the spool. He roamed the ship, careful not to get in the way.

McGrath snapped a picture of Beuckman pouring sulfa powder on a wound. He took another of Hollowell leading Sless to the mess deck to lay him on a table. He kept snapping pictures, one after another, his mind shut down. He was a picture-taking machine.

BEDELL MADE HIS way up the ladder to the gun deck, on his way to the bridge to tell Herring about the damage on the bow. The gun deck was a bloody mess. The information would have to wait.

He sprinted to Beuckman. It looked like Kepner was dead, but Beuckman felt a pulse. He was barely alive and needed to be taken to the mess deck. Bedell ordered two crew members to help carry him.

Bedell spotted Schoenleben stumbling, walking in circles. He could see his friend's uniform was covered in rivulets of blood. White fluff, the stuffing blown out of his life jacket, stuck to his face.

More terrifying was the awful cavity blown into his left side. Bedell could see Schoenleben's heart beating in there. Bedell sidled up beside him, put his arm around his waist, and said, "Come on, buddy . . . I got you."

The two walked slowly down the ladder. When they reached the fantail, they stopped. Bedell knew they couldn't make it to the mess deck, which was filling up with the wounded. There were so many, every table had a body sprawled on top. Instead, Bedell lowered Schoenleben to the deck, making sure that his back was propped against the bulkhead. Bedell removed a syrette of morphine from his pocket and poked it into Schoenleben's leg. He knew his friend was going to die. He wanted him to be comfortable.

Bedell sat with Schoenleben and reminisced—that Christmas day they'd spent stranded on a reef, on their way to Saipan for a church service. They sat in that little boat with the outboard motor for two hours, waiting for someone to notice their plight. They'd passed the time talking about their favorite singers and made a list of their favorite songs.

Schoenleben managed a weak smile.

Bedell reminded Schoenleben of the recent letter from his wife, saying he had a son. "Remember how you ran around the ship, waving the letter over your head? Remember?"

Suddenly, Schoenleben opened his eyes, smiled, and stared at Bedell's face. "Howie," he said. "Howie. Howie." He closed his eyes.

No one had to tell Bedell why Schoenleben uttered those words before he died. Schoenleben's baby boy was named Howard.

Bedell felt his heart break. Howie Schoenleben would never know his father. Bedell squeezed Schoenleben's hand tightly, kissed the side of his face, and laid him down on the deck. He looked down at his buddy and made the sign of the cross.

He gathered up more bandages and headed back outside.

HERRING WAS WAITING for Bedell, but he didn't need a report to know the gunboat was in serious trouble.

In just a few minutes, the 449 had sustained major damage. Herring could see the casualties scattered on the decks below the bridge. He could see the fires and the smoke, hear the shouts and cries, the clatter of steel striking steel. Men were rushing all over the gunboat, risking their lives as they treated wounded sailors and carried them to safety.

Despite the suffering and mayhem, they still had a mission to accomplish. All the guns were knocked out except one 20mm in the aft. If Vanderboom could fix the wiring for the rocket launchers, they'd at least have some firepower.

In the meantime, Herring wanted to get more manpower onto the casualties in the gun deck and continue the search for survivors on the bow. He stepped to the rear of the bridge and onto the top rung of the ladder leading to the gun deck. Leaning over the railing, Herring yelled down to the sailors in the standby brigade, huddled in the fantail: "I need more men to help the wounded!"

Several terrified crewmen ran forward to assist, and then Herring shouted: "OK. That's enough. The rest of you . . ."

He never finished.

30

SOMETHING HUGE EXPLODED on the bridge. A simultaneous roar, shock wave, and blinding light.

Another Japanese mortar had hit the 449, this one the deadliest of all.

The starboard side of the tower blew apart, catapulting Herring from the bridge. Wires strained and popped, iron screeched, and the mast of the 449 collapsed and tumbled over the side, taking the American flag with her to the ocean floor.

The ship shuddered and slowed, then sat motionless in the water.

It was 10:59.

They'd taken three direct hits in five minutes. The first mortar destroyed the 40mm gun on the bow and set the ship on fire. The second knocked out the rest of the ship's 40mm guns. But the third was catastrophic.

The gunboat was no longer able to fight.

Bedell was on the fantail when the mortar slammed down. Chunks of steel flew over his head, a body fell ten feet from the bridge to the gun deck below. Whoever that was, he needed help. Bedell bolted up the ladder to the gun deck and knelt by the man.

It was Herring, and he didn't look good.

The skipper was unconscious, but still breathing. His left shoulder was ripped open, white pieces of jagged bone protruded from the wound. Bedell grabbed Herring's wrist to check his pulse. It was slow.

Bedell glanced up at one of the sailors finding his feet. "Find Beuck-man!" Bedell barked at him.

He couldn't believe it. In just a few minutes, the mission had spun out of control. They were in the crosshairs of Japanese coastal guns. The gunboat was so close to the beach that enemy machine-gun fire zipped across the hull or ricocheted off the ship. Shrapnel sprayed the sides of the gunboat from the near misses.

The other gunboats were in trouble, too. Bedell could see that the 438 had been hit by a large-caliber artillery round. The 450, 474, 441, and 457 had been struck multiple times. He could see smoke and flames pouring from the other LCIs. Despite the heavy fire, they all maintained their positions.

But Bedell knew his gunboat was in deep trouble. One more hit—this one in the right spot—and the 449 would be history. They still had 120 rockets on board, and a shitload of ammunition. Yes, he had flooded the forward magazine, but explosives were stored all over the ship. It was time to get out.

Beuckman appeared. Bedell had to find the other officers. "Take care of him, Henry. I'll be right back," he told the medic.

Bedell took the ladder to the bridge two steps at a time. He needed to get there fast, to tell Yarbrough he'd have to take command of the gunboat. But when Bedell reached the top, he stopped in his tracks. He gasped.

The mortar had blown a huge hole in the starboard side of the bridge. Signalman Arthur Lewis was lying facedown in a pool of blood. Yates, the demolition team observer, had taken a direct hit. Parts of his body were scattered over the deck like a jigsaw puzzle. And then there was Yarbrough.

Yarbrough was propped against a wall in a sitting position, head slumped, chin resting on his chest. It looked like he was asleep. But Yarbrough's gut was open, his intestines had spilled onto his lap.

Bedell scrambled over to his friend and dropped to his knees. "Byron, I'm so sorry. So sorry," he whispered. "Oh, for Chrissakes." Auburn, Bedell thought. Ohio State. Big Ten versus the South Eastern Conference . . . God, how Yarbrough loved Auburn. He loved jumping into the ocean, going for long swims. And Betty Jones, that girl from Cordele, Georgia, who he never met . . . he loved her, too. The hours Yarbrough spent reading those letters, smiling or chuckling, the hours he spent writing letters back. How many times did Yarbrough ask Bedell for advice about Betty? Oh, God, poor Betty. Who'd tell her this? There beside Yarbrough's body, Bedell was overwhelmed with grief. He stopped hearing the explosions, the screams of the wounded. He let two great sobs erupt from some deep part of his gut. He got back on his feet. He had to shake it off, think clearly. There was still so much to do.

Bedell took a deep breath, moved to the edge of the bridge, looked at the deck below. Herring was sitting up with his eyes open, trying to talk to Beuckman. A good sign! But then Bedell looked up. The mast was gone. No radio antennae. No lanyards for raising signal flags. They had no way to communicate with the other ships.

The signal light was still there, mounted on the railing, but when Bedell wheeled the light around to face him, shards of thick glass crashed to the deck. The bulb and glass cover were shattered, the wiring exposed, ripped apart.

Damn it, we're in trouble, he thought. *How the hell are we going to get help?*

Then he heard Lewis, down on the floor. The signalman was moaning. Bedell rushed to him. He bent down and examined Lewis's wounds. Shrapnel had sliced into his legs. He needed tourniquets or he would soon bleed to death.

Bedell jumped up and leaned over the edge of the bridge. "I need a couple of men up here with a stretcher," he shouted.

As two sailors ran up the ladder, Bedell looked at the destruction below. Bodies were strewn all over the decks. Sailors were carrying the wounded to the mess deck, or dragging hoses, trying to douse the flames. He glimpsed one young sailor clawing at the steel decking with his bare hands, trying to dig a foxhole for protection, screaming and crying.

If that wasn't bad enough, Bedell could feel the ship begin to list to starboard.

Could they be sinking? He thought about it for a moment, then came up with an idea. They could use mattresses to stuff holes in the hull. So

Bedell leaned over the bridge again, this time pointing to Lemke and another sailor on the gun deck: "Go below and grab some mattresses and meet me on the bow."

Lemke and the sailor ran down the ladder to the deckhouse, and then another to the crew's quarters. They each grabbed an armload of mattresses and headed topside.

Meanwhile, Bedell struggled to the bow across the slippery deck. He did everything he could to keep his balance. But just before Bedell reached the bow he stopped short, and spit out a string of obscenities. In all the chaos, he forgot he had turned on the sprinklers to flood the forward magazine. That's probably why the gunboat felt like it was listing. The compartment up there was full of water by now.

"Drop those," Bedell told Lemke. "We won't need them after all." He didn't have time to explain. "Move those hoses. We need to pump out this water." The seamen scrambled to connect hoses to the pumps, Bedell noticed something strange. The ship was not moving. They were just sitting still.

"Why the hell aren't we moving?" he shouted.

No one responded. Most of the officers were down. Herring was fighting for his life. Cooper was lost overboard, and Corkins and Yarbrough were dead. Cromer had been directing the 20mm fire in the back of the gunboat, but Bedell hadn't heard any 20mm fire since the conning tower was hit. Maybe Cromer was hurt, too. He knew Duvall was in the pilothouse, but he hadn't seen him at all.

Bedell headed to the pilothouse to find out what was going on. Vollendorf was an experienced helmsman, but maybe there was trouble with the engines. If that was so, Bedell knew he'd have to go down to the engine room and oversee repairs.

BEUCKMAN WAS OVERWHELMED. He fought back panic as the bodies piled up. He didn't know how many sailors had been killed or wounded, but he kept finding more who needed help. His mind flashed to that afternoon in Pearl Harbor, the explosion in West Loch, when so many men were killed and injured. That disaster took place on a navy base, with hundreds of doctors, nurses, and emergency personnel on the scene. There were hospitals with equipment to save lives. But on the 449, he was the lone person on board with any real medical training. And with the equipment at hand, Beuckman could only provide first aid. Many of these wounded needed major emergency surgery if they were to live.

Herring was badly hurt, too. As soon as Beuckman knelt beside him and opened his medical bag, the skipper told him to get the hell away. He refused to be treated. He ordered Beuckman to take care of the others first.

"What, you want to die, Geddie? You want to get me court-martialed?" But Herring was adamant. His men came first. Yeah, he hurt, but he knew others were in worse shape. They needed Beuckman's help more than he did. Herring stared into Beuckman's eyes and told him to go. "That's an order," he said.

Beuckman propped Herring up against an ammunition locker and promised he would keep checking on his condition. As he was leaving, Beuckman turned to a sailor and told him to keep an eye on Herring. And if Herring passed out, the sailor was to find him quickly. Then the pharmacist's mate turned around and scanned the gun deck for survivors. After a few steps, Beuckman realized that in the aftermath of the third explosion, the entire gun deck—in fact the entire ship—had turned into a horror movie set.

Across the decks were smears and layers of coagulating blood, shimmering and shifting like gelatin. The stench was overwhelming. The strong, metallic blood smell combined with burned flesh, diesel fuel, sulfur, and feces. Along the edges of the decks were scattered teeth, tendons, hair, fingers. Beuckman bit back a wave of nausea.

Before the third explosion, he'd run from body to body, applying tourniquets and wrapping bandages around wounds. He had to pick up the pace. He passed by the lifeless bodies of Corkins, Minnick, and Trotter.

As he approached the pilothouse, he saw long strips of film fluttering across the way like party streamers. McGrath, the young photographer, was dead. The contents of his satchel were spilled across the deck.

A few feet away Beuckman spotted Brockmeyer slumped over the body of a sailor he had been giving first aid to. The Marine was still, his torso ripped by shrapnel. Finally Beuckman caught sight of someone alive: Wilcox and Seaman Second Class James Griffin Jr. They were on the deck moaning, blood seeping from wounds on their legs and arms. They were the men Herring had sent forward to help carry the wounded, seconds before the third mortar slammed into the gunboat. Beuckman moved quickly to Wilcox, knelt down, and opened his medical bag.

DOWN IN THE engine room, five men were living the nightmare of the trapped. Over the din of the engines they could hear underwater explosions. Machine-gun fire rattled against the side of the gunboat. The boat shuddered with each hit. The commotion was playing into their worst fears: being abandoned to the darkness, going down with the ship.

With Bedell topside, Robert Carrell was in charge of the black gang. The explosions were worrisome, especially that last one, with shrieks and groans of major structural damage. But what concerned him most wasn't noise, it was silence. They weren't moving. The engine order telegraph had shifted to *Stop* many minutes before, and hadn't budged since. Carrell had buzzed the officers in the pilothouse and bridge, but no one responded. He double-checked to see if his headset was working. He pulled the jack out of the slot on the wall, then plugged it back in. He didn't think that was the problem. Carrell asked for a volunteer to go topside to find Herring.

Holgate didn't hesitate. He'd been worried about his friend Hoffman, so he offered to go. Carrell took off his headset and told Holgate to be careful, to get a report and get back as quickly as possible. "I knew something bad was going on. I just didn't know how bad," Carrell recalled.

As Holgate bolted up the steps to the fantail, his heart began racing. There were bodies sprawled on the deck, but he didn't see any officers. He dashed up a ladder to the gun deck. Herring was there near the top, but Holgate thought he was dead. He glanced up at the bridge, but most of the bridge was gone. Nobody was up there.

He saw Seaman First Class Daniel Skluzacek firing his 20mm gun at the shore, the only man still stuck in the primary mission. He was the only one shooting. All of the other guns were silent, unmanned. Holgate glanced at Iwo Jima, then the other gunboats. Mortars and shells were exploding on every side. The other gunboats were flaming and smoking. Reality struck Holgate: This was full-on combat. How the hell did this happen? This was supposed to be a quiet little recon mission.

A pall of black smoke passed over the ship, adding to the surreal effect. Cromer appeared, walking in a daze, his shoes sloshing in blood. It looked like he might have been hit, but Holgate couldn't tell if the blood that spattered his uniform was Cromer's or someone else's. Cromer was an officer. Holgate saluted, ready to ask for a report. "Sir," he said. "We need an update in the engine room."

"What do I do?" Cromer answered him. He shuffled past as if Holgate wasn't even there.

It was all too much for Holgate. He felt a deep, sharp pain behind his heart, and sensed that something bad had happened to his friend. Holgate had to find out. He made his way toward the 40mm gun on the starboard side of the ship, passing lifeless bodies. He found Hoffman right there by his gun, his arms, legs, and back studded with shrapnel. Holgate dropped to the deck and reached under Hoffman's armpits to lift him up. Hoffman didn't move. Holgate heard himself wail. His friend was dead.

Shells exploded around them, spraying them with water. Holgate cradled his friend's head and rocked back and forth, sobbing.

ON THE BRIDGE of the 457, Nash could see black smoke billowing from some of the ships. Urgent messages crackled over the radio, gunboat captains calling for help. It looked like the Japanese had an invasion's worth of artillery raining down on one little flotilla.

At first, Nash thought it was friendly fire, that U.S. destroyers were "firing short of Iwo Jima." He jumped on the radio and relayed the message to Captain Hanlon, aboard a destroyer positioned just a few thousand yards behind them.

As commander of the underwater demolition teams' recon mission, Hanlon's job was to protect the frogmen. Hanlon ordered his ships to raise their fire because they were hitting the gunboats.

But even after Hanlon's orders, shells continued to rain down on the gunboats. At that point, Nash knew the fire was coming from Japanese shore batteries.

The barrage showed no signs of letting up. Nash peered through his binoculars to gauge how many had been hit. But he was in a bad position to judge. His ship was on the far right, its bow facing the island. Each of the seven gunboats on the firing line was spaced five hundred yards apart from the next one. The best vantage point would have been in the middle of the pack, where the 438 was now facing Yellow Beach 1. Then Nash would have had three ships flanked to his right, the three others flanked to his left.

Meanwhile, Hanlon was on the bridge of the *Gilmer*, watching the battle unfold. The gunboats were being shredded, especially the 449. After seeing its mast fall, Hanlon sent Malanaphy, the Flotilla Three commander, an urgent message: "Relieve LCI-449." The gunboat would be replaced on the line by the 469, one of five LCIs in reserve. The 449, and Nash, needed to be contacted immediately with the orders.

The time of Hanlon's message: 11:03—eight minutes after the first enemy shell hit the 449.

But it would be a while before Nash would hear the order. The radio was jammed with bad news. "All of our guns are out," said a radio operator on the 474. The same with the 438, the gunboat carrying Draper Kauffman. The message from the 473 was dire: It was "taking water rapidly and will have to be towed from the beach." All had casualties. Then a shell hit Nash's gunboat. He got on the radio himself and told Hanlon: "We've been hit and are taking on water."

The Japanese attack was relentless. The gunboats kept fighting as well as they could. They would stay in position as long as the recon mission was still a go. The frogmen were just reaching the shore, ready to collect information critical to the invasion just two days away.

But at this point, Nash didn't know how long they could hold out.

FROM OPPOSITE ENDS of the gunboat, Bedell and Blow reached the same conclusion: They weren't moving.

They arrived at the pilothouse at the same time.

Like Bedell, Blow had been running back and forth, making sure the able-bodied men were fighting fires or helping Beuckman with the wounded.

"Do you know why we're not moving?" Blow asked.

"I have no idea. I'm going to find out," Bedell answered.

Bedell swung open the door. "Duvall! Why the hell—" He stopped in midsentence.

Silver spears of light streamed through holes punched in the bulkhead. They illuminated the murky room just enough to reveal a horrific scene. To his left, sitting in a chair by the radio, was what remained of Paglia. The radioman's arms hung limply at his side, blood dripping from his fingers. His head was gone.

Bedell wanted to slam the door shut on the scene, turn, and vomit. But not just yet. He took another step inside. Glass crunched under his feet. Everything inside the pilothouse was shattered.

Holtby was alive, but in awful shape. Part of his jaw was blown off, his teeth scattered in pieces on the floor. Holtby was trying to reach up to feel his face, but his right forearm was almost severed. Blood poured from his wounds. He was pale, barely alive.

Vollendorf lay nearby, clutching his legs. He tried to stand, but his legs would not support him. When he tried to move, blood spilled onto the floor.

"Bill, don't move. We're going to get you help," Bedell said.

But then Bedell realized someone was standing near the helm. It was Duvall, staring blankly into space. He was unaware of his surroundings, in shock, blood streaming down his legs. His hands shook violently as he grasped the controls of the ship. Duvall's training was telling him to move the gunboat, but he couldn't get his body to respond.

A shell exploded off the port-side rail. Seawater blasted in through the broken glass.

Bedell made a quick decision. If they didn't get out of there now, they'd all be dead. Duvall was a lieutenant junior grade, Bedell's superior officer. Bedell knew he could be court-martialed for this, but he had to take control.

"Duvall, get out of there and let Blow in," Bedell said.

Duvall didn't respond, or even acknowledge their presence.

Blow moved beside Duvall and tenderly removed Duvall's hands from the steering mechanism. They moved toward the door. There on the floor by Duvall's feet was Paglia's severed head.

Bedell guided Duvall outside the pilothouse, where several sailors were waiting. The men took Vollendorf, Holtby, and Duvall to the mess deck on litters.

When they were gone, Bedell opened the portholes, then turned to Blow. "Get us out of here."

Blow gave him the thumbs-up sign and blocked out everything around him. He scanned the gauges, cracked his knuckles. When he reached for the engine-order telegraph, he saw it pointed to *Stop*. How the hell did it get to that position? The boat should have been moving forward. The only thing he could figure was that Holtby's arm had accidentally hit the setting when the explosion threw him backward and into the wall. It was sheer luck that the setting ended up where it did. If the telegraph had been set to *Ahead Full*, or even set to *Ahead Slow*, the 449 would have beached itself on the black sand of Iwo Jima.

Blow let out a low whistle as he reached over to grasp the handles of the helm. He hadn't done this in a while. He started talking to himself, remembering how to make a 180-degree turn from dead in the water. One engine would have to move one step faster than the other, with a hard right rudder. Blow took a deep breath, then moved the engine-order telegraph to *Port Ahead 2/3, Starboard Back 1/3, Hard Right Rudder*.

In the engine room, Carrell saw the hands of the engine-order telegraph move. He whooped with joy—somebody was alive up there! It was the signal he'd been waiting for. He shouted the positions to his men.

The engines roared to life. The 449 was moving again.

The gunboat turned slowly until the bow was pointed away from Iwo Jima. Then Blow moved the engine order telegraph to *Ahead Full*.

In the engine room, Carrell shouted the new orders, and the gunboat ground forward.

Blow let out a long breath. They'd solved one problem, but now faced a whole new slew.

If this had been the real Iwo Jima invasion, the ocean would have been covered with ships of all types: transports, tankers, LSTs, LSMs, LCTs, cruisers, destroyers, battleships, frigates, and, most importantly, hospital ships. But the invasion was still two days away. The water was sprinkled with destroyers and other fire support ships. Right now, every vessel on the eastern side of Iwo Jima was busy blasting the shore, protecting the demolition teams.

Blow didn't know where to go to get help. All he knew was he had to get away from Iwo Jima, out of the kill zone. He put his head down and took off like a jackrabbit.

By now, even the grizzled veterans aboard were feeling scared. Every shot from the Japanese made the wounded cry out in fear. They could not differentiate between the sound of incoming and outgoing fire. All the artillery in the world seemed to be aimed at the 449.

In the meantime, Blow had no instructions on how far to go, but the screams of the wounded spurred him on. Soon, they were a mile from the island, two, then three. Slowly, the sounds of war faded into the distance. It wasn't enough. They had to keep going.

NOW IN COMMAND of the ship, Bedell had assumed the responsibilities of six officers.

Yarbrough, Corkins, and Cooper were dead. Duvall was so shell-shocked he didn't know his own name. Cromer was down. Herring had lost so much blood he was fading in and out of consciousness.

Bedell was the only able-bodied officer left. He checked on the wounded in the mess deck, then bolted back to the pilothouse. Blow stood inside, peering straight ahead, gripping the controls.

Bedell thought fast. They had to find help. Without the radio, they had no way to find out the positions of any vessel that might be able to take casualties. Bedell scanned the horizon. He tapped Blow on the shoulder. "Frank, do you see that ship?" he said, pointing out to sea.

Blow squinted, then spotted it. It looked like a destroyer.

"Yeah," he said.

"Take us to her," Bedell said, then wheeled around and headed out the door.

On the gun deck, Herring struggled to hang on to consciousness. Darkness rushed in at him, but at the last second, he'd shake his head from side to side and open his eyes for a moment. The sailor assigned to watch him paid close attention. He didn't know how the captain was still functioning. Soon the blood loss took its toll. Herring closed his eyes. The sailor bolted to the mess deck. When Beuckman heard the news, he ordered two sailors to grab a stretcher and follow him.

Beuckman prayed that Herring was still alive. He found him breathing, but very weak. Beuckman was happy to see that the captain was unconscious. It was the only way he'd be able to treat the bull-headed bastard. Now maybe Herring would have a chance.

Up at the very tip of the ship, Hallett opened his eyes, roused by the spray and cold wind. He'd blacked out after the first shell hit, and was left for dead on the prow. He sat up, looked around, and remembered. He was alive! The flutter of joy didn't last long. His arms and hands were burned. Sharp pains shot through his body. He was in rough shape, and he had to get himself to help. He pulled himself upright, feeling for balance.

The deck was scattered with pieces of raw flesh and slippery with blood. Hallett felt sick. He held on to bulkheads, lockers, rails, picking his way over the dead.

He was still groggy as he climbed the ladder to the gun deck. When he reached the top, he was stunned. The scene aboard there was one of unimaginable horror. Some men crouched at their positions, frozen in death. The bridge and conning tower, usually a buzzing beehive, was deathly quiet. Smoke belched from the holes blown in the ship, bodies lay smoldering. Underfoot was a bog of gore.

That morning Hallett was laughing, joking around with Banko, the gun crew. Now they were probably all gone. Not just dead, but mangled, blown apart, unrecognizable.

He trudged through the blood, but the pain stopped him when he reached aft of the conning tower. Hallett slid down and leaned against a railing to catch his breath. He looked at the horizon. They were moving fast, he realized. The ship was headed away from Iwo Jima.

NOW THAT THEY had a destination, Bedell had to solve the problem of communications. The antennae had gone under with the mast, so there was no use going down to the radio shack. The signal light was smashed. There was no point in opening the flag bag because the lanyards were now on the ocean floor with the mast.

There was only one hope: semaphore flags and a signalman. There were three signalmen on board, but Bedell didn't know where they were, or what shape they were in. He knew Park and Walton had been stationed near the pilothouse, near the locker where the flags were kept. Bedell headed there, followed by Beuckman and several sailors. They found Park on the starboard side of the pilothouse. He was missing a leg, unconscious, in a condition Beuckman said was "likely unsurvivable." The second signalman was slumped against the pilothouse beside Park.

Bedell squatted, careful not to kneel in the muck. He lifted Walton's head and stared at his face. It was a sickly pale color. There was a little hole in the crown of Walton's helmet. A piece of shrapnel had punched through the metal and sliced into his brain.

"He never knew what hit him," Bedell said to Beuckman. "He was a good kid." He paused for a moment and looked up. "How's Lewis?" he asked.

Beuckman shook his head. "Listen, Leo, his legs are shredded and his abdomen is really tore up."

"We need him. If there's just a way . . . He's our only hope," Bedell said.

Beuckman wasn't sure, but so far, Bedell's instincts had kept them alive. He said if Lewis was conscious, they could ask him to help, but he wasn't going to force him. Bedell agreed. They ran down the ladder to the fantail, into the deckhouse and to the mess deck. Lewis was sprawled on a table, woozy with pain. Beuckman had put tourniquets on both his legs and tried to patch up his other wounds. But Lewis was still bleeding. He looked up, puzzled at the faces gathered around him.

Bedell wasted no time. "Art, this is a hell of a deal, but you're our only signalman now. All of our communications equipment is destroyed. The only way we can communicate is by semaphore."

Before Bedell could finish the sentence, the wounded signalman responded: "I'll do it."

Bedell glanced up at the sailors hovering near. "Find me something Lewis can use as a flag," he said. The men searched the mess deck and returned quickly with a handful of big dishrags.

Lewis glanced at the cloths. That would work . . . Then he peered up at his shipmates. "Help me up, fellas. I can't stand on my own."

They carefully lifted the signalman by his arms. When he was upright, Lewis draped his arms over their shoulders for support. They wanted to make sure there was no pressure on his legs. Still, the pain was excruciating. It felt like someone had sledgehammered his legs. He fought for breath. But he urged them to keep going.

They carried Lewis from the mess deck. Once outside they had to get Lewis up two ladders and over the slippery decks. Lewis was floppy. They kept a firm grip on his shirt back and waistband as they wrestled him up to the bridge.

Finally they were there on the bridge with a big ship in the distance. Bedell spotted a pair of gunboats only a few hundred feet away, and he decided to take a chance.

"You ready?" Bedell asked Lewis. He nodded his head yes. So Bedell handed him the rags and the men hoisted Lewis on their shoulders. Lewis could see LCI-346.

Lewis began waving the rags. "Urgent. Multiple casualties. Immediate medical help needed." He squinted, looking for a sign that someone on the 346 saw the message. Finally a signalman replied. After deciphering the response, Lewis glanced down at Bedell. "Sir, they state they will get help for us."

But they didn't have time to wait. "We're going to keep going," he shouted to Lewis.

As the 449 approached the next gunboat, Lewis re-sent the SOS message. The signalman on 348 responded: "Proceed to the nearest large ship."

Easier said than done, Bedell thought. Without a radio, they'd be lucky to find one in time. All they could do was push forward. Minutes were ticking by. The small window for treating the wounded was closing. Most of the injured had catastrophic wounds. If they didn't get help soon, most of them would die.

The only hope now was that big ship Bedell had pointed out to Blow. They seemed to be getting closer.

THE USS *WILLIAMSON* was an old destroyer, built in the waning days of Woodrow Wilson's administration. In the early part of the war it had been stationed in Alaskan waters, refueling float planes. It later escorted convoys across the Pacific Ocean. Now it sat at anchor ten miles east of Iwo Jima, again as a gas station for pontoon aircraft.

The job was a cakewalk. The *Williamson* was safely out of range of the Japanese big guns, and float planes were few and far between. When a sailor on the bridge saw a small boat speeding in their direction, he immediately alerted his commander.

Lieutenant Commander William Ayer peered through his binoculars and fumed. This patch of water and sky was restricted to float plane traffic. He told his radioman to order the gunboat to get the hell out of the restricted area.

The radioman tried frantically to communicate with the ship, but no one answered the messages. They flashed the message by signal light. Again, nothing.

By now, Ayer was furious. He could not imagine a U.S. Navy ship neglecting to communicate with another vessel.

Meanwhile, Bedell had returned to the pilothouse, encouraging Blow to move in closer to the destroyer.

When the 449 was about one hundred feet from the *Williamson*, two sailors again hoisted Lewis onto their shoulders. He signaled the ship with the dishrags.

Up on the bridge of the destroyer, the lookout saw why their messages had gone unanswered. The LCI pulling up to them was a battered mess. Their mast was gone. He glimpsed what looked like two men holding up a signalman. He told his commander.

"What do they want?" Ayer asked.

Moments later, a signalman on the *Williamson* replied: "It's urgent, sir. They need help with their wounded."

Lewis was struggling to keep his eyes open. Blood was seeping through his bandages. It was hard to even hold the cloths. But he had to stay alert. He knew the *Williamson* had read his message. He was just waiting for their response.

Suddenly, Lewis saw his counterpart on the *Williamson* relaying a message. "They're sending over a small boat with a medical team, but don't have facilities aboard their ship to handle all of our casualties," Lewis said.

Bedell was disappointed. On one hand, Beuckman would get additional medical help. That was a relief. But most of his men needed more than just bandages. They needed surgeons. How long could they survive with just first aid? It had been nearly an hour since the first hit, and many were slipping into comas. How long would it be until the 449 reached a ship with enough doctors and equipment to adequately treat them?

Within minutes, Pharmacist's Mate First Class Robert Lacy and Hospital Apprentice Arthur White were ready to go. They stuffed supplies into medical bags and made their way to a small boat that had been lowered into the water. A doctor was already in the craft, waiting. After they walked down a ladder to get on board, the boat headed to the LCI idling in the water, just ahead.

As the team approached, they weren't sure what they'd face. But if the condition of the gunboat was any indication, they were in for a long day. The ship looked like it had been used for target practice.

The medical team handed their supplies to the sailors on the other side. One by one, they leapt to the ship. As soon as the doctor and his two assistants were on board, Beuckman gave them a quick rundown of the situation. It was grave. He didn't know how many men were killed, but at least two dozen were wounded, probably more. Most were in the mess deck, sprawled on tables, on the floor, anywhere he could find room. Who knew how many were still on the well deck, gun deck, and bow. He said Herring, the ship's captain, was in bad shape, too.

Beuckman led the team into the deckhouse and down the corridor to the cramped mess deck. The trio was shocked at what they saw. None had ever dealt with so many critical cases at once.

During invasions, military planners prepare for massive casualties. They set up field hospitals in the rear, staffed with sufficient doctors and medical help. They make sure every platoon has medics to provide first aid on the battlefield. In the navy, every invasion has special ships to aid the wounded as quickly as possible.

But no one had planned for something like this, a small boat with heavy casualties. No one had expected the gunboats to take catastrophic damage. If they had, they would have assigned more than one pharmacist's mate, or set up the one man with a lot more training and equipment.

HOLLOWELL HAD BEEN scrambling, helping move the casualties below. There were so many, it was hard to keep up. Some of the men didn't know they were injured. Hildebrand wandered in a daze. He had blacked out after the bow was hit, and couldn't remember a thing. Hollowell helped him get to the mess deck.

Cromer was out on the gun deck, so shell-shocked he was oblivious to his own injury. Cromer's pants were soaked in blood. Hollowell took him below. Every now and then Hollowell stopped to whisper words of encouragement to Johnson. Hollowell could tell his friend was getting worse. He was fading in and out of consciousness.

As the medical team boarded the ship, Hollowell noticed one of the patients was missing: Sless. For an hour or more Sless had squirmed on the tabletop, shouting, "The ship is going to sink. I don't want to go down with the ship. I don't want to die." Hollowell would calm him down for a few minutes, but then Sless would start up again.

Now Sless was gone. Hollowell asked a few of the men if they had seen him, but they shook their heads no. So he told Bedell about it. "I'll keep my eyes open for him," Bedell said, "but in the meantime, see if you can find him."

But when Bedell wheeled around, there was Sless, holding his hands over his exposed intestines.

"You're going to leave, aren't you? You're going to leave me on the ship. I don't want to go down with the ship!" shouted Sless, whose frantic cries were beginning to unnerve some of the sailors already teetering on the brink.

Much as he wanted to simply slap the sailor into silence, Bedell knew he had to calm the situation, not escalate it. He draped his arm around

Sless's shoulder and led him to his own cabin beside the mess deck. He gently placed Sless in Yarbrough's bunk. Bedell took a Bible from his desk drawer.

"Swifty, I want you to lay here and hold this. When you feel scared you hold this Bible tight and pray. It's the word of God. I am not going to leave you on this ship. If this ship goes down, I will go right down with you."

Bedell's soothing words worked. Sless clutched the Bible and closed his eyes.

Bedell left the room and headed straight to the pilothouse. The fresh medical help was like sticking a finger in a dike, he thought. They were helping stabilize some men, but it was clear that many of the wounded were not going to make it unless the 449 got to some surgical facilities.

When he got to the pilothouse, Blow was still at the helm, the gunboat idling. He looked impatient and peevish.

"Awaiting orders, sir," he said. Bedell squinted out one of the portholes. He spotted another ship in the distance. "That one, Blow. Head for it." Blow didn't waste any time. He moved the lever to *Ahead Full* and the engine roared to life.

As the 449 began moving, Bedell stepped outside. He couldn't stay in the pilothouse very long with Paglia's head on the floor. He marveled at Blow's tolerance for the stench and blood. He knew if they didn't get help soon, not only would more men die, but Blow would crack. You just couldn't stay enclosed in a place like that for too long without losing your mind.

The ship in the distance was their last chance. He hated bouncing the gunboat from ship to ship, like a redheaded orphan. He might be reprimanded for taking control of the 449, but it had seemed like the only thing he could do. People were dying. He couldn't just sit still and wait for orders, doing nothing at all.

LEWIS HEARD A familiar voice. Bedell. He opened his eyes and saw the ensign hovering over him.

"We need you one more time, Art," Bedell said.

Lewis was groggy, unsure if he was really awake. Not sure where he was. After the medical team boarded the 449, the crew had carried Lewis back to the mess deck. They'd checked his tourniquets and tightened his bandages, but there really wasn't much else they could do. Without surgery, Lewis would die.

Bedell was in a jam. He knew every move aggravated Lewis's condition, but without Lewis's help, the signalman wouldn't get the help he needed to live. So Bedell crouched beside Lewis and told him they were in trouble again. They were headed to another ship, and they still needed his skills. "We have to see if they can handle all our casualties," Bedell said. "I won't ask again, Art. I'll leave you alone after this, I promise."

The two sailors who had been carrying Lewis were there, waiting. Lewis said yes, he'd do it again. If the men could hold him upright, he'd try his best.

"Thank you," Bedell whispered.

Bedell stood up, then trotted for the pilothouse to help Blow pull alongside the ship.

With medical personnel on the scene, Beuckman finally had a chance to circle back and check on Kepner. He was horrified to see that his friend had been moved. He was lying among the dead.

"No, God," he said. He laid his hand on Kepner's neck, hoping for a pulse. And yes, his heart was pounding away in there, but it was a weak signal.

"You!" Beuckman yelled to one of the sailors who'd only joined the gunboat in the last few weeks. "What's your name?"

"Charles Halcomb, sir."

With all the chaos, Beuckman sort of chuckled at the formality. "Your job is to stay with Kepner, watch these tourniquets, and if blood starts to come out, tighten them up like this." After giving Halcomb a quick demonstration, Beuckman was ready to move to another patient. But before he left, he wanted to make sure no one would move Kepner again.

"Do not leave his side," Beuckman ordered. "Got it?"

Halcomb took a deep swallow and tried to sound sure. "Got it."

Meanwhile, the mess deck looked like a giant surgery.

As Lacy and White treated the wounded, they felt liquid dropping on their heads, shoulders, and hands. At first, they ignored it. But it seemed to be picking up. They looked up to see what was leaking.

The shrapnel had punctured holes in the gun deck. There was so much blood up there it was dripping through. It wasn't only in the mess deck. Blood and seawater ran down the bulkheads in every room in the deckhouse. On the galley counter, Bozarth and Vogel's pies and cakes turned red.

Lemke and the others were still finding casualties topside and moving them below. Lemke ran through the crew quarters from room to room, tearing blankets from the racks to cover the bodies of the injured, to keep them warm.

Bedell told Lemke to start grabbing pillowcases, too, for when this was over, for when they were finally safe. They'd use them to collect body parts. That might be the only way to identify some of the men, he said.

Lemke froze at that idea. He'd been fighting the urge to throw up. He was a fastidious man, someone who had to be neat and clean, who craved order in his life. Somehow Lemke had found the strength to slog through the gore to help his friends, his hands sticky and slippery. Blood was caked under his fingernails, it smeared his uniform. Somehow he had even been able to push intestines and cold, spongy body parts back in gaping wounds. But he didn't know how much more he could take.

NASH WAS ANXIOUS and angry. No one could find the 449. After the order came through to pull the 449 off the firing line, no one knew what had happened. The 449 was seen heading away from Iwo Jima. That was an hour ago.

Nash sent a radio message to the other gunboats: "Has anyone seen or heard from the 449 lately?" The reply: No. Jesus. Maybe the gunboat had sunk. Nash didn't want to be negative, but so far, everything about this day had gone pear-shaped.

The action had been nonstop. For more than an hour, the Japanese had pounded the gunboats with heavy-caliber shells and mortars. So many were damaged, all five reserve gunboats were pressed into action. When one was pulled off the line, it was replaced by another.

All twelve of the gunboats assigned to the recon mission had been hit, including Nash's. A shell had torn into the port-side hull, flooding the crew quarters. Nash's men had scrambled to pump the seawater out. At one point, Nash radioed Hanlon with the sobering message "We are sinking."

Many of the gunboats had extensive damage to the hulls, equipment, and electrical systems. One was going down. The radio jabbered endlessly with messages about casualties.

It still wasn't over.

Somehow the little gunboats continued to hang in there, firing away at enemy positions with whatever guns remained. The 469 was hit and started taking on water. It was pulled from the firing line, but after the crew stopped up the holes with mattresses the captain sent a message to Hanlon, requesting permission to return to the fray. Permission was granted. The 469 was hit three more times.

To protect the LCIs, Hanlon ordered his ships to fire white phosphorous shells on the right flank of the beach. He hoped the wind would pull the smoke over the area and obscure the gunboats. Despite the smoke, the heavy fire continued.

Meanwhile, the frogmen were on the beach collecting their critical pre-invasion information. As long as the frogmen were on shore, the gunboats would stay.

Finally, Nash received a message from the radio operator on the LCI-348. He said they had exchanged semaphore messages with the 449. The gunboat was heading out to sea, looking for medical assistance because of heavy casualties. It had no way to communicate with other ships because its mast was blown off.

Heavy casualties? The two words jumped out at Nash. Even though he was Group Eight's commander, he still considered the 449 his boat. Those were his crew. He'd trained most of them. He had spent so much time with the officers, bonding with them as they jumped from island to island in the Pacific Ocean. He wondered if Herring was safe. What about Yarbrough, and Blow?

Before Nash had a chance to respond, the radio operator said they were leaving to search for the 449. Nash took in the words quietly and with no show of emotion. "Very well," he said matter-of-factly. But he knew he'd be waiting anxiously for the information.

THE MEN WAITED on the bridge. One more time they'd hoist Lewis on their shoulders—if he didn't pass out first. Lewis was weakening, Bedell could see it. The signalman's eyes were closed, his body limp. They were drawing closer to the big ship. Bedell had no idea if this one would be able to take the wounded, but no matter: This was their last stop. A few hundred yards out, Bedell turned to Lewis: "All right, Art, it's time."

The signalman nodded his head, acknowledging that he could hear Bedell. Meanwhile, the ensign could feel the gunboat lose speed as Blow prepared to come alongside the other ship.

Bedell told Lewis the message would be the same as it was before: They needed help. They had heavy casualties.

Lewis said he was ready. If he was going to do it, it had to be now. So he gave the men the signal to lift him. His arms were so heavy he could barely hold them over his head. But he clutched the now-bloody rags tightly in his hands and began moving them in perfect order.

Aboard the USS *Terror*, a minesweeper, the lookouts informed the captain that a ship resembling an LCI was approaching. Commander Horace Blakeslee was puzzled. They hadn't received any message from a gunboat. Then *Terror*'s signalman spotted Lewis. He peered at his hand movements and then shouted to Blakeslee: The ship was in trouble. They had casualties, lots of them.

Blakeslee told his signalman to give the gunboat permission to move alongside.

Lewis stared at the ship, waiting for the response. He didn't know how much longer he could stay alert. Then came his counterpart's message: Permission to come alongside the ship for assistance. When Lewis relayed the message, Bedell felt like crying.

All across the minesweeper messages were sent and phone lines buzzed. Sailors scampered up and down ladders, retrieving gear and medical supplies. One of the officers, looking through his binoculars, was horrified to see a blood-spattered signalman held aloft by two sailors. It was obvious that all of the gunboat's communication equipment had been damaged.

"Almost there, Blow. Ease us in," Bedell shouted down to the pilothouse.

The starboard side of the 449 was almost parallel to the other ship. But suddenly, the men along the rail began frantically waving their arms over their heads, shouting for the 449 to keep away. Bedell couldn't believe it. What the hell was going on? He needed Lewis again. The men had just placed him on the deck, so spent he couldn't sit up by himself. Bedell knelt beside the battered man.

"Look up, Lewis! Just tell us what they're saying! Tell us why they won't let us alongside!"

Lewis didn't say a word, but gave Bedell the thumbs-up sign. Bedell turned to the sailors and motioned for them to lift the signalman. When they did, the *Terror* signalman was already waiting. Before Lewis had a chance to raise his arms, his counterpart had already sent him a message. Lewis peered at the flags, then glanced down at Bedell: "Rockets." They'd have to get rid of the rockets on the starboard side of the 449 before the other ship would let them get close.

Bedell threw his hands up in disgust. "Damn it to hell!" he growled. Another damn obstacle. But he wasn't going to quit. Not this close to the end.

"Get Lewis below and get the doctor to him, fast," he told the sailors. "Be gentle. This guy's a hero." Then Bedell bolted down the ladder to the gun deck. When he opened the door to the pilothouse, he ordered Blow to stop.

The gunboat was grounded.

BLOW COULDN'T BELIEVE it. How the hell were they going to get rid of the rockets? They couldn't just toss them overboard. The impact of the rockets hitting the water from the deck could trigger an explosion. They'd have to find a way to lower each one carefully into the water. But even that wouldn't be safe. Good thing they'd only have to get rid of half of the ship's 120 rockets. Still, it could take a shitload of time.

Bedell knew he was right. Vanderboom was the rocket expert, but Bedell couldn't remember seeing him at all. He didn't know if Vanderboom was still alive. But Blow said he'd spotted him a little earlier near the rocket racks. He was trying to fix the wiring just in case the gunboat returned to action after the wounded were evacuated. So Bedell told Blow to stay put, that he'd find Vanderboom and bring him to the pilothouse.

Again, Bedell scuttled down the ladder. He didn't know how many times he had gone up and down in the last hour or so. He was physically and mentally drained. But each time he felt like collapsing, his adrenaline kicked in.

By the rocket launchers, he saw Vanderboom right away. He was on his knees, fiddling with wires. Bedell didn't stop to say hello. "Vanderboom, come on. I need you," he barked. The rocket man jumped up. "What can I do?" he asked.

"How can we get rid of sixty armed rockets really fast? What do we do with them?"

Vanderboom thought about it for a moment. It would be painstaking and dangerous, but there was a way, he said. Someone would have to jump into the old ramp with the rocket launchers and gingerly pull out each rocket, one at a time, and pass it to another who would insert a safety wire into the projectile, to prevent the propeller from spinning and detonating under the ship. Then another crew member would tie a long piece of string to the stabilizer and lower the rocket, nose first, into the water. Once the explosive tip was submerged, the sailor could just let go. The rocket would sink, harmless, to the ocean floor.

They could do it like a bucket brigade. Everyone along the line would have a job. But only the most experienced sailors should take part, Vanderboom warned. They needed veterans with steady hands. Bedell knew Vanderboom was right, but he wondered if anyone matching that description was still alive on board. Bedell told Vanderboom to grab the safety wire and twine and they'd meet by the rocket launchers.

Bedell had to draft sailors quickly. As he bounded into the deckhouse, he combed his memory for sailors who weren't dead or wounded. There weren't many. He knew he'd tap Blow, and Skluzacek, the gunner from the rear. If Overchuk could walk, he'd use him. On the way down the corridor, Bedell spotted Holgate and Hildebrand. Hildebrand said he was feeling better now—he probably had a concussion, but he was able to help. Bedell sent the pair of them to the rocket launchers.

In the mess deck, Bedell saw Cromer lying on a table, blood coming from an area around his crotch. Sheesh, Bedell thought, those other guys knew they were going to die, and this guy somehow knew he was getting his balls shot off!

Bedell spotted Overchuk leaning against a bulkhead. "Can you walk?" he asked.

Overchuk's leg was throbbing, but he could tell by the tone in his voice that Bedell needed him. "Yeah. I'm fine."

"OK. Follow me."

As the men assembled outside, Bedell climbed up to the pilothouse and told Blow he needed his help. Blow followed Bedell. Getting down that ladder was becoming harder. Blow was getting tired, maybe even a little shaky. When he saw Vanderboom standing with his hand on a rack of rockets, Blow knew he should feel afraid. But he just didn't have the energy.

They were short on time, so Bedell let Vanderboom explain the dangerous task ahead. But when Vanderboom was finished, the men didn't say a word. They were worried. Bedell stepped in with his no-nonsense approach, trying to ease their fears.

"As long as the safety wire is put in correctly, and as long as we don't bang them against the ship or the water surface, these rockets are safe," he said. "If they were gonna blow up, they would've done it already. Besides, everyone else is depending on us."

Vanderboom gave everyone his assignment. They'd work in two teams. Vanderboom and Blow would remove the rockets from the racks; Skluzacek and Overchuk would insert the safety wires, and Hildebrand and Holgate would tie the twine and lower the explosives into the water.

Before they started, Vanderboom showed Skluzacek and Overchuk the correct way to insert the safety wire, and Hildebrand and Holgate where to tie the twine.

They started out slow and tentative. No one wanted to do it wrong. Overchuk stopped and asked Vanderboom a couple of times if he was doing it right. They picked up the pace after a little while, like an assembly line in a factory.

Meanwhile, as a precaution, Bedell moved up to the gun deck. If anything went wrong, he didn't want himself and Blow to be in the same place. Someone would have to guide the gunboat.

After nearly fifteen minutes, Blow stood up and lifted his muscular right arm high into the air in a triumphant thumbs-up sign. Bedell bolted to the pilothouse and moved the engine-order telegraph to the *Ahead Slow* position. But this time, Bedell wasn't going to wait. He grabbed the controls, then began easing the 449 toward the other ship.

As the gunboat began moving, Bedell glanced at the other ship through a porthole. The deck was filled with sailors who had watched in silence while the crew of the 449 slowly, methodically disposed of each rocket.

Meanwhile, Blow made his way into the mess deck and told the medics they'd start evacuating the wounded in just a few minutes.

When the 449 was lined up alongside the other ship, Bedell moved the engine-order telegraph to *Stop*. Then he bounded from the pilothouse and descended the ladder one last time. Bedell stepped onto the fantail and saw a great wall of steel rising alongside—the other ship was so much higher than the 449. How were they going to transfer the wounded?

His fears faded at the grinding sound of turning gears. He looked up and smiled. A crane was moving a pallet full of men onto the gunboat.

Now, nearly ninety minutes after the first shell had hit them, the 449 was safe.

= 31 =

THE FROGMEN WRAPPED up their recon mission on the Iwo Jima beaches. With Japanese shells still raining down on the American gunboats, it looked like the beach was a safer place to be.

The frogmen didn't find mines or reefs that could disable landing crafts in the water. But they had scrambled ashore and collected bags of sand that military planners would use to analyze the terrain. They sketched charts and maps on Plexiglas slates while LCPRs, the frogmen's fast little boats, moved back and forth parallel to the beach, dodging Japanese mortars, machine guns, even rifle fire. Finally, after more than an hour on Iwo Jima, the frogmen swam back to the battered LCPRs.

The men aboard the gunboats thought the frogmen would never finish, but word finally came over to "wind down the mission." Gunboats with working guns had kept firing as long as the ammunition and manpower held out. Damaged LCIs initially called off the firing line had returned to action.

Kauffman was impressed by the gunboats' tenacity. He said the LCI skippers and crews showed "extraordinary heroism."

"They kept coming back onto the line, no matter how badly beaten-up they were. As long as they had a gun to fire, they would come back on the line. It was really a darned inspiring thing to see," he wrote in a report.

Meanwhile, all across Iwo Jima, Japanese soldiers shouted and cheered in their caves and bunkers. The enemy ships had turned around. Their fire was accurate. They could see the flames and smoke . . . they'd stopped the invaders!

Kuribayashi sent a message to Tokyo: The American ships had been turned back.

The propaganda machine embellished the details.

The Domei News Agency broke into programming to announce: "On February 17 in the morning, enemy troops tried to land on the island of Iwo. The Japanese garrison at once attacked these troops and repelled them into the sea."

The broadcaster added that five warships, including a battleship, were sunk. Newspapers in Japan followed with similar accounts, and soon Tokyo was announcing to all the wire services across the globe that they had turned back an American invasion.

But on Iwo Jima, Kuribayashi knew the truth.

Yes, they had stung the Americans. But the Americans were not going away. He knew the full force of the U.S. military was on its way. Any day now.

AS SOON AS the pallet landed with the medical personnel and supplies, Bedell sent them to the mess deck. He told them there could still be some sailors alive on other parts of the ship, but he just didn't know for sure. He glanced down at his watch and wiped grime off the lens. It was 12:50. He'd need to remember the time when he filed his after-action report.

A report. He'd have to remember everything. The morning was a blur. The 449 was hit three times. They had to get out of the line of fire. When they made it out, they raced from ship to ship, trying to find proper help for the wounded.

Bedell turned to one of the men. "What's the name of your ship?"

"USS *Terror.*"

How appropriate, Bedell thought.

The sailor stood there in his perfect, pressed uniform, staring at him. Bedell realized he probably looked like shit. There was blood and grease and God-knows-what on his uniform. He'd singed his face and hands; his eyebrows were probably gone. He looked the sailor in the eye.

"Sheesh, don't you have things to do?"

"Yes, sir," the sailor said, before he wheeled around and headed below.

Lieutenant Commander Horace Warden stepped off the pallet and onto the 449. He was a surgeon on Rear Admiral Alexander Sharp's staff, sent to gauge the extent of the injuries. Warden spotted Bedell, the only officer in sight. They exchanged courtesies.

"Who's in command here?" Warden asked.

"I am," Bedell said. The officer hid his surprise. Bedell was only an ensign; he looked so young. "What happened to your captain? Where are the other officers?"

"I'm the last man standing," he said. "I'm the only officer who hasn't been killed or wounded."

Warden paused for a moment. "Looks like you had one hell of a day," he said.

Bedell nodded. "Yes, sir, a hell of a day."

Warden quickly went over the procedure: Move the wounded on stretchers to the fantail. Load them two at a time onto the pallets, then hoist them to the ship for treatment.

Warden told Bedell he'd struck it lucky: The *Terror* was the command ship for a fleet of minesweepers, and they had extra supplies and training just in case they had casualties. They were a floating hospital, with doctors, a surgical room, and recovery areas.

"Your men will get the help they need," Warden said.

Bedell felt a wave of exhaustion roll over him. Another doctor stepped up: Lieutenant Junior Grade Robert Rickert. "Where are the casualties?" he asked. Bedell took him and Warden down to the mess deck. The doctors moved calmly from patient to patient, consulting with the medical team from the *Williamson*. They soon had a priority list: at least a dozen surgical cases, probably more. They'd go first.

The doctors identified Herring among the wounded, shifting in and out of consciousness. He had to be stabilized before transfer, and the skipper didn't make it easy. Herring insisted on being the last wounded man off the ship.

The "walking wounded" assembled at the fantail. Hollowell and Holgate together moved Johnson to the deck. Holgate noticed a large gash in

Johnson's right arm. He grabbed a piece of board from the first aid supplies and splinted and bandaged the deep wound. He wondered why no one had thought to splint it before.

For the next half hour Bedell watched the evacuation. The *Terror* team worked like a well-tuned assembly line. The metal chains clanked and groaned as the pallet was lowered and raised. The men on the stretchers hung on as hard as they could, if they had any awareness.

Lewis was barely alive. Wilcox opened his eyes for a moment, then shut them as he felt the chains take hold and his body lift and swing over the decks like a bale of cargo. The pallet was going to break, he thought—after all this, he'd end up dumped into the sea!

Cromer and Duvall were next. Cromer was still in shock. Corkins was dead, he knew, and Cooper was missing. He was hit in his upper left thigh, and it hurt like hell . . . but he had to be grateful. A few more inches to the right, and his worst fear would have been realized. Duvall was heavily medicated. When he opened his eyes, they were vacant. Cromer caught his gaze and whispered, "Good luck." Duvall didn't respond. They were hoisted skyward.

Next up were Holtby and Kepner. Halcomb was right by Kepner's side, faithful to Beuckman's orders, but now it was time to say goodbye. "You're going to be OK. Then you're going home. You're done with the war," he said to Kepner. The cook opened his eyes for a moment, but he didn't smile.

"You're going home," Halcomb said again.

When the signal came, Halcomb stepped back and watched the pallet lift. He felt someone nudge him. "Hey pal, you want a butt?"

Halcomb was startled out of his reverie. It was a frogman, holding a pack of Lucky Strikes. Just like normal life. Halcomb forced a smile, glanced at the pack of cigarettes, and said, "Thanks, but I don't smoke."

The offer meant a lot to Halcomb, though. It was that man's way of saying "hang in there, you're going to be all right."

Hallett lay in a wire stretcher, trying to recall what had happened. He'd blacked most of it out. Hell, he had been unconscious for almost the whole battle. Now and then, though, ghastly images of dead shipmates came to his mind. How many were gone?

He wanted to know about Banko, but he was too afraid to ask. He didn't want to know, not yet. Glancing to his side, he saw Boatswain's Mate Second Class John Fisher, one of the original crew members, on the next stretcher. He was barely conscious. Bulky white dressings made his hands look like bowling pins. As the pallet moved, Hallett wondered if every damn one of them was hurt. Was there anyone on the gunboat who wasn't hit?

The loading crew picked up the pace until Herring was the only wounded man left to go.

"It's time," Rickert called out.

"Is that everyone?" Herring asked.

"Yes."

Herring nodded his head, "I'm ready," he said.

As Herring was loaded onto the stretcher, the survivors—Bedell, Blow, Beuckman, Overchuk, Lemke, Hightower, Skluzacek, and a few others—gathered near. They didn't know if this was goodbye for now, or maybe forever. Tears filled their eyes. They touched the skipper and offered words of encouragement.

"Good luck, Geddie," Blow said softly.

"Don't worry about a thing," Bedell said.

"You're gonna make it, Skip," Overchuk said.

Herring was fighting back a lump in his own throat. They'd been prepared, and they'd performed. In the rain of metal and death, his men acted with courage, with honor. They'd risked their lives to save one another. He lifted his head from the stretcher. "You fellas take care" was all he said.

ALL THE WOUNDED had been transported, all of the fires had been put out. It was time to gather up the dead.

The bodies would be taken to the *Terror* and laid out on the deck. Someone from the crew would help identify them.

The job was a rock-bottom detail. It wasn't just putting bodies on stretchers, it was body parts—heads, legs—dog tags. If a body was burned or dismembered beyond recognition, they'd have to rummage through the dead man's pockets to find a wallet, a letter, something with a name on it. In due course the navy would track down the man's family and tell them their husband, son, or brother was dead. Killed in action.

The 449 didn't have many seamen left standing, and Bedell wasn't going to force his men to participate in the cleanup—they'd seen enough. Bedell turned to the *Terror* for help. Admiral Sharp responded quickly and assigned several men to the death detail.

But after that job was done, the 449 crew would still have to hose down and clean up the ragged ship. The 449 would move to a dry dock for repairs and, after that, back to sea with a new assignment. Iwo Jima was just two days away, and other invasions stood on the horizon. The navy needed every ship it had, and every sailor.

Bedell didn't have many sailors to offer. Of the seventy-one men who'd embarked that morning on the mission—including Yates, Brockmeyer, and McGrath—at least forty-one had been killed or wounded. Even the ones who claimed they weren't hurt didn't escape injury. Throughout the day Lemke pulled bits of shrapnel from his uniform. He and Blow both had cuts and bruises up and down their bodies.

They could have said no, but none of the survivors opted out of the death detail. They volunteered. This was their ship, these were their friends and colleagues. It was the least they could do for them now. So Blow, Overchuk, Carrell, Lemke, Skluzacek, Holgate, Hollowell, and several others stayed aboard to finish the job. Admiral Sharp sent over Oliver Steele, Charles Sheaters, Olympic Barson, and several others from the *Terror*.

It was a gruesome assignment.

Steele started with the pilothouse. He stepped through the door and froze. A headless radioman sat at his post. The floor was covered in blood, flesh, and scraps of uniform. On the deck nearby, Sheaters sized up the burned and bloated body of Tominac. As he pulled him from his seat, the skin on his arm sloughed off in Sheaters's hands.

Sheaters bit back his nausea and kept working. He could feel the grisly scenes searing themselves onto his brain.

They moved a charred, headless body they found near the bow. Bodies were scattered all over the ship. "Loose parts" found scattered across the decks were shoveled into chum buckets and tossed overboard. Heads and limbs were put into pillowcases and mattress covers.

Lemke was nauseated. His hands shook. He tried to fight it, but just like that first day aboard, on the way from Pearl Harbor to Saipan, he leaned over the railing and heaved. No one said a word. Bedell went below to retrieve the Bible he had handed to Sless. He needed it. In the galley he spotted the cakes and bread, now gone black with blood. He wheeled around and walked back outside.

It was starting to get to him. He hadn't thought about the horrors when he was trying to get the gunboat out of harm's way. But now that the pressure was off, it was all coming back at him with perfect clarity: Every minute, every second of the morning. The bright white light, panicked faces, horrific impossible wounds, blood running down the walls and through the ceilings. Bedell had to keep his emotions in check. There was still too much to do.

High-pressure hoses dropped from the *Terror* to all parts of the 449. Bedell and his men grabbed them and turned on the water. They sprayed the ship from top to bottom in wide, sweeping arcs—decks, pilothouse, bulkheads, and fantail. After an hour of steady washing and scrubbing, the floors still showed dark red along the seams.

MALANAPHY HAD LISTENED in disbelief to the radio as the battle unfolded. Now he began compiling preliminary numbers on the destruction for his commanders: Nine of the twelve gunboats were badly damaged. Scores of men had been killed and wounded.

He hoped they could repair the LCIs, get them back into action as quickly as possible. His report listed the damage as well as the repairs facing some of the gunboats:

441: Major rewiring.
449: Communications gear destroyed. Conning tower shot up.
450: Rocket launchers damaged.
457: Damage to forward waterline on hull. Guns destroyed.
466: Extensive hull damage.

469: Engine room damage.
474: Sunk.

They already faced a shortage of 40mm and 20mm guns, as well as communications equipment. Larger ships seemed to get preferential treatment. The gunboats—the "Waterbug Navy"—always had to wait. Malanaphy asked for the higher command to intercede if they wanted to see the gunboats back on the line anytime soon.

Repairs were just the start of their troubles. A total of seven hundred sailors and officers had manned the twelve gunboats. Malanaphy said they'd need at least two hundred to replace all the dead and wounded. They'd probably need two hundred more to replace those too shell-shocked to ever return to action.

On the *Estes*, Admiral Blandy reviewed the losses. This wasn't supposed to happen. His ships had been bombarding Iwo Jima for two days with shells that could penetrate several feet of concrete. American planes had been intermittently bombing Iwo Jima for months. The attack on the gunboats revealed a startling truth: The Japanese heavy guns were still up there. They had concealed gun positions all over the island, including on Mount Suribachi. If those guns remained intact, it would be "murder on the beach" when troops landed on the morning of February 19, Marine Lieutenant General H. W. "Howling Mad" Smith warned Blandy.

When the admiral first drew up his battle plans, Marine commanders had warned that three days wasn't long enough to take out the heavy-caliber Japanese guns—they needed at least ten days of steady bombardment. But Blandy's staff assured him three days would be enough. He went with their recommendation.

But now Blandy knew Iwo Jima was going to be a meat grinder. If they didn't do something about those guns, it would be a massacre. Blandy called an emergency meeting. All of his commanders were there, including Smith, Malanaphy, and Hanlon. Blandy told them about the Japanese guns. He reminded them they only had one more day of bombardment before the invasion. Then he went around the table and asked each one what he should do.

When it was Marine Lieutenant Colonel Donald Weller's turn, he said the Japanese had made a critical error they could use against them. When they used heavy artillery to fire on the gunboats, they exposed all their secret positions. Using battle records and arithmetic, they could track the trajectory of the artillery, calculate the coordinates, and identify each target. U.S. battleships could move closer to shore and pound the new targets at point-blank range. Going in close would be risky, but that was the price of real effectiveness.

Blandy listened carefully. He and the commanders pored over the ships' firing reports and air reconnaissance photos. Postponing the invasion was out of the question, Blandy said. He had a schedule, and he was going to keep it.

The admiral issued an order: Battleships would move in at dawn and pound Mount Suribachi. Now that they knew where the heavy guns were, they would destroy them once and for all.

HIGHTOWER STEPPED OFF the pallet and onto the deck of the *Terror*. His eyes were immediately drawn to the straight line of bodies on the deck, under the sun. Someone ought to cover them up, he thought. He wanted to look away, but couldn't. He stared at their bloated, distorted faces, and began to feel guilty. They were dead, but he was still alive. Not only alive, but not hurt. Not even a scratch. How the hell did that happen? he asked himself.

Nothing about the day made any sense.

Just a few hours earlier these guys were alive, at their battle stations, waiting for orders. They were scared, but they were young, and invincible, every man thought he'd get through it. Hightower was overwhelmed with grief. The men on the tiny gunship had become as close as brothers. They had laughed together, listened to one another snore, carried one another home after a night at the bar. They'd read their letters out loud, even "Dear John" letters, and unabashedly showed snaps of their girlfriends and wives. They knew every detail of one another's life. Now their strong, suntanned bodies were broken and ugly. Hightower thought about their families, how they would break down when they answered the door and saw the messenger there with his fateful Western Union telegram. He let himself weep. He didn't care who saw him.

Hightower gathered his wits and turned to leave, but an officer from the *Terror* approached him.

"Are you ready?"

The officer had boarded the 449 earlier in the afternoon, looking for a volunteer for a disturbing detail. Hightower was the first person he approached.

"I hate to ask, sailor. But we need someone who knew these fellows to help us officially identify them. Would you be willing?"

Hightower said he would. Now he wasn't so sure. He'd just now pulled himself together, and didn't like the idea of going through all that again. He thought about it for a moment. If he didn't do it, someone else from the 449 would be assigned to it.

Hightower said he was ready.

He followed the officer and two Medical Division sailors to the bodies. The first one, Hightower said, was Yarbrough. "He was our executive officer," he said softly. "He was a good man."

One sailor wrote down the name on a clipboard, while the other bent over the body to remove one of the dog tag identification medals from a chain around Yarbrough's neck. One tag was kept for burial records; the other remained with the body. The sailor searched through Yarbrough's pants pockets for his wallet, good luck charm, coins, jewelry—personal effects to ship home to his family.

They moved next to Corkins. Then Young. Paglia.

They stopped when they reached a burned, headless body. There were no dog tags. One of the sailors glanced at Hightower. "Any idea who this is?"

Hightower looked closely, then shrugged. There were no visible tattoos. No jewelry. But when the sailor reached into the man's pants pocket, he pulled out a small book. He began flipping through the pages. "It looks like a prayer book," he said.

Hightower took a deep breath. He knew who it had to be. Before he had a chance to say a word, the sailor read the name inside the front cover: Lawrence Bozarth.

Hightower felt a sharp pain in his stomach. He turned away from the men, overwhelmed. This was just too much. Bozarth was so admired, so devout, so loved. He'd stop everything he was doing when one of his shipmates asked him to pray for something. He covered for them at night when they had shore leave. That very morning he'd smiled that innocent smile at Hightower and asked: "How ya doing?"

He was dead, his body grotesquely burned, but his holy book was unscathed. Hightower couldn't help but think of the irony. Bozarth had looked straight into the Gates of Hell, and his prayer book was the only thing that didn't burn. Scripture was the only thing left of him, his "word of truth." Without it, his parents would have received a telegram with the words: "missing in action." This way, his parents, siblings, friends, would have some peace.

The officer laid a hand on Hightower's shoulder, asked him if he'd had enough. Hightower regained his composure. He continued along the line as the navy man jotted down names. Schoenleben, Vogel, Minnick, Tominac.

THE GUNBOAT HAD been scrubbed down. It was far from spotless, but they were running out of time. Bedell received his orders late in the afternoon. A relief crew would come on board the 449 and sail her to another ship for repairs.

Only a handful of the crew was left. The rest were dead or wounded. In a few weeks, the remaining crew would probably be given survivors' leave. They'd go home for good.

But not Bedell. He was an officer and too many had been killed and wounded.

It was close to 16:00 when Lieutenant James Reed came on board the 449 with a dozen temporary replacements. He introduced himself to Bedell. For now, Reed would be skipper. No one was sure if Herring would survive, and if he did, he'd be sent home to recuperate. The new men would fill key positions on the 449—helmsman, signalman, and radioman.

Bedell took Reed for a tour, to inspect the damage. They walked forward, and Bedell listed the names of the men who were killed and hurt there, earlier that long, long day. When they reached the bow, Bedell pointed to the blackened hole near the ammunition locker. It was the first place the gunboat was hit, he said. It triggered a fire that took a long time to get under control.

A damage control team was hard at work documenting the destruction. They were pumping water from the bow and measuring the diameter of the holes punched in the gunboat's skin.

Seaman First Class William Cserney walked along behind Reed, listening to Bedell's narrative. He was worried about being assigned to the 449. It was only temporary, but it didn't seem very safe. The ship had taken so many hits, he wondered how it could function effectively. He didn't say anything to his shipmates, but several of them expressed similar fears.

"What if the engine conks out and we drift into the beach? We'll be killed," a friend warned Cserney. Another asked if the engines still worked at all.

"The engines work just fine," Cserney told them. "They pulled her off the line because of the hits, not because of the engines."

But that didn't ease their fears. They'd seen the ship hosed down, but they were still finding pieces of skin and hair. Maybe all that violence and death had somehow worked itself into the bulkheads and steel. The men concluded the 449 was a ghost ship, a bad-luck boat. That explained their anxiety. They were glad to be short-timers. They were afraid the bad luck might stick to them.

In the months that followed, every rainfall sent red-tinged water running through the decks and down the bulkheads. It didn't matter how many times they scrubbed the boat. The blood of the dead sailors traveled with them. Out at sea, late at night, eerie voices spoke in the pilothouse, out on the gun deck, right up on the bridge with the officers.

There could only be one explanation. The 449 was haunted.

ONCE THE DISASTROUS recon mission wound up, Nash was pulled in a dozen directions at once. He had reports to read and write, debriefings with the men, and meetings with the commanders, including Malanaphy. All of Group Eight's gunboats needed repairs. All were dealing with casualties. But when Nash finally learned the 449 was lashed to the *Terror*, he headed straight there.

He didn't know what he would find. The 449 was the only gunboat in his group that hadn't reported back to him. As Nash's ship approached the *Terror*, he saw the big numbers painted on the front of the gunboat: 449. It was the only way he would've recognized her.

He was shocked. The bridge, his old bridge, was gone. The mast was gone. There were holes punched right through iron cladding, and black smudges left by fires. What the hell had happened?

Nash's gunboat pulled alongside the 449. The commander strode out to the fantail and jumped the gap onto his old boat. He stood there for a moment, trying to get a feel for the place . . . he felt like a stranger. "Where is Lieutenant Herring?" he asked the nearest sailor.

The man shrugged. "I don't know who he is."

Another new crew member jumped in. "I heard he got hit bad, sir."

"How bad?" Nash snapped.

"I don't know, sir."

"Who the hell is in charge?"

"Ensign Bedell. He was on the 449 during the battle. But he's talking to Lieutenant Reed."

"Reed?"

"He's taking over command, sir."

Just then, Bedell and Reed walked out of the deckhouse to the fantail. Bedell snapped a salute, but Nash was in no mood for formalities.

"Herring, how is he, Bedell? How's the lieutenant?"

"Herring was blown out of the bridge, sir. His left shoulder was ripped open. He probably has internal injuries. He's unconscious now."

Bedell saw the pained look on Nash's face.

"What about Yarbrough?"

"He's dead, sir."

"Damn . . . Duvall?"

"Wounded."

Nash wasn't particularly close to the sailors. He kept a wall between himself and the enlisted men. He had to do that. It was the best way to command a ship. If you got too close, they might not listen. Still, there were a few other names he tossed out, men he respected: Beuckman, Kepner, Johnson, and Blow.

"Beuckman saved a lot of lives today, sir. And Blow took the helm and got us here. Neither of them is hurt. But Johnson lost a lot of blood. He might lose an arm."

Bedell took a breath.

"Kepner . . . I don't know if he'll make it, sir. He was hit bad, his legs are probably going to be amputated."

Nash absorbed the information, trying hard to hide his emotion. He changed the subject.

"What happened, Bedell?" he asked simply.

Bedell recounted everything, from the first mortar to the final drop of rockets into the sea. He told how Beuckman saved lives, how Blow steered the ship away from trouble, how a badly injured Herring refused treatment until all his men were cared for. He told him how the communications were destroyed, and how Lewis, with deep wounds on his legs, was hoisted up on the men's shoulders and used rags to relay urgent messages to ships. What Bedell didn't tell Nash was his own role—how his quick thinking and decisive leadership saved the ship and most of the men aboard.

Nash was impressed. He was proud to have been the first commander of the 449. He had trained many of the men who performed so well under fire.

"Thank you, Ensign, for the update," he said. "I'm heading over to the *Terror*."

"Very well, sir. It's a pleasure to have you aboard," Bedell said.

Nash turned again to the young ensign. He looked him in the eyes, then shook Bedell's hand. "Good job," he said. Nash didn't give many compliments. When he gave one, it meant something.

Nash jumped back onto the 457. Bedell turned his attention back to Reed. As soon as some of the crew returned from the *Terror*, they would be on their way.

THE RECOVERY WARD beds were filling up fast. The *Terror* was used to handling wounded, but they were busier than usual. Surgeons removed shrapnel and sometimes limbs, set bones, stitched wounds, and tried to keep dying men alive. The newly repaired men were then taken to Recovery, where they were tucked into beds arranged in neat rows.

Hallett was a bundle of morphine and bandages, lying in a woozy stupor in his Recovery bed. John Fisher, another 449 crewman, was in the bed to his right. He seemed to talk endlessly, but Hallett couldn't understand a word. Then Fisher leaned over and poked him. "Something's wrong with Park," he said.

Hallett sat up on his elbows and opened his eyes just wide enough to see across the room. Several people stood around Signalman Carl Park's bed. They were shaking him, trying to wake him up. A doctor came in, pulled out a stethoscope, and placed the bell against Park's chest. After a few seconds, the doctor removed the earpieces, folded the stethoscope up in his hands, and shook his head. Hallett slumped back in bed, closed his eyes, and sighed. Another one gone.

Commanders sometimes came to the Recovery Ward to talk to their men. When Nash entered, he walked slowly down the narrow room, peering at the faces in the beds until he found Herring's. He was unconscious. A unit of plasma hung from a hook on the wall.

He didn't want to disturb Herring, so Nash leaned over and whispered to a hospital apprentice, "How's he doing?"

"Sir, he's got a serious injury. He has a long road ahead of him."

It wasn't what Nash wanted to hear. He had forged deep ties with Herring. In a way, he was like a younger brother. Of all the people he'd met in the navy, Herring was the only one he could imagine staying in touch with after the war. "Take good care of him," he told the attendant. "He's one of the good ones." He left the room.

THE SUN WAS sinking. Commanders and sailors gathered on the fantail. Along the rail were sixteen bodies, each wrapped in white sailcloth, the ends sewn closed with a heavy five-inch shell inside. Each was draped with an American flag.

A gentle wind rippled the water. The commanders took their positions near a podium. Nash could see several gunboats near the minesweeper, along with the 449. Men huddled near the railings to watch and hear the ceremony broadcast over the loudspeakers.

A voice crackled over the ship's speakers: "All hands, prepare for burial service on the main deck."

In the recovery room, Banko and several of the wounded were helped to their feet and escorted to the main deck, but most of the injured couldn't move. They stayed in bed and listened to the service.

The men on the gunboats strained to hear the broadcast, too.

There was no chaplain aboard the *Terror*, so Admiral Sharp conducted a ceremony that had been part of naval tradition for centuries. When the injured were settled into chairs, Sharp stepped to the microphone and placed a Bible and some papers on the podium.

He glanced at a page. Then in a soft, soothing voice, he asked everyone to bow his head in prayer. He asked God to let the men rest in peace, to let the fallen know that their brothers and comrades honored their service. Sharp then beseeched the Lord to give solace to the families that would grieve the loss of their loved ones.

He then opened his Bible to Psalm 23. "The Lord is my shepherd; I shall not want. He maketh me to lie down in green pastures: He leadeth me beside the still waters . . ." As the admiral slowly continued his recitation of the passage, Nash looked at Iwo Jima in the distance. The sun seemed to be dropping into the mouth of Mount Suribachi, which was perfectly outlined by the brilliant last beams of yellow and orange light.

"Yea, though I walk through the valley of the shadow of death, I will fear no evil: for thou art with me; thy rod and thy staff they comfort me."

The admiral read on. Hallett, Johnson, Vollendorf, Duvall, and the others lay quietly, staring at the ceiling, remembering the men about to be buried at sea.

Bozarth's schmaltzy records. Swimming parties and mail call with Yarbrough. The laughter, the late nights sitting in their bunks, or topside talking about Owens's beautiful Nina, Schoenleben's new baby. Pearl Harbor nights, hitting the bars. Late-night patrols, exhaustion, "Cotton-Eyed Joe" and "All of Me" played soft in the dark on Hoffman's harmonica.

"Surely goodness and mercy shall follow me all the days of my life: and I will dwell in the house of the Lord for ever . . . Amen," said Sharp's voice.

The admiral closed the Bible. He reached for his papers. He took a deep breath and started reading a poem that seemed to have been written about the gunboats, how they handled themselves on this awful day. Most of the men recognized the poem right away. They'd learned it in school, in elocution class:

> *Half a league, half a league,*
> *Half a league onward,*
> *All in the valley of Death*
> *Rode the six hundred.*
> *"Forward, the Light Brigade!*
> *Charge for the guns!" he said.*
> *Into the valley of Death*
> *Rode the six hundred.*

Sharp's voice carried to every corner of the minesweeper and every gunboat alongside. Bedell, Blow, Lemke, and Overchuk could hear the admiral's voice on the 449. So could the men in the recovery room. If they listened closely, the Japanese on Iwo Jima could hear it, too.

> *"Forward, the Light Brigade!"*
> *Was there a man dismayed?*
> *Not though the soldier knew*
> *Someone had blundered.*
> *Theirs not to make reply,*
> *Theirs not to reason why,*
> *Theirs but to do and die.*
> *Into the valley of Death*
> *Rode the six hundred.*

By this time the sailors were having a hard time holding back tears. Not with the bodies on the deck. Not with everything they had seen, and everything they knew they'd face. As Nash looked around, he could see men quivering, brushing away tears.

Cannon to right of them,
Cannon to left of them,
Cannon in front of them
Volleyed and thundered;
Stormed at with shot and shell,
Boldly they rode and well,
Into the jaws of Death,
Into the mouth of hell
Rode the six hundred.

As Banko sat there, he wondered what would happen to him now. He was headed to a hospital at Pearl Harbor for recovery. He was glad Hallett had made it, but he grieved for the others. He didn't know if he would ever get over this.

When can their glory fade?
O the wild charge they made!
All the world wondered.
Honour the charge they made!
Honour the Light Brigade,
Noble six hundred!

The stirring words complete, Sharp stood at attention and ordered: "Firing party! Present arms!" Instantly, the seven sailor riflemen snapped to attention and held their rifles out in front of them with the barrels pointing skyward. Simultaneously the men who could stand stood at attention.

Four sailors picked up the first flag-draped body that rested atop a plank.

As the sailors stepped to the rail, Nash brought his arm up in a crisp, straight salute.

The wood was dipped toward the rail and, as the sailors clutched the flag, the body of Lieutenant Junior Grade Byron Chew Yarbrough slipped off and dropped into the ocean.

The sailors then stepped to the next body: Ensign William Corkins.

One by one, the sailors were given to the sea: Bozarth, Schoenleben, Hoffman, Walton, Paglia, Brockmeyer, Yates . . .

Park was the last to be buried. When his body slipped off the board and plummeted into the ocean, an officer from the ship's company stepped forward, faced the ocean, and snapped a salute. An honor guard followed with three volleys of fire. The noise startled the men.

Then, silence. No gunfire. No explosions. No roar of engines. No birds. No aircraft overhead. The only sound was a bugle playing Taps, the long, mournful notes carried in the lilting breeze.

For a brief moment, with the sun setting over the calm Pacific Ocean and a riot of pastels splashed across the sky, the dead sank slowly to the ocean floor.

They were at peace.

Many of the others would be stuck in hell for the rest of their lives.

EPILOGUE

THE IWO JIMA invasion was one of the bloodiest battles in the Pacific Campaign. It began at dawn on February 19, 1945, and lasted thirty-six days. More than 26,000 Americans fell in the battle; 6,800 were killed. Of an estimated 22,000 Japanese fighters, only 216 survived. This was the only Marine battle in the War in the Pacific where American casualties outnumbered the Japanese.

Iwo Jima was immortalized by Joe Rosenthal's Associated Press photograph of U.S. Marines raising Old Glory atop of Mount Suribachi. In the seven decades since, historians, filmmakers, authors, and scholars have analyzed, reconstructed, and celebrated aspects of the monumental battle.

What happened two days before the invasion is a footnote now, nearly forgotten.

But without the reconnaissance mission, the death toll would have been much higher.

The U.S. Congress awarded twenty-seven Medals of Honor for the Iwo Jima campaign, more than any other single operation during the war.

The first recipient was Lieutenant Junior Grade Rufus Geddie Herring. The *Congressional Record* used breathless prose to describe his heroism:

"Herring directed shattering barrages of 40mm and 20mm gunfire against hostile beaches, until struck down by the enemy's savage counterfire, which blasted the 449's heavy guns and whipped her decks into sheets of flame . . . His unwavering fortitude, aggressive perseverance and indomitable spirit against terrific odds reflect the highest credit upon Lieutenant Herring and uphold the highest traditions of the United States Naval Service," the award said.

Herring wasn't the only one on the 449 to be honored. Seven sailors and officers were awarded Silver Stars and Bronze Stars. They were:

Ensign Leo Bedell: Silver Star
Signalman Arthur Lewis: Silver Star
Pharmacist's Mate Henry Beuckman: Silver Star
Lieutenant Junior Grade Robert Duvall: Silver Star
Boatswain's Mate Second Class Frank Blow Jr.: Bronze Star
Electrician's Mate Paul Vanderboom: Bronze Star
Seaman First Class Daniel Skluzacek: Bronze Star

Nash received the Navy Cross. LCI (G) Group Eight received the Presidential Unit Citation, one of the highest military awards, for "extraordinary heroism" in support of the underwater demolition teams on February 17, 1945.

Even though the "lightly armored" gunboats sustained major damage "from well-concealed and strongly fortified Japanese positions," the LCIs kept fighting.

"Only when the beach reconnaissance had been accomplished, did LCI (G) Group Eight retire after absorbing . . . devastating punishment," the award said. Their action "bravely led the way for the invasion two days later."

All told, 43 men in Group Eight died, 152 were wounded. The 449 was the hardest hit—20 killed and 21 wounded—nearly two-thirds of the men aboard.

The day after the attack on the gunboats, Rear Admiral William H. P. Blandy ordered several battleships closer to Iwo Jima to pound Japanese positions exposed the day before. Once the coastal guns were destroyed, Blandy gave the green light for the invasion.

"Without this error by the Japanese, it is probable that many threatening coast defense weapons would have remained to take a very heavy toll of men and supplies from the outset of the ship-to-shore movement. This was unquestionably the most significant role ever played by the bold underwater swimmers and their close-support gunboats in the course of the Pacific War," historians Peter A. Isley and Philip A. Crowl wrote in their book, *The U.S. Marines and Amphibious War, Its Theory and Practice in the Pacific.*

After a month of horrific fighting, Kuribayashi's prediction came true. Iwo Jima became a major U.S. air base. By the end of the War in the Pacific in August 1945, nearly 2,400 American B-29 bomber landings had taken place at Iwo Jima. Many came in under emergency conditions that might otherwise have meant a crash at sea. Kuribayashi reportedly committed ritual suicide, but his body was never found.

That apocalyptic day in February 1945 had a profound effect on hundreds of lives. Nowhere was that more evident than with the crew of LCI-449.

Ralphal Johnson never played baseball in the Negro Leagues.

He spent months in a series of hospitals, and he returned to Decatur, Texas, a broken man.

His face was disfigured, and he could barely move his right arm. Even in blistering heat he wore long-sleeved shirts, to hide the scars. He got married in 1948, had a son and a daughter, and worked odd jobs around town, trying to earn enough to support his family.

The community was still segregated, and tension was high. Whites feared that returning black sailors, soldiers, and airmen would no longer tolerate Jim Crow conditions. There was a rash of lynchings, but the change had come. National newspapers broadcast the shameful violence through the nation. The publicity fueled the fire that ignited the national civil rights movement.

But Johnson was quiet and withdrawn. He began drinking heavily. His marriage ended and his struggles continued. He rarely talked about the war, but his family knew something bad had happened at Iwo Jima. Besides the physical scars, there were the emotional ones. Every Fourth of July, he'd flee town to get away from the noise, his family said.

"He used to get in his car, wouldn't say anything to anybody. But we knew where he was going. He would go way in the country where he couldn't hear all that, where he couldn't hear the firecrackers," said Bobby Johnson, one of his younger brothers.

In November 1970, Johnson drove his truck five hours to at a Veterans Administration hospital in Dallas, Texas, complaining of chest pains. He made it to the hospital parking lot, but passed out in the truck. He was in there for hours until passersby noticed him unconscious. He was taken inside. But he never regained consciousness. Doctors discovered that it wasn't only Johnson's heart that had failed. He had lung cancer. Johnson died November 24, 1970. He was forty-six years old.

His family never knew what happened at Iwo Jima. They didn't know he was a trailblazer, that he'd fought alongside white sailors in major battles.

His body was taken home. A small headstone marks his grave.

Today we call these symptoms "post-traumatic stress disorder," or PTSD. The condition afflicted thousands of World War II veterans, but it was decades away from being identified by mental health experts. The trauma they'd experienced had no acceptable outlet, so a generation of soldiers and sailors buried their memories deep inside their minds. Most refused to discuss the war with loved ones or friends, afraid of appearing weak or unmanly. Still, the psychological symptoms—flashbacks, nightmares, and depression—reminded them almost daily of what had happened.

When Johnson's ammo loader Junior Hollowell returned home, he didn't talk about the war either. His family knew he'd served at Iwo Jima, but not much more. He became a machinist, married, raised a family. Except for a single visit to Lawrence Bozarth's family, he lost contact with all the men on the ship.

"Pappy never shared anything with me about his military service, other than perhaps an occasional drunken disconnected phrase, 'swab the deck,' and 'been all over the world,' and 'tossed buddies' guts and body parts in buckets,'" recalled his daughter Tricia Miers.

Another daughter, Terri Sengbush, remembered her father's repeated references to one of the sailors killed on his ship: a family man. "My dad talked about how horrible it was that a man with a wife and children would have died, and that he was spared."

He kept saying it should have been him who died out there.

"I really believe that my dad's war memories messed with his nervous system," she said. "He would wake up swinging [his fists]. He had dreams and would say weird things in his sleep. He told me that when he drank alcohol it helped him to forget the horrible things he saw and lived through. I think he questioned why his life was spared."

For Norm Holgate, the pain never went away. The loss of his best friend Clarence Hoffman haunted him for the rest of life.

When the news of Hoffman's death reached his mother, she was stunned into disbelief. She wrote a letter to Holgate, asking him if it was true, if her boy was really dead. She needed to know what happened, from someone who was there. She wanted details.

"Well, I couldn't answer it. I just . . . at that time I just . . . you know . . . ," Holgate recalled, his voice trailing off. "I wished I was one of those guys that died at the time."

Holgate gave Hoffman's mother's letter to a chaplain and asked "if he would please answer it for me . . . that the young man was dead. And he said, 'Oh sure I'll take care of it.' So that was the last I heard about that," he recalled.

No one knows just what Holgate did for the first five years after the war. "For a while, he just disappeared," said his sister, Maggi McKinzie. "We didn't know whether he was alive or dead."

But he reappeared in their lives again, with stories about traveling along the Pacific Coast, working for a while as a disc jockey. Then, just like his father, he opened up a repair shop. He could fix just about anything, especially radios. Things got better. He married, had children. When his father was dying, Holgate took him in, even after everything he had done to the family, McKinzie said. "He just forgave him," she said.

The years went on, and Holgate's health began to fail. The doctors found cancer.

While there still was time, Holgate's children arranged a once-in-a-lifetime trip for their father. They flew to Hawaii, then boarded a special flight, an expedition to Iwo Jima. He didn't know anything about it until they circled the island to land.

Holgate was stunned. He walked off the plane and down to the beach. Soon as his feet hit the sand, he dropped to his knees, closed his eyes, and prayed. He prayed for all the men who died on that terrible island. He apologized to his old friend Hoffman for never contacting his mother. He prayed for Hoffman's soul, and asked for forgiveness and peace for his own.

Holgate died on February 21, 2011. He was 84.

Clifford Lemke's family threw a party to celebrate his homecoming. Eleanor and little Mary joined Lemke's parents at their home in Wisconsin and invited two dozen people over. A photographer captured the scene: The partygoers crowd the porch outside the house, with Lemke and his father, Fred, right in the center. Everyone is smiling except the haggard young sailor and his dad.

Lemke put his carpentry skills to work in the postwar building boom and made a good living. He settled just outside Milwaukee, where he and Eleanor raised six children.

Lemke was a quiet, orderly man, responsible and hardworking, but he drank heavily. His family called him a "functioning alcoholic." When a war movie came on the television he would occasionally watch, but the battle scenes were too much for him. His eyes filled with tears, then he'd leave the room. He often slept alone, his wife driven to sleep in another room because Lemke thrashed and cried out through the night.

Lemke eventually retired and moved to Torrance, California, to escape the long Wisconsin winters. There was no peace for him there. When his wife died of cancer after fifty-five years of marriage, Lemke fell to pieces.

One morning, he woke up, got dressed, and sat down at the kitchen table. He wrote a note, then placed it with his watch and wallet on the table. He called police and told them that when they arrived they'd find his body. As a police cruiser pulled up in his driveway, Lemke put a .22-caliber pistol to his head and pulled the trigger.

Lemke was an introvert going in, but he returned from the war deeply changed, his wife once told their daughter. His suicide devastated his family.

His daughter Deborah Blocker wept one afternoon and told her son Dennis Blocker it was the war that finally finished off her father. His relationship with his children had been strained because of his drinking, and he drank to anesthetize himself, to dull the pain of some terrible, unmentionable memory.

"Dennis, I don't care how you do it, but I want you to find out what Daddy went through during the war," she told her son.

Blocker knew his grandfather had served in the navy, but nothing else. His mother didn't know much more. But that day began Blocker's long journey into his grandfather's past, and the gunboat's role in a battle that scarred the lives of so many.

An avid history buff, Blocker remembered his grandfather signing a book about World War II. When he opened it, he saw his grandfather's signature and the inscription: "SIC Cliff Lemke LCI-449, '43 to '45."

In 2001, he got a lucky break.

Blocker lives in San Antonio, Texas. He was on his way to the library when he passed an older man wearing a hat embroidered with the words: "National LCI Association." Another man passed, wearing the same hat. Then another. Blocker stopped two of the men, Bill Brinkley and David Cox, and discovered the group was just then holding their annual national reunion in San Antonio. The excited young researcher told them his grandfather had served at Iwo Jima, and he was even then researching his role in the battle.

"Which gunboat was your grandfather on?" Cox asked Blocker.

"He was on the 449," he answered. Brinkley frowned and asked a question that would set the tone for Blocker's research: "Did he survive?"

Brinkley and Cox promised Blocker they'd get a list of the survivors of not only the 449 but of all the gunboats that participated in the underwater demolition teams mission on February 17, 1945. With that list in hand, Blocker conducted interviews with more than one hundred men in Flotilla Three, Group Eight, including key members of the 449, men who knew his grandfather.

The stories these men told revealed just why his grandfather lived in so much pain.

"He became close with so many people on the boat, and then watched them die. He had to put their body parts in a pillowcase. You can try to forget, but can you?" Blocker said.

Blocker then contacted me, Mitch Weiss, and asked for help. As a

Pulitzer Prize–winning investigative journalist, I'd covered dozens of military-related stories and investigations. I had also written four critically acclaimed nonfiction books about the military, including one detailing a failed Special Forces mission in Afghanistan.

Blocker's research was fascinating reading.

I started into my own research. I pulled documents, conducted interviews, read transcripts of Blocker's interviews, and found hundreds of additional letters from Herring's family as well as the first commander of the 449: Lieutenant Willard Vincent Nash.

I realized that the 449 was a microcosm of America, men from all walks of life. There were older men with families who could have sat out the war, but didn't. There were young men so patriotic they couldn't wait to enlist. Some were affluent and educated, and others were the sons of dirt-poor farmers or factory workers. There were Catholics, Protestants, Jews, and unbelievers. At the height of segregation in America and the military, white Southerners fought alongside the only African-American on board, Ralphal Johnson, who was such a good shot, he manned one of the gunboat's 20mm guns.

They all were brought together on a cramped, tiny gunboat, a tin can stuffed with explosives and charged with one goal: shoot Japan to its knees. They ate together, feasted, baked bread together, swapped stories, and shared intimate details of their lives as the 449 advanced across the Pacific Ocean. These were not elite, special-unit sailors. They were regular guys, young men, mostly eighteen, nineteen, and twenty years old, with officers who were not much older.

Even with stacks of official documents and interviews, I kept coming back to the letters. They were filled with hope and despair, uncertainty about the war's outcome and their own mortality.

One set of letters was a dialogue of doomed romance, two lovers who never saw each other face-to-face.

Betty Jones and Lieutenant Byron Chew Yarbrough hit it off right away. It was no surprise. They were solidly middle-class Southerners, from leading families in small towns, Betty in Cordele, Georgia, and Yarbrough in Auburn, Alabama. And both were in their mid-twenties, single, and lonely.

They began writing to each other in September 1944. Five months later, in Yarbrough's last letter to Betty, he hinted that he wanted to marry her. In a letter he wrote to his parents on the same day, he asked them to pick out a present for her.

But Yarbrough was killed in February, when a Japanese shell hit the conning tower where he stood. Betty had no idea. During the war, many families didn't know until weeks later that a loved one had been killed or was missing in action. They continued to write letters, continued to pray for their safe return.

So well after Byron Yarbrough died, Betty Jones continued sending him cheerful letters.

"The news from the European front is really good and has been lately. Maybe that part will be over real soon. Then I hope those Japs are thoroughly taken care of, and you can come home for good. Oh, what a happy day that will be," she wrote on February 17, 1945.

A day later she penned: "And how is my Navy Lieutenant in the Pacific? I have come to the conclusion that if given my choice, I much prefer writing you each day, than to do anything else. The time I spend each day writing you does so much for me. If I feel bad or if I am in bad humor and sit down for a chat with you, I feel like a new person when I am through with my letter."

On February 24, 1945, she received a package from Yarbrough's parents.

"I know that somewhere in the Pacific is a man, my man, who is the sweetest person I've ever known. Today I received a little package in the mail. It was postmarked Auburn, Alabama, but I know the thought behind it came from a certain Navy man somewhere in the Pacific. Honestly, Byron the pearls are beautiful."

Her parents were looking forward to meeting him, she said. "Naturally they don't read your letters, so they wonder what kind of a person it is who has the power of personality or something, that can get Betty Jones to write them every day. They just don't know you as I do or they would understand why it is that I live all day looking forward to the time of night when I can sit down and write you."

By early March, she had begun to worry. And she made one request: When he returned to the United States, she wanted a new photograph of him. "I want one I can put in a frame on my bedside table. I'm content now with your snapshots and I'm so proud of them, but one of these days I want a big one that I can see from across the room even. Goodnight, my Byron, and always remember I send you my love."

Her letters started coming back to her, marked "returned to sender." Something bad had happened. Yarbrough's family finally called with the news: Her Byron was dead. Killed in action at Iwo Jima.

Betty never got over it, her family said.

She grieved like a widow. Years later, Betty moved to Atlanta and took a job as a secretary. But in the late 1950s, her family, worried that she was drinking too much, brought her back to Cordele.

"She was a beautiful girl. She was so smart," recalled her sister-in-law Nancy Jones. "Everything just went downhill."

Betty never got married. She died in 1995. When her family began packing away her belongings, they opened her cedar chest in the attic. There, wrapped in a blue ribbon, were Yarbrough's letters. She had saved every one. She even kept the ones that were returned to sender.

"It was so sad. She just never got over him," said her niece, Nancy Dupree.

In the years following Iwo Jima, Seaman First Class Robert Minnick's mother told everyone her boy was still alive. She said he had fallen overboard and was probably on a deserted island waiting to be rescued, said his sister, Marilyn Cornell.

"She kept thinking he would be found alive," she said.

It took some time, but she came to the realization that her son was killed in action. But one day, Cornell heard noises coming from the attic. Her mother was up there, kneeling on the floor before a storage trunk. She was sobbing, pressing her nose against her son's old clothes.

"You cannot imagine her pain," her daughter said.

Seventy years later, Mary Cooper could still remember when and where her telegram arrived: March 11, 1945—exactly a year after her husband enlisted. She was visiting Cooper's parents and sister in Truro, Iowa. They were sitting in the living room when the knock came on the door. When Mary answered, a man was there, holding a telegram.

"I just sort of knew in a way. I went outside and I started running outside the house, crying and making a lot of noise," she recalled. Cooper's sister Eulalia put an arm around her shoulders and told her to come inside the house. "That's what I remember. She got me calmed down a little bit."

Ensign Frederick Cooper was missing in action, the telegram said. There was almost nothing more said, but Mary knew her husband was dead.

She returned to Orange City, Iowa, where Cooper was a teacher before he joined the navy. "People in the town were very kind and helpful to me and thoughtful about my situation," she said.

They never found his body.

Germany had surrendered on May 7, 1945; the Japanese did the same on August 15, 1945, but only after the United States used a devastating new weapon: the atomic bomb. Worried about staggering casualties if they invaded Japan, the United States on August 6 dropped a nuclear bomb on the Japanese city of Hiroshima. Three days later, the bomb was dropped on the city of Nagasaki.

The navy changed Cooper's status to killed in action on March 7, 1946.

A week later the town held a memorial service at the American Reformed Church in Orange City, Iowa. School officials and students remembered him fondly.

"Mr. Cooper loved the profession in which he was engaged," Superintendent C. H. Madden told the audience. "Had his life been spared, he was destined to go far in it."

Student Frederick Bower said: "It is very hard for us to realize that Coach Cooper will not return to us. We cannot understand why one who played such an important part in the lives of the youth of our country should be called away from his life's work so soon."

Cooper's father, the Reverend Frederick Cooper Sr., said the final words: "His hope was strong and his courage and ambition high. Then came the gathering storm of human passions, suspicion, greed, and hate, with fury of destruction and death. He threw his young life into this conflict where he thought it would mean the most. He was caught in the storm and carried out to sea. Somewhere in the great ocean his body is lost, but his soul will live forever."

Mary Cooper was now a widow, a single mother. She decided to go back to school, to Manchester University, and major in education. In her senior year, she met the man who became her second husband. She taught elementary school for twenty-eight years. Over time, she settled into her new life. Memories of Cooper faded.

After her second husband died a few years ago, Mary began reclaiming memories of her first marriage.

She remembered fondly that necklace Cooper had sent home from Guam, a string of beautiful pearls.

At Christmas 2014 she decided to do something special. She sought out similar necklaces, and sent one to each woman in her family, with a note about her first love and the necklace that he had sent her so long ago. "I wanted them each to think of Frederick when they would wear the necklace," she said.

Soon after the war ended, a man named Donald Cromer contacted her. She met him in Chicago, during a layover in a train journey.

Cromer told her he'd made a pact with her husband and another officer, Ensign William Corkins. If any of them were killed, the survivor would meet with their wives to tell them what happened.

Mary Cooper sat in a hotel lobby with little Rebecca squirming on her lap, and listened while Cromer told her a somewhat cleaned-up version of the battle. It was supposed to be a routine mission, but it turned out to be anything but that. Her husband died with honor, he said. He told her he was sorry.

It didn't make her feel better—her husband was never coming back. But at least she knew what had happened. She thanked the man, and continued on her journey. She never heard from him again.

Her train trip included a visit to Corkins's wife, Dotty, who lived outside of Cincinnati. She was having a hard time dealing with her husband's death. With two young children at home, she didn't know how she was going to raise them, Mary said. The widows commiserated. "At that point in our lives, there was so much uncertainty."

Dotty eventually remarried, and Corkins's two sons grew up knowing little about their father. They had no idea what happened to him at Iwo Jima, said Jim Corkins, a doctor. Young Corkins found old letters his father had written to family members during the war, as well as poems he had penned as a teenager.

His father loved nature, and talked about someday becoming a farmer. He'd majored in agricultural engineering at Ohio State. But like so many, his dreams died with him that morning at Iwo Jima.

John Overchuk never made it to Broadway. He taught dance at an Arthur Murray studio for fifteen years. He married another dance instructor, then took a job in a motorcycle parts factory after the birth of his son. Overchuk didn't tell his family about Iwo Jima, but that day was never far from his mind.

"We were very close friends all of us. I mean we sat on the toilets in the open with no dividers right next to a guy," he joked.

But then he turned deadly serious.

"I think about the 449 all the time. A day doesn't go by that I don't think about it . . . We lost so many people that day," he said, adding that over the years, he's been "haunted by the images." The nightmares.

"I dreamed I was in the galley lying on a bench by a table asleep. I awoke when we were being attacked at Iwo Jima. My brains were coming out of my head and I was trying to push them back in," he said.

Overchuk died May 8, 2010.

Like so many others, Frank Blow packed up his Bronze Star and stuffed it in his closet with the rest of his war memories. He married his girlfriend Mary Hodges and then picked up where he'd left off before the war. He became a master plumber. He raised three children, bought a house outside Philadelphia and a boat for weekend excursions up the Delaware River. Blow didn't talk about the war with his family. They didn't know he was a hero at Iwo Jima.

He died from a heart problem in May 2001. He was 77.

Willard Nash, too, became another of his generation's silent men.

Nash took a leave in June 1945 to receive his Navy Cross in New York. Dorothy Wallace was waiting for him.

She joined Nash and his sister and brother for an evening, but he was called home suddenly—he phoned Dorothy from the hotel bar to cancel their weekend plans. He'd leave on the next train, he said.

Dorothy impulsively decided to see him one last time. She threw on a bright yellow dress, grabbed her sunglasses and bag, and ran for the subway. She swept into the hotel bar just in time to find Nash and his brother getting ready to leave. Nash seemed pleased, but Dorothy wasn't sure she'd done the right thing. She wasn't sure at the end of the day if he was interested in seeing her again.

Nash wrote her a flirtatious letter a few days later that put her doubts to rest.

"It was a wonderful leave while it lasted," he wrote, adding that he was thankful the navy gave him the leave to get the award. As soon as he arrived home, he did his laundry, he said. "It turned out very well, all except one red streak near the left shoulder. Mother noticed it and commented that it looks like a red pencil mark. I didn't think it was, but didn't bother to tell her that lipstick will usually wash out."

Within a year of the letter, they were married in Forest Hills, New York. They settled in Saginaw, Michigan, where Nash served as city attorney from 1946 to 1978.

The couple raised two children. Nash joined the Saginaw Bay Yacht Club and sailed the Great Lakes, while Dorothy volunteered with community groups and wrote a newspaper column.

Nash died in December 1986 at age 76. Dorothy died in 2002, and left behind her writings and a scrapbook of her romance with the "dashing young Navy lieutenant."

His friend, Lieutenant Junior Grade Rufus Geddie Herring, was for years hailed as a hero. The handsome young officer with the Medal of Honor was the best and the brightest: a young college graduate who excelled under pressure.

But it took nearly two years for Herring to recover from his wounds. At one point, doctors didn't know if he would make it. He spent years undergoing grueling physical therapy to try to regain the use of his left arm. "With his injury, he couldn't raise his arm so high," recalled his son Stan Herring.

He put his recovery time to good use, writing letters of condolence to the families of crew members killed in the battle. The families corresponded with him for years, and he always tried to answer their questions. They were his men, and he felt responsible for them.

During physical therapy at Bethesda, Maryland, he met a no-nonsense navy nurse named Virginia "Ginny" Higgs, a native of Parkersburg, West

Virginia. She was the first in her family to graduate college. She pushed Herring hard and saw him strive to get stronger.

Herring eventually returned to Roseboro, North Carolina, but he wrote letters to Ginny, upbeat accounts of life in the small Southern town. He didn't write about the war. The only hint of his trouble came in a line in one of his letters: "You know what I've been through."

They married on March 15, 1947, in Roseboro, in a wedding that his mother turned into the social event of the season.

"She went downtown and went through the city water book. Anybody that had water, she made sure they had an invitation. She didn't leave anybody out. She just wouldn't exclude anyone," Stan Herring recalled.

And Herring truly did have a wonderful life.

He took over the family lumber business, then opened a furniture store. He raised poultry, and later opened a feed dealership and a swine operation. He had two sons and a daughter.

"He was a very quiet and very humble man," his son recalled.

After a long battle with cancer, Herring died on January 31, 1996. He was 74.

He never did go sailing with his old skipper. He'd left that part of his past behind.

Leo Bedell stayed in the Pacific until the Japanese surrendered in August 1945. Once back in Akron, he made good on his mail-order engagement to Mary Jo Costigan. The pair eventually had ten children.

Bedell worked for two insurance companies, before starting his own business: Hastings-Bedell Insurance. Bedell found solace in service. He was a devout Roman Catholic, and a member of the St. Vincent de Paul Society for more than fifty years, helping to feed and house the poor of the parish.

Bedell's family knew he had received a Silver Star for heroism, but he preferred not to discuss that part of his past.

But when Blocker, the researcher, contacted Bedell in 2004, he opened up and shared his experiences. It was the first time his family had heard any of the stories. "There was so much we just didn't know," recalled his son Terry Bedell.

Bedell reached out to other crew members. He attended an LCI Association reunion in 2006 in Branson, Missouri, where he saw William Hildebrand, Bruce Hallett, and others he hadn't seen since the day of the battle.

After the reunion, Hildebrand phoned Bedell every year on February 17 to thank him for "another year of life." He'd send Christmas cards with the same thankful message. Bedell had saved his life, and he still is grateful. He has undertaken an effort to get Bedell's Silver Star upgraded to the Medal of Honor or at the very least a Navy Cross.

Bedell wasn't sure how he felt about that. He was embarrassed by the praise, even if, yes, he did do those daring deeds, way back when. To Bedell, that fateful day was a string of horrors. At night, he saw the faces of the dead in his sleep.

"When you live through something like that, it stays with you forever," Bedell said.

Bedell passed away on October 14, 2014. He was 93.

When Beuckman returned, he decided to live in his childhood home: East Saint Louis, Illinois. He lived a simple life. He set up a business, going door-to-door selling home goods. Like so many, he wanted to put the war behind him. If anyone asked about his service or his Silver Star, he'd shrug. Nothing much to talk about, he'd say.

Beuckman worked hard and stayed close to his brothers and sisters. After his wife died, he remarried, and his family grew. He later moved to his mother's farm. He was surrounded by stepchildren, grandchildren, and great-grandchildren. Beuckman died in January 1998. He was ninety years old.

His stepdaughter Susan Anderson said he was a quiet, thoughtful man. But he kept in touch with his best friend on the gunboat, Clarence Kepner, whose legs were terribly injured.

When everybody had told Beuckman that Kepner was "too far gone," he had said no, that Kepner was going to make it. He stayed by his friend's side. "He could not turn away from his dear friend," Anderson recalled.

Years later, Kepner said he owed his life to Beuckman.

Kepner's legs were amputated in surgery, but somehow he survived, just as Beuckman had promised.

He spent many months in the hospital. Kepner fretted about going home. How would his young wife react to him? How would he fit into ordinary life again without legs? But he vowed that he'd make the most of the life he had left. He had been given a second chance. If not for Beuckman's actions, he would be dead.

Once home, he was fitted with prosthetic limbs and used them to their limits. He had children and his daughters fondly recall him climbing trees with them, swimming, playing tennis. He learned how to ride a motorcycle. Nothing slowed him down. The family moved to Los Angeles, California, and he worked at the Northrop Corporation in Hawthorne, California.

Kepner's blood type was AB negative, a rare match for all other types of blood. He enrolled with the American Red Cross and was on an emergency donor call list.

When the Vietnam War was raging in the 1960s and early 1970s, Kepner worked with the Veterans Administration, helping returning amputees learn to live with prosthetic limbs. When Kepner died in 1988, dozens of uniformed veterans attended the service.

Many of the men lived with a nagging sense of loss.

Once Charles Hightower returned home, he screwed up his courage and called Ralph Owens's mother. He explained what had happened to her son. He promised to drive out to see her one day, but that day never came.

"I will always kind of halfway regret that I didn't go and tell his mother," he said. "I phoned her on the phone and talked to her and I got the satisfaction of telling his mother about what happened. But I wanted to really go and sit down and talk to her and his girlfriend, Nina."

The battle was the defining moment in his life.

"I went in as a little kid, and I had to become a man pretty quick. I had to do some things that you just don't do when you're a kid. And that's all I was, a kid. I had just turned eighteen," Hightower said.

He recalled what he told Cooper that afternoon on the gunboat so long ago: that in battle, you fight for the men to your left and right.

"I met a lot of fine men. I guess some of them might have been pretty rough. But when you're fighting side by side, buddy, you're just as close as you can get. You'd just die for them. That's all."

After the war, he opened "Charlie's Barbershop" in Russellville, Arkansas. It was a fixture in town for fifty-seven years. He got married to his girl

Billie, raised a family. He started going to military reunions, and found it helpful to share company with other old warriors. He was able to open up to them. He died in 2012.

Many families grieved for years.

Bozarth's father was overwhelmed with guilt. He had tried to convince his son not to enlist, but the boy was relentless. He'd pestered his father until he gave in, and then? Then he was dead.

"You know, we never had a memorial for Lawrence back in 1945," said Evelyn Schoonover, the eldest of Bozarth's sisters. "Our dad would not talk about death, and especially Lawrence's death. He had to sign for Lawrence to go into the service, and he felt bad about that all of his life."

After the war, Elaine Butler, "the girl from San Diego," had contacted the Bozarth family, wanting to know if Lawrence had been discharged. They had to break the news to her: He'd died in combat.

Elaine went on with her life, married, had children. She never forgot the handsome young sailor who walked into the broom shop that day in San Diego. She kept in touch with Bozarth's family over the years. They exchanged letters, updates on weddings and babies and graduations, but they lost touch in the mid-1990s.

At age ninety, Elaine still remembered many of the details of those weeks in San Diego. She could recall Bozarth standing by her family Victrola, playing that one gospel song over and over, as he explained how it reminded him of his family.

"I thought he was going to be the one," she recalled. "I can still see his sweet face."

Shortly after the war, a tall lanky fellow showed up unannounced at the Bozarth family front door. He said his name was Junior Hollowell, and that he was a friend of their son Lawrence. The family knew the name—it had appeared in many of Bozarth's letters. In one of his last, Bozarth asked his sister if she would write to Hollowell.

Leona Bozarth asked him in and sat him down at the kitchen table, made him a cup of coffee. Hollowell reached into his pocket and solemnly placed an object on the table in front of Bozarth's mother, Leona. It was her son's wallet. Hollowell said he knew from experience that wallets typically did not make it home to relatives. Too many thieves along the trail home would steal and loot such items.

Leona picked up the black billfold and felt the soft, well-worn leather in her fingers. Inside were pictures of the family and a few dollars. One of the sisters went to retrieve their father, but he refused to meet with the visitor. The wounds were too fresh.

Hollowell told them how much everyone on the ship respected Bozarth, how he prayed with everyone and was always positive, even in the heat of combat. Before he left, he said something to Bozarth's mother that would haunt her for years.

"He said he never believed the body identified as Lawrence was Lawrence, and told Mom never to give up hope that he would show up sometime," recalled Bozarth's sister, Mildred Cosper.

Hollowell was trying to ease her pain. Instead, Bozarth's mother held out hope.

"She would just about accept his death, and then you would hear of someone showing up that was on an island or some strange tale and she would hope again," Cosper said.

In 2005, the Bozarth family was invited to a ceremony the researcher Blocker organized dedicating a plaque to the 449 at the National Museum of the Pacific War in Fredericksburg, Texas.

The Bozarth family pulled up in two cars. An elderly woman emerged from the second, a thin, five-foot frame with gray hair. It was Leona Bozarth. She was ninety-nine. The two women escorting her were her daughters.

The following day at the ceremony, she was introduced to the crowd and given a rousing round of applause. After the ceremony, she and her family had a quiet moment by the plaque for the 449. They pointed to Lawrence's name, ran their fingers slowly over it, and posed for pictures.

There, surrounded by his shipmates and their families, surrounded by people who knew their pain, they were finally able to say goodbye.

Handsome young beach boy Fred Walton's family also had trouble coming to terms with their loss. They expressed their grief in writing. Shortly after his son's death, Albion Walton put his thoughts to paper. First, he called his piece: "Restoration." But he crossed it out, and called it "*Vivat*"—the Latin command to live.

In my humble home I found a picture today. With trembling hands I held it. Torn at the edges, soiled and cracked. A picture of our youngest son as a little boy of two years. A few months ago, as a sailor in his country's navy, he joined the legion of those who gave their all. The picture lay in a closet for years; forgotten and dust ridden. How tenderly I caressed it, fearful lest I could not restore its torn edges and broken spots to their former state, my hands shook. For hours with painstaking care I toiled to restore this picture, so priceless now until at last we could see his tiny face smile back at us.

Suddenly over me swept the realization that out there in the horror of the battle's carnage and terrifying explosions I would see God kneel beside our boy amid the battle's roar. With deft fingers in infinite tenderness he lifted our loved one's torn, broken and bleeding body to restore again his mortal spirit and make it an immortal whole. As a great surgeon wields the scalpel and needle when he mends a broken body, so God restored the shattered souls of our loved ones lost in battle. He knelt, gathered them gently in his everlasting arms and carried them home.

Walton's brother made it home from the war. His other brother graduated from the U.S. Naval Academy. And on holidays, the entire family gathered at Albion and Jean Walton's house—sons and daughters, in-laws and grandchildren. But there was always a hole in their lives.

For years, right around Walton's birthday, Jean wrote what she called "Letters to My Deceased Son." It was a way of coping with the pain. In February 1969, she wrote:

Time says that in a few days my Fred will be forty-three years old—but no that cannot be so because to me he will always be just nineteen, nineteen years of love and laughter, singing his happy songs and making us all laugh with his cute happy funny ways.

He went away one day, brave and proud that he could fight for his country, we waited and prayed that he would come home to us, just a few months went by, then the telegram came telling us he's not coming home to us but home to God.

There have been good days and bad days since then. Sometimes we can laugh when we talk of the cute, funny things he used to do, but then other days we long for him so much, and tho years have passed the tears come and we miss him so much it seems we can't stand it.

His birthday will be on Feb 6th and because we can't have him with us we do ask our good Lord to love him and let him know that we love him also. And his memory is so very dear.

Happy birthday darling, your mom and dad do love you so much, remember how we used to listen to your records, I can remember one record very well "Heartaches" because that is what I get if I sometimes fail to remember that our Father is taking care of my sweet one. Good night and all good tomorrows.

The families of the dead only had memories. They tried to remember the last time they saw their brother, son, or husband. They tried to remember the last words their loved ones said before leaving. Memories fade over the years. Now, with the passing of time, there are few people still alive who remember the dead. Some, like Signalman Arthur Lewis, have passed out of living memory.

After Lewis was wounded, he somehow found the strength to keep going. He found the strength to lift those bloody rags to signal for help. He was awarded the Silver Star for his heroism. But two months after Iwo Jima, two months after his legs were amputated, Lewis died of complications in a naval hospital in Corvallis, Washington.

Lewis's parents and sister, Vivian, were comforted by Herring's stirring words: "Lewis was my personal signalman . . . Where the correct signal counted, Lewis had that job. I trusted none of the others," he wrote.

The Lewises kept his memory alive among themselves, but now they, too, are dead. And Arthur Lewis is just a name, one of 407,316 U.S. service members killed during World War II.

Lareto Paglia's parents, brothers, and sisters honored his memory by saving his artwork—watercolors and charcoal sketches. They hung them on walls, showed them to nieces and nephews. And when the nieces and nephews had their own children, they told them stories of a talented young man who gave up a promising career to fight for his country.

Some of the injured recovered completely.

Banko spent long months healing from his wounds. He was honorably discharged from the navy in April 1946. He took advantage of the GI Bill and enrolled at Yakima Valley Junior College in Yakima, Washington. During summer breaks he worked for the U.S. Forest Service on the Snoqualmie National Forest. He finished his degree in wildlife management and forestry in 1950 at Washington State College.

He went right to work, accepting a job as a biologist and game protector in northeast Washington. A close encounter with well-armed duck poachers led him to transfer to the Forest Service. It was there he found his true joy.

Banko married in 1963 and had four children. In 2003, he learned that Hallett lived a few hours from him. They reconnected. After talking with his old buddy, Banko decided to put into words what happened to him at Iwo Jima. He wrote nearly forty pages.

"We always had such a good view from the ship's bow," Banko recalled. "We thought it was great at the time. Now, when I think about it, standing at the bow wasn't such a great thing."

He died on December 6, 2011, at age 86.

Hallett also took months recovering from his injuries. But unlike his friend, he stayed in the military. He was honorably discharged from the navy in 1947, then enlisted in the army in 1950 to join its Criminal Investigation Division. When Hallett left the army in 1966, he worked for U.S. Customs until he retired in 1980. Along the way, he got married, had three children, and moved to Bremerton, Washington, about two hundred miles west of Wenatchee, his childhood home.

Like so many others, Hallett was haunted by his past.

He'd blacked out after the first shell landed on the bow, and when he regained consciousness he staggered along the deck, passing friends who had been killed and wounded. He vividly remembered the body parts.

"These were guys you spent so much time with. You knew everything about them. Then to see them like that, it hurts," he said.

He didn't have much reason to call up the past until the phone rang one day, and a man on the other end asked a simple question: "Were you on the 449?"

Hallett put down the phone and threw up in the kitchen sink.

It was the beginning of his journey. He began opening up about the war. His memories formed a large part of this work.

"You know, I was eighteen years old when I went into combat. By the time of Iwo, I was an old vet. I had just turned twenty, and that was my fifth invasion. Looking back at it, it's still hard for me to imagine. It really is," he said.

Hallett said he coped with his postwar culture shock with long walks along the Pacific Ocean. One day, he decided to write a poem about Iwo Jima. It was his way of healing.

Perched on a bluff above the ocean in 1946, he put his thoughts to paper.

Nearly seventy years later, he sat on his back porch and recited the last lines, a verse that he said summed up the horror that now is fading into history:

> *They met us there on that island beach*
> *They met us with shot and shell*
> *I thought I'd dropped from the top of earth*
> *Down to the heart of hell.*

ACKNOWLEDGMENTS

This book was years in the making, and I'd like to thank a number of people who helped me along the way.

I am grateful for Dennis Blocker, who brought the story to my attention. You worked so hard for so long to make sure the men of LCI-449 were not forgotten. Mission accomplished.

A special thanks to Rebekah Scott, an extraordinary writer, editor, and friend. Your guidance, insight, and wisdom helped shape the book.

Kevin Maurer provided critical support. As always, you offered important advice. I couldn't have asked for a better colleague, or friend.

I've learned from so many others over the years, including Michael D. Sallah, one of the nation's best investigative journalists. As I was writing, I could hear your voice, reminding me about character, plot, tension. You're an incredible teacher and friend.

To Adam Bell and his wife, Julie Reed Bell, I'm grateful for your friendship. It has helped carry me through some difficult times over the years.

I offer my gratitude to my mother Sonya, brother Alan, and sister Roslyn. You have always been there for me. I can never repay you for all of your encouragement and support.

As I was researching and writing the book, I kept thinking of my father, Morris Weiss, who served five years in the U.S. Army in World War II. Like so many from his generation, he didn't talk much about his service. But later in life, he opened up. A machine gunner, he recounted fighting across the central Pacific. He talked about being stuck in foxholes in godforsaken places like Okinawa, trying to shoot down dive-bombing Japanese planes. He was so proud of serving his country. He passed away in 2008, but I could feel his presence while I was writing. Thank you, Pop.

I credit the men who served on LCI-449, most notably Rufus Geddie Herring, Willard Vincent Nash, Byron Chew Yarbrough, Ralphal Johnson, Leo Bedell, Lawrence Bozarth, Frank Blow, Charles Banko, Bruce Hallett, Norman Holgate, Clarence Hoffman, Arthur Lewis, and Clifford Lemke. I will carry the memories of your sacrifice and courage for the rest of my life.

I'd also like to thank my agent, Scott Miller of Trident Media Group, who recognized the value of the story, and I'd like to express my gratitude to the team at Penguin Random House for their editorial support, including Brent Howard, my book editor, who truly understood the importance of the story.

I'm thankful for my children Brittany, Meredith, Samantha, and William, who inspire me. I only wish that my daughter Jessica was here. She passed away in 2006. When she was alive, we'd spend countless hours talking about politics and history. Jessica, you'll always be in my heart. We all miss you.

Lastly, but most importantly, I am forever indebted to my wife, Suzyn Weiss, an extraordinary and courageous woman. Without her love, support, and patience, this book would not have been possible.

BIBLIOGRAPHY

BOOKS

Baker, A.D. III. *Allied Landing Craft of World War Two*. Annapolis, Md.: Naval Institute Press, 1985.

Blassingame, Wyatt. *The U.S. Frogmen of World War II*. New York: Random House, 1964.

Brooks, Victor. *Hell Is Upon Us. D-Day in the Pacific June–August 1944*. Cambridge, Mass.: DaCapo Press, 2005.

Bush, Elizabeth Kaufmann. *America's First Frogman. The Draper Kauffman Story*. Annapolis, Md.: Naval Institute Press, 2004.

Camp, Dick. *Iwo Jima Recon. The U.S. Navy at War, February 17, 1945*. Minneapolis, Minn.: Zenith Press, 2007.

Dyer, George Carroll. *The Amphibians Came to Conquer*. Washington, D.C.: GPO Publishing, 1991.

Edgerton, Robert B. *Warriors of the Rising Sun: A History of the Japanese Military*. New York: W.W. Norton, 1997.

Friedman, Norman. *U.S. Amphibious Ships and Crafts*. Annapolis, Md.: Naval Institute Press, 2002.

Goldstein, Donald M., and Katherine V. Dillon. *The Pacific War Papers. Japanese Documents of World War II*. Washington, D.C.: Potomac Books, 2004.

Horie, Yoshitaka. *Fighting Spirit: The Memoirs of Major Yoshitaka Horie and the Battle of Iwo Jima*. Annapolis, Md.: Naval Institute Press, 2011.

Isley, Jeter A., and Philip Crowl. *The U.S. Marines and Amphibious War, Its Theory and Its Practice in the Pacific*. Princeton, N.J.: Princeton University Press, 1951.

Kakehashi, Kumiko. *Letters from Iwo Jima*. London, England: Weidenfeld & Nicolson, 2007.

Kakehashi, Kumiko. *So Sad to Fall in Battle: An Account of War Based on General Tadamichi Kuribayashi's Letters from Iwo Jima*. New York: Ballantine, 2007.

Lorelli, John. *To Foreign Shores. U.S. Amphibious Operations in World War II*. Annapolis, Md.: Naval Institute Press, 1995.

Lund, Paul, and Harry Ludlam. *War of the Landing Craft*. London: W. Foulsham & Co., 1976.

McGee, William. *The Amphibians Are Coming!* Santa Barbara, Calif.: BMC Publications, 2000.

Morrison, Samuel Elliot. *History of United States Naval Operations in World War II, Volume III, The Rising Sun in the Pacific 1931–April 1942*. Edison, N.J.: Castle Books, 2001.

Morrison, Samuel Elliot. *History of United States Naval Operations in World War II, Volume VII, Aleutians, Gilberts and Marshalls, June 1942–April 1944*. Edison, N.J.: Castle Books, 2001.

Morrison, Samuel Elliot. *History of United States Naval Operations in World War II, Volume VIII, New Guinea and the Marianas. March 1944–August 1944*. Edison, N.J.: Castle Books, 2001.

Morrison, Samuel Elliot. *Victory in the Pacific*. Boston: Little, Brown and Company, 1960.

Newcomb, Richard F. *Iwo Jima*. New York: Nelson Doubleday, 1983.

O'Brien, Francis, A. *Battling for Saipan: The True Story of an American Hero*. Novato, Calif: Presidio Press, 2003.

Rielly, Robin L. *American Amphibious Gunboats in World War II. A History of LCI and LCS(L) Ships in the Pacific*. Jefferson, N.C.: McFarland & Company Inc., 2013.

Rooney, John. *Mighty Midget U.S.S. LCS 82*. USA: J.A. Rooney, 2000.

Ross, Bill D. *Iwo Jima, Legacy of Valor*. New York: Vintage Books, 1986.

Sherrod, Robert. *Tarawa: The Story of a Battle*. New York: Bantam Publishing, 1994.

Taylor, Robert A. *World War II in Fort Pierce*. Charleston, S.C.: Arcadia, 1999.

Wright, Derrick. *Tarawa 1943: The Turning of the Tide*. Oxford, England: Osprey, 2000.

ARCHIVES AND DOCUMENTS

National Archives and Record Administration, Washington, D.C. This archive includes U.S. Navy, U.S. Army, and other military files related to World War II and the War in the Pacific, including the Battle of Iwo Jima.

After-Action Reports, Iwo Jima UDT Support Mission:

LCI (G) 346

LCI (G) 348

LCI (G) 438

LCI (G) 441

LCI (G) 449

LCI (G) 450

LCI (G) 457

LCI (G) 466

LCI (G) 469

LCI (G) 471

LCI (G) 473

LCI (G) 474

UDT 12

UDT 13

UDT 14

UDT 15

Action Report, Commander LCI (G) Flotilla 3 (Commander Task Unit 52.5.1), 24 February, 1945.

Action Report, Commanding Officer, LCI (G) 348, Lt. (j.g.) Alvin Rosenbloom, Underwater Demolition Support on Iwo Jima, 17 February, 1945.

Action Report, Commanding Officer, LCI (G) 457, Lt. (j.g.) Gerald M. Connors, 27 February, 1945, Enclosure B Medical Officer's Report on Casualties and Treatment Given.

Action Report, UDT #14 in the Iwo Jima Operation 16 February to 1 March 1945.

Boat Group Commander Summary Report, Lt, (j.g.) C. H. Shepard, III, USCG, Operational Data, USS *Arthur Middleton.*

CINCPAC War Diary, February 1945.

Commander Task Force Fifty-Four, *Report of Operations in the Iwo Jima Campaign.*

Commander Task Force Fifty-One, Commander Amphibious Forces, US Pacific Fleet, *Report on the Capture of Iwo Jima.*

Commander Task Force Fifty-Two, *Report of Operations in the Iwo Jima Campaign.*

Deck Log, LCI (G) 449, August 1943–March, 1945.

Deck Log, USS ESTES.

Deck Log, USS TERROR, February 1945.

Deck Log, USS WILLIAMSON.

Iwo Jima Naval Gunfire Support, Expeditionary Troops Report, Fleet Marine Force Commander UDT Pacific, History of Pacific Operations.

Logistics Report, From G-4, Headquarters, Expeditionary Troops, Task Force 56, *Iwo Jima Operation.*

Office of the Commander Amphibious Group One, *Report of Operations of Task Force 52 in the Iwo Jima Campaign from 10 February to 19 February,* March 7, 1945.

Radio Log, USS *CAPPS* (DD-550), 17 February, 1945.

Rear Admiral Harry W. Hill, *Report of Tarawa Operations*, December, 13, 1943, Enclosure A, p.-f-.

Rear Admiral Harry W. Hill, *Report of Tarawa Operations*, December, 13, 1943, Enclosure A, p.-g-.

Visual Reconnaissance Report of Observer With UDT #12, March, 29, 1945, Company "B" Amphibious Reconnaissance Battalion, Fleet Marine Force, Pacific, Enclosure "A" to Appendix 10 to Annex Charlie to 5th Amphibious Corps Landing Forces Special Action Report.

Visual Reconnaissance Report of Observer With UDT #14, March, 29, 1945, Company "B" Amphibious Reconnaissance Battalion, Fleet Marine Force, Pacific, Enclosure "A" to Appendix 10 to Annex Charlie to 5th Amphibious Corps Landing Forces Special Action Report.

War Diary, LCI Flotilla 3, January 1944–March 1945.

War Diary, LCI Group 8, January 1944–March 1945.

War Diary, USS *TERROR*, February 1945.

War Diary, USS *WILLIAMSON*, February 1945.

PERSONAL LETTERS

Betty Jones

Byron Yarbrough

Carl F. Park

Carleton "Lee" Yates

Dorothy Wallace

Ernest "Buck" Yates

Fred Walton

Frederick Cooper

Lawrence Bozarth

Leroy Young

Nancy Yates

Robert Duvall

Robert Minnick

Rufus Herring

Willard Vincent Nash

William Corkins

INTERVIEWS

OFFICERS AND CREW OF LCI (G) 449:

Alfred Max Fox

Anthony Joseph Serine

Arthur Guajardo

Bruce Henry Hallett

Bruce W. Taylor

Charles "Chuck" Banko

Charles E. Halcomb

Charles Hightower

Daniel P. Skluzacek

David M. Fletcher

Ensign Donald J. Cromer

Ensign Leo W. Bedell

Hillman Ryan

James Edward Naughton

John Andrew Overchuk

Junior Ray Hollowell

Maxwell Ball

Norman G. Holgate

Richard W. Holtby

Robert Lee Carrell

Robert Duvall

William E. Hildebrand

William Mayo Vollendorf

William Wilcox

FAMILY MEMBERS AND FRIENDS OF LCI (G) 449 OFFICERS AND CREW:

Officers:

Ensign Donald Cromer: Cheryl Cromer (daughter-in-law); Doris Kutschall (sister); Donald Kutschall (nephew)

Ensign Frederick Cooper: Mary Uhrig (wife); Rebecca Shearer (daughter); Frederick England (nephew); Diane Alderman (niece)

Ensign Leo W. Bedell: Terry Bedell (son); Alice Bedell (daughter-in-law); Ann Bedell (daughter); John Bedell (grandson)

Ensign William Corkins: William Corkins II (son); James Corkins (son)

Lieutenant Junior Grade Byron Chew Yarbrough: Clarke Yarbrough (brother); Margaret Yarbrough (sister-in-law); Cecil Yarbrough III (nephew)

Lieutenant Junior Grade Robert Duvall: David Duvall (son); Susan "Sue" Duvall (daughter)

Lieutenant Rufus Geddie Herring: Max Herring (son); Stan Herring (son); Cora Essey (childhood friend)

Lieutenant Willard Vincent Nash: Jim Nash (son); Carol Miller (daughter)

Enlisted:

Alfred Fox: Ruth Fox (wife)

Arthur Trevor Lewis: Arthur Trevor Myatt (nephew)

Bruce Goodin: Trudy Baker (sister)

Bruce Hallett: Phyllis Hallett (wife); Kelly Ling (daughter); Carol Campbell (daughter)

Carl Park: Josephine Park (sister); Marijane Park (sister); Wendy Stoner (niece)

Charles Banko: Russell Banko (brother); Marcy Gibson (daughter); Andrea "Andie" Rymill (daughter)

Charles Halcomb: Christine Halcomb (wife)

Charles Hightower: Virginia Hightower (wife); Randy Hightower (son); Ricky Hightower (son); Ronnie Hightower (son)

Charles Vogel: Evelyn Mae Hendricks (sister); Keith Evans (relative); Heather Evans (relative)

Clarence Hoffman: Oliver Berger (childhood friend); Dolores Berger (childhood friend)

Clarence Kepner: Vicky Wallace (daughter); Rose Jobert (daughter); Jerry Kepner (nephew)

Clifford Lemke: Deborah K. Blocker (daughter); Ellen Dodson (daughter); Peggy Conte (daughter); Clifford Lemke II (son)

David Fletcher: Virginia Fletcher (wife); Michael Fletcher (son); Sharon Fletcher (daughter-in-law)

Frank Blow Jr.: Peggy Blow (wife); Connie Dermovsesian (daughter)

Frank Weber: Lee Weber (son); Donna Glover (niece)

Frederick Walton: Mary Walton (sister-in-law); Will Walton (nephew); Francis Schade (childhood friend)

Glen Trotter: Candy Lee Ellison (relative)

Harold Chambers: Karen Dietz (daughter)

Harry Hilliard: Nedra Hilliard (wife)

Henry Beuckman: Susan Anderson (stepdaughter)

Howard Schoenleben: Howard Schoenleben II (son)

James Griffin: Robin L. Griffin (son); Susan Sitler (daughter)

John Flook: Gene Flook (son); Richard Flook (brother)

John Shire: Joyce Sauerwald (daughter)

Junior Hollowell: Terry Sengbush (daughter); Patricia Myers (daughter)

Lareto Paglia: Romeo Paglia (brother); Daniel Paglia (brother); Jim Paglia (brother); Lucy Hite (sister); Anthony Paglia (nephew)

Lawrence Bozarth: Leona Bozarth (mother); Evelyn Schonover (sister); Mildred Cosper (sister); Mary Lorencz (sister); Robert Bozarth (brother); Rev. Joseph Bozarth (brother)

Leonard Sless: Kathleen Sless (wife); Anne Scott (daughter); Steve Sless (son)

Leroy Young: Evelyn Moon (fiancée); Jay Young (nephew)

Meredith Luckner: Tommy Luckner (son)

Norman Holgate: Maggi McKenzie (sister)

Paul Vanderboom: Mary Vanderboom (wife); Daniel Vanderboom (son); Patricia Wilkum (daughter)

Ralph Owens: Vernade Owens (sister); Opal Ratliff (sister); Wayne Owens (nephew)

Ralphal Johnson: Maurice Johnson (brother); Bobby Johnson (brother); Cora Yarbrough (sister); Rodney Johnson (grandson); Janet Minor (childhood friend); R. J. Bell (childhood friend); Donna Williams (childhood friend)

Robert Carrell: Wendy Carpenter (daughter)

Robert Minnick: Marilyn Cornell (sister); Peggy Lintner (niece); Julie Seabrook (niece)

William Hildebrand: Joanne Hildebrand

William Tominac: Nicholas Tominac (brother)

William Wilcox: Mary Cannell (daughter); Randy Wilcox (son)

Observers:

Edward Brockmeyer: Mary Roell (niece)

Lee Yates: Nancilynn Dunn (stepdaughter)

Leo McGrath: Susan McAdams (niece)

OFFICERS AND CREW MEMBERS OF LCIs AND OTHER SHIPS IN THE IWO JIMA RECONNAISSANCE MISSION: FEBRUARY 17, 1945:

Abbott Sparks USS *ESTES*

Alex A. Bartosiewicz LCI (G) 466

Alfred C. Galedrige LCI (G) 466

Alvin E. Rosenbloom LCI (G) 348 (skipper)

Arbie G. Bates LCI (G) 450

Arnett S. Weeks LCI (G) 474

Bernard J. Powers LCI (G) 438 (skipper)

Carl G. DeGolyer LCI (G) 466

Charles Brinly USS *TENNESSEE*

Charles E. Crandall LCI (G) 471

Charles T. Sehe USS *NEVADA*

Charles B. Sheaters USS *TERROR*

Chester Kobierecki LCI (G) 441

Clarence Stewart LCI (G) 457

Clayton L. Cinnamon LCI (G) 457

Conley James LCI (G) 469

Don Picker LCI (G) 466

Earl G. Launceford LCI (G) 457

Earl W. Reneau LCI (G) 469

Ed Brush LCI (G) 450

Edward Peden LCI (G) 457

Elden F. Connelly LCI (G) 473

Elwin Wayman LCI (G) 348

Ensign Zench USS *John D. Henley* (DD-553)

Floyd Leomazzi LCI (G) 441

Floyd G. Robbins LCI (G) 457

Frank A. Cattern LCI (G) 346

Frank J. Pacholski USS *ESTES*

Franklin M. Kulp LCI (G) 441

George D. Kern LCI (G) 450

George E. Metzger USS *TERROR*

George E. Tanner LCI Flotilla Three Staff

George Menhorn LCI (G) 438

George Panos USS *TENNESSEE*

Glenn Donaldson LCI (G) 450

Harry W. Meyer LCI (G) 469

Harry M. Wenner USS *ESTES*

Herbert J. Fischer LCI (G) 441

Ivy Roberts LCI (G) 450

Jack McMahon USS *TERROR*

James R. Cala LCI (G) 457

James B. Cheyney LCI (G) 438

James Stanfield LCI (G) 466

James M. Trammell LCI (G) 471

Jerome J. O'Dowd LCI (G) 457 (skipper)

John F. DeJournett LCI (G) 457

John L. Manuel LCI (G) 450

John Moriarty LCI (G) 457

John J. Pasacic LCI (G) 441

Joseph Kvidera LCI (G) 450

Joseph Sizer LCI (G) 457

Joseph Thornburg LCI (G) 438

Kenneth E. Huff LCI (G) 473

L. C. Martin LCI (G) 441

Larry M. Hermes LCI (G) 471

Len Rochon LCI (G) 450

Lester E. Taylor LCI (G) 469

Linwood F. Cox LCI (G) 474

Loran V. Brevick LCI (G) 348

Loran E. Schuh LCI (G) 438

Louis F. Pobuda LCI (G) 438

Lyle G. Tilden LCI (G) 441

Lyle A. Wood LCI (G) 457

Lyman E. Blanton LCI (G) 346

Marion B. Hopkins LCI (G) 471

Melvin F. McKinnon USS *ESTES*

Nick J. Gawlik LCI (G) 441

Nick Grosso LCI (G) 450

Noah J. Joyner USS *ESTES*

Norman Sperre LCI (G) 441

Olympic Barson USS *TERROR*

Paul E. Hinchcliffe LCI (G) 438

Percy Montgomery LCI (G) 466

Philip J. Morgan LCI (G) 441

Poley Davis LCI (G) 438

Richard E. Brinson USS *TERROR*

Richard Swartzel *UDT 14*

Robert D. Deviney LCI (G) 457

Robert Dotson LCI (G) 471

Robert Gaunt LCI (G) 348

Robert J. Harker LCI (G) 474

Robert S. Hudgins LCI (G) 471

Robert P. LaClede LCI (G) 441

Robert Main LCI (G) 450

Roy L. Anderson LCI (G) 450

Roy Gladen LCI (G) 450

Royal D. Kissinger LCI (G) 469

Stanley J. Nels LCI (G) 466

Thomas W. Elmore LCI (G) 450

Thomas N. Lennox LCI (G) 466

Timothy J. Sullivan LCI (G) 474

Travis I. Austin LCI (G) 471

Vaughn Hampton LCI (G) 450

Vester C. Kelly LCI (G) 441

W. Lou Bales LCI (G) 466

Wallace Exum LCI (G) 457

Wayne W. Ross LCI (G) 450

William A. Carrico LCI (G) 438

William C. Bishop LCI (G) 471

William Brinkley USS *NEVADA*

William Cserney USS *TERROR*

William Dudley LCI (G) 469

William P. Langfeldt U.S. Navy Operations Dept.

William L. Waters LCI (G) 473

William Snodgrass LCI (G) 438

Zoltan Noga LCI (G) 441

OFFICERS AND CREW MEMBERS OF OTHER LCIs:

Albert E. Clasing LCI (G) 726

Bernard W. Wenrich LCI (G) 454

Bruce K. Cottington LCI (G) 462

Carl E. Cleveland LCI (G) 468

Cecil Read LCI (G) 365

Clifford H. Toth LCI (G) 461

Craig B. Rector LCI (G) 470

Darius C. Rigby U.S. Marine Corps, Twenty-Second Marine Regiment

David Cox LCI (G) 633

Douglas D. Eoff U.S. Marine Corps, 2nd Marine Regiment

Douglas Mayo LCI (G) 468 (skipper)

Earl Carlin LCI (G) 472

Floyd C. Rohrbach LCI (G) 441

Forrest D. Coontz LCI (G) 726

Gabriel J. Chapa LCI (G) 470

George Richard LCI (G) 373

Gordon L. Smith LCI (L) 43

George M. Wratten LCI (G) 365

Hal Bleyhl LCI (L) 812 (skipper)

Harry S. Hande U.S. Marine Corps, 8th Marine Regiment

Henry A. Mullins LCI (G) 439 (skipper)

Herman Rosenberg LCI (G) 454 (skipper)

Homer Clark LCI (G) 372

James T. Flannery LCI (G) 464

James A. Prime LCI (G) 373

James Talbert LCI (L) 618

John H. Belke LCI (G) 464

John Crunkleton LCI (G) 80

John Cummer LCI (L) 502

John A. Hay LCI (G) 462

John R. Nimiskern LCI (G) 439

John B. Stilley LCI (G) 726

John J. Wilkes LCI (G) 452

Joseph Goldberg LCI (G) 372

Larry H. Curry LCI (G) 470

Larry N. Shroy LCI (G) 470

Layne L. Caldwell U.S. Marine Corps, 22nd Marine Regiment

M. Edward Corbitt U.S. Marine Corps, 22nd Marine Regiment

Manual H. Hirata U.S. Marine Corps, 2nd Marine Regiment

Norman S. Moise U.S. Marine Corps, Second Amphib Tractor Battalion

Norman E. Ward U.S. Marine Corps, Second Amphib Tractor Battalion

Pasquale Maietta LCI (G) 461

Patrick Gallo LCI (G) 347

Paul T. Harig LCI (G) 454

Phillip A. Oliva LCI (G) 439

Robert F. Fritchen LCI (G) 372

Robert H. Bollum U.S. Marine Corps, 10th Marines Artillery

Russel G. Banwart U.S. Marine Corps, 18th Marine Regiment, Engineers

Sheldon L. Severson U.S. Marine Corps, 22nd Marine Regiment

Stewart N. Long LCI (G) 460

Thomas N. Fortson LCI (G) 365 (skipper)

Vito P. Colamussi LCI (G) 77

Wallace E. Nygren U.S. Marine Corps, Second Amphib Tractor Battalion

William R. Emrich LCI (G) 365

William A. Mercer LCI (G) 439
William F. Sorsby LCI (G) 347
William Wertz LCI (G) 464

PERIODICALS

Grosvenor, Melville Bell. "Landing Craft for Invasion." *National Geographic*, July 1944.
Marquand, John P. "Iwo Jima Before H-Hour." *Harper's*, May 1945.
Niedermair, John C. "Reminiscences of John C. Niedermair." *Naval Architect— Bureau of Ships*. Interview #4 conducted by John T. Mason of the U.S. Naval Institute.
Ruge, Jack. "Battlewagon Off Iwo." *Army Weekly*, May 15, 1945.
Sparks, Baxter Abbott. "Water Ballet Off Iwo Jima." *United States Naval Institute*, 1945.
Survival on Land and Sea. Office of Naval Intelligence, U.S. Navy, 1944.

NEWSPAPERS AND WIRE SERVICES

Akron Beacon Journal
Anniston Star
Associated Press
Bureau County Republican
Elkhart Truth
Maryland Gazette
Medina County Gazette
New York Times
Oklahoman
Park Falls Herald
Saginaw News
San Antonio Express News
San Antonio Light
Shelbina Democrat
Sioux County Capital Democrat
St. Louis Post-Dispatch
Western Observer
Wise County Messenger

INDEX